BETWEEN
THE FLOODS

The Civilization of the American Indian Series

BETWEEN THE FLOODS

A HISTORY OF THE ARIKARAS

MARK VAN DE LOGT

UNIVERSITY OF OKLAHOMA PRESS : NORMAN

Library of Congress Cataloging-in-Publication Data
Names: Van de Logt, Mark, 1968– author.
Title: Between the floods : a history of the Arikaras / Mark van de Logt.
Other titles: Civilization of the American Indian series ; v. 282.
Description: Norman : University of Oklahoma Press, [2023] | Series: The civilization of the American Indian ; volume 282 | Includes bibliographical references and index. | Summary: "A history of the Arikara people from the time of their traditional origin, a great flood, to the flooding of their lands by the Garrison Dam in the 1950s"—Provided by publisher.
Identifiers: LCCN 2022028849 | ISBN 978-0-8061-9173-7 (hardcover)
ISBN 978-0-8061-9490-5 (paper)
Subjects: LCSH: Arikara Indians—North Dakota—History. | Arikara mythology. Classification: LCC E99.A8 V36 2023 | DDC 305.897/9320784—dc23/eng/20220721
LC record available at https://lccn.loc.gov/2022028849

Between the Floods: A History of the Arikaras is Volume 282 in The Civilization of the American Indian Series.

The paper in this book meets the guidelines for permanence and durability of the Committee on Production Guidelines for Book Longevity of the Council on Library Resources, Inc. ∞

Copyright © 2023 by the University of Oklahoma Press, Norman, Publishing Division of the University. Paperback published 2024. Manufactured in the U.S.A.

All rights reserved. No part of this publication may be reproduced, stored in a retrieval system, or transmitted, in any form or by any means, electronic, mechanical, photocopying, recording, or otherwise—except as permitted under Section 107 or 108 of the United States Copyright Act—without the prior written permission of the University of Oklahoma Press. To request permission to reproduce selections from this book, write to Permissions, University of Okla-homa Press, 2800 Venture Drive, Norman OK 73069, or email rights.oupress@ou.edu.

In loving memory of my mother, Marie van de Logt-Loeffen (1933–2020)

TiwNAsaakaríčI,   Today we remember them,
NikuwetireeWAtwaáhAt,   The ways of the old ones who were,
AniinuuNUxtaahtwaáRA   The good ways that were ours

FROM THE SONG "MEMORIAL TO THE OLD SCOUTS"

CONTENTS

Maps – xi
Preface – xiii

Introduction: Oral Traditions and Arikara History – 1
1 The First Flood and Arikara Origins – 9
2 Mother Corn and the Formation of Arikara Culture – 26
3 Microbial and Foreign Invasions, 1500–1700 – 53
4 Strangers, Smallpox, and Sioux, 1700–1781 – 69
5 Bitter Years: The 1781 Smallpox Epidemic and Its Consequences – 87
6 Meeting the Long Knives, 1800–1823 – 110
7 The Fur Trade Era, 1824–1864 – 142
8 Military Alliance with the United States, 1864–1881 – 169
9 Defending Arikara Land and Culture, 1864–1900 – 196
10 Cultural Revival, 1900–1934 – 225
11 The Second Flood: Betrayal of the Arikara Nation, 1934–1953 – 256
12 After the Flood – 278
    Afterword: Looking toward the Future with One Eye to the Past – 294

Notes – 297
Bibliography – 331
Index – 353

MAPS

Points of Interest in Arikara History – 2

Too Né's Map, circa 1806 – 124

Fort Berthold Indian Reservation before and after the Garrison Dam – 275

PREFACE

Kuwiteetuunú'a'

—FORMULAIC STATEMENT SOMETIMES
USED TO START A TALE

When Sahniš storyteller Lillian Brave (also known as One Kernel of Corn Woman) sat down with linguist Douglas R. Parks to relate ancient Sahniš tales, she often prefaced her stories with the term *kuwiteetuunú'a'*, which means "The village was coming in a long procession." The exact etymology of the phrase is unclear, but it most likely referred to the time when the Sahniš migrated from their place of origin to their eventual location on the Missouri River. The phrase immediately reminded Sahniš listeners that they were an ancient people. They had come a long way.[1]

Throughout history, the Sahniš were more widely known as the Arikaras. Indeed, scholars parsing the historical record will find many variants of the name Arikara, including Arickara, Ricara, Arickaree, Ree, and numerous other forms. The name Arikara means "horn" or "antlers" and may have originated when they lived on or near the Elkhorn River in present-day Nebraska, though it is also possible that this river was named after them. Today most Arikaras prefer to call themselves Sahniš, a name that simply means "the people."[2] Throughout the book, however, I use the name Arikara, because it is the one used most often in both Indian and non-Indian circles and it is accepted by the Sahniš themselves as a perfectly legitimate designation.[3]

Though this book uses the orthography created by Douglas R. Parks to spell Arikara words, I make one concession here. In Parks's orthography, capital letters refer to whispered sounds. In this book, however, I capitalize some Arikara words and terms for grammatical and stylistic reasons.

In most histories, the Arikaras are usually lumped together with the Mandans and Hidatsas, with whom they presently share the Fort Berthold Indian Reservation in North Dakota. It is true that since the mid-1800s, the histories of these nations have often overlapped and that many Arikaras have intermarried with their Mandan and Hidatsa neighbors. However, even into the present, the Arikaras maintain a separate cultural and historical identity, of which they continue to be proud. The Arikaras have a distinct and noteworthy history that deserves treatment in a separate book.

My own association with the Arikaras started in 2002 when I accepted a postdoctoral fellowship at the American Indian Studies Research Institute at Indiana University. The institute's directors, Raymond J. DeMallie and Douglas R. Parks, introduced me to the Arikara community at Fort Berthold and asked me to research the history of the Arikara scouts who served with George Armstrong Custer at the Little Bighorn. Eventually my research expanded, and I was asked to write a tribal history for Arikara students at the White Shield High School on the Fort Berthold Indian Reservation. Naively, I accepted this assignment, not realizing that the orthodox method of research, which relies almost completely on documentary evidence (government records, memoirs by non-Natives, newspapers, and so on), was inadequate to reconstruct the history from the Arikara perspective. Numerous conversations with Arikara people, some of whom became close friends, convinced me that I had to dive more deeply into the oral traditions and histories of the people to get the complete story. Hence, after I finished my first draft in 2007, this book underwent many changes. With each subsequent revision, oral traditions took on a more prominent role, until I finally realized that they should be a starting point for discussion rather than a complement to the bibliographic record.

This book treads new territory, presenting Arikara history not only by itself but also by the methodology that I followed. Rather than adhering to the conventional practice of privileging non-Native bibliographic sources, I placed the oral traditions at the center of the narrative and supplemented them with the bibliographic record. I suspect that this methodology will draw criticism, especially because so many of the oral traditions—sometimes referred to as myths (a word that actually means "story" rather than "fabrication")—pose major problems of interpretation. After all, how does one explain the presence of the fantastic, such as the monsters, cannibals, witches, talking animals, sacred beings descending from the heavens, and other magical creatures and events in these stories? In addition, does not the passage of time and the faulty nature of human memory distort the historical events related in these oral traditions? Are such records at all reliable, let alone usable? I present answers to these questions in the introduction. For now I merely wish to say that my analysis of certain Arikara traditions, though admittedly interpretive and therefore open to debate, has nevertheless yielded interesting new insights into the Arikara past. These insights concern the significance of the Black Hills to the Arikaras; the route the people took during their migration to the plains; their earliest contact with whites; the impact of metal tools, guns, and horses; the slave trade; the return of Mother Corn during wars with the Lakhotas; and more.

I chose to end this history with the completion of the Garrison Dam in 1953. The dam created Lake Sakakawea, which flooded nearly a third of the reservation and most of its fertile lands. It was a traumatic event in Arikara history. Ever since, the Arikaras and their Mandan and Hidatsa neighbors have struggled economically as well as culturally. The loss of cultural vibrancy and spirit stemmed in part from the fact that the dam, and the lake it created, scattered families across long distances. The Garrison Dam disaster was a turning point in the history of these nations.

As harmful as the Garrison Dam was, it was hardly the first destructive event in Arikara history. There had been many before, including events that led to the separation of the people from their Pawnee, Wichita, and Caddo relatives. Occasional droughts and other natural disasters caused tremendous suffering and even devastating wars, such as one that led to the massacre at Crow Creek around AD 1325. Disaster struck again with the arrival of infectious diseases introduced by European invaders. The invaders' horses, guns, and metal tools further caused major disruptions and resulted in the reshaping of the Arikara world. The appearance of the Lakhota and Dakhota Sioux on the plains would alter the geopolitical landscape of the Arikaras forever. A war in 1823 troubled Arikara relations with whites for nearly a half century. The US government's assimilation policies ravaged Arikara culture after the Indian Wars. Finally, global events (such as World War I, World War II, and the Korean conflict) did not leave the people of Fort Berthold undisturbed.

Paradoxically, a major flood allowed for the birth of the Arikara people in their creation story, but a second flood caused by the Garrison Dam nearly destroyed them. Yet they survived, though their self-esteem and their culture suffered a terrible and near-fatal wound.

Still, for all the trauma the dam caused, it may have also signaled a new beginning. The rising waters of Lake Sakakawea had a precedent in the Arikara creation story. A long time ago, Neešaanu NačitákUx, "the Great Chief Above," sent a terrific flood to earth to renew the world. With Neešaanu's approval, Mother Corn, the great prophetess of the Arikaras, placed the people underground. There they lived as seeds until Mother Corn deemed it time to coax them up to the surface of the earth. After they emerged, Mother Corn taught the people the proper way to live. She gave them their institutions and customs, and showed them how to worship. In other words, Arikara culture emerged after a terrifying flood destroyed the world. Likewise, in recent years there has been a rebirth of Arikara culture and tradition led by younger generations inspired by the examples of the elders. It has been an obstacle-filled road, for sure. There have been sharp turns and frequent roadblocks along the way, with the oil fracking business and its pollution and social disruptions being the most recent. Still, these younger generations are now leading the resurgence of Arikara culture. I do not feel adequate to tell their story. It is up to them to tell it. They can do it much better than I can.

It has been a long journey since 2002, when I was a naive young scholar fresh out of graduate school. Twenty years later I am more wrinkly and slightly less naive. Luckily, I had much help along the way. Numerous people, Native and non-Native, pointed me in the right direction. I owe them many thanks and I am grateful for the opportunity to acknowledge them here.

First and foremost I must thank my *inaani* Loren Yellow Bird, a park ranger and Native American interpreter at Fort Union National Historic Site in Montana. An accomplished historian himself, Loren has always supported my work and cheered me on. In many instances I deferred to Loren's expertise on Arikara history and culture. He generously shared his own research and insights with me. I could not have completed this book without his help.

Delilah White-Yellowbird, retired language and culture teacher at the White Shield High School at Fort Berthold, has been a source of support for me since we first met in 2003. Her dedication to her students and her people is truly exceptional and was always in the back of my mind while I wrote this book. Delilah never ceased to encourage me when I felt hopeless because I had bitten off more than I could chew. I also owe a debt of gratitude to Wendell White and Sidney Howard, who enabled me to spend a few weeks at Fort Berthold interviewing people and collecting information. Wendell arranged a vehicle for me, and Sidney graciously opened up his home to me. Their hospitality and generosity were heartwarming.

At Fort Berthold, I received the help of many people. Some shared their stories with me. Others read the manuscript and made suggestions on how to improve it. I gladly take the opportunity here to thank Rodney Howling Wolf, Brad Kroupa, Russell Mason, Pearl Ross, Margaret Starr, Rhoda Star, Jasper Young Bear, Don Yellowbird, Gloria Young Bird, Yvonne Fox, the Reverend Duane Fox, Myrtle Painte, Max Dickens, Marilyn Hudson, Pansy Goodall, Dawn White, Sianna Conko, and Susie Paulsen. Thanks also to the White Shield school board, teachers, and staff for all the work they have done to preserve the Arikara language and culture and for passing them on to the younger generations.

Several Pawnee friends were instrumental in shaping my ideas about ancient Arikara history, when the Arikaras were closely associated with the Pawnees. Pawnee historian Roger Echo-Hawk first opened my eyes to the significance of Native American oral traditions. Roger has been a steadfast cheerleader and critic of my work, and I am truly blessed to count him among my dearest friends and to call him *iraari*. Pawnee archaeologist Carlton Gover profoundly shaped my thinking about early Pawnee–Arikara migrations and prehistory. Carlton is headed for a promising career, and I look forward to reading his future work, which, like Roger's and mine, is founded on a deep and abiding respect for tribal oral traditions.

Institutional support was crucial. The groundwork for this book was laid while I was a postdoctoral fellow at Indiana University. I was fortunate to work with experts in the field who helped me become a better scholar in ways they probably never anticipated. I want to thank Douglas R. Parks and Raymond J. DeMallie for taking an interest in my work and hiring me. I also wish to thank Noemie Waldhubel, Christina Burke, Dennis Christafferson, Heidi Kwon, Sally Anderson, Indrek Park, Nicky Belle, John Erickson, Wally Hooper, Linda Cumberland, Travis Myers, Cynthia Ramlo, and Josh Richards for their companionship during my time in Bloomington. My friend and Lakhota specialist Rani Andersson deserves special mention. Times sure have changed since Rani and I shared an apartment. We never anticipated that both of us would hold professorships someday—or chase our children around the house. Rani is a prolific historian, and this book is partly the result of my quest to keep up with his impressive publishing record.

Qatar Foundation provided me with generous financial support over the past decade. In addition, I owe thanks to my colleagues and friends at Texas A&M University—in the Liberal Arts Department in Qatar and in the History Department in College Station, Texas. They include Troy Bickham, Hyun Wu "Paul" Lee, James and Meg Rogers, Adam Seipp, Lorien Foote, Sherry Ward, Deanna Rasmussen, Joe Ura, Jessica Herzogenrath, Brittany Bounds, Sara Hillman, Hassan Bashir, Phillip Gray, Michael Telafici, Leslie Seawright, Joseph Williams, Zohreh Eslami, Khadija El Cadi, and Olena Snitko. Many thanks also go to Alessandra Jacobi-Tamulevich at the University of Oklahoma Press, who watched me struggle with this project for more than a decade; Peg Goldstein, who copyedited and improved the manuscript; and cartographer Erin Greb, who created the maps.

Finally, if writing the history of a person at a specific point in his or her life is a difficult undertaking, writing the history of an entire nation spanning centuries is utter foolishness. Yet many years ago, I set out to do just that. In the end, I could not have accomplished the task without the patient support of my wife, Tet. While I plugged away at this book, Tet in effect raised our daughter, Keira. Both sacrificed much to let me pursue my dreams. Without their love my life would be practically meaningless.

Doha, Qatar
March 2021

INTRODUCTION

ORAL TRADITIONS AND ARIKARA HISTORY

This is what I used to hear.

—FORMULAIC STATEMENT FREQUENTLY
USED AT THE END OF AN ARIKARA STORY.[1]

Winters are long and cold in North Dakota. Temperatures can drop to −30°F or even lower on some nights. Among the Arikaras, *psí'u'* (winter) is the season for storytelling. Before Lake Sakakawea forced the Arikaras to move from the sheltered bottomlands along the Missouri River "up top," where icy winds blow across the snow-covered landscape, people used to gather in the evenings to spend pleasant hours around the fire. One such evening in the late 1800s, they came together in the lodge owned by Strikes Two's wife. While women prepared dinner for the visitors, Bull Neck, Enemy Heart, and Bear's Teeth entertained the guests with stories.[2]

Bull Neck kicked off the round of storytelling. One time, he said, he had trouble killing a buffalo. Each time he got close, the animal ran away. Finally he caught it in a ravine, where it was harder for the animal to spot him. He shot the animal and commenced to skin it when he saw it had a third eye in its side. "No wonder we could not approach the buffalo any closer," Bull Neck proclaimed, "This one has an eye in his rump!" The listeners laughed.

Having captured the attention of the audience, Bull Neck continued with several more humorous stories. Each time he concluded a tale, the people in the room laughed. At last Enemy Heart spoke up and told a few humor-tinged stories of his own. Feeling challenged, Bull Neck retorted with two more stories, one in which an apparently dead buffalo came back to life, giving him a dreadful scare, and another in which he dragged home a sleeping coyote by its tail. Once again his tales drew many laughs.

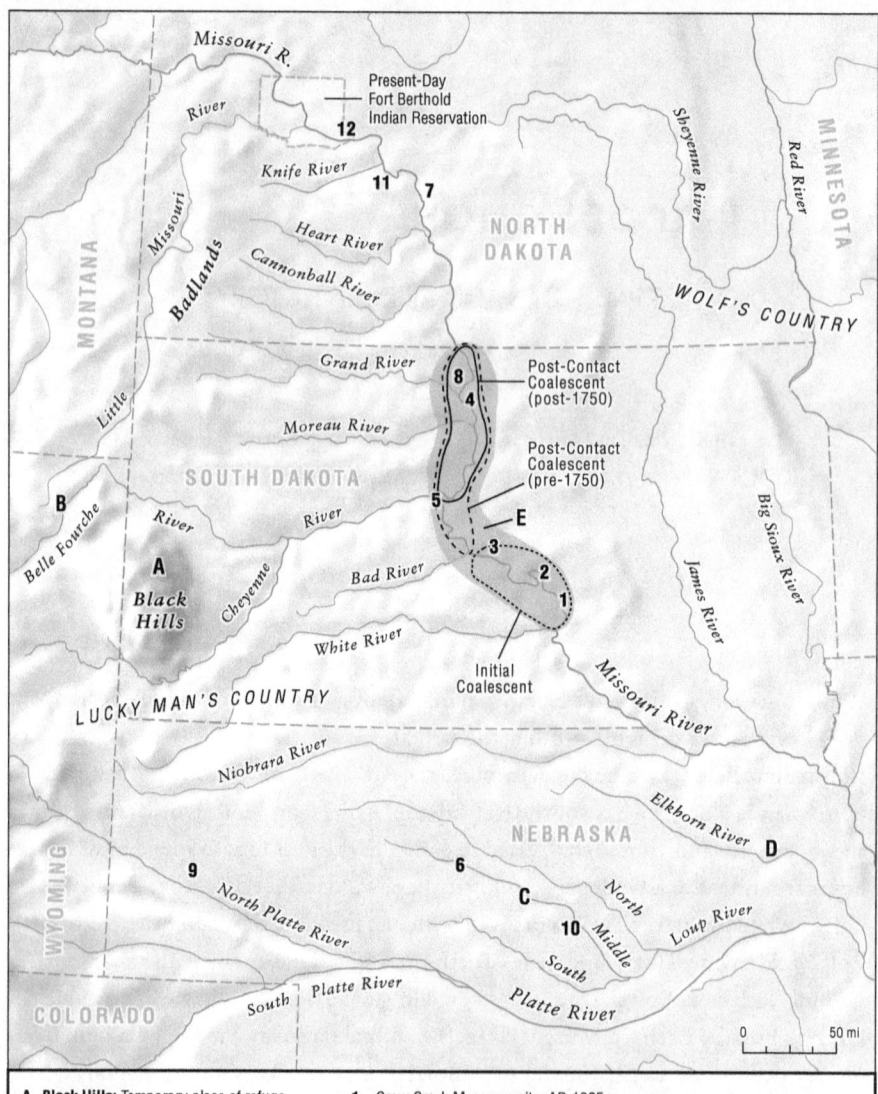

A Black Hills: Temporary place of refuge during an epidemic in the 1600s	1 Crow Creek Massacre site, AD 1325
B Devil's Tower: Possibly temporary place of refuge according to Arikara oral traditions	2 Location of Arikaras in 1714 (Bourgmont and De L'Isle), abandoned c. 1750
C Skiri Pawnee territory: Place of refuge for the Arikaras in the mid-1790s and 1833–36	3 Location of an Arikara town visited by the La Verendrye brothers in 1743
D Elkhorn River: Arikaras were named after this river or instead gave their name to this river; possible location of Arikara hunting groups when contacted by Lone Man of the Pawnees	4 Larson site, c. 1750–86; site of a massacre of Arikaras in the 1780s
	5 Location of Crazy Bear's town, 1794–96
	6 Arikara group seeking refuge among Skiri Pawnees, 1796–99
	7 Arikara group seeking refuge among the Mandans near Painted Woods, 1796–99
	8 Location of Arikara towns in 1799–1823 and 1824–32
	9 Approximate location where Bloody Hands contacted Skiri Pawnees in 1832
E Extent of Arikara territory during the "Coalescent Tradition" (AD 1300–1800)	10 Among the Skiri Pawnees, 1833–36
	11 At Fort Clark, 1837–61
	12 At Fort Berthold (Like-A-Fishhook Village), 1862

Points of Interest in Arikara History

Key historical points of interest for the Arikara, including locations of Arikara settlements over time.

But the final story of the night was left to Bear's Teeth, an "old warrior" and "hereditary chief." It was a story of a young man who received power from an eagle. The eagle instructed the young man to wear an eagle feather in his hair. The young man did as instructed and procured an eagle feather. He cut it at the end and tied it to his hair. That night the eagle again appeared to him in a dream. It told the young man that he should not have cut the feather. He would in turn be cut by the enemy. The next day the Sioux attacked the town. The young man rushed out and chased one of the enemies. At one point, the two contestants dismounted and drew their knives. In the fight that followed, the young man was stabbed in the left arm, but he killed the Sioux. That night the eagle appeared to him again and assured him that he would not die. And so it happened: the young man lived and became a leader among his people.

These stories entertained and instructed. Even Bull Neck's delightfully self-deprecating stories taught listeners that the world housed a great number of mysterious powers who determined success or failure in human life by bestowing sacred blessings on those worthy and brave enough to receive them. These powers, the storytellers knew, commanded respect. They did not take slights lightly. Thus, when the young man in Bear's Teeth's story wronged the eagle, he paid for his mistake by suffering a wound in a battle with the Sioux.

THE POWER OF STORY

One day in the winter of 1915, a white visitor told Episcopalian missionary Aaron McGaffey Beede that Indians did not record history. "The Indian has no yesterday," he said. "He knows his own generation, and has a little idea of the generation before."

Beede disagreed. He had visited the Arikaras frequently and was close friends with Byron Wilde and his wife, Anna. Whenever the Arikara sacred bundle was opened, Beede informed his visitor, the priests would relate the nation's history, which stretched back for at least one thousand years. According to Beede, the full version of this account, which also contained prayers and songs, would take fifteen hours—spread out over three to five evenings—to recount.

Knowledge of this story came at a price, however. One was obliged not to tell or write what he heard, Beede said. In the past a man who was privileged to hear this sacred history instantly became a member of the tribe's "historical society." With it came great responsibilities. A newly initiated "historian" had to leave and fast for a time and then kill a fat elk and bring it to the "historical lodge," saying, "This is food for my mother," indicating his appreciation to the bundle for sharing its secrets with him.[3]

Although one was sworn to secrecy to protect the integrity of these sacred histories, Beede nevertheless encouraged fellow scholars interested in Arikara culture and history, such as Orin G. Libby and Herbert C. Fish of the North Dakota State Historical Society, to hear the Arikara legends when the sacred bundles were opened. But he warned them that they were not allowed to reveal what they learned. Fish asked what good this knowledge was if he was not to reveal it. It was a dilemma that frustrated Beede as well. It continues to frustrate scholars today.[4]

Presently, most Arikara sacred stories that have been passed down are only imperfect versions—fragments really—of the originals. They are largely stripped of all their sacred and religious content and are, at best, *CliffsNotes*-style versions. Still, they constitute the best materials in existence. Although fragmented and frustratingly obscure, they nevertheless contain valuable clues about the Arikara past.

Not all stories were of such deeply sacred significance. There were many other kinds of stories as well: hero stories, accounts of battles, tales of mysterious encounters, and bawdy coyote stories full of slapstick and crude sexual humor. Some of these stories were an individual's private property, but many were not. Indeed, Arikaras were prolific storytellers who relished telling tales. Sometimes they borrowed stories from other nations, but in many cases they themselves were the sources of tales that people elsewhere adopted. Among the tribes that appropriated stories from the Arikaras were the Lakhotas. Several stories now labeled "Lakhota tales" actually originated among the Arikaras. Among these is the famous story of the Standing Rock (after which the Standing Rock Indian Reservation is named), about a mysterious young woman and her dog who turned to stone after she was married to a man against her wishes.[5]

In all cultures around the world, stories hold great power. Stories instruct, amuse, caution, comfort, clarify, and explain. They are repositories of a civilization's customs, beliefs, laws, and attitudes, as well as records of historical events. The Arikaras valued their storytellers. They believed that good storytellers and orators had been gifted with special talents by the sacred powers. Hence gifted storytellers occupied a special place in society.

In this book, I rely greatly on Arikara storytellers who shared their tales with me and my scholarly predecessors. Only the names of a few dozen storytellers have survived. Among the earliest ever mentioned in historical documents is Eagle Feather, who in 1804 traveled to Washington City, where he met with officials in Thomas Jefferson's administration. Contemporary sources describe him as a lively and engaging storyteller. Unfortunately, Eagle Feather died in Washington City in 1805 and today is best remembered for a detailed map of the Arikara world that he left behind. Not until the late 1800s do the names of Arikara storytellers appear more frequently in the historical record. Their names show up throughout this book.

Among the most important collections of Arikara stories were those recorded by James Rolfe Murie and George Dorsey in 1903 and published the next year as *Traditions of the Arikara*. In the 1990s, linguist Douglas R. Parks published a four-volume set of Arikara narratives. Both works are cited extensively throughout this book. Other traditions appeared in journal articles or were never published at all. The latter include oral history interviews conducted between the 1950s and 1990s.

Between 2003 and 2007, I conducted interviews with Arikara elders, including Yvonne Fox, Gail Valenzuela, Anita Howard, Pearl Howard, Myrtle Painte, Martina Ross, Gloria Young Bird, Pearl Ross, Margaret Starr, Rhoda Star, Gerald White, Wendell White, and Jasper Young Bear. None of these interviews were ever published.

ORAL TRADITIONS AND METHODOLOGY

Many mainstream historians continue to be skeptical of oral traditions as historical sources. They question the accuracy of oral traditions. After all, they argue, human memory is faulty and often changes with the passage of time. People forget certain details while highlighting, exaggerating, or perhaps even imagining others. Thus oral traditions are problematic historical sources. These historians favor bibliocentric research methodologies that focus on the written word. However, the cancerous growth of internet memes, "fake news," and disinformation (both deliberate and unintentional) in recent years shows that the written word itself has suffered much in terms of reliability. Because of our focus on the written word, we have also lost our appreciation for spoken memories passed down over the generations.

In Plato's *Phaedrus*, ancient Greek philosopher Socrates pointed out the danger of placing too much confidence in the written word. When Thoth, the Egyptian god of wisdom, invented writing, he claimed it would make Egyptians wiser and give them better memories. But fellow god Ammon corrected him. Thoth's invention would introduce forgetfulness in those who learned to write: "They will not practice using their memory because they will put their trust in writing.... You provide your students with the appearance of wisdom, not with its reality."[6]

We are the children of Thoth. We have become distrustful of cultures that reconstruct the past from memory rather than the (false) security of the written word. The fact is that historians ought to use both.

Preliterate cultures were more accustomed to committing information to memory than we are today. Before they were written down, lengthy poems such as the *Iliad*, *Beowulf*, the *Nibelungen Saga*, and the *Edda* were performed by storytellers who had memorized every word. Likewise, Arikara storytellers and historians (there is no great difference between the two) committed their stories to memory. Cheyenne historian Stands All Night is still remembered for his detailed knowledge of tribal history and lore. He was an Arikara, born in the 1760s, who married a Cheyenne woman and lived among his wife's people until his death, at more than one hundred years of age, in 1869.[7]

In more recent history, Alfred Morsette Sr., was known for his phenomenal memory and his encyclopedic knowledge of Arikara stories and songs. Parks, who started working with Morsette in 1976, was thoroughly impressed with his ability to commit stories to memory. After he heard a song, he told Parks, he "soaked it up like a sponge" and retained it in his memory. He contributed more than sixty stories and numerous songs to Parks's collection of Arikara recordings. In traditional Arikara fashion, Morsette would only recount stories in the winter months, roughly between October and March.[8]

Apart from the limits of human memory, critics believe that oral traditions are unreliable historical sources for other reasons. They argue that storytellers often alter old texts to accommodate the tastes, preferences, and concerns of modern audiences. Furthermore, the presence of monsters, speaking animals, magical transformations, and so on defies reality and place the reliability of the entire story in doubt. In addition, how does one determine which story is most accurate when multiple different versions exist? Finally, because many of these stories cannot be verified by other records, whether printed or archaeological, one cannot determine whether they are based on real events or imagined ones.[9]

Because of the above concerns, critics tend to treat these stories more as cultural artifacts reflecting a people's values rather than as historical sources. Lakhota philosopher Vine Deloria Jr., dismissed this viewpoint as being too narrow and short-sighted. "It seems strange," Deloria observed, "that the ancient peoples would spend so much time writing about the inner mysteries of life and find little time to record the events and incidents of their times."[10]

The concerns of critics must be weighed against other considerations as well. First, sometimes oral traditions are the only sources we have about a people's past.

To not use them would deny us at least some insights into their history before stories were put down on paper. Second, just because some oral traditions may be false, that does not mean that *all* oral traditions are false. Likewise, if some *part* of an oral tradition may not be true, that does not mean that *everything* in the account is false. Although Homer's *Iliad* is largely fictional, it nevertheless refers to an actual event called the Trojan War. Similarly, if Margaret Mitchell's *Gone with the Wind* were the only surviving text mentioning the American Civil War, it would nevertheless tell us a great deal about that terrible conflict (though much of it obviously biased and otherwise problematic). Finally, written texts are often unreliable as a result of bias, misrepresentation, falsehood, and exaggeration as well. They too often reflect the tastes of their writers as well as the audiences for whom they were written. In short, both written and oral sources must be approached with caution.[11]

Finally, there is the problem of the "fantastic" in many Arikara accounts. As I showed in an earlier book, *Monsters of Contact* (2018), even this can sometimes be linked to historical events and processes. Contact "monsters" were symbolic representations of traumatic events of such cataclysmic or paradigm-defying proportions that people borrowed the language of myth to describe and explain them. Thus epidemic infectious diseases became angry whirlwinds or monstrous, man-devouring animals, while murderous foreign invaders clothed in metal armor and armed with mysterious weapons became cannibals and witches.[12]

Readers must be aware that many of my interpretations of Arikara oral traditions in the early chapters of this book are speculative. I acknowledge that they are not definitive. Indeed, it is possible that eventually other scholars may produce better explanations. If so, I am comforted by the fact that my suggestions have renewed interest in these important cultural and historical artifacts. Historians should always be open to other interpretations, and I am willing to be persuaded as well. The purpose of my research is to advance knowledge rather than satisfy some political agenda. In this regard I agree with Pawnee historian Roger Echo-Hawk that "it is appropriate for academic institutions to respect the principle that accurate history is researched, not negotiated."[13] Although I am aware that my interpretations are open to discussion, I am nevertheless convinced that not using these remarkable sources would be foolish as well as ethnocentric.[14] Therefore, until more convincing interpretations come along, I am quite comfortable presenting mine.

To sum up my methodology for the first part of the book: I placed oral traditions first, after which I relied on conventional (non-Arikara) historical sources as well as insights from archaeology, linguistics, anthropology, and other scientific disciplines. Where I could, I privileged Arikara voices. Sometimes this worked. Sometimes it did not. In my experience, most of the time the Arikara sources got it right. In the second part of the book, I relied less on oral traditions and more on oral histories. Because oral histories are based on testimonies by contemporaries and witnesses of certain events, the use of these sources is much less controversial among historians. Many of the oral histories I consulted were never published.

I must conclude with one last observation. To many contemporary Arikaras, the old traditions are part of sacred history. Indeed, I have met Arikaras who believe that these stories must be taken literally. To them, historicizing traditions through interpretation is problematic. I acknowledge these concerns and offer my explanations as suggestions only. Though I have not met any yet, a few Arikaras may even consider my interpretations sacrilegious. I hope they nevertheless understand that my treatment of these stories is based on a deep respect, if not awe, for their beauty, their wisdom, and their ability to speak to us over the centuries. In my experience, however, most Arikaras appreciate thoughtful discussions of these stories. Indeed, I hope that both Arikara and non-Arikara readers will find much to enjoy in this book.

1 THE FIRST FLOOD AND ARIKARA ORIGINS

> You shall have my corn to plant so that you will grow and multiply.
> —MOTHER CORN

ARIKARA ORIGINS

Arikara oral traditions say that the universe was created by Neešaanu NačitákUx, "the Great Chief Above." The Arikaras usually addressed him simply as Neešaanu, "Chief."[1]

In the beginning, Neešaanu created the stars, the earth, and the four corners of the universe. Then he created life. First he made a race of giants and placed them on earth. This first creation was imperfect. The giants believed they were as powerful as Neešaanu himself. They began to ridicule him. To punish them for their pride, Neešaanu turned them into stone. They became mountains and rocks.[2]

Neešaanu's second attempt at creating a race of worthy beings also fell short of perfection. Though smaller, these beings also mocked him. To punish them, Neešaanu drowned them in a flood.

The earth was now covered entirely with water. There are different versions of what happened next. In the 1880s, Arikara priest Two Crows told how only a duck and a mosquito were left alive. The duck lived off what he found on the seafloor. The mosquito lived off the foam that formed on the waves. Tired of eating foam, the mosquito persuaded the duck to take him under his wing and dive down to the land. When they reached the bottom, the water dried up instantly.[3] In Yellow Bear's 1903 version, two ducks were sent by Wolf and Lucky Man to bring up mud. With this mud, Wolf and Lucky man created the land along the Missouri River.[4]

Next, Neešaanu created the first man, the first woman, and all the animals. The first people were Spiderman and his wife. But they were dirty and smelled very bad. Wolf taught them how to cleanse and purify themselves with sage. This transformed the man and woman. Because of Wolf's medicine, they were now able to have sex and have offspring.[5] The descendants of Spiderman and Spiderwoman lived with Neešaanu in the sky. Then Neešaanu told Thunder to take all beings to earth. But when Thunder's lightning bolt struck the earth, it pressed too deep into the soil, which was still soft from the flood. Thunder cried out in sadness, and ever since one can hear his cry whenever lightning strikes.[6]

The people now lived under the surface of the earth. At this time, they had not fully formed yet. They were merely seeds living underground. They lived in darkness and longed for the day when they would be brought into the light. Their prayers were answered when, one day, Neešaanu sent Mother Corn to help them.

At first, Mother Corn appeared only as a voice, encouraging the people to move up. Several animals began to dig. Long-Nosed Mouse was the first to break through to the surface of the earth. Making the first hole gave him his sharp nose. Mole dug next, but he was blinded by the sun, and his eyesight has been poor ever since. Badger then followed and widened the hole. But the sun burned his head and cheeks until they were black. Finally the hole was large enough for the people to emerge. Some of the people, however, chose to remain underground. They became burrowing animals.[7]

When they reached the surface, the people saw pathways where other people had come out of the ground. Some had emerged with the help of Buffalo, while the Arikara people were guided by Mother Corn.[8]

After leading them from the earth, Mother Corn led the people on a long and difficult journey. Three times they ran into great obstacles. The first was a steep ravine. But a kingfisher tore up the bank with its sharp beak and so created a path. The next obstacle was a dense forest. It was overcome by an owl, which created a road with its wings. Finally, the people came to a wide river or lake. This time, a loon created a path for them.[9] At each obstacle, some people remained behind and turned into animal species that inhabited these places.[10]

Finally, Mother Corn led the people to the Missouri River. The people saw that it was wonderful and called it the Mysterious River or Sacred River. Here they settled, and Mother Corn gave them corn and other crops to grow. "You shall have my corn to plant so that you will grow and multiply," she said. She also taught the people how to hunt buffalo, cook meat, and prepare the skins. Each time they stopped to camp, Mother Corn taught them sacred ceremonies, in which offerings were made of smoke, corn, and meat.

One group of people emerged last from the earth. They trailed all the others and camped at the abandoned sites of those who had gone before them. There they would eat the sacred meat that had been left behind. By doing so, they absorbed all the ceremonial teachings of Mother Corn. Thus they became the leading group among the Arikaras. This group provided the head chief of the nation as well as the leading priests. This band was called Awaáhu, which the Arikaras today translate as "Left Behind."[11]

One of Mother Corn's most important teachings was to make smoke offerings to Neešaanu, the four directions, and all the other sacred powers, including Mother Corn herself. But one day, the people committed a sin by leaving behind two dogs and forgetting to offer smoke to them. These dogs were Sickness and Death. Ever since, they have stayed with the people.

In some versions of the creation story, disease and death appear in the form of Whirlwind, who turned against the people in anger. To save the people, Mother Corn changed herself into a cedar tree. At the same time, a meteorite, which the Arikaras addressed as Grandfather Rock, fell from the sky. Some of the people found shelter against Whirlwind in the tree and on the rock, but others were killed or dispersed by the violent storm. The scattered survivors turned into other tribes, such as the Šaahé (Cheyennes), Pichia (Psi'a' or Assiniboines), Wooden Faces (Iroquois), and Witchcraft-People (the Čirikuúnux or Wichitas).[12]

Now that disease and death had come into the world, Mother Corn gave the people sacred bundles to effect cures. After she had thus blessed the Arikaras, Mother Corn entered the Missouri River and returned to the heavens.

After Mother Corn's departure, the people invented games and began to gamble. Soon they quarreled and began to kill one another. The animals living with the people became frightened and fled. A few people also fled and formed new tribes. Observing these developments from above, Neešaanu once again dispatched Mother Corn to earth, with new instructions for the people.

Mother Corn now gave the Arikara people laws and rules to live by. She created the office of the chief to enforce the rules and lead the people by example. She also taught the people to be respectful of Neešaanu and the sacred powers, to be brave when defending themselves against enemies, to be industrious, to look after the needy, and to be honest and generous toward one another.

After she had taught the Arikara people, Mother Corn sacrificed herself in a war. According to Four Rings, she led twelve followers into battle and was killed. According to Hawk, she was killed when enemies attacked the Arikara town. Both informants agree that after Mother Corn's remains were buried, corn and other

Four Rings, Arikara, priest of the Hu'ka'wirat sacred bundle, circa 1910. Four Rings's account of the bundle and its ceremony, published by Melvin Randolph Gilmore, remains one of the premier Native American esoteric texts and the most important description of the Mother Corn ceremony of the Arikaras. State Historical Society of North Dakota, A2395–00002.

vegetation sprang up from her grave. Following Mother Corn's example, the Arikaras interred the bodies of the deceased into the womb of the earth, from which the people had originally emerged.

ARIKARA CREATION ACCOUNTS AS HISTORICAL SOURCES

As obscure as the Arikara creation story is, it nevertheless provides some important clues and insights into early Arikara history. Unfortunately, the absence of convenient historical markers does not allow for an easy chronological reconstruction. Complicating analysis is the fact that different versions of the creation story exist today. It is hard to tell which one is more accurate. Finally, these stories mix religious symbolism and history. Indeed, the Arikaras consider their creation story to be *sacred history*. For the historian, however, it is difficult to parse the historical from the religious.

In his analysis of the Arikara creation stories, Pawnee historian Roger Echo-Hawk proposed that these accounts refer to events in "deep time," including the crossing of the Beringian ice corridor. The creation stories indeed offer suggestions for such primeval migrations. After emerging from the ground, Hawk told in "Origin of the Awaho-Bundle People," the people ran into a great barrier. "There was wide, thick ice and deep water," he said. Bear's Tail added that when the people emerged, "they were upon an island in big waters." Both of these descriptions, Echo-Hawk suggested, may refer to the Beringian ice corridor. Next the people faced "Blue Mountains," which Echo-Hawk identified as the Rocky Mountains. Then the people were blocked by a great chasm, which Echo-Hawk speculated was the Grand Canyon. Finally the people reached the Missouri River country, where they separated into different tribes, including the Arikaras and Pawnees.[13]

Echo-Hawk's theory that the Arikara creation stories refer to events in deep time receives further support from the Cut Nose tales, which seemingly refer to paleolithic events. Hawk said in 1903 that before the people crossed the lake, the chasm, and the forest, they encountered a monstrous being living near the primordial lake. Its name was Cut Nose, and it had long horns that "seemed to touch the heavens." Hawk's monster was either a prehistoric giant buffalo or, more likely, a mammoth or mastodon. In any case, from underneath this monstrous animal sprang buffalo that hunted and devoured humans. It was the buffalo's aggressive behavior that forced the people to migrate. Only after crossing the obstacles with the help of the animals were the people able to elude the buffalo.[14]

In accounts related by Star and Snowbird, the people eventually overcame these primordial buffalo with the help of the sacred powers. In Star's account, a mysterious man (possibly Neešaanu himself) appeared to give a boy bows and arrows, with which the people defeated the buffalo. In Snowbird's version, the daughter of the chief of the buffalo gave the young man the bow and arrows, which the people used to chase and scatter the buffalo. After the buffalo scattered, the buffalo chief's daughter married the young man and they created the knot-in-the-tree bundle, which allowed subsequent Arikara priests to lure buffalo herds.[15]

Of course, it is possible that the Arikaras invented such tales after discovering petrified remains of mammoths, mastodons, or prehistoric giant buffalo in geological formations exposed by fluvial erosion. Perhaps the presence of human-made Clovis-like fluted projectile points in these remains further stimulated such imaginations.[16]

What is undisputed, however, is that the Arikaras at one point paused in the Southwest. In Hand's 1903 account, the people traveled to a chasm, where Kingfisher created a land bridge so the people could cross. As mentioned above, Echo-Hawk theorized that this was the Grand Canyon.[17] However, based on what Hand said next, it is possible to further pinpoint this event to Canyon de Chelly in northeastern

Arizona or Canyon of the Ancients in southwestern Colorado. According to Hand, after Kingfisher created the bridge across the chasm, it said, "All the people who want to join me may remain here, and we will stay and make our homes in these banks." The remains of these homes can still be observed today. Every year thousands of tourists swarm the ancient Anasazi cliff dwellings at Canyon of the Ancients, Mesa Verde, and Canyon de Chelly. These, Hand's account indicates, were made by Kingfisher's people. They were the ancestors of modern-day Pueblo Indians. Perhaps it is here that the Arikaras learned to raise corn, though modern-day Arikaras argue that the Pueblo nations learned this skill from them.

According to Hand, the Arikaras next encountered a heavy timber. If one accepts that the Kingfisher episode is linked to the Anasazi cliff dwellings, then the timber was probably the forests of western Colorado, including the San Juan National Forest. Here an owl assisted the people by creating a path for them among the trees. Western Colorado is indeed home to a great number of owl species, including the flammulated owl, the great horned owl, the barn owl, the western screech owl, the long-eared owl, the short-eared owl, the northern saw-whet owl, the snowy owl, the northern pygmy owl, the Mexican spotted owl, and the forest-dwelling boreal owl. Other species, such as the short-eared owl, the western burrowing owl, and the eastern screech owl, prefer open landscapes, including grasslands, and are therefore found primarily in the eastern half of Colorado. [18]

Also intriguing is Hand's mention of the invention of a "ball game" after Mother Corn left for the heavens. Although this was probably the game of shinny, it nevertheless resembles the Meso-American ball and hoop game of the Olmecs, Aztecs, and Mayas in one regard: it resulted in human sacrifice. "When one side was beaten," Hand said, "it immediately began to kill those of the other side, and whose language they could not understand."[19] This suggest Meso-American connections.

That at some point the Caddoan ancestors of the Arikaras paused in the American Southwest is confirmed in two Pawnee accounts. The Arikaras, Pawnees, Wichitas, Kitsais, and Caddos at this point formed a single nation. In the 1880s, Chawi Pawnee elder Secret Pipe Chief told ethnographer George Bird Grinnell that long ago, the people "were far off in the southwest, and came from beyond two ranges of mountains. When they scattered out, each party became a tribe. At that time the Pawnees and the Wichitas were together. We made that journey, and went so far east that at last we came to the Missouri River."[20] Bear Chief, a Skiri Pawnee elder, claimed that their ancestors came from the beyond the Rio Grande. They moved north and eventually reached the Mississippi River where the Missouri runs into it.[21] These stories parallel Arikara traditions and indicate that their Caddoan ancestors spent some time in the Southwest, from where they migrated eastward until they reached the Mississippi River.

Along the way, the Caddoans broke off into separate nations. The Caddos settled in what is now Louisiana, Arkansas, eastern Oklahoma, and Texas. The other Caddoan groups ascended the Mississippi River before moving up the Missouri River and onto the central plains. When they reached Kansas, the Wichitas branched off and turned south, settling in southern Kansas, Oklahoma, and northern Texas. Meanwhile, the ancestors of the Pawnees and Arikaras moved into Nebraska. According to archaeologists they settled in Nebraska around AD 900. Once there, the Arikaras eventually branched off, moving up the Elkhorn River before reaching the Missouri River, which they followed into South Dakota.

The oral traditions of the related Pawnee, Wichita, and Caddo nations shed further light on early Arikara history. Like the Arikaras, the Caddos believed they had entered the world from the earth. They emerged through the "mouth of a cave" in a hill, which they call Cha'kanĭ'nă, or "The Place of Crying."[22] Interestingly, the Arikara accounts by Hand and Four Rings similarly mention much "wailing and crying" after the people reached the surface of the earth. The Caddo story, however, locates this place "on a lake close to the south bank of [the] Red River, just at its junction with the Mississippi."

As in the Arikara story, Caddo tradition says that people and animals lived together as family before they emerged from the earth. When the people discovered the entrance to the cave leading up to the surface of the earth, they decided to ascend and come out. Leading the way was an old man who carried fire and a pipe in one hand and a drum in the other. Behind him came his wife, who carried corn and pumpkin seeds. Then followed the rest of the people and the animals. Some animals, however, were trapped underground when a wolf closed the hole behind him. These animals remain underground today. Those on the surface cried for a long time for their friends below, thus giving the place its name. Subsequently, like the Arikaras, the Caddo inter their dead in *ină'*, or earth, because it is the place of their origins.[23]

The traditions of the closely related Skiri Pawnees are even more useful for reconstructing early Arikara history by providing additional details. To be sure, there are differences between the Arikara and Skiri Pawnee accounts, but many of these can be explained by the fact that during their separation (estimated to have occurred between AD 1450 and 1550), the two groups divided up the sacred bundles. As they divided up the bundles, they carried different parts of the creation story with them. This explains the greater emphasis on Mother Corn among the Arikaras, while the Skiri Pawnees emphasized the roles of Evening Star and Morning Star.

Both Skiris and Arikaras believe in a single supreme creator. The Skiri version of Neešaanu NačitákUx is Tiraáwaahat, "The Universe and Everything Inside."[24] Both traditions detail that the world was first populated by giants who mocked the creator and were subsequently destroyed in a flood for their prideful behavior.[25] After destroying the giants (whose fossilized bones still litter the landscape today), the creator made humans up in the heavens.[26] Like the Arikara account, the Skiri creation story describes people being carried to earth by lightning, though the details of these events are different.[27] Both traditions contain migration stories, but whereas in the Arikara account Mother Corn led the people to the Missouri River, the Skiri tradition describes a journey, filled with hardship, of a young man who eventually united male and female people. Incidentally, both accounts also describe, albeit differently, the "invention" of sex for procreation.[28]

The Skiri accounts indicate that after a long journey, the ancestors of the Pawnees and Arikaras arrived at a place where they received their ceremonies and divided into different groups. According to the Arikara story told by Hand, this place "where there is only one mountain" was located on the Republican River in present-day Kansas. The most likely location for this event was Guide Rock, on the northern side of the Kansas–Nebraska border. Incidentally, this is also the location of Pahur, one of the sacred animal lodges of the Pawnees.[29]

At this place, the Pawnees and Arikaras separated. The Skiri tradition mentions how the people divided into separate groups and dispersed. The Arikara account, as detailed earlier, says that the people started gambling and killing one another. Whatever the reason, disagreements caused the ancestors of the Pawnees and Arikaras to veer in different directions. The Arikaras settled near the Elkhorn River in northeastern Nebraska and from there followed the Missouri River into South Dakota.

In 1903 Sitting Bear told of how he visited the ancient Arikara territory in Nebraska. "At this village site we found four large mounds where there had stood the four lodges of the bundle lodges," he said. "The oldest of the men told us that once the Arikara lived here; that while they were having their medicine ceremonies in one of these lodges a Sioux or one of some other tribe came and went through the village."[30]

After their separation from the Pawnees, the Arikaras grew estranged from their southern relatives. At some point, however, the sacred powers again reconnected the two groups. In a Skiri Pawnee town on the Platte River in present-day Nebraska, a Skiri band lived under the leadership of a chief named Closed Man. Closed Man would become a great prophet. Under his leadership, relations between the various Skiri towns and their Arikara relatives were formalized.[31]

According to Skiri tradition, one day a hunter from Closed Man's town met a stranger—probably an Arikara—from a different town. They discovered that they could understand each other. The hunter rushed home and reported to Closed Man that there were other people on earth who were similar to them. Shortly thereafter, Closed Man had a vision in which Bright Star (Evening Star) explained to him that these people had been created by other powers and that they had received bundles but did not know the ceremonies that came with them. Bright Star instructed Closed Man to call the different Skiri and Arikara groups together so they could receive their ceremonies. Following his vision, Closed Man moved his people northward, across the Loup River, where they established a town on Beaver Creek in present-day Nebraska. From here he sent errand men to the other Skiri towns, inviting them to come and receive their ceremonies. The errand men also visited the Arikara towns. Several agreed to come, but two Arikara groups, which occupied towns on the Elkhorn River, refused to participate because "their god had given them certain powers, so that they could hold their ceremonies themselves."[32]

The other groups gathered at Closed Man's town on Beaver Creek. All brought their bundles. They erected four poles that symbolized the four corners of the world. Closed Man painted these poles in the colors of the types of corn associated with these semi-cardinal directions:

yellow (corn)		black (corn)
	x	
white (corn)		red (corn)

At this place, the people dressed in different animal skins and reenacted the creation story. They made Closed Man chief, and he selected one man to be the lead priest. When all towns had taken up their positions in this great ceremony, they "performed the first great ceremony, under the direction of the first priest, and the owners of the various bundles were taught the ceremonies which were there performed in connection with other bundles." After each group received its songs and ceremony, they scattered again.[33]

An Arikara tradition by Bear's Tail refers to this gathering. This account shows that at least some Arikara groups attended Closed Man's council. According to Bear's Tail, the Arikaras received their ceremonies and bundles in "Pawnee country." In one of the bundles they gathered the skulls of a long-nosed mouse, bear, mole, badger, and fox. Bear's Tail said, "These were wrapped up in a bundle and when the Pawnee invited them to attend the bundle ceremony they went and received their

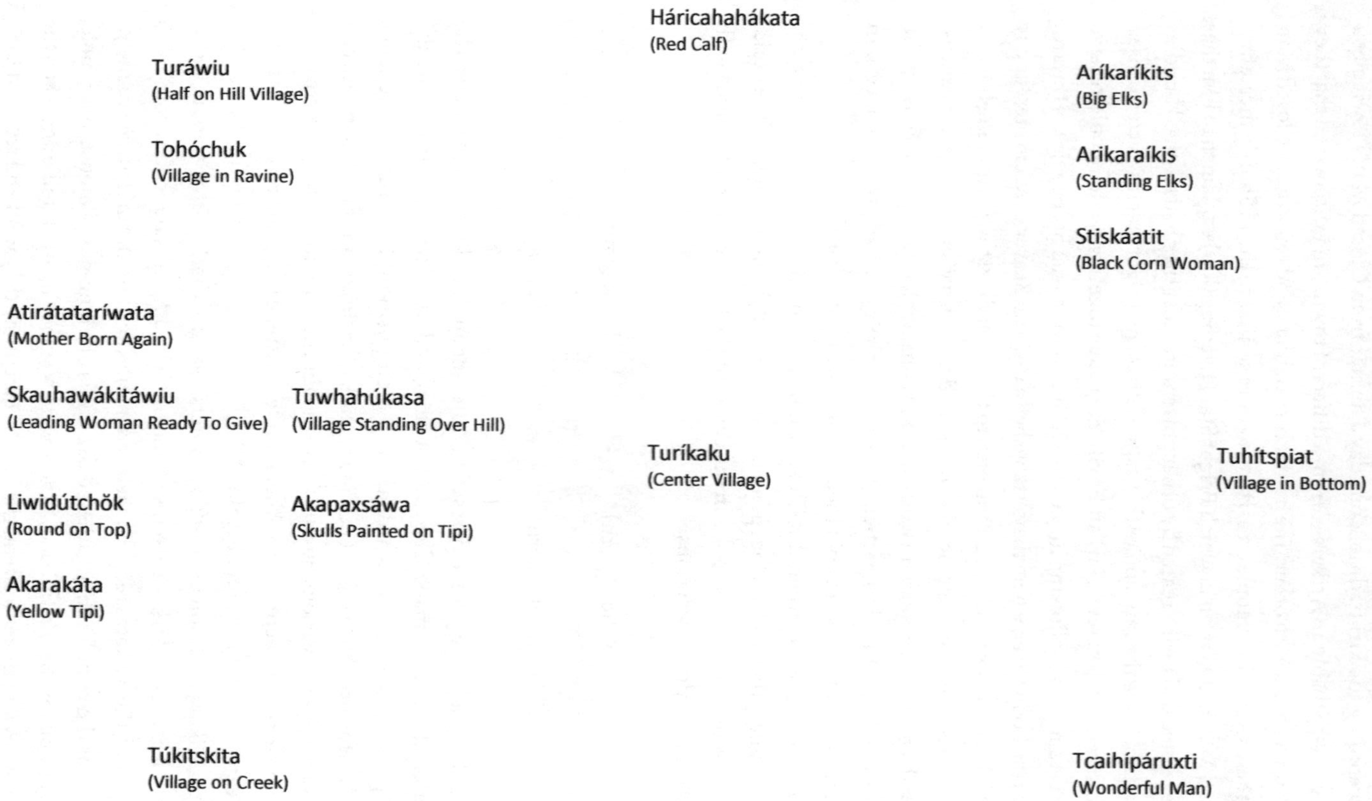

Háricahahákata
(Red Calf)

Arikaríkits
(Big Elks)

Arikaraíkis
(Standing Elks)

Stiskáatit
(Black Corn Woman)

Turáwiu
(Half on Hill Village)

Tohóchuk
(Village in Ravine)

Tuhítspiat
(Village in Bottom)

Turíkaku
(Center Village)

Atirátataríwata
(Mother Born Again)

Skauhawákitáwiu
(Leading Woman Ready To Give)

Tuwhahúkasa
(Village Standing Over Hill)

Akapaxsáwa
(Skulls Painted on Tipi)

Liwidútchŏk
(Round on Top)

Akarakáta
(Yellow Tipi)

Tcaihipáruxti
(Wonderful Man)

Túkitskita
(Village on Creek)

Geographic location of the Pawnee towns and associated Arikara bands according to the Closed Man story as told by Roaming Scout.

ceremony. Mother-Corn and also a ceremony were given to them. All the bundles received their rituals, each being different from the others."[34]

The word "received" in Bear's Tail's account is confusing because it incorrectly implies a hierarchical relationship between the Arikaras and the Pawnees. It is more accurate to see this as the moment when the Skiri Pawnees officially acknowledged the Arikaras as a distinct people. At Closed Man's council, the Arikaras formally secured their ownership and rights to the bundles that symbolized their covenant with Mother Corn. At the same time, both peoples—Skiris and Arikaras—recognized their affiliation and formalized their friendship. What the Arikaras "received," in short, was recognition as a distinct entity within the Pawnee–Arikara constellation.

Scholars disagree about when the Arikaras and Pawnees parted and formed separate tribes. But based on Arikara oral traditions and linguistic theories, it appears that this separation occurred in phases between AD 1450 and 1550,[35] though some groups may have broken away as early as the early 1300s. The Arikara creation story states that the people moved in different groups or bands. As mentioned, the last of these bands, the Awaáhu, became the chief group among the Arikaras. They would provide the head chief of the Arikara nation as well as its leading priests.

It is interesting to note that the Skiris claimed that the Arikaras broke away from them, while the Arikaras claimed the reverse and that the Skiris left first. Despite the separation, Arikara–Pawnee relations remained close, as the Closed Man tradition indicates. Indeed, the Arikaras and the Pawnees continued to share many cultural similarities.[36]

LINGUISTIC AND ARCHAEOLOGICAL EVIDENCE IN SUPPORT OF THE ORAL TRADITIONS

Modern scholarship supports the idea of southern or southwestern ties for the Arikaras. Ethnobotanist Melvin Gilmore determined that the sacred tobacco of the Arikaras (*Nicotiana quadrivalvis*) was originally found only in Mexico.[37] Furthermore, the Arikaras may also have practiced a form of human sacrifice similar to the Morning Star ceremony of the Skiri Pawnees, which scholars usually also associate with Meso-America.[38]

The most compelling evidence for the southern hypothesis, however, is the dispersion of the Caddoan nations along a south–north axis: from the historic Caddos in eastern Texas, western Louisiana and Arkansas, and southeastern Oklahoma; to the historic Wichitas in northern Texas, Oklahoma, and central Kansas; to the Pawnees in north-central Kansas and Nebraska; and finally to the historic Arikaras along the Elkhorn River in northeastern Nebraska and the Missouri River in central South Dakota.

One way to date divisions between the different Caddoan nations is a linguistic method called glottochronology. This method compares languages and looks for similar words (cognates) and determines to what degree words and grammar have changed. The method is controversial because the formula used to assign a number of years to these changes is debatable. After all, sometimes languages change rapidly while at other times the changes occur more gradually. Still, glottochronology offers some rough dating estimates. In conjunction with the oral traditions and the archaeological record, the overall picture comes into focus.

Based on their analysis, linguists believe that the Caddo Indians left the main group first, between three thousand and thirty-five hundred years ago. The Wichitas separated around nineteen hundred to two thousand years ago. The Kitsais (now an extinct group) separated about twelve hundred years ago, while the Pawnees and Arikaras separated between three hundred and five hundred years ago.

According to linguist Douglas R. Parks, the Arikaras separated from the Pawnees before the Skiri Pawnees split from the South Band Pawnees. Still, the linguistic and cultural similarities between the Skiris and the Arikaras strongly suggests that they separated from each other. The Skiris share more similarities with the Arikaras than with the South Band Pawnees, with whom they were reunited in the nineteenth century.[39]

Though still in its infancy, genetic research is also providing clues to the southern origins of the Arikara people. In 2018 Arikara tribal member Michael Yellow Bird, dean and professor of the Faculty of Social Work at the University of Manitoba, used a genetic testing service to learn more about his ancestry and to see if his father's claims that the Arikara people originally came from South America were true. The results revealed that Yellow Bird's DNA matched with that of ancestors in Mexico and Central America, from places such as Michoacán, Jalisco, Puebla, Durango, Oaxaca, Zacatecas, Guanajuato, Nuevo Leon, Chihuahua, and Mexico City. Even if these results do not suggest a South American origin, they do indicate that Mexico may have been "a stopping point for the tribe."[40]

The archaeological record sheds further light on early Arikara history. Of course, the farther back in time archaeologists venture, the less clear the record becomes. It is impossible to link the Arikaras directly to the Paleo-Indians who roamed the plains in search of game or with the nomadic big game hunters of the Archaic period (8000–500 BC).[41] It is likely that the ancestors of the Pawnees and Arikaras entered Nebraska during the Plains Woodland Tradition (circa 500 BC to AD 1000). Here they hunted, gathered, and occasionally practiced horticulture. The most marked difference with the preceding Archaic period is the appearance of new and improved technologies, some of which seem to have come from the eastern woodlands, though the Pawnees–Arikaras may have also passed corn horticulture eastward. By the middle Plains Woodland period, between AD 1 and 500, the influence of Hopewellian cultures seems evident: new styles of pottery and projectile points appeared, as well as burial mounds. Toward the end of the Plains Woodland Tradition, people lived for longer periods in semipermanent homes, which they tended to reoccupy after the hunting season was over. Though hunting and gathering remained primary forms of subsistence, horticulture became more important. A major technological change was the appearance of bows and arrows during the late Plains Woodland period (circa AD 500–1000). Ceremonial life also seems to have become more complex during this time.[42]

Archaeologists believe that the ancestors of the Pawnees and Arikaras had firmly established themselves on the central plains by AD 900. Compared to earlier occupants, they cultivated improved corn varieties obtained from the Southwest. They divided their time between growing crops, gathering, and hunting. They lived in village or hamlet-size semipermanent settlements ranging from central Kansas into central and northeastern Nebraska. These small semipermanent villages were unfortified and did not follow a specific plan. There were no open central plazas. These settlements were located near streams to take advantage of the moisture for gardening purposes. Most of the houses were rectangular, though occasionally there were circular ones. Both types were of the earth lodge variety, and they included storage pits and central fireplaces.[43]

Around 1400, these people abandoned Nebraska. Environmental changes may account for this development. Starting in the 1300s, extensive droughts resulted in resource depletion. Game animals became scarce. Crop yields diminished or failed altogether. Scarcity created tensions within and between communities. Compounding the crisis was increased warfare with Oneota invaders, the ancestors of the Iowas, Otoes, Missourias, Omahas, and Kansas.

Archaeologists believe that some of the ancestors of the Pawnees and Arikaras moved into South Dakota, where they formed the so-called Coalescent Tradition. Here they met the Mandans and Hidatsas. Relations with these tribes vacillated between peace and war. During a conflict in 1325, a force whose identity is unknown attacked a proto-Arikara town at Crow Creek, South Dakota. Perhaps the attackers were Mandans or Hidatsas, or perhaps they were—as the gambling episode in the Arikara creation story suggests—a rival Caddoan group. If so, this episode may have

Mother Corn ceremony depicting the cedar tree from the Arikara creation story. The dancers belong to one of the doctor societies and bring gifts and carry bundles of sage. In the background is the medicine lodge, upon which a camp crier sits and watches the

signaled the rift between the Arikaras and the Pawnees. Another group turned south and eventually became the South Band Pawnees. In 1541 Francisco de Coronado learned of these Pawnee groups (the Harahey) from the Wichita Indians. By 1600 the Pawnees had moved back to Nebraska. This might have been when Closed Man tried to forge a confederacy between the Pawnees and the various Arikara groups. As described above, he was only partially successful.[44]

Between 1400 and 1550, Arikara groups (it is too early to speak of them as a single nation) pushed the Mandans and Hidatsas out of South Dakota and into North Dakota. The Arikaras firmly established themselves in central South Dakota.[45]

Around 1600, the towns and material culture of the Pawnees and Arikaras seem to have reached the shape described by the first European visitors. Small dispersed settlements made up of square lodges, with cord-roughened pottery and notched arrowheads, during the Central Plains Tradition became larger consolidated towns composed of round earth lodges, with stamped pottery and unnotched arrowheads. One noticeable difference between Arikara and Pawnee settlements was that Arikara towns tended to have a ceremonial plaza in front of a large ceremonial lodge. The Arikaras may have adopted this tradition from the Mandans or developed it on their own per instructions from Mother Corn. Indeed, the plaza and ceremonial lodge were the backdrop for the annual Mother Corn ceremony of the Arikaras.

proceedings. National Anthropological Archives, Smithsonian Institution, MS 154064B #08510631 and 08510632.

Archaeologists call the period on the central plains between 1300 and 1800 the Coalescent Tradition because tribes gathered (coalesced) to form larger communities. This was the time when distinct identities, including that of the Arikaras, emerged. Archaeologists further subdivide the Coalescent Tradition into shorter periods called variants. These variants also involve spatial dispersion and therefore sometimes overlap. The Initial Coalescent Variant (circa 1300–1600) and Extended Coalescent Variant (1450–1650) overlap in years but not in region. They are followed by the Post-Contact Coalescent Variant (circa 1650–1800) and the Disorganized Coalescent Variant (which began after a devastating smallpox epidemic of 1781).[46]

During the Initial Coalescent Variant, towns were built on top of terraces overseeing rivers. These towns had defensive works, including palisades, ditches, and occasionally bastions. As opposed to the Central Plains Tradition, most lodges were circular, though occasionally square ones are found.

The Extended Coalescent Variant developed farther north slightly later. Interestingly, these townsites had defensive works on only their northern and southern borders. Towns between these frontiers did not have palisades, bastions, or ditches. These towns were usually small, consisting of no more than twenty-four circular earth lodges, though these were usually occupied by multiple families. It appears that the towns of the Extended Coalescent Variant were initially built by the Mandans and Hidatsas, who were pushed north by groups that would eventually form the Arikara nation.

Although these Caddoans became the sole occupants of the regions abandoned by the Mandans and Hidatsas, they continued to build heavily fortified towns. Archaeologist Richard A. Krause wrote that this suggests that these people had a "penchant for internecine warfare, a propensity to fight their cultural compatriots as well as outsiders, a commitment perhaps to principles of social order that stimulated military action."[47] If so, the people who eventually formed the Arikara nation were not always on friendly terms with one another.

The Post-Contact Coalescent Variant started around 1650 or 1675, depending on which archaeologist one asks. By this time a distinct Arikara identity seems have formed, although most towns were still largely semiautonomous. Each had its own sacred bundles and its own ceremonies associated with these bundles; each made its own political decisions. Indeed, it might be better to speak of a loose confederation of communities sharing similar organizations, practices, and religious concepts, even though differences in speech may have continued. Archaeologists have identified about sixty Arikara townsites along the Missouri River valley in South Dakota, dating from the late seventeenth century to the end of the eighteenth century. There were four clusters of towns: one near the mouth of the Grand River, another just below the mouth of the Cheyenne River, a third north of the mouth of the Bad River, and the last in the vicinity of the Big Bend of the Missouri. On average, these towns had about forty lodges each. The lodges tended to be somewhat smaller than those of the Mandans and Hidatsas. They may have held on average ten people. Archaeologist Donald J. Lehmer suggests that twenty-two (about one-third) of these towns were occupied at one time, leading him to conclude that at their height, the Arikaras numbered about eighty-eight hundred people. At this time, European-made objects had become more common. Indeed, the Arikara towns became centers of trade. Most of these developments are discussed in later chapters.[48]

To recapitulate: Arikara oral traditions strongly suggest southern and southwestern connections before the people arrived on the central plains. Before they reached their final station, however, the Caddos and Wichitas separated and formed nations of their own. The Pawnees eventually divided into northern and southern branches. The northern branch, in turn, developed into the Arikaras and the Skiri Pawnees.

Such separations are recurring themes in the Arikara creation stories. However, on occasion different tribes also came together. Sometimes these bonds were temporary—for purposes of trade, for example—while on other occasions they became more permanent, for example when Closed Man created the Skiri Pawnee confederacy or when the Arikaras allied themselves with the Mandans and Hidatsas in the mid-1800s. In any event, the Arikaras had a long and complex history—in which groups separated and united—before Europeans arrived on the continent.

The Closed Man tradition of the Pawnees suggests that the groups that eventually formed the Arikara nation broke away between 1450 and 1550, though earlier groups may have moved away as early as the early 1300s. Linguistic and archaeological evidence supports this thesis. Rather than sudden, the separation was more likely gradual, with extended families leaving at different stages to form separate communities elsewhere. Indeed, it might be better to talk about an Arikara "confederacy" at this time rather than a unified and integrated "nation." Even the term "confederacy" suggests a unity that was more imagined than real. Not until the Arikaras formally received the bundles and the traditions of Mother Corn and integrated these into a religious system can we speak of a distinct Arikara cultural identity. Indeed, it was Mother Corn who would become the focal point of the Arikara religious and ceremonial complex.

2 MOTHER CORN AND THE FORMATION OF ARIKARA CULTURE

> Just as the white people talk about Jesus Christ, so we feel about the corn.
> —TWO CROWS, ARIKARA PRIEST, 1893.[1]

In 1924 Arikara priest Four Rings explained the importance of Mother Corn to the Arikaras. She instructed the people "with words of wisdom in matters of religion and of the high and deep things in life." She reminded everyone of their duties toward Neešaanu and the other holy beings; taught the Arikaras to respect not only one another but all living things; showed them how to construct the holy lodge, whose architecture was a model of the universe; and taught that this universe was divided into four corners, each of which was associated with different powers. Her greatest gift, however, was corn. It nourished and sustained the people. It was a gift made in self-sacrifice, for Mother Corn sacrificed herself in battle. When the people arrived at the spot where she had been killed, they found a corn stalk growing there. This corn plant, Four Rings explained, symbolized Mother Corn's promise that she would forever act as a mediator between the people and the Chief Above and that she would forever be "their unerring but unseen guide." Through her sacrifice, Mother Corn also showed the people that there was life after death.[2]

By the early 1600s, Arikara identity revolved around the worship of Mother Corn. It signaled the Arikaras' development as a distinct and unique culture. This is a good moment to pause and take a closer look at the civilization that the Arikaras forged. Much of the following discussion is based on what scholars learned from late nineteenth- and early twentieth-century sources. This approach is problematic because it suggests that Arikara culture was "frozen" over the centuries. It was not. Like all cultures, it was subject to changes due to shifting social, economic, and political circumstances. Still, by the seventeenth century, the foundations of Arikara culture had been laid.

SACRED GEOGRAPHY

At the heart of Arikara geography was the Missouri River. The Arikaras called it the Mysterious River or Sacred River. The lands on opposite sides of the Missouri were created when Wolf challenged Lucky Man to a contest to create land. With mud brought up from the bottom of the lake by a duck, Wolf commenced making the land on the north side of the river. "Form into land, and let it be prairie," Wolf spoke, "and let the buffalo roam over this prairie!" Then it was Lucky Man's turn. Lucky Man, who was probably a manifestation of Neešaanu, created the land south of the river with the help of another duck. From the mud, Lucky Man shaped hills and mountains. Then he admonished Wolf for making his land level, so that in winter the buffalo would be driven from it by cold winds. "When the people come they shall choose to live on the south side of the Missouri River," Lucky Man said, "for there are hills and valleys, so that their ponies, dogs, and buffalo can find shelter in the hills and mountains." The Missouri River thus became both the heart of the Arikara universe and its northern and eastern boundary.[3]

On the opposite side of the Missouri River very different peoples lived. Among these were the Oneotas (ancestors of the Iowas, Otoes, Missourias, Omahas, Poncas, Osages, and Kansas), as well as the Dakhota Sioux. Farther northeast were the Lakhotas and Cheyennes. Not until later did the Lakhotas and Cheyennes cross the Missouri River, in what turned out to be a Rubicon moment for the Arikaras.

The Arikara creation story suggests how different nations were created. Some had followed the buffalo after they emerged from the earth. Other nations were created after the people began gambling and killing each other. Finally, humans separated again when Whirlwind dispersed the people. Among the nations so dispersed were the Assiniboines, the Cheyennes, the Iroquois, and the Wichitas. In any event, numerous tribes and peoples bordered Arikara territory. Not all of these peoples arrived and lived there at the same time. The Mandans and Hidatsas, for instance, were ancient to the region, while others arrived at later dates. Some, such as the Padoucas (Apaches), Kiowas, and Comanches, came from the north and stayed for a while before moving south. Later, after their towns became centers of trade during the post-contact period, the Arikaras learned about numerous other peoples beyond.

One Arikara group broke away from the tribe and went north. These were the Niitaxkstaáwo, "They Who Went after Sinew." The true identity of this group and what exactly happened to them remain enigmas. Some Arikaras say that these people became the Sarcee of Canada, but there is no cultural or linguistic relationship between the two peoples to suggest a shared ancestry.[4]

The Missouri River winds through the Arikara creation story like a giant aorta. It reminds people of their epic migration story and connects them to the past. At the end of the Mother Corn ceremony, for instance, the Arikaras tied the worn-out shoes of little children to the sacred cedar tree before tossing it into the river. It would float downstream past their Pawnee relatives to show them that the Arikaras were thriving. Some Arikara families still practice this ritual: they place old Christmas trees onto the frozen river before the spring thaws melt the ice, allowing the river to carry the trees downstream.

The Arikaras considered the Missouri River their most sacred geographical feature. Its floodwaters fertilized the bottomlands where people kept their gardens. Its valleys attracted wildlife and game. Trees and shrubs lined its banks, providing useful resources as well as shelter from cold winds in winter. The waters of the river were also used to cleanse bundles. Without water there was no life.

But the water also housed dangers. In the Missouri River lived a number of mysterious snakes. One of these was Nuutawáčeš, a giant water serpent to whom war parties made small sacrifices of tobacco or meat when they wished to cross the river safely. According to Yellow Bear's 1903 account, two boys once came upon the monster, which was blocking their path. One of the boys suggested piling logs onto the snake's back and setting it on fire. The boys did so, and the fire burned a path right through the snake. Then one of the boys ate the cooked snake meat. Over the next few days he slowly transformed into a serpent himself. Before his transformation was complete, he instructed his friend to put him into the river. "I am to rest in the middle of the Missouri River," he said. "Whenever the people cross the Missouri River they must say 'My brother, let me step over you.' They will then always cross over the river without any danger of drowning."[5]

A similar version of this tale was told by Antelope, but this version contained not one but several monstrous water snakes. These stories of mysterious and powerful water serpents show that the rivers had tremendous hidden powers. Incidentally, these water snakes occasionally bestowed blessings on people. The water snake also became one of the powers in the annual Arikara medicine lodge ceremony.[6]

In the 1990s, Joseph Reed (1931–1999) told the story of a mysterious giant snake living in the water near Twin Buttes. One day some veteran Arikara army scouts were hunting near this place. One of the scouts camped a little away from his friends. The next morning he found the remains of his friends. Their bones had been picked completely dry. The snake had sucked the life out of them. According to Reed, evil still lurks near this place and causes people to die violent deaths.[7]

Perhaps more treacherous than the water snakes were the "water dogs," who also lived in rivers and streams. Two-Hawks explained in 1903 that whenever someone heard or saw a water dog, they usually died not long thereafter. A young man named Poor Bear reportedly died soon after seeing one coming out of the river. Not long after that, a young woman fetching water heard the dogs chattering in the deep near the place where Poor Bear had first seen them. She ran home afraid and told what had happened. According to Two Hawks, the girl fell sick and died shortly afterward.[8]

Like other animal powers, water dogs could bestow power upon people. These powers were mostly used for evil purposes, as exemplified in a story told by Strikes Enemy. In the story, a mischievous man had committed many crimes, so the people conspired to kill him. After luring him to a feast, they ambushed him. The man fled into the river. There, on the river bottom, he found a tipi inhabited by dogs. The dogs healed his wounds and pledged to help him. When the man returned to town later, the people were even more afraid of him. The man began to commit crimes worse than before. This time, no one dared to harm him. One day this man gathered his relatives and broke away from town. The man's followers later attacked the town, killing several people. Because of this man's bad deeds, the people separated and would never meet again. Apart from illustrating the pernicious nature of water dogs, the story also illustrates the sociopolitical dynamics that occasionally caused towns to break up.[9]

In the late twentieth century, Alfred Morsette shared a tradition about a lake where many Arikaras drowned. An Arikara war party was on its way home after having failed to find the enemy when they came upon a hill. It was a beautiful hill covered with much vegetation. Because the hill looked like the back of a giant turtle, the men were reluctant to climb it, until a young man—"one who does not believe in things," Morsette explained—climbed on top and persuaded the others to follow. One man refused. "Certainly this turtle is holy," he warned. "You're going to do something to yourselves." The others ignored him. Suddenly the turtle moved and turned toward a big lake. As it slid into the lake, the men on its back tried to climb down, but their feet were stuck and they disappeared into the cold water. The man who had refused to join them watched his friends disappear into the darkness. He mourned all night for the lost men. In the morning, a voice from the lake spoke to him. It told the mourner to go home and tell the people what had happened. It urged them to respect sacred things. Though the men were now condemned to stay in the lake forever, the voice said, they would help the survivor whenever he stopped by the lake and prayed to them.[10] Around 1806 Arikara chief Eagle Feather, or Too Né, included this lake on a map he drew, which is now housed in the National Library of France. Despite Too Né's map, the precise location and identity of the lake remain uncertain.

In the 1990s, Joseph Reed related the story of a strange and deadly whirlpool in the Missouri River caused by a mysterious animal. In a tale similar to the turtle story, Reed told how a group of young men were determined to see what it was all about. They threw a large log into the river and climbed on top of it. As they floated down the river toward the mysterious whirlpool, people watched from the riverbank and prayed for their safety. When the men came near the whirl, they spotted a large white buffalo on the river bottom. In a panic, the men jumped off the log and swam to safety. There they told the people what they had seen and warned them never to go near that place again. "This is how [the elders] taught us," Reed explained. "They told us stories about what *not* to do."[11]

Rivers, streams, lakes, and springs, then, were not merely valuable sources of water, food, and other useful things. They were also places of power and meaning. Mysterious beings lived in them and had to be approached with respect.

ARIKARA RELIGION

Although the Arikaras distinguished between natural and supernatural realms, the distinction was not always obvious. The supernatural was always present around them. Anything out of the ordinary was potentially "mysterious" or "holy."

The Arikaras believed their earthly existence was only a vague reflection of the real world inhabited by the many sacred powers.[12] The most powerful, of course, was Neešaanu, the creator. Mother Corn, the four directional powers, and other celestial powers followed him.

It is inaccurate to call Arikara religion polytheistic. Neešaanu was the great mysterious life force whose self-sacrifice made *all* life possible. He was the ultimate source of everything. While it is true that the Arikaras distinguished between a number of sacred powers that are often incorrectly called gods, these sacred powers all had their origin in Neešaanu.

Neešaanu created these subsidiary powers by sacrificing parts of himself. His most powerful creations were Mother Corn and the four directional powers that supported the universe.[13] Below Mother Corn and the directions ranked celestial powers, such as the stars, the sun, the moon, comets, the Milky Way, lightning, clouds, and wind. Ranked below the celestial powers were terrestrial powers, usually animals, although it appears that inanimate objects, such as rocks, plants, trees,

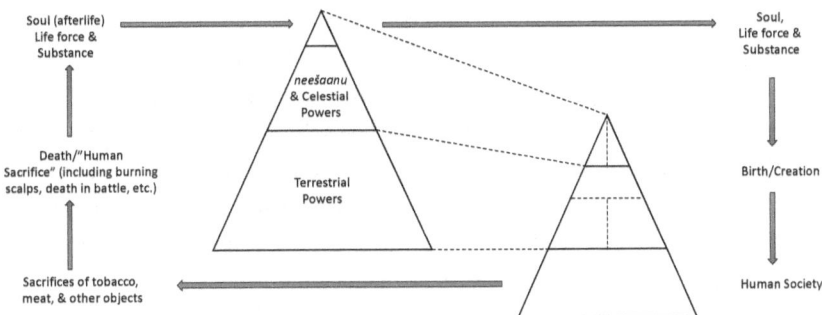

Creation: the role of sacrifice in the cycle of birth, death, and rebirth. All life and substance originated with Neešaanu NačitákUx ("the Great Chief Above"), who consequently permeates everything. What Neešaanu created through sacrifice had to return to continue creation. The left pyramid depicts the sacred powers flowing downward from Neešaanu to the celestial powers (stars and so on) and the terrestrial powers (animals). The right pyramid shows Arikara social hierarchy based on spiritual power and how it is linked to the sacred powers.

rivers, and streams, also contained power. The powers of Mother Corn, the four directions, and the celestial objects were the domain of tribal priests, whereas the terrestrial powers belonged to the domain of doctors and other blessed individuals.

In order for Neešaanu to continue the cycle of creation, humans had to make sacrifices to restore and revive his powers. Sacrifices were an inextricable part of every Arikara ceremony. For example, tobacco was burned at every ritual occasion. Also common were sacrifices of corn and buffalo meat. And although the ethnographic record is rather obscure about the subject, scalp sacrifices and the "sacrifice" of people on the field of battle probably served a similar purpose of enabling Neešaanu to create again.

Although Neešaanu was the all-powerful creator, the Arikaras usually directed their prayers to Mother Corn. She was their "culture hero" or prophetess, who guided the people both materially and ethically. Whereas Neešaanu created nature, Mother Corn taught the people culture: farming, hunting, gathering, tool making, and so on, as well as rules for society to live by, the proper attitudes toward relatives and strangers, and the correct way to worship the sacred powers.

In 1924 Patrick Star, custodian of the Awaáhu village bundle, explained how Neešaanu created Mother Corn by rubbing his hands on his sides, after which a grain of corn came out of his mouth. He rubbed the grain of corn with earth and it became an ear of corn. Finally he blew on the ear of corn and it took the form of a woman.[14]

Perhaps Mother Corn was another manifestation of Neešaanu, just like Jesus, according to Christian doctrine, is a manifestation of God. In fact, some Arikaras compared Mother Corn to Jesus. "Just as the white people talk about Jesus Christ," said Arikara bundle priest Two Crows in the 1880s, "so we feel about the corn."[15] In 1925 Four Rings also drew parallels with Jesus (especially as referenced in John 6:35), describing how Mother Corn said she was "the giver of life.... You shall pray in my name. When you are in need or have desire for anything, if you ask God above in my name, you shall have it, but those who do not believe in me shall be in want."[16]

The symbol of Mother Corn underscores the significance of corn in Arikara culture. "You shall have my corn to plant," said Mother Corn in Hand's version of the Arikara creation story, "so that you, by eating it, will grow and also multiply."[17] According to Star's account, Mother Corn created red, yellow, black, and white corn by vomiting when Whirlwind struck the people. The suggestion is that corn strengthened the people against diseases. By eating the corn, the people entered into communion with Mother Corn and the sacred powers.[18]

Corn was such an essential part of Arikara identity that other tribes referred to the Arikaras as the "Corn People." In Plains Indian sign language, the signal for Arikara was the same as that for shelling or husking corn.[19]

In short, corn (*niishu*) was the pillar of Arikara subsistence and religion. It was Neešaanu's greatest gift to the people. Through selective breeding, the Arikaras developed as many as eleven varieties of corn. Some of these, such as Ree corn, were able to withstand extreme weather conditions. Ree corn matured early and, under favorable conditions, yielded fifty to seventy bushels per acre. On average, fields yielded twenty-five bushels of corn per acre, and this still left a surplus that could be stored for leaner years or be used in trade.[20]

Numerous ceremonies were associated with corn cultivation, but the most important ceremony among the Arikaras was the one dedicated exclusively to Mother Corn. The Mother Corn ceremony was a ritual of public thanksgiving for the year's crop. It involved the ritual butchering of a buffalo and the sacrifice of a portion of the buffalo meat (the tongue, trachea, heart, and lungs, all attached together) to the sacred powers. The meat was carried inside the lodge and placed before the altar upon which the contents of a sacred bundle were spread out. These objects included a pipe, tobacco, an enemy scalp, and two ears of sacred corn. The man who had pledged to sponsor the ceremony provided the meat. Songs were an essential part of the ceremony. During one song sequence, women mimicked cultivating the corn with hoes. Only women who had kept their gardens clean and orderly were entitled to dance. One woman, carrying eagle down, took the place of Mother Corn. The

The wife of Little Crow demonstrating the use of a wooden mortar and pestle to pound corn in 1948. Several varieties of corn lie nearby. Anthropologist W. R. Hiller recorded this and other traditional practices before parts of the reservation were flooded following construction of the Garrison Dam. State Historical Society of North Dakota, 00039 0002 00029.

ceremony also involved a dance in which male dancers mimicked a buffalo hunt. The ceremony was concluded by a feast of meat and corn mush, after which the objects used in the ritual were carefully returned to the sacred bundle. Ceremonies dedicated to Mother Corn were performed three times a year.[21]

The Arikaras had their own ideas about how the universe was ordered and what forces kept it in place. This order was represented by the four semi-cardinal directions. Each of these four directions was associated with a specific color and specific cosmic forces.[22]

The arrangement of the four directions served two purposes. First, it showed the four stages of human biological and cultural development. The northeast corner represented the process of human development, from the embryonic stage to the moment when the fully grown people reached the Missouri River. The southeast corner was associated with the development of Arikara civilization, from simple

Table 1
Arikara Cosmology Depicting the Four Semi-Cardinal Sacred Directions and Associated Powers
As a system of classification the four directions allowed the Arikaras to understand the universe and how everything was related. When the system was brought out of balance through abusive human action, disasters such as famines, droughts, and storms would result.

NORTHWEST						NORTHEAST
White						Black
	Wind				Night	
		Birds/Insects		Mother Corn		
			Echo			
WEST—Altar						Cedar and Rock—EAST
			Rain	Healing		
		Animals/Buffalo		Vegetation		
		Thunder/Water			Sun	
Red						Yellow
SOUTHWEST						SOUTHEAST

gatherers to sophisticated cultivators of crops. The southwest corner represented how the relationship between humans and animals, especially the buffalo, developed, and it included the invention of hunting. The northwest corner, finally, represented the highest stage of human development: the ability to echo, or transfer, wisdom and knowledge of sacred matters to subsequent generations through ceremony.[23]

Second, the four-directional scheme served as a system of classification, allowing the Arikaras to group objects, much like Mendeleyev's periodic table classified the elements and Linnaeus's taxonomy grouped animal species. The Arikaras fitted all the elements of nature into this scheme. Thanks to Neešaanu and Mother Corn, these elements were in balance. The ancient Arikaras understood that if this balance were disrupted, the consequences could be devastating: if order was upturned, primordial chaos might return.

Priests were charged with keeping the elements of the universe in balance. Their ceremonies honored and restored the vitality of these forces. Because of their vital role, the sudden death of a priest was a cause of great concern, especially if he had not yet passed on his knowledge to a successor.

The powers of the universe were harnessed or captured in sacred bundles. The Arikaras distinguished between two basic types: village (tribal) bundles and personal bundles.

Village bundles held great significance not only for the people of a particular town but also for the entire nation. These bundles represented the highest cosmic powers that worked for the well-being of the tribe, including Neešaanu, Mother Corn, and the four sacred directions. Some of these bundles ensured plentiful crops through adequate rainfall or the absence of animal plagues. Others guaranteed successful hunts, helped towns ward off disease, and gave the people strength and success in the defense against enemies.

Each bundle had its own creation story, which explained how a certain community came into existence. The objects included in the bundle usually referred to elements of its creation. When opened in 1921, the Awaáhu bundle contained the following items: five large gourd rattles, a buffalo calfskin quiver with an inner lining of fox skin, several sacred arrows, nine bird skins (from several hawks, a grebe, and probably two Carolina parakeets; each of the bird skins had an ear of corn as well), two additional ears of corn tied to sticks, a catlinite pipe, a dried buffalo tail, a stick with several scalps attached to it, a wooden bow, two large clamshell halves, two small beaver skulls, a meat hook made of a hawk claw attached to a stick, two unidentified rodent skins, several braids of sweetgrass, and three gardening hoes made from buffalo shoulder blades.[24]

Because there were at least twelve Arikara towns at one time, there may have been as many as twelve bundles. However, it is possible that at some point there were even more bundles, as more towns (perhaps as many as twenty at one time) may have existed. By 1921 there were only six or seven bundles left.[25]

The village or tribal bundle was owned by a hereditary chief, a direct descendant of the person who had the original vision to create the bundle. But the chief was only the keeper. The secrets and ceremonies associated with the bundle were known only to the bundle priest. In effect this amounted to a system of separation of powers in Arikara society. Whereas the chief was responsible for political affairs and the daily operations of the town, the priest was responsible for leading the main religious ceremonies. Both men occupied offices of great responsibility, and it seems likely that they consulted each other on major decisions. It is unclear how this separation of powers came into being, but it is likely that the original bundle visionary divided the responsibilities among two sons. Ceremonies conducted by priests were moving affairs for the Arikaras who attended them. As events of great spiritual meaning, these ceremonies "inspired deep religious fervor, delicate poetic imagination and dramatic art," wrote ethnobotanist Melvin Gilmore after attending a ceremony in August 1921.[26]

Personal bundles ranked below village bundles in significance. Unlike village bundles, personal bundles benefited the individual rather than the community as a whole. Personal bundles were owned by individuals who had been blessed with a vision from an animal spirit. The animal appeared to a worthy person in a dream or vision and instructed the visionary to create the bundle. The animal spirit also taught the visionary all the secrets associated with the bundle. Such bundles granted individuals success in doctoring, hunting, warfare, or other activities. Like village bundles, they were often inherited, but unlike village bundles, they could also be purchased from another person. The purchaser paid the bundle owner (usually an old man nearing the end of his life) a certain amount to learn the secrets of the bundle. Even though these bundles were less powerful than village bundles, ordinary people relied much on personal bundle owners for assistance in their daily affairs.

The Arikaras believed that all beings possessed souls. They called the soul *siišu'* and believed that it was immortal. Arikara informants told Edward Curtis in 1908 that the soul "is responsible for all the acts of a man during life." They explained that "it resides in the breast, and appears in the spoken word, in the look of the eye, in the movement of the muscles." The soul also rattled in the throat of the dying in its attempt to escape. Shadows were vaguely identified with souls.[27]

Because they emerged from the womb of the earth the Arikaras preferred to bury the dead in the ground. Scaffold burials were common only in winter when the ground was frozen. In such cases, the bones of the deceased would be buried later. The Arikaras painted the face of the deceased with sacred red ocher, wrapped the body in a buffalo skin, and placed it in the grave either on its back or sideways with legs flexed. The head of the deceased usually pointed eastward to welcome the rising sun in the morning. Gifts, such as tools, ornaments, beads, and other objects, were placed in the grave as well. The grave was then covered with split logs, dirt, and rocks.[28]

Unlike the body, which was returned to the earth, the soul returned to the heavens from where it had originated. The Arikaras believed that the soul or spirit of the dead stayed around for four days before traveling to the spirit world. On the fourth day, friends and relatives gathered for a feast known the Last Supper. Even today after a death, the people gather at sunset to eat the favorite food of the deceased person. The food is brought in and placed in the center of the room, where it stands covered. At sunset all go out and face west. Prayers are spoken. As the sun descends, the deceased enters the room to partake in the dinner. The food must remain covered until a specific time. When it is uncovered, the spirit "tastes" the food. Then everyone present eats. At the end of the dinner, people are smudged before leaving. How similar this present-day wake is to the original tradition is impossible to say, but by all appearances it is a very old custom.[29]

Gilmore described a ceremony held by friends and family of the deceased within a week or two after a death. This was a ceremony to comfort the mourners or, as the Arikaras say, "to wipe away the tears." At this ceremony, people came together for prayer, presents were given away, a sacred bundle was opened, and the creation story was recited. People also drank from an ear of corn (Mother Corn) that had been dipped into a bowl of water. A feast of meat ended the ceremony.[30]

The Arikaras did not believe in a hell. All people entered the spirit world after death. In the afterworld, the dead would be reunited with their loved ones. A story told by White Owl around 1900 explained how the dead called for living relatives to join them. White Owl himself visited the land of the dead during a sickness. He saw singers who were calling the living. "They wanted me to go into the lodge," White Owl said, but someone told him not to enter the lodge with the singers. "Do not go into the lodge," the man told White Owl. "You must not stay here; you must be going to your country."[31]

ARIKARA SOCIETY

Arikara society was hierarchical. Unlike modern-day Western societies, this stratification was based on spiritual power rather than material wealth. The social pyramid mirrored the stratification of the sacred powers. Individuals climbed the social ladder if there was proof they had been favored by the sacred powers. The highest offices were reserved for individuals who held spiritual power bequeathed by Neešaanu, Mother Corn, the four directions, or other heavenly beings. Further down the ladder were individuals blessed by the animal powers. At the bottom of the pyramid were people who had not been favored by any of the sacred powers. Finally there was a group of outcasts, including those who had violated social and cultural norms: thieves, loose women, murderers, cowards, witches (people who used medicines for evil purposes), and the "scalped ones."

Although wealth was not a decisive factor in determining status, in theory it was possible for a person of means to climb the social ladder by purchasing sacred power from knowledgeable people. In reality, because they had spiritual power, the people on the upper steps of the ladder tended to be more successful economically.

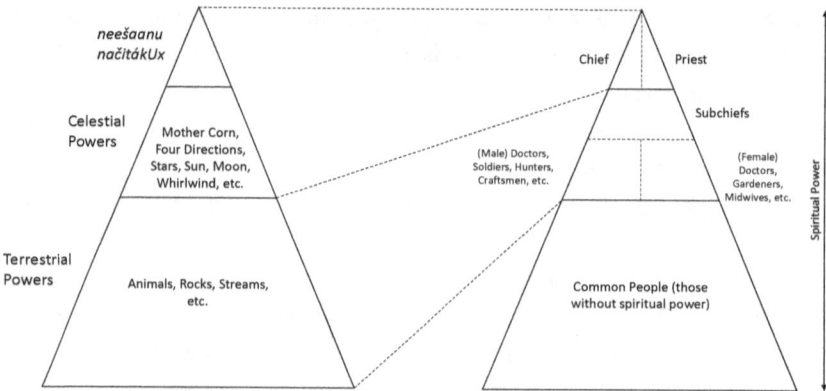

Cosmic hierarchy and Arikara social status based on spiritual power. Spiritual power rather than wealth determined one's position in Arikara society. Arikara men and women took risks or spent time, energy, and personal wealth to obtain spiritual power.

However, this situation was mitigated by the fact that the sacred powers mandated that wealthy people should share their wealth with others. It was not strange to find a chief who lived in poorer conditions than a commoner, because the responsibilities of his office required him to give his wealth away. Thus, when a chief told European and American government officials that he was "poor," he meant that he was a good chief because he had given his possessions to his people. Unlike European monarchs, who extracted their wealth from the common people through taxation and tribute, Arikara chiefs had to be generous.

At the bottom of the social pyramid were people who had not been favored with a vision. They formed by far the largest segment of Arikara society. Although they could be affluent, they were considered "poor" because the sacred powers had not blessed them with spiritual powers. Most commoners tended to be poor materially as well. Generally, they owned the least fertile lands, because when chiefs assigned garden spots at the beginning of the planting season, commoners were the last ones to receive their allotments.

Although difficult, upward mobility was not impossible. For a poor man to climb the social ladder, he had to garner spiritual power. He could do so through inheritance, purchase, or dreams and visions. Power could also be transferred through sex. In that case, women served as the vessels through which power was channeled from one man to another.

There was yet another way: men (and sometimes women) could get ahead by placing themselves in the hands of the sacred powers, making periodic sacrifices, working hard, taking risks, and showing a willingness to suffer. As a general rule, only people willing to make sacrifices at great personal risk or expense, whether in the hunt, warfare, or otherwise, would show themselves worthy to an animal power and thus climb the social ladder.

One way for a man to draw the attention of the sacred powers was to go to war. This path in life was the most hazardous but potentially also the most rewarding. By going to war, a man sought to prove that he was worthy of the favors of the supernatural. He willingly subjected himself to the hardships of the warpath and the dangers of battle. He had to be prepared to sacrifice his own life. If he lost his life, his death bestowed honor upon him and his family. If he returned successfully, this was considered proof that he had been blessed. He might dedicate the spoils of war (booty, scalps, captives) to the sacred powers, which would only increase his standing. Because warfare was an important avenue to achieve status, chiefs sometimes found it difficult to keep ambitious men from going to war.

A less dangerous way to advance socially was to purchase a bundle (with the accompanying songs, rituals, and secrets) from a doctor, warrior, or other successful person. This, however, was a time-consuming and expensive process because the apprentice promised to support his mentor for the duration of his education. Few men could afford to purchase a bundle. A man could not move up the ladder by marrying a woman from a higher segment.

Successful warriors, doctors, hunters, gardeners, midwives, and others had proven that they were favored by the terrestrial (mostly animal) powers. They owned bundles that made them successful. Hunting large game animals such as bison required skill and bravery, especially before the arrival of horses on the plains. Success in the hunt, as in everything else in life, depended on the sacred powers. The best hunters often possessed secret knowledge that enabled them to track and approach game and kill it with a steady hand. With the help of the sacred powers, some men also become expert weapon makers. The sacred powers also taught fishermen to make traps and catch fish in large numbers.

Doctors (*kunaananá*) were among the most admired members of this class. Apart from visions, doctors usually obtained medical knowledge through purchase of a medicine bundle and its rites. The process involved the gradual transfer of power from the doctor to an apprentice. At the conclusion of the transfer, the original doctor had lost all his power. Usually, but not always, sons purchased medicine bundles from their fathers. Female doctors were called *skunaananá*.

Doctors who derived their powers from the same spirit guardian usually formed medicine societies. There were several such fraternities among the Arikaras. In 1909 Curtis listed nine societies: Ghost, Black-Tailed Deer, Buffalo, Swamp Bird,

Principal Medicine (led by Beaver), Duck, Owl, Mother Night or Young Dog, and Bear.[32] Twelve years later, in 1921, Gilmore also saw nine, but some of the names were different: Ghost, Deer-Elk, Buffalo, Crane-Bald Eagle-Cormorant, Beaver-Otter, Duck, Owl, Rabbit-Sioux, and Bear.[33] Membership in one of the medicine societies was also by purchase.

During late fall medicine societies gathered at the town's ceremonial lodge to perform public spectacles in which they displayed their supernatural powers through sleight of hand. This so-called medicine lodge ceremony lasted several weeks and was attended by many people in town. In the ceremony, doctors frequently challenged each other to feats of magic, such as making things disappear and reappear, shooting people with guns or arrows and curing them on the spot, reattaching dismembered limbs, calling animals, and bringing objects of clay or other materials to life. Although doctors were well respected for their curative abilities, they were also feared because of their ability to bewitch.[34] Doctors with a proven record of success and kindness might be elected to serve on the town council.

Some men owed their status to their records in war. The best warriors sometimes organized war parties into enemy territory in search of treasure, scalps, and captives. These spoils they distributed in the hope of gaining the favors of members of the town. If ambition did not kill them first, such warriors hoped to be appointed to the council of subchiefs.

Women could also obtain spiritual power. Their power was usually associated with female professions such as gardening, house construction, midwifery, pottery making, and sewing. Some women became respected doctors. Occasionally a

Interior of the Arikara ceremonial lodge during the Mother Corn ceremony in 1923. Different doctor societies occupy specific stations within the lodge. State Historical Society of North Dakota, 10190 0055000 00730.

woman also earned war honors, which entitled her to speak up in meetings usually reserved for men.

Subchiefs (*neešaanu naahukoosu'*, or "soldier chiefs") assisted the head chief in running the daily affairs within a community. The subchiefs formed a council that advised the chief on matters of policy. They were selected from the group of hunters, doctors, and warriors of age and experience who had led exemplary lives. They were required to be hardworking, generous, kind, patient, and thoughtful. A candidate who had significant spiritual power but lacked these moral characteristics would not be considered for the position of subchief.

A separate group were "criers" and "errand men" (*taroosihUx*), who assisted chiefs, priests, and sometimes doctors in political and ceremonial functions. Criers announced decisions made by the chief and the town council and called people for certain ceremonies and other important events. Errand men prepared the ceremonial lodge for upcoming ceremonies. Both positions were honorary and awarded to men with distinguished records of service.

At the top of Arikara society stood the chiefs (*neešaanuu načitawi'U*) and priests (*kuna'Uxwaarúxtii'u'*). Chiefs were owners of tribal and village bundles associated with the powers of the heavens. Priests knew the secrets of these bundles and conducted the ceremonies associated with them. Thus the chiefs and priests cared for the well-being of the town or nation as a whole. Together the chiefs and priests formed the aristocracy in Arikara society.

Chiefs personified Neešaanu on earth. They were expected to maintain peace and order, compel the people to live by the rules instituted by Mother Corn, and work for the benefit of the people. The office required them to be patient, kind, deliberate, and above all generous. At the beginning of the horticultural season, they assigned land to the families of the town. They also presided over the council composed of the *neešaanu naahukooìsu'*. Unlike the village chief, soldier chiefs did not inherit their positions but were appointed. They advised the village chief on village affairs and enforced decisions made in the council.[35]

There was a hierarchy among the village chiefs on the tribal level. The chief of the Awaáhu (Left Behind) band was regarded by all as the head chief of the tribe and presided over the tribal council. This council was composed of the various band and village chiefs. The exact number of bands is unclear, but twentieth-century informants told Gilmore that at one time there were twelve. Each band was composed of one or more towns. Each town had its own chief.[36]

Comparable in importance to town chiefs were town priests. Their office was hereditary too. While the chief owned the village bundle, only the priest knew its ceremonies. The ceremonies and rituals performed by the priests ensured the well-being of the town. Priests conducted ceremonies to ensure bountiful crops and successful buffalo hunts and to keep diseases away from town.

Like that of chief, the office of priest demanded great discipline, self-restraint, and strength of mind. "The priests felt the gravity and responsibility of their station," wrote Gilmore in 1925. A priest had to be "dignified but kindly . . . patient and long-suffering . . . unselfish and self-abnegating [and] courageous in defense of the rights of others." In addition, "he must hold no grudges, he must have no envy or malice in his heart, he must be forgiving toward those who wronged him, he must be magnanimous; never be haughty and prideful, but humble and considerate." Finally, he "must not allow himself ever to be drawn into bickering and strife, but always show an example of self-restraint."[37]

Outcasts were social deviants who had violated certain taboos or disgraced themselves in some way. The Arikaras believed, wrote the Reverend Aaron M. Beede in 1916, that since all laws were made by the sacred powers, any crime against the community amounted to sin. By extension, any offense against the sacred was a crime against the community.[38]

Arikara society valued chastity in women and looked down on women who did not follow this morality. Women were encouraged to select a partner who had proven himself as a provider and protector. Women who were careless about sexual matters were thought to have "no sense." Giving birth out of marriage was considered a stain on the entire family. Disgraced women, although they were allowed to remain in the town, were often eschewed by others. It was not dishonorable for a woman to divorce her husband (and vice versa), however. Some sources suggest that it was acceptable for an Arikara man to allow a wife (plural marriages were possible) to have sexual relations with one of his relatives or an esteemed guest. Such cases were uncommon but considered a form of honoring someone. Because the Arikaras believed that sexual intercourse was one of the ways through which spiritual power could be transferred from one person to another, poor men sometimes allowed a wife to have sexual relations with another man. But this last practice was rather a desperate last resort rather than a preferred method to transfer spiritual power.[39]

Cowardice was a grave violation of the martial code of honor among the Arikaras. A coward was often scorned as having the "heart of a woman." He would not be asked to join war expeditions or invited into a military society. However, mitigating circumstances might prompt a man to turn away from a military expedition. A man who decided to leave a war party after receiving a dream or bad omen was not considered weak or cowardly.[40]

Witches were people who used magical power (*niitunísu'*, or "evil medicine") for evil or selfish purposes. Often these were doctors. Jealousy, ambition, frustration, sexual fixations, and hatred turned good doctors into witches. Some witches used their powers to get rich by causing illness in victims and then charging them for the cure. The usual method of witching someone was through the use of "magic arrows." These were usually made of human body parts, which the witch blew in the direction of the person he wanted to harm. These objects lodged themselves in the victim's body, causing injury followed by a painful death. Witches used these powers secretly and thus continued to occupy a high rank in Arikara society until they were exposed. Once exposed, a witch faced the scorn of the people and even possible retaliation from a victim's relatives, because death by witchcraft was considered murder. Because they dealt with disease and death, many doctors were feared as potential witches.[41]

The "scalped ones" were people who had been mutilated in war but restored back to life by one of the sacred powers. Consequently, they were no longer humans but spirits. Because the Arikaras believed that they possessed potentially harmful spiritual powers, scalped people were forced to live away from the community, where they would not be a threat to ordinary humans. Scalped people often lived a lonely existence in caves near rivers and streams. They appeared from their hiding places at night to steal food and other supplies from town or to kidnap women as a remedy for loneliness. Arikara tradition has a great body of scalped men stories, often meant to scare little children and correct their behavior. Occasionally, however, scalped men bestowed their supernatural powers on worthy individuals.[42]

ARIKARA GENDER ROLES

Women and men performed different tasks in Arikara society. Women's tasks were often associated with the forces of life: they gave birth to children (and sometimes sacrificed their lives in the process), acted as midwives, raised crops that sustained the people, and owned and kept the house. Men, in contrast, killed animals for food and might be called upon to kill enemies or sacrifice their own lives in defense of the people. Arikara women were taught from childhood that they should honor a husband, "because he will suffer so much for you. He must fight to defend the home and the fields, and he will very likely die in battle," an Arikara informant told the Reverend Beede in 1915.[43]

Though they were not necessarily homosexuals, men who followed the path of women (*kUxát*; sometimes called two-spirit people today) were not expelled by the Arikaras. They were merely thought to be under the influence of a supernatural power, such as a deer or the moon. Likewise, some women (*skUxát*) followed the ways of men.

One must not apply these gender roles too rigidly. In reality, gender roles were flexible. Women could be doctors, and there were some esteemed female doctors among the Arikaras in the twentieth century. A few women even distinguished themselves in battle, and it is said that in the nineteenth century, the Sioux actually feared Arikara women for their abilities in war.[44] Likewise, husbands frequently helped their spouses in clearing and maintaining gardens or doing household chores. Men also maintained gardens of their own, albeit to grow tobacco, which they raised for religious purposes. And if necessary a woman might take up a weapon to defend people in case of attack.

Still, although a woman might show her bravery in battle and a man might show his talents as a gardener or cook, each was still valued first for the qualities associated with their gender. Thus a woman was valued first for her qualities as a worker and guardian of her chastity, while a man was judged primarily for qualities such as bravery and generosity.[45]

These ethics were instilled in children from an early age. "A boy prayed that he might grow up to be a brave, generous, useful and honorable man," one of Gilmore's Arikara informants said, while "girls prayed to grow into kind, quiet, hospitable and useful women." In addition, children of each gender were taught "reverence, respect for wisdom and age, deference to old persons, helpfulness to the needy, the sick and afflicted, [and] kindness to all."[46]

BANDS AND TOWNS

Though a distinct Arikara identity had emerged by the 1600s, it is incorrect to speak of the Arikaras as a single nation. In fact, rivalries, tensions, and conflicts between different Arikara communities continued.[47] At best the different groups formed a loose confederation of autonomous bands. The number of bands shifted over time, as some joined together while others split up. It also appears that groups separated from the Skiri Pawnees at different times before joining the Arikara constellation. Only a few band names survive in the historical record.[48]

Each band had its own origin myth, sacred bundle, chief, and priest. Many spoke different dialects. Linguistic analysis shows at least two basic Arikara dialectal groups from which all other dialects derived. The speech of some Arikara bands closely resembled the speech patterns of the Skiri Pawnee, while others spoke a more distinctly Arikara dialect. Each band consisted of one or more towns. Fourteen Arikara band and town names have survived in the historical record.

Known Sahnish Band or Town Names	Translation
AxtarAhi	Concave Foot
Wa'hukAxa	Sides of Head Shaved
Awaáhu	Left Behind
tUhka'takUx	Village against a Hill
Tu'nu'ka'takUx	Village on Creek Bank
nAhu'ka'tA	By the Water
CinIhna'htakUx	Ash Wood on Hill
tUhkAstha'nu'	Buffalo Sod Village
Na'karikA or Ha'karikA	Tree with Branch Sticking Out
Hu'ka'wirat	Eastern
Warihka'	translation unknown
Sitni'sapIt	They Broke the Arrow
Wi'ta'u'xU	Long-Haired Man
Naka'nusts	Small Chokecherry

When the chiefs of the different bands came together in council, each chief held a specific place in the council circle. In the council, chiefs discussed matters of war, peace, trade, the annual tribal hunt, where to locate towns when time came to move, new applicants to the council, and any other issue that might arise.

Table 2
Seating Arrangements of the Chiefs of the Different Bands in the Tribal Council

NORTHWEST	NORTHEAST
Tukátuk ("Village at the Foot of the Hill")	Tukstánu ("Sod-House Village")
Tšinina'ták ("Ash Woods")	Nakanústš ("Small Cherries")
Wítauh ("Long-Hair People")	Nišapst ("Broken Arrow")
Principal Chief (from Awaáhu Band)	
Hu'káwirat ("East")	Awaáhu ("Left Behind")
Warihka ("Horn-Log")	Hokáat' ("Stake at the Shore")
Nakarík [?]	Sciriháuh ("Coyote Fat")
SOUTHWEST	SOUTHEAST

Source: Gilmore, *Notes on Arikara Tribal Organization*, 344–45.

It was not always easy to get chiefs to agree on a single policy. Although the chief of the Awaáhu band was considered head chief, his authority was limited. He had to maneuver diplomatically to reach a consensus. In matters that did not affect the Arikara people as a whole, the bands could act independently.

The diagram above shows the seating arrangements of the chiefs of the different bands in the tribal council according to Gilmore.[49]

In the 1500s the Arikaras claimed much of the lands west of the Missouri River, from the Elkhorn River in northeastern Nebraska up to the Big Bend of the Missouri River in central South Dakota.[50] From all appearances, the Arikara hunting grounds stretched as far west as the Black Hills.[51]

We know little about these early Arikara towns. Only two obscure references to the Arikara settlement in the Big Bend of the Missouri River exist. Strikes Two and Sitting Bear told South Dakota historian Charles E. DeLand about the Big Bend settlement around 1905. The Arikaras called the Big Bend settlement Fox Woman, after another tribe (possibly a Kiowa band) that at some point frequented the area. Straight east from the bend was a big timber where once three different peoples lived. Strikes Two listed them as "Pawnees, Sinin, and Arikaree." Their exact identification is unclear. Strikes Two's grandfather, a man named Chief Horse, was born at Fox Woman some years before the 1781 smallpox epidemic. When he was about three years old, his people moved from Fox Woman to the mouth of the Bad River, where they built a town they called Long Village because of its width. It took seven arrow shots to reach from one end of the town to the other.

Sitting Bear added that Long Village had no fewer than three medicine lodges, indicating that the new town was composed of the remnants of three different towns after the 1781 epidemic. Here his grandfather Star was born. When Star was three years old, the people moved to the mouth of the Grand River, where they built two settlements on opposing sides of a creek. There Sitting Bear's father, Rushing Bear, also known as Son of Star, was born. Sitting Bear summed up the confederate nature of the nation in a final statement. "We were the same tribes that they used to call different names," he said. "We are about ten different tribes [bands], but we are the same tribe that used to have ten names."[52]

ECONOMY AND MATERIAL CULTURE

The Arikaras lived in earth lodges during the spring and fall and in buffalo hide tipis in the summer and winter. Women owned both types of lodges and were in charge of building and repairing them. Tipis were used when the people traveled during the annual summer hunt or when they camped in the bottomlands along the river during the winter season. The size of earth lodges varied according to the size and wealth of the family or families living in them.

The largest earth lodge structure in town was the holy lodge. Here important ceremonies were conducted. This structure, which was always located in the town's center, was erected at public expense. Located in front of it was a large plaza for ceremonial processions and activities. The entrance of the holy lodge always faced in the direction of the rising sun. A fireplace was located in the center. The west wall, directly across from the entrance, was the most sacred place in the lodge. The altar and the sacred bundles were kept in this part of the lodge. The ceiling represented the sky or Neešaanu. It was supported by four large posts, which were placed in the four semi-cardinal directions around the fireplace. In short, the floor plan of the ceremonial lodge reflected Arikara cosmology.[53] Ordinary earth lodges generally followed the same floor plan, although the direction of the entrance sometimes varied.

Town plans changed over time. During periods when warfare was endemic, the Arikaras built their earth lodges close together and constructed fortifications such as moats and palisades. Occasionally these palisades were reinforced with bastions. During extended periods of peace, these defensive measures were dropped and lodges were scattered over greater distances.[54]

The Arikaras had a mixed economy that included gardening (horticulture), hunting, gathering, fishing, and trade. These activities were considered gifts from Neešaanu and involved elaborate ceremonial preparation by priests possessing calendrical knowledge stored in the sacred bundles. They determined when the fields had to be cleared, seeds planted, and crops harvested, or when it was time to go on the annual buffalo hunt.

Arikara seasonal activities were as follows:

April–May	spring planting season
June–July	summer hunt
August–October	harvest and trade season
November–December	late fall/early winter hunt
January–March	winter camps in bottomlands[55]

The horticultural season began in April, after the spring rise of the Missouri River had fertilized the bottomlands. Although land was owned communally, the head chief assigned each family a plot of land according to the family's needs.[56]

The Arikaras grew corn in little hills about one foot to eighteen inches in diameter, in which they placed nine grains of corn. The hills resembled little earth lodges. One kernel was placed in the middle, representing the fireplace. Surrounding it was a square of four seeds representing the four central support poles. An outer ring of the four remaining seeds represented the lodge walls. The hills were placed about two steps apart. Squash and beans were planted between them. Sunflowers were planted at the edges of the gardens. Until the plants began to sprout, each garden bore a striking resemblance to a miniature earth lodge village.[57]

Gardens were the domain of women, and they owned the fruits of their labor. Each day they left for the fields at sunrise, returned home to take care of the household when it got warm, and returned later to complete work in the fields. In May the fields were hoed at least twice, until the plants were tall enough to withstand further weed growth. The Arikaras did not fertilize or irrigate their gardens.

Hunting was the domain of men. By far the most important game animal was the *tanáha'* (bison). Its meat was an important source of protein. Choice parts were the hump, heart, and tongue. Raw liver dipped in gall was considered a delicacy. Marrow from bones was used to butter corn. Bison fat was used for cooking, and bison meat was sliced into thin strips to be dried.[58]

Bison were in effect giant, four-legged bovine hardware stores that provided raw materials for numerous applications: skulls served as altars;[59] hides made robes,

Black Calf Woman, widow of Arikara chief Sitting Bear, demonstrating the process of fleshing a hide with an elk horn scraper for historian Orin G. Libby, August 1916. Born in 1850, she married Sitting Bear in 1866. Sitting Bear (born 1839) died in 1915. State Historical Society of North Dakota, B0127-00001.

tent covers, blankets, moccasins, shields, packing cases, pillows, thongs, ropes, and bull boats; fat was used as a base for ointments; bones made needles, flint chipping tools, awls, and fleshers; shoulder blades made excellent hoes; horns were turned into spoons, cups, ornaments, and containers for paints, ointments, and medicines; sinew made thread, bowstrings, and ropes; water containers were fashioned out of bladders; paunches were used as cooking vessels, in which water was brought to a boil by dropping in hot stones; hoofs were boiled to make glue. Even dried buffalo chips were useful as a clean and odorless fuel for fires.

Women usually butchered the killed bison, prepared the skins, and dried the meat. All parts of the animal were used except for the flesh underneath the front legs, which according to Arikara lore were the remains of earlier humans, victims from the time when buffalo still ate humans. Because there were no horses, dogs carried the spoils of the hunt on travois. By the end of July, the hunters returned to their towns in time for the corn harvest. [60]

The harvest season began in late summer. In early August, squash was gathered, sliced, and dried for storage. During the second week of August, a portion of the corn was harvested. This green corn was cooked immediately, but part of it was also dried and stored as "sweet corn." During September and October, the remainder of the corn was harvested. No cobs were left behind. Seed cobs were braided together in strands before drying. The remainder of the corn was dried on scaffolds, threshed, placed in bags, and cached in underground storage pits.[61]

At the end of the harvest, the trading season began. If the harvest was plentiful and enough remained to be traded with other tribes, the priests conducted a *piireeškáni'*, a calumet (pipe) or peace ceremony. It was more properly an adoption ceremony, in which one side assumed the role of father and the other the role of child, thus establishing kinship relations that ensured a peaceful exchange of goods.[62]

A second bison hunting season started in the late fall and early winter, before the weather became too cold. The hunters and their families followed the bison. Hunters may have used snowshoes to travel through the snow. The hides acquired during the winter hunt were especially valued because they were thick with hair.

During the coldest months of the years, the Arikaras camped in the bottomlands, where they subsisted on crops and meat they had collected in the preceding seasons. This was a time of much socializing and the season in which the people told stories, both ancient and new. It was unlucky to tell stories in other seasons.

In addition to hunting large game animals, Arikara men fished and trapped eagles. Eagle feathers were highly prized, and the Arikaras trapped eagles from shallow pits covered with branches, grass, and leaves. They lured eagles by shaking dead rabbits.[63] The Arikaras used both lines and traps to catch fish. According to Gilmore's informant White Bear, ritual preparations, such as sacrifices of tobacco and other objects, were essential for a successful catch. Fish were boiled or were coated with mud and cooked under burning coal.[64]

The Arikaras also gathered plants for nutritional, medicinal, and ceremonial purposes. Among the plants that the Arikaras collected for food were prairie turnips, wild onions, lamb's-quarter, wild grapes, Jerusalem artichoke, and a wide variety of plums, berries, cherries, and nuts. Plants gathered for ceremonial purposes included wild sage, which could drive away diseases and was used to purify rooms and sacred objects. Arikara tobacco, which was an essential component in any religious ceremony, was not gathered but grown in special gardens tended by men.[65]

WARFARE

The Arikaras believed that warfare was part of the great cosmic drama of death and rebirth. According to the Arikara creation story, Neešaanu NačitákUx created sickness and warfare "so that there may be death among the people, lest they should increase and fill the world and starve."⁶⁶ Thus Neešaanu was both creator and destroyer. Death was necessary to continue the process of creation.

The Arikaras, who explained everything in religious terms, also ascribed religious meaning to warfare. Going to war was a ceremonial activity. Like all ceremonies, this one involved careful ritual preparation: warriors often consulted one of the sacred bundles before leaving; they carried with them pipes, tobacco, warpaint, and other ceremonial objects; on the march, they observed taboos associated with warfare, and they stopped periodically for prayers and to make smoke sacrifices. Battle casualties were sacrifices to the sacred powers. (The word *sacrifice* in fact means "to make sacred.") It did not matter whether the sacrifice was an enemy or oneself. A man who was killed in battle had brought great honor upon himself and his family. The ceremony ended with a joyful reunion with friends and relatives, the sharing of the spoils of war, and a celebration in thanksgiving to the sacred powers for granting success.

Though death in war was honorable, the Arikaras considered it the highest skill to steal from an enemy while avoiding bloodshed. Nevertheless, every Arikara going on a stealing expedition was fully aware of the fact that his life and those of his comrades lay in the hands of the sacred powers and that they might become sacrifices themselves if the powers so dictated.

In Arikara creation, Neešaanu urged men to go on the warpath so they could attain the status of chiefs.⁶⁷ In 1903 Hand confirmed this claim. According to Hand, one day Neešaanu appeared to the people carrying a scalp. "This," Neešaanu said, "the chief must have . . . for the man who takes the most scalps and captures the most enemies shall become a chief."⁶⁸

Another strong incentive for men to go to war was marriage. Until a man had displayed bravery in battle, Arikara women showed little interest in him. Cowardice was scorned. The quest for treasure, captives, and scalps could be another incentive for war. The Arikaras sacrificed the scalps they took from the enemy in battle to renew their compact with the supernatural powers.⁶⁹ Sitting Bear described the sacrifice of a scalp in 1903: a priest burned the scalp, allowing people to pass their medicine bags through the smoke while he called on the sacred powers.⁷⁰

Through stories and folk tales, Arikara boys were taught that the warpath was dangerous but honorable. They were told not to fear death, to be brave in battle, to be loyal to their comrades, and to always place their faith in the sacred powers. Among the practical skills they acquired were stealth, endurance, and the ability to manufacture, use, and repair weapons. The arsenal of the Arikara warrior consisted of a bow and arrows, some spare bowstrings, a war club, a spear, and a shield. Shields became smaller after the acquisition of the horse; large shields were unwieldy on horseback. Battleaxes, knives, and guns did not become part of the warrior's equipment until the arrival of the Europeans. When boys reached the age of fifteen, they joined one of the military societies (*nanís̆u'*), where they received instruction in the art of war. Each society had a distinctive staff or lance, which it carried into battle. These staffs were important rallying objects for members of the society. Arikara warrior societies fostered a sense of brotherhood and cohesion in battle.[71]

No Arikara warrior entered the fight without some form of supernatural protection, usually in the form of a personal bundle. These bundles usually contained paint, luck-bringing charms, herbs, and other medicines to treat wounds incurred in battle. The presence of their comrades, the faith placed in their personal medicines, and the military ethic impressed upon each individual since childhood made the Arikaras formidable warriors.

Pre-contact territorial wars could be extremely violent. At the Crow Creek archeological site in South Dakota, scientists discovered a mass grave containing the remains of 486 individuals in an old proto-Arikara earth lodge village dating to circa AD 1325. All remains showed evidence of massive trauma, including skull fractures and scalp marks. The relative absence among the victims of females suggests that the attack was staged to capture women. Further analysis showed that the plains experienced an extended period of drought at the time of the massacre, providing a possible explanation for the war: as droughts continued, large game animals became scarce and fields became less and less productive, malnutrition caused diseases and lowered fertility rates, and warfare may have ensued as towns began to compete with each other for the best available horticultural lands and hunting grounds. This pattern of drought and warfare was confirmed in other archaeological sites on the plains.[72]

The scale of violence at Crow Creek indicates that, despite highly efficient subsistence patterns, the Arikaras occasionally faced hardships and struggles. Their realization that they were vulnerable to disturbances in the universe made them a deeply religious people. For this reason, they placed their faith and their fate in the hands of the Almighty.

In the seventeenth century, Arikara existence would grow more precarious with the arrival of the *sahništaaká* ("white people") at the edges of their universe. In the wake of European arrival, the Arikaras would be confronted with hitherto unknown diseases, displacement by foreign invaders, and powerful new technologies, all of which posed a threat to them and their institutions.

3 MICROBIAL AND FOREIGN INVASIONS, 1500–1700

> Mother Corn stood up and spoke, saying, "Nesaru and the gods, I want help, for the Whirlwind is coming to destroy my people!"[1]
>
> —"THE ORIGIN OF THE ARIKARA," TOLD BY STAR

THE ANGRY WHIRLWIND

When Star related his version of the Arikara creation story in 1903, he told how Whirlwind became angry at the people for failing to offer her smoke. She turned herself into a dark and violent storm, intending to kill the people for their slight. Luckily, Mother Corn came to the rescue. She stepped forward and turned herself into a cedar tree. Then a voice thundered from the sky, and out of the heavens fell a big black rock. The people found shelter in the tree and on the rock. Though the storm killed many people and scattered others in different directions, the Arikara people survived because of Mother Corn and Grandfather Rock. Ever after, the Arikaras reenacted this event in the Mother Corn ceremony. They cut a cedar tree and placed it in front of the ceremonial lodge. Next to the tree they placed a large rock, which they decorated with paint. Members of the different doctor societies danced around the tree and the rock. Photographer Edward S. Curtis published visual images of the ceremony in 1909, and ethnobotanist Melvin Gilmore filmed it in 1924.

Though most Arikaras accept this story literally, the events described by Star have a historical basis that can be understood only when they are read symbolically. In this interpretation, Whirlwind represents an infectious disease introduced by European invaders while Cedar Tree and Grandfather Rock, who provided refuge and shelter to the Arikaras, represent a well-known American landmark: the Black Hills.

This chapter discusses the impact of European invasions upon the Arikaras in the 1600s. Even before they established contact, the Arikaras felt the presence of Europeans. Spanish, French, British, and Dutch imperial projects resulted in massive population shifts and demographic upheavals in the East that caused a chain reaction moving westward. Some Native nations, displaced by Europeans, in turn displaced other tribes farther west. Increased warfare and enslavement created refugee "scatter zones" elsewhere. Though far removed from early contact areas, the Arikaras nevertheless felt their impact: New tribes amassed on the eastern borders of Arikara territory. Metal goods changed plains economies. New technologies, such as firearms and horses, altered the region's balance of military power. Finally, germs introduced by Europeans would shatter the world that the Arikaras had built so meticulously.

CEDAR TREE, GRANDFATHER ROCK, AND ARIKARA SACRED GEOGRAPHY

Long before the Lakhotas claimed it as their most sacred place, the Black Hills were of great spiritual significance for the Arikaras. Though less central to their existence than the Missouri River, the Black Hills were nevertheless part of Arikara sacred geography. They were a place of refuge and shelter—a last resort.

Much knowledge was lost after the Lakhotas appropriated the Black Hills and Arikara population figures dropped below four hundred in the early 1900s. As elders died, they took knowledge of their nation's past with them. Still, the significance of the Black Hills was preserved, albeit in coded terms, in Arikara creation stories.

As mentioned in the previous chapter, the geocultural history of the Black Hills started when Lucky Man created the land south (and west) of the Missouri River. According to Yellow Bear, Lucky Man lined the land on the south side with hills and mountains. Here, Lucky Man said, the people would find shelter in hard times.[2]

Although the Black Hills are not specifically mentioned in the Arikara creation story, they nevertheless play a central part in the scene where Mother Corn turns herself into a cedar tree and Neešaanu descends from the heavens in the form of a rock. Cedar Tree and Grandfather Rock are the Black Hills.

Covered with coniferous trees that give them a dark appearance all year round, the Black Hills are located a mere 160 miles from the seventeenth-century Arikara towns near present-day Pierre, South Dakota. At least some Arikara groups found refuge here when the first major epidemics struck the nation. Here they quarantined themselves and waited for the infection to pass. The story told by Star provides some important clues. "The people then ran up to the Cedar-Tree and around the rock," Star said. "The Whirlwind came, and some of the people ran away, some going north, some west, some south and some east, and when the Whirlwind struck these people it changed their language. The people who stood upon the Cedar-Tree and the Rock remained as the Arikara."[3]

According to Four Horns, the Arikaras found shelter among the trees and the rock. Unfortunately, not everyone escaped the ravages of disease. Although the people crawled under the branches of the trees at Mother Corn's direction, "The Black-Wind came and took many people, notwithstanding," Four Horns said.[4]

The choice of the Black Hills as a place of refuge was obvious: here there was food and shelter in abundance. The high-altitude microclimate of the Black Hills provided shelter not only for the Arikaras but also for deer, antelope, and buffalo populations in periods of drought. Here summers were cooler and rainfall more lavish. Vegetation offered a range of berries, roots, and wild plants fit for human consumption. Here, too, there was water, timber, a wide variety of game and vegetation, and rocks for making stone tools.[5] It was these assets, especially the presence of buffalo all year round, that would attract the Lakhotas to this region two centuries later. In time the Black Hills became the center of the Lakhota universe, and they claimed it had been theirs forever, but the Arikaras have a more ancient claim to the area.[6]

Archaeologists have found little evidence directly linking the Arikaras to the many petroglyphs strewn all over the Black Hills.[7] Still, based on what the Arikara creation story tells us, the link is there. For example, swirl petroglyphs may refer to the Whirlwind episode. Swirl symbols in Plains Indian pictographs often denote a range of diseases: smallpox, cholera, measles, and possibly dysentery. The swirls also resemble whirls caused by strong winds. Truth be told, however, most experts on petroglyphs do not agree with this theory.

The Arikaras called this area Inawaakatiitúhat (meaning "hills black"), or simply Waakatít, because from a distance the lush growth of cedar trees gives a dark veneer to the otherwise light-colored geological formations.

In their reenactments of the Whirlwind episode, the Arikaras used a rock to represent the Black Hills. In the Mother Corn ceremony, the priests placed it next to a cedar tree and painted it for the performance. They called it Grandfather Rock or Big Black Meteoric Star. There is a remote possibility that they brought this rock back from the Black Hills. It still exists and is now in the possession of the Chase family on the Fort Berthold Indian Reservation.

Leaving their towns whenever infectious diseases struck was one of the few available options. Unfortunately, by the late 1700s the Black Hills were under the control of the Lakhotas, who jealously guarded this area as a sanctuary for themselves. So when a devastating smallpox epidemic struck the Arikara people in 1781, the Black Hills were effectively closed off to them. The fact that the Arikaras were barred from the Black Hills sanctuary made the 1781 epidemic more devastating than earlier ones. Still, the Arikaras continued to avoid infection by leaving their towns. In 1837 Bear's Tail was thirteen years old when his family learned that smallpox was coming from the East. "We all left our village and went north in order to get away from the smallpox," he said in 1903. Though the Black Hills were now forbidden territory, the Arikara refugees luckily found sufficient buffalo along the way to weather the storm. Indeed, Bear's Tail's father consecrated a buffalo on this occasion. During the ceremony, the priests once again called upon Mother Corn for aid during these trying times.[8]

It is difficult to determine which disease outbreak prompted the Arikaras to seek refuge in the Black Hills. In an earlier publication, I speculated that it was the smallpox epidemics of the 1700s, especially the well-documented 1780–81 epidemic. A second reading of the episode now leads me to believe that it took place a century earlier, because the oral traditions fail to mention the Sioux (who only later controlled the hills) but instead mention the Iroquois, who were at the height of their power in the 1600s. Pushing back the date is also justified by the fact that a number of historians now believe that epidemics hit the plains between 1600 and 1650.[9]

Another epidemic, probably smallpox, struck the southern plains and made its way up the Missouri River between 1687 and 1691.[10] Infectious diseases followed existing Native trade routes, and the Missouri River was one of the main arteries of trade. Smallpox could travel great distances in contaminated bison robes, other clothing, and other articles.

In the early 1600s, Nebraska was still largely empty, with one group of Pawnees (mostly South Band) living near the Wichitas in Kansas and Oklahoma and another segment (mostly Skiris) living near the Arikaras along the Missouri River in central South Dakota. Interestingly, the suggested smallpox epidemic of the mid- and late 1600s roughly coincides with the repopulation of Nebraska by the Pawnees. This suggests that these epidemics broke up and scattered towns, prompting some Pawnee groups, including the prophet Closed Man, to repopulate Nebraska.

Although there is no Euro-American documentation of these earlier epidemics on the northern and central plains, Arikara oral traditions place these events in the seventeenth century. Star's version of the Arikara creation story is the most important here because it specifically mentions the then-powerful Iroquois, suggesting this as the most likely date for the events described by Star. When Whirlwind scattered the people, Star said, she turned them into different nations. Among these were the Šaahé (Cheyennes), the Pichia ("People of Cold Country," also known as the Psi'a's or Assiniboines), the Čirikuúnux ("Witchcraft People" or Wichitas), and the "Wooden Faces" (Iroquois). Of these nations, the Cheyennes and Assiniboines were also making inroads into the northern and central plains in the mid- to late 1600s. Though the Iroquois never crossed the Missouri River, their reputation shows the power they projected at this time. Not only had the Iroquois subjugated, dislodged, or annihilated neighboring tribes by the late 1600s, but they were also key figures in a burgeoning slave trade that trafficked numerous Indians, including Pawnees and Arikaras, from the plains into Canada.[11] Furthermore, the absence of the Lakhota and Dakhota Sioux in Star's account is conspicuous. We can explain this only if the Whirlwind episode referred not to the 1780–81 epidemic but to one at least a century earlier. The Sioux would not become a major nuisance until the 1700s and became a serious threat only after the 1780–81 smallpox epidemic.[12] In short, a close reading of the oral traditions suggests that Whirlwind struck the Arikaras first in the seventeenth century, only to return in the eighteenth century.[13]

Thus, during epidemics, the Arikaras left their towns and dispersed in smaller units, seeking shelter in mountainous terrains where there was ample food, water, and shelter. This strategy worked rather well until the 1780s, when the geopolitical situation on the plains had changed to the detriment of the Arikaras.

MYSTERIOUS STRANGERS

The onset of infectious diseases roughly coincided with the appearance of Europeans on the plains in the 1600s. We do not know who these persons were, but once again the Arikara creation story provides some clues.

The first officially documented contact between Arikaras and Europeans was in 1743, but Arikara oral traditions suggest that they first met the *sahništaaká* ("white people") much earlier. In 1903 Hand recollected that at one point during their migration, the people spotted a mysterious stranger in the distance: "At this place the people saw a man who was very tall and whose hair from his mouth reached down to his waist, and they exclaimed, 'Wonderful!' And they were afraid of him. They thought this man was from the heavens."[14]

Most Arikara people today believe this mysterious stranger was Jesus, who had come to invite the people into his church. He was bearing gifts, Arikara stories say, but because the Arikara people refused to meet him, Jesus turned away and left.

That night Jesus appeared to a man in a dream and said he had felt bad when the people refused to meet him. He had come to bring gifts, but because the people had slighted him, he would give his gifts to another people: the whites. That, the Arikaras say today, is why white people had special skills that allowed them to make many wonderful things while the Arikaras remained poor.[15]

Skeptics will question this version of events. If the stranger was indeed Jesus, then the most plausible explanation is that the story is apocryphal and was added to the creation corpus after the Arikaras had been introduced to Christianity by missionaries in the mid- to late 1800s. Most Arikaras today, however, insist it truly happened as it was told by Hand and others. "It is not a tale, but a true story," Frank Heart assured anthropologists in 1952. Heart had learned this story when he was a boy. It was told to him by Two Crows, an Arikara priest in the late 1800s. "It is a sacred story," Heart emphasized. Arikaras like Heart take this story as gospel.[16]

There is a third possibility to explain this mysterious encounter. This version will satisfy neither Arikara believers nor non-Arikara skeptics who think this story was simply added later. This is the—admittedly speculative—possibility that the story indeed recollects the first time the people met a white man carrying "gifts" of powerful objects hitherto unknown to the Arikaras. In this scenario, the bearded stranger was not Jesus but rather a *coureur de bois*, as unlicensed—and often undocumented—French traders were called. This obscure character later morphed into Jesus. This theory bridges the gap between oral tradition and modern-day scholarly skepticism.

Though the first officially documented European visitors were the La Vérendrye brothers, Francois and Louis-Joseph, who in 1743 met an Arikara group they called the Little Cherry People, anecdotal evidence suggests earlier contacts between Arikaras and Frenchmen. After all, French explorers such as Rene-Robert Cavalier, sieur de La Salle, visited the confluence of the Missouri and Mississippi Rivers in 1686. Indeed, it is in the writings of La Salle's companions Louis Hennepin and Anastasius Douay that we find possible mention of the Arikaras. While ascending the Colbert (Mississippi) River, La Salle's expedition reached the "famous river of the Masourites" (Missouri), which was described as follows:

> [It is] at least as large as the river into which it empties; it is formed by a number of other known rivers, everywhere navigable, and inhabited by many populous tribes—as the Panimaha, who had but one chief and twenty-two villages, the least of which has two hundred cabins; the Paneassa, the Pana, the Paneloga, and the Matotantes [possibly Otoes], each of which, separately, is not inferior to the Panimaha. They include, also, the Osages, who have

seventeen villages on a river of their name, which empties into that of the Massourites, to which the maps have also extended the name of Osages. The Akansas [Kaws] were formerly stationed on the upper part of one of these rivers [the Ohio], but the Iroquois drove them out by cruel wars some years ago, so that they, with some Osage villages, were obliged to drop down and settle on the river which now bears their name.[17]

Scholars have struggled to identify the Panimahas, Paneassas, Panas, and Panelogas, though there seems to be a consensus that the Panimahas were most likely the Skiri Pawnees and the Panas the South Band Pawnees. The identity of the Paneassas and Panelogas remains uncertain. They could have been Chawi, Kitkehahki, or Pitahawirat Pawnees, but they could also have been the Arikaras. In any case, it is important to point out that to La Salle, the Missouri River was already "famous" and its tributaries were already "known." The presence of these nations, therefore, was no longer a matter of surprise.

A few years after LaSalle, French officer and explorer Louis-Armand de Lom d'Arce, baron de Lahontan, claimed to have sailed up the "Long River" (which some scholars believe was the Missouri) in 1688. During his journey he met a people called the Eokoros.[18]

While reportedly rowing up the Long River, Lahontan saw on the left bank some "Hutts" (probably tipis) about "a quarter of a League" from the riverbank. Approaching the settlement with ten of his men and his Outagamis (Fox Indians), Lahontan found fifty to sixty hunters, who "prepar'd to receive 'em, with their Bows and Arrows." Luckily, a violent confrontation was avoided. The Eokoros presented Lahontan's crew with deer they had just killed. The hunters told Lahontan that they had left their towns to hunt. Lahontan presented them with gifts of tobacco, knives, and needles, "which they could not but admire." The hunters left satisfied but returned the next evening with about two thousand Eokoros, who immediately started dancing when they saw Lahontan's company. Lahontan sent his Outagamis ashore while a few leading Eokoros boarded his canoes and traveled toward their "chief Village," which they reached at midnight. Despite invitations from the chiefs to stay in town, Lahontan instructed his men to set up camp near a little stream about "a quarter of a League" from the settlement. Only Lahontan's Indian escorts, the Outagamis and Outaouas (Ottawas), visited the Eokoros that night.

The next day Lahontan presented the "Grandees of this Nation" with knives, scissors, needles, and tobacco. The chiefs were "infinitely well pleas'd with our arrival in their Country [because] they had heard the Savages of other Nations speak very honourably of the French." Lahontan stayed until November 12, when he boarded his canoes to resume his journey upriver. The chiefs had given him more corn and dried meat than he needed. As Lahontan's company sailed upriver, some six hundred Eokoros escorted them along the shore. It took a few days to pass through Eokoro country. They passed several more towns, also located on the left bank, but did not disembark. At the last town, Lahontan stopped to obtain more information from their "Great Governour" about the nations upstream. The chief, "a venerable old Gentleman," told him that sixty leagues upriver lived the Essanapes. Because the Eokoros were at war with the Essanapes, the old chief could not provide Lahontan with an escort. Instead he supplied the company with six captives whom Lahontan could return to the Essanape people to ensure his safe passage.[19]

Before Lahontan boarded his vessels to resume his travels, the Eokoro chiefs provided some information about their people. They "had twelve Villages peopled by 20,000 Warriors," Lahontan reported. This number was much diminished as a result of warfare with the Nadouessis, Panimahas, and Essanapes. The people were "very civil," with an "Air of Humanity and Sweetness." They lived in long earth lodges that were round at the top. Men and women were naked except for loin cloths. They were well organized politically: "There seems to be something of Government and Subordination among this People; and they have their Houses fortified with the branches of Trees, and Fascines strengthen'd with Fat Earth."[20]

Twenty thousand warriors may seem like an exaggeration, even if one includes the Skiris and South Band Pawnees. Perhaps the total sum of men, women, and children among the Pawnees and Arikaras might reach that number. Still, the facts of Lahontan's description—that the hunters were able to quickly rally two thousand people and that there were twelve towns—indicate that the Arikaras were numerous. They were powerful too. Though warfare with enemy nations had reduced their population somewhat, there was no mention of diseases that would ravage the Arikaras later. Perhaps Lahontan himself (or his sources) inadvertently introduced germs to the Eokoros. Still, the geopolitical situation was volatile. Fortifications, nervous hunters who were ready at an instant to do battle, and mention of warfare make it clear that the region was ripe with tensions.[21]

For good reasons, many historians question the reliability of Lahontan's account. They contend that Lahontan never visited the region but merely based his account on what he learned from either coureurs de bois, Indian slaves who hailed from the region, or other tribes familiar with the Arikaras. They point out many inaccuracies that render Lahontan's map of the region practically useless. In short, the sceptics have identified plenty of reasons to approach Lahontan's account with caution.[22]

Other historians, however, contend that Lahontan's narrative nevertheless contains valuable and accurate information. Some of it was not verified until much later. Lahontan's descriptions of tribes on the Pacific coast, for example, are remarkably accurate in certain details. Though his map of the Long River is indeed inaccurate, pro-Lahontan historians believe he was actually describing the Missouri River (which he entered around present-day northeastern Nebraska) without realizing these were one and the same.[23]

Even if Lahontan lied about his supposed journey, his description of the Arikaras probably came from well-informed sources. The description of lodges made of earth (though round rather than "long"), the presence of twelve Arikara towns, and their reliance on corn matches known facts about the Arikaras. This information could only have come from coureurs de bois who had visited the nation.

Archaeology provides further evidence of French visitors. Not only is there a noticeable increase in the number of European-manufactured goods after 1675, but archaeologists also identified the remains of a European visitor who made contact with the Arikaras at the Swan Creek site in present-day Walworth County, South Dakota. In a grave, they discovered the remains of male between forty and fifty years old, with Caucasoid features, who had been buried between 1675 and 1725. He was most likely a coureur de bois, a fugitive from the law, or a fugitive Spanish slave. Such early visitors probably carried few goods but may have been of considerable use because of their knowledge of European technologies—that is, the "gifts" that the Arikara oral traditions mention.[24]

CAPTIVES AND SLAVES

Further evidence of contact between the Arikaras and Europeans can be found in the records of the French and Spanish slave trade.

Enslaving enemy captives had long been standard practice among Native American peoples in North America. For example, at the site of the 1325 Crow Creek Massacre, archaeologists noted the absence of women between the ages of fifteen and thirty-four, indicating that their capture was one of the objectives of the attack.[25] The Skiri Pawnees occasionally took female captives to sacrifice in the Morning Star ceremony, which reenacted Morning Star's epic journey to create humankind. Likewise, the Arikaras probably took enemy captives as well, frequently adopting them into the nation, where they might rise to positions of wealth and status.[26]

In the seventeenth and early eighteenth centuries, however, Arikaras and their Pawnee relatives were mostly victims of the French and Spanish slave trade. The

French assigned the name Panis to Indian slaves, which led many scholars to believe that the Pawnees were in fact the main victims of the Native American slave trade. However, the term seems to have been used for Native slaves of any tribe deemed an enemy of France or beyond French influence. The term conveniently provided the French "a degree of legal clarity intended to allow Indian slavery without the continual justification of each captive's enslavement under the law of nations."

In contrast, some scholars suggest that the designation Panis derived from the fact that Pawnee Indians were the main *suppliers* of slaves. Undoubtedly, the Pawnees were involved in exchanging enemy captives at Spanish markets. The evidence for Arikara involvement in the trade is less certain.[27]

The debate over whether Pawnees (and Arikaras) were slaves or enslavers is unlikely to be settled soon. It is not unreasonable to assume that they were both. The fortunes of the Arikaras, Pawnees, and their Wichita relatives followed the tides of European contact. Before they acquired horses or guns, these nations were at the mercy of better-equipped enemies. In the late 1600s, for example, the Pawnees suffered terribly from attacks by mounted Padoucas (Apaches) operating from bases in eastern Colorado, northeastern New Mexico, and western Nebraska and Kansas. The Apaches traded Pawnee captives for horses at Spanish markets, especially Santa Fe. Not until the Pawnees acquired guns from the French did the momentum shift in their favor and turn them into prominent slave traders. Of course, the supply of guns, gun parts, and ammunition was irregular, and during times of scarcity, the balance again tipped to the other side.[28]

Like the Pawnees, the Arikaras may have suffered from Apache slave raids. Ironically, most Apache tribes were horticulturalists who occasionally hunted buffalo. Among these Apache groups were the Jicarillas, Cuartelejos, Faraons, Sierra Blancas, Carlanas, Natagés, Llaneros, and Palomas. These nations became trade intermediaries between the Spanish at Santa Fe and the Plains Indians to the north and east.

The Apaches were among the first Plains Indian nations to acquire horses from the Spanish. They paid for these horses with slaves captured from neighboring tribes. Horses gave the Apaches a military advantage that they used successfully against the Poncas, Omahas, Pawnees, and Arikaras.[29]

It is unclear how many Arikaras ended up at slave markets in Santa Fe as a result of Apache attacks. These attacks lasted for several decades, until the Missouri Valley nations also acquired horses. The pendulum finally swung in the other direction after French traders introduced guns to the nations of the Missouri Valley. Guns allowed renowned Omaha chief Blackbird to defeat the Apaches in 1777.[30] The Kansa Indians were especially successful in countering Apache attacks because they had steady access to guns and powder. The tables had turned: now the Kansas and Pawnees successfully raided the Apaches for slaves.[31] Pressure from the Comanches forced the Apaches southward as well. By the mid- to late 1700s, the Apaches were in full retreat. As they moved south, they became vassals of the mighty Comanches.[32]

A separate group, the Plains or Kiowa Apaches (not to be confused with the Kiowas proper), led a strictly nomadic existence, relying primarily on the buffalo hunt. The robes they secured in this manner they traded to other nations. Until they acquired more horses, they lived in tipis and used dogs as pack and draft animals. They were not always on friendly terms with their horticultural relatives, who were jealous of their pivotal position in the buffalo hide trade. In early colonial sources, Plains Apaches were often called Padoucas (or some variant thereof), a term that means "enemy" in various Siouan languages. There has been some confusion over the term in the literature. Although scholars are now certain that these were Plains Apaches, by the late 1700s the name Padoucas was occasionally—and erroneously—applied to the Comanches.[33]

Padouca relations with the Arikaras were complex. Though they may have occasionally raided the Arikaras for captives, on balance their relations with the Arikaras seem to have been friendly and mutually beneficial. In 1719 Jean-Baptiste Bénard de La Harpe reported that the Padoucas traded horses with the Arikaras on the northern plains. Another reason for the Padoucas to seek friendship with the Arikaras was pressure from enemy tribes, especially the Comanches, which left them isolated and vulnerable. While the horticultural Apachean groups moved southward, the Padouca contingent had moved northward and into the vicinity of the Arikaras by 1717. Maps made that year by Guillaume De l'Isle and Le Sieur Vermale show ten Padouca camps west of the Arikaras and two other camps to the southwest.[34] Here they continued their nomadic lifestyle, which also enabled them to avoid contact with enemies. A much later Spanish report, dating from 1785, listed "small forts" of "Pados" on the Bad River. A decade later they moved to the southern branch of the Platte River before finally moving to the southern plains another decade later with the Kiowas, with whom they had forged an alliance.[35]

More Arikaras turned up as slaves in markets controlled by the French in Canada, however. Indeed, French colonial sources abound with references to Panis (male) and Panise (female) slaves. Only incidentally do these records allow us to identify the correct ethnicity of these slaves with certainty. Hence we know that in 1718 French priest Jean-Baptiste Robillard baptized a "vicara" (Arikara) slave into the Catholic parish at Lachine near Montreal. It seems likely that many more Arikara captives

Arikara women doing a scalp (victory) dance. They carry scalp sticks and wear warpaint, headdresses, and hairstyles usually reserved for warriors. Generally, only women related to victorious warriors got to carry scalps. National Anthropological Archives, Smithsonian Institution, MS 154064B #08510613.

were traded at French markets in Green Bay, Michilimackinac, and Detroit.[36] Most of these Arikaras were taken by the Sioux in conflicts discussed in the next chapter.

In turn, Pawnees and Arikaras occasionally traveled into Illinois country to trade slaves to the French. Pierre Deliette, a French fur trader who spent years in Illinois country in the late 1600s, wrote that the Pawnees and other Missouri River tribes frequently were the target of slave raids but in turn also visited to trade slaves.[37]

Arikara oral traditions published by Dorsey show that captives were not always integrated but often occupied lower-status positions in Arikara society. In the story of Rabbit Boy, told by Elk, this subordinate status of captives is made apparent. In this account a young man received sacred power from a rabbit that enabled him to become a successful warrior. His war exploits caught the attention of the daughter of an enemy chief. This girl instructed an Arikara captive-servant to notify Rabbit Boy of her romantic interest in him. The Arikara servant notified Rabbit Boy, who under the cover of darkness snuck into the enemy camp and spent the night with the chief's daughter. By Plains Indian custom, Rabbit Boy was now married into his wife's nation. He even went on war expeditions against the Arikaras and frequently returned from these raids bearing scalps, over which his adopted tribe danced in celebration. What his wife's people did not know was that these scalps actually belonged to their relatives who had been captured by the Arikaras. In short, Rabbit Boy killed only captives enslaved by the Arikaras. Rabbit Boy's in-laws therefore were celebrating the death and humiliation of their own people.[38]

The story of Rabbit Boy provides glimpses into the status of captives in Indian societies on the northern plains. Although sources show that many captives were indeed integrated, Elk's account of Rabbit Boy's exploits suggests that captives were sometimes treated as servants who were expendable.

NEW TRIBES ENTER THE PLAINS

Far more than the French and the Spanish, it was British colonization that sent waves of dispossessed Indigenous peoples across North America. Whole nations were forced to leave their homelands. Sometimes they left in a great hurry, leaving behind their possessions as well as loved ones unable to march. They sought to escape the cycle of war, disease, famine, and death triggered by the British desire for land and resources. What they found, however, were other nations already occupying the territories where they sought shelter. The result was new cycles of invasion and conquest, in which native inhabitants were displaced by the immigrants. This tragic chain reaction reached Arikara territory in the mid- to late 1600s.

The first newcomers were the Kaws, Osages, Omahas, Poncas, Iowas, Otoes, and Missourias. They had been pushed out of their homelands by eastern tribes armed with European-made guns. The newcomers settled in the lower Missouri River country south and east of the Arikaras. Interestingly, the appearance of these nations did not set the region aflame with war. Apparently, the country along the Missouri River and the western plains was able to absorb the newcomers and provide them—for the time being at least—with safety and comfort. Perhaps surprisingly, Arikara relations with the newcomers was relatively peaceful. Relations between the Arikaras and the Omahas and Poncas, the nearest of the new tribes, were especially friendly. These tribes even adopted the earth lodge dwelling of the Arikaras, and Omaha oral tradition states that the Arikaras taught them to cultivate corn. They also received a distinct type of tobacco (*Nicotiana quadrivalvis*) from the Arikaras. Beyond these outward changes, however, the new tribes remained culturally distinct and firmly attached to their own social and religious institutions.[39]

The process through which the Arikaras established these peaceful relations was the piireeškáni', or calumet ceremony. According to Arikara oral tradition, Mother Corn showed the people how to make pipes of catlinite stone, found in present-day southwestern Minnesota. Mother Corn then taught them the ceremony. Its purpose was to extend kinship relationships beyond the ordinary biological family affiliation or consanguinity.

Piireeškáni' means "many children" and refers to the symbolic adoption of one group by another. Two feathered pipes, one representing the sky (male) and the other representing the earth (female), were used in the ceremony. The priest performing the ceremony carried the two pipes and waved them in the air; the moving feathers imitated the flapping of wings. Mother Corn was represented by a painted ear of corn to which a downy eagle feather was attached. Throughout the ceremony, the priests sang songs, accompanied by gourd rattles and a drum. At the high point of the ceremony, both sides exchanged gifts and placed them at the feet of the chiefs and their children. The ceremony was usually performed between two tribes before conducting trade. The kinship bonds formed during this ceremony were reportedly very strong. As a result, the piireeškáni' is often called a peace ceremony. From the Arikaras it spread to the Omahas, who called it *wawan* ("to sing for someone"). Other tribes adopted it, though in somewhat different forms.[40]

Unfortunately, the region was able to sustain only a limited number of people. Soon more nations appeared while others, such as the Blackfeet, expanded their realms. Among the new peoples entering the region or expanding on the plains were the Apaches, Kiowas, Comanches, Plains Crees, Plains Ojibwas, Assiniboines, Arapahos, Gros Ventres, Cheyennes, Dakhotas, and Lakhotas. This second wave proved far more disruptive than the earlier one.

Although this second immigrant wave entered the plains from different directions, at slightly different times and for different reasons, eventually they all adopted nomadic lifestyles that challenged the semisedentary ways of the Arikaras and other older occupants. The appearance of the horse obviously facilitated the nomadic way of life. Like magnets, horses drew tribes toward the plains. Although some of the newcomers had led a nomadic existence all along, relying upon the dog and human power for travel, others, like the Cheyennes, made the transition from a sedentary to a nomadic lifestyle in less than three generations.

The sudden influx of these peoples upset the peace on the plains. Intertribal conflicts increased as nomadic tribes competed with sedentary nations (as well as each other) for access to horses, guns, hunting grounds, and slaves. The Arikaras and other horticultural tribes were soon swept up into this cycle of violence.

Arikara relations with some of the newcomers were friendly. The Kiowas entered the plains from the Yellowstone and Rocky Mountains. They settled near the Black Hills around 1700. From here they visited the Arikaras, with whom they established mutually beneficial trade relations. The Arikaras provided the Kiowas with corn and other produce while the Kiowas supplied the Arikaras with meat and bison hides. Later, the Kiowas also provided the Arikaras with horses obtained from Spanish markets in New Mexico. The Kiowa called the Arikaras *k'atá* ("biters"), which supposedly referred to the latter's consumption of corn. Relations between the two groups were close and there was much intermarriage. In fact, the presence of these Arikaras resulted in the formation of an entire band named the K'atás, who eventually became very wealthy and powerful. This band occupied the first place in the camp circle and to it belonged several "great chiefs" who ruled the Kiowas. In the 1890s, James Mooney wrote that this group constituted the "aristocracy" of the Kiowa nation. The Arikara name for the Kiowas was Ka'íwA or Ka'iwó'.[41]

Another nation (more accurately a confederation of groups) with whom the Arikaras established friendly relations was the Šaahé, or Cheyennes. The Cheyennes originally lived in Minnesota, where they cultivated wild rice and lived in bark-covered lodges. They were pushed west by the Ojibwas and the Assiniboines. After entering the plains, a few Cheyenne groups adopted the arts of earth lodge construction, corn and bean cultivation, eagle trapping, pottery making, and possibly the calumet ceremony from the Arikaras. Arikara specialists also showed the Cheyennes how to prevent burns when removing meat from a kettle by applying a paste of prairie mallow leaves to their hands. The Cheyennes also adopted some Arikara mythological elements into their own origin story, including the creation of land by a duck and their emergence from the earth. From their Mandan and Hidatsa neighbors to the north, the Cheyennes obtained the Okipa and Sacred Arrow Ceremonies. As with the Kiowas, relations between the Arikaras and the Cheyennes found their expression in intertribal marriages and people joining the other tribe. One Arikara who joined the Cheyennes, Stands All Night, is still remembered by present-day Cheyennes as a tribal historian and folklorist.[42]

The newcomers who ultimately had the greatest—and most disruptive—impact on the Arikaras were the Sanánat, or Sioux, more accurately the Lakhotas and Dakhotas. Like the Cheyennes, the Sioux were originally a woodland people. Before they moved west, they lived in present-day Minnesota and Wisconsin, where they cultivated wild rice and gathered maple sugar. Under pressure from the Ojibwas and attracted by the trade in beaver pelts, buffalo hides, and slaves, the Sioux turned their attention westward in the seventeenth century. The Lakhotas led the way.

Following them were the three Dakhota groups: the Yanktons, Yanktonais, and Santees. At the end of the seventeenth century, Sioux hunting parties periodically entered Arikara territory in search of buffalo.

The first recorded contact between the Arikaras and the Sioux occurred in 1694. It would be a warning sign of things to come. That year Sioux winter counts report a battle between the Padanis and a Sioux group, the Padani mni-e-wicayayapi. According to the John K. Bear winter count, "They chased the Arikaras into the water." This entry is significant for two reasons. First, the Sioux term "Padanis" can refer to the Arikaras or Pawnees, showing the similarities that caused the Sioux to (incorrectly) lump the two nations together as one. In this case, however, it is certain that the Arikaras are meant. Second, the entry shows that Arikara relations with the Sioux were troubled from the beginning. It would soon get worse. Indeed, for the next century and a half, relations with the Lakhotas and Dakhotas would come to dominate Arikara life.[43]

CONCLUSION: A CHANGING WORLD

In the seventeenth century, the Arikaras were thriving. They inhabited numerous towns along the Missouri River, where they enjoyed the many blessings given by Mother Corn. In spring the people cleared the fields and planted crops, in summer they traveled westward in search of bison, in fall they returned home in time for the harvest and the annual feast of the doctors. After the snows fell, they enjoyed long evenings with feasts of corn and meat around the fireplace. Unfortunately, only a handful of the stories they told on these winter nights has survived into the present.

But there were signs of change. Bearded foreigners bearing strange and powerful gifts appeared. Through established trade routes, the Arikaras were able to obtain small quantities of these goods. In the wake of the strangers, enemy tribes such as the Padoucas (Apacheans) and tribes from east of the Missouri River, raided their towns in search of slaves to trade to the sahništaaká, the white people. A malicious infection struck the nation at least once in the seventeenth century, forcing the Arikaras to temporarily abandon their towns on the Missouri River and seek refuge in the Black Hills. There they waited out the storm until it was safe to return to the Mysterious River. Around that time, new nations began to arrive on their eastern and southern frontiers. With some of these newcomers, the Arikaras established cordial relations. However, by the late 1600s, new and more aggressively expansionist peoples—the Lakhota and Dakhota Sioux—had arrived. They would unleash a whirlwind of a different kind that would challenge Arikara supremacy.

4 STRANGERS, SMALLPOX, AND SIOUX, 1700–1781

> Then he opened the door and when he peeked inside he saw them. Oh, dead people! There were many dead human bodies piled up inside, human beings whom the man had apparently killed. But the boy certainly did not know what tribes the different kinds of humans were.
>
> —ALFRED MORSETTE, "BLOODY HANDS AND THE STAR BOY"

BLOODY HANDS AND THE STAR BOY

In the mid-1970s, Arikara storyteller Alfred Morsette shared a tradition he had been taught by his grandmother Squash Blossom. The story told of a mysterious boy who came from the heavens and had many adventures on earth. His name was Star Boy, and he was the son of the Morning Star.

On earth Star Boy was put to work by a mysterious and heavyset man named Whirlwind. This man owned a white horse, which he kept locked away. Driven by curiosity, Star Boy snuck into the enclosure and spotted the horse. It instructed him to feed it hay. After it had been fed, the horse told Star Boy to don Whirlwind's armor and place a saddle on its back. As they fled from Whirlwind's camp, strange black clouds followed them, but Star Boy and the horse managed to escape unharmed. After taking Star Boy to a human village, the horse remained on the plains but assured Star Boy that it would assist him whenever enemies attacked. In the village, Star Boy befriended Bloody Hands, a poor boy who lived with his grandmother. One day enemy warriors under the leadership of Iron Shirt attacked the town. Star Boy called on the spirit horse, and suddenly a black horse appeared with armor attached to its saddle. Star Boy put on the armor, and in the battle that followed he killed and scalped Iron Shirt. However, upon his return, nobody believed Star Boy had killed Iron Shirt. More battles followed. Star Boy killed Iron Ear, Iron Hand, and Iron Hair, all powerful enemies. Each time the spirit horse helped him. Star Boy eventually married the youngest daughter of the chief and fathered two children before returning to the heavens. Before leaving, he instructed his wife on how to raise the children. He transformed Bloody Hands to look like him, so that Bloody Hands too became a great warrior and eventually became chief of the village.[1]

Though Morsette's story is obscure and seemingly mythical, it is clear that it takes place after Europeans had arrived in the Americas. Indeed, a closer reading of this story reveals its historical rather than supernatural roots. Whether Squash Blossom, Morsette's grandmother, realized it or not, the story told of a runaway slave—probably from New Spain—who introduced horses and iron armor to the Arikara people. In this interpretation, the heavyset man who enslaved Star Boy was a white man. He may have been named Whirlwind because he was very powerful or because—like Whirlwind in the Arikara creation story—he was associated with infectious diseases. Like whites, this man owned horses, metal armor, and firearms. When Star Boy absconded with the horse and armor, his pursuers fired at him with muskets that caused clouds of black smoke to appear behind him. Having made his escape, Star Boy used his newly acquired powers—horses and metal armor—to defeat the enemies of his people, many of whom also owned metal armor. Before returning to the heavens, Star Boy left his gifts with Bloody Hands, who in turn used them to become a great man among his people.

As mentioned in the previous chapter, the Arikaras felt the presence of the sahništaaká ("white man") long before they met him. Europeans introduced new trade items, new plant and animal species, new ideas, and, most devastating, new germs. The consequences of European arrival for the Arikaras were significant. The white man's presence increased intertribal rivalries in trade and war and caused Arikara dependency on European guns. The original Arikara view of white people as powerful beings (a notion questioned by some scholars but not by me) soon made way for a different view of them as greedy, unreliable, and treacherous. Of all the aspects of European contact, none was more dramatic than deadly germs. Diseases introduced by the sahništaaká caused tremendous suffering, massive depopulation, social dislocation, and military decline.

Despite all these pressures, Arikara culture remained essentially intact. The Arikaras continued to rely on corn horticulture and worship Neešaanu, Mother Corn, and the other sacred powers. Indeed, it was their faith that sustained the people through this turbulent and desperate period.

POWERFUL OBJECTS

European invaders introduced many objects that impacted Arikara culture. Best known are guns and horses. But there were others, including metal weapons of war: knives, axes, clubs, spear points, arrowheads, and armor.

Often references to metal weapons are obscure in Arikara oral traditions. In some cases it requires imaginative reading that few historians are willing to exercise. In one oral tradition, for example, an evil father killed his daughter's suitors with a sharpened leg. One day the girl's latest husband spotted his father-in-law inside his lodge, sharpening his leg. The young man's wife warned him that her father was evil and killed her husbands with his leg. The young man attempted to escape, but the murderous father-in-law went in pursuit. He quickly gained on the young man, despite moving on sharpened legs. When he was about to strike the deadly blow, his leg missed and struck a tree instead. The tree told the young man to leave. It would hold the old man until he died. Thus liberated from the evil father-in-law, the young man took his wife and mother-in-law back to the people.

The reference to the sharpened leg is puzzling. Though I am speculating, it may have been based on a type of stirrup common on the southern and central plains in the 1700s and early 1800s. Spanish cavalrymen and their Native allies often rode horses on metal *estribos de cruz* ("cross stirrups"), which were used to knock down and injure enemies in battle. Perhaps the Padoucas (Plains Apaches) first used these weapons against the Arikaras. These weapons were so horrifying that in 1772 the Spanish authorities outlawed their use and in 1778 even banned their manufacture.[2]

The Arikaras often refashioned European technologies for their own use.[3] Although metal kettles gradually replaced homemade clay pots, the Arikaras also used kettles as raw material from which to make arrowheads or other metal objects. Beads almost entirely replaced quills as decorative material. They were used to make earrings, necklaces, hair ornaments, and other jewelry. However, instead of simply adopting readymade beads, the Arikaras fashioned new beads from beads they acquired through trade. They ground blue beads into a powder, added water to form a paste, and shaped it into the desired forms before firing them on a copper plate. Over time, the Arikaras became master beadmakers, fashioning beads of all kinds of shapes, sizes, colors, and designs.[4]

Metal tools transformed the lives of women. More durable and efficient than traditional stone and bone tools, metal awls, kettles, axes, scrapers, hoes, knives, needles, and thimbles not only made work lighter but also allowed women to spend less time manufacturing tools. Women were now able to focus more on producing other vital resources, especially corn during the farming seasons, and processing meat during annual hunts. These tools elevated the role of women in the domestic economy. As corn production expanded, corn increased in importance as a medium of exchange. Meanwhile, trade dyes replaced native dyes and new textiles gradually replaced deer and bison skins. Wool blankets and cotton shirts were not only lighter and more comfortable to wear, but they were also easier to clean and dried more quickly.

The object that may have had the greatest impact was the *tinaáku'* (gun), but it did not become of vital importance until the late 1700s, when the conflict between the Arikaras and the Sioux intensified. Although bows and arrows continued to be used, especially in the bison hunt, the gun was important in warfare. Bullets flew faster than arrows, were less easy to dodge, were less likely to be deflected by wind or vegetation, and caused more damage on impact. Indian shields stopped arrows but could at best only deflect bullets. Using guns required relatively little training and much less arm strength than using bows, and because bullets traveled considerably farther than arrows, the gun was a useful defensive weapon. Furthermore, guns allowed hunters and warriors to crawl up to animals and enemies and shoot at them from a prone position. Finally, the old smooth-bore muskets could be loaded with shot or gravel, effectively turning them into shotguns, thus increasing their effectiveness at close range.[5]

But guns also had disadvantages. They were heavy and noisy. They produced thick clouds of smoke, which quickly gave away the position of the shooter. The most important disadvantage, however, was the gun's low rate of fire. Whereas trained men could discharge between twelve and fifteen arrows a minute, a gunman could fire his weapon merely two or three times. As a result, Arikara warriors and hunters continued to carry bows and arrows as well. Nevertheless, as guns improved over time, they became *the* weapon of choice. Consequently, Native Americans became dependent on white traders for guns and powder.[6]

The Arikaras considered guns powerful objects. They desired only guns of the highest quality. Guns, gun parts, bullets, and bullet molds were sometimes included in the graves of warriors. The supremacy of the gun over the bow is further illustrated by the fact that the term *tinaáku'* ("bow") came to designate a gun, while the bow itself came to be called *tinaáts* ("little gun").[7] Like the Mandans, the Arikaras may have consecrated guns in special rituals to increase their accuracy and effectiveness.[8]

Guns changed Arikara military tactics. The spear disappeared as a shock weapon but survived in the form of coup sticks, society insignias, and a tool for killing buffalo. More significantly, the Arikaras abandoned close-formation tactics and perfected the use of guns on horseback. For this reason they preferred short-barreled muskets that were lighter, could be pointed at a target more rapidly, and could be loaded more easily. They often shortened the barrels of long guns by removing several inches from the muzzle. Even after the introduction of rifled breech-loading guns, many warriors preferred smooth-bore muzzle-loading muskets because they allowed the use of buckshot. Furthermore, warriors could mold bullets for these guns themselves and determine the amount of powder for each load. In addition, rifled guns were more difficult to load on horseback than smooth-bore muskets. According to some observers, Indians loaded their muskets by spitting bullets into the barrel, a feat that would be impossible with rifled guns, which required the use of a ramrod. The saliva made the bullet stick to the powder.[9] Unlike some tribes, the Arikaras did not count the capture of an enemy gun as a war honor. However, a man who had been struck or wounded by a bullet had the right to wear a small wooden stick or a red-stained eagle plume in his hair. Interestingly, the Arikaras considered arrow wounds to be greater war honors than bullet wounds, possibly because receiving an arrow wound required closer proximity to the enemy.[10]

Whereas making arrows required spiritual power, the Arikaras quickly learned to cast bullets with bullet molds. They protected their guns from rusting by greasing them with animal fat. They also learned to repair broken gunstocks with wet rawhide; the drying hide shrunk, tightly connecting fractured parts. When a gun was beyond repair, its parts were used to mend other guns. Sometimes gun parts were used to make other objects. For example, brass butt plates and flattened gun barrels made fine scrapers and fleshers.

"SACRED DOGS"

In one story, Morsette told of a time when buffalo were still killing and eating people. When the animals came together to discuss how the world should be, a horse spoke up and challenged the buffalo to a race. If the buffalo won, they could continue to eat people. If the horse won, the buffalo would eat grass. Although the buffalo were strong, they were no match for the horse. After the buffalo lost, humans jumped on horses and began to chase buffalo with bows and arrows. Ever after, the people rode horses to hunt buffalo. After the race, four horses took up different stations in the sky: a black horse went east, a palomino went to the south, a sorrel stood in the west, and a white horse went north.[11]

Some scholars believe that the Arikaras owned horses as early as the 1680s, but others believe that horse ownership did not become common until after 1700. The

Arikaras probably first obtained horses from their Pawnee neighbors, who were much closer to the main center of the Spanish horse trade in Santa Fe. From the Pawnees they also acquired horse gear (saddles, lariats, and so on), and learned how to ride, care for, train, doctor, and breed horses.[12]

The horse reinforced and intensified existing Arikara cultural traits. Horses reduced the need for dogs and lightened burdens for women by making transportation of domestic goods easier. Horses also allowed the Arikaras to travel greater distances in search of buffalo herds during the annual summer hunt and added the "surround" to the Arikara repertoire of buffalo-hunting techniques. For this work, hunters selected and trained specialized "buffalo runners," horses that had great endurance, intelligence, and agility and were not easily spooked by buffalo. The Arikaras also continued to use dogs as pack animals. Although the number of horses per person remained small among the Arikaras, scholars noted that the adoption of the horse led to higher levels of arthritis in the lower joints and sacroiliac joints in men as a result of horseback riding.[13]

Although the Arikaras called the horse *xaawaarúxti'* ("holy dog"), they never kept horses in large numbers except for trade purposes. Their semisedentary lifestyle did not lend itself to the maintenance of large herds. Horses required fresh grass for forage and thus needed to be moved often and sometimes over great distances. The Arikaras preferred to sell surplus horses as soon as possible. The only exceptions were horses used for hunting, war, and breeding. These horses were often kept inside the lodge during cold weather and to prevent them from being stolen by enemy raiders. Mules were desirable pack animals because they could carry heavier loads than horses.

The Arikaras were in constant danger of losing their horses to diseases, hunting accidents, battle wounds, starvation during winter, old age, and theft by enemy tribes. The Arikaras replenished their herds through breeding, horse raids, and trade. There is no evidence to suggest that they captured and broke wild horses. Undoubtedly, it was much easier to buy trained horses from visiting tribes.[14]

Like guns, horses changed Arikara warfare. Horses turned the Arikaras from foot soldiers into cavalrymen. Swift strikes and surprise attacks became more common than pitched battles.[15] Horse raids became the most common type of military action. Here the objective was to capture the enemy's horses, especially his buffalo runners and warhorses. Because these horses were kept near the lodge of their owner, capturing them required great skill and bravery.[16] Sometimes Arikara raiders made their escape quietly, but other times they stampeded the enemy's herd to throw the camp into disarray. When escaping from the enemy, the raiders did not stop until

Horses, guns, and metal tools (including the knife held by one of the warriors) became highly desirable objects in the eighteenth century. In this ledger drawing from the early 1870s, two Arikara raiders sneak into an enemy camp, trying to steal a valuable warhorse or buffalo runner, as indicated by the fact that the animal is staked near its owner's tipi. Such actions required stealth, skill, and daring, often provided by a man's spiritual power. National Anthropological Archives, Smithsonian Institution, MS 154064B #08510628.

the next morning. Horses that tired out were abandoned or killed. Horses that had run all day in hot weather were not allowed to drink until they had rested; otherwise they would die the Arikaras believed.[17] Although it took considerable skill and supernatural protection to become a successful horse raider, the capture of horses did not earn special war honors. It did, however, enable individuals to raise their social status by giving away horses, purchasing sacred bundles, and increasing marriageability.[18]

Rather than steal horses from enemy tribes, the Arikaras preferred to trade for them. Here too we see that the Arikaras fell back upon Neešaanu's greatest gift, corn, to obtain what they needed. Their success as corn producers allowed them to obtain large numbers of horses, which they then sold to other tribes. Thus horses were incorporated into the Arikara trade system and the Arikaras became one of the principal suppliers of horses on the northern plains.

At Arikara towns, three important products, each representing fundamentally different economic activities, met in one place. Guns represented European proto-industrialism. Horses represented the pastoral-nomadic lifestyle of the Lakhotas and Cheyennes. Corn, finally, represented the horticultural tradition of the Arikaras. Of all these activities, only the horticultural tradition of the Arikaras was truly ancient.

Usually, the horse and gun trades draw more attention of scholars than the corn trade. Undoubtedly, these items (guns especially) were important to the Arikaras. But corn was vital to them. Corn allowed the Arikaras to participate in the trade not only as middlemen but also as producers. Because corn played a crucial role in this triangular trade system, the Arikaras saw no need to fundamentally change their way of life. In fact, the trade intensified Arikara corn horticulture.

Trade with Europeans not only allowed the Arikaras to add watermelons to their crops but more importantly allowed the Arikaras to increase the production of corn to obtain European trade goods. Archaeologists have found a higher ratio of scapula bone hoes in post-contact sites than in pre-contact sites, which might indicate that the Arikaras stepped up their "agricultural production to meet the demands of the intertribal trade."[19] The additional work required to produce these surpluses was conducted exclusively by women, who were responsible for clearing, maintaining, and harvesting the fields. Women began to cultivate larger areas and as a consequence spent longer hours gardening. Archaeologists have discovered that the increased work even changed bone growth among the women.[20]

ARIKARA RELATIONS WITH THE SANÁNAT (SIOUX)

The Sioux were a large but loosely connected confederation of bands. The Lakhotas (or Tetons) were the westernmost of the three divisions. They consisted of the Oglalas, Sicangus (also known as the Brulés or "Burnt Thighs"), Miniconjous, Hunkpapas, Itazipcos (also called the Sans Arcs or "No Bows"), Oohenumpas ("Two Kettles"), and Sihasapas ("Backfeet"). The middle division, sometimes mistakenly called Nakotas, was composed of the Yanktons and the Yanktonais. Finally, the eastern division, the Dakhotas (also known as Santees), consisted of the Mdewakantons, Wahpekutes, Wahpetons, and Sissetons. Together the three divisions referred to themselves as the Očhéti Šakówiŋ, or the "Seven Council Fires."

By the 1730s these three divisions lived west of the Mississippi River. Here the Yanktons, Yanktonais, and Santees adopted a lifestyle similar to that of the Arikaras. Most of the Lakhotas, however, adopted a nomadic lifestyle.

Sioux–Arikara relations were complex. The Santees and the Yanktonais were generally friendly. But the Yanktons were not, though on occasion attempts at peace were made. Usually, peaceful interludes did not last long.

Arikara relations with the Lakhota bands are even more difficult to untangle in part because the seven Lakhota sub-bands were loose social and political organizations in which chiefs had little coercive authority and individuals were at liberty to act on their own account. Internal disagreements often resulted in bands breaking up. Indeed, families and individuals easily moved between bands. They often disagreed on the issue of war and peace with the Arikaras. For most of the eighteenth century, the Arikaras and the various Lakhota bands were in a state of "armed peace" with one another. Occasionally, tensions flared, resulting in raids, battles, or opportunistic individual acts of violence. This state was interrupted only when a temporary truce was concluded in order to conduct trade. Apart from corn, horses were the objects that the Sioux desired most from the Arikaras during the first half of the eighteenth century.[21] As early as 1718 or 1719, Sioux winter counts tell us, the Sioux visited Arikara towns to obtain horses.[22]

In sheer numbers, the Sioux nation was larger than the Arikaras. Still, the Arikaras were able to field numerous able warriors, making them a formidable opponent on the middle Missouri. Consequently, pitched battles between the two sides were rare. Unless they had a clear military advantage, the Sioux preferred small-scale attacks over large-scale offensives. Sioux warriors preferred ambushing lone Arikara hunters or surprising women working their fields. Until 1780, most fights were skirmishes rather than battles. Though most of these attacks seem opportunistic, they were nevertheless part of a larger Sioux strategy. It was a strategy aimed at putting the Arikaras on the defensive, frustrating Arikara access to French and British traders, and preventing them from uniting with other sedentary tribes—such as the Mandans and Hidatsas—into an anti-Sioux alliance.

Arikara oral traditions mention engagements with the Sioux but do not specify when they took place. Sioux winter counts provide additional information, but these too are fragmentary. Still, they suggest that conflicts between the two nations were common after the first recorded battle in 1694.[23] Indeed, for nearly a century, battles with the Arikaras take up a prominent place in winter counts.[24]

The Battiste Good winter count for the year 1712–13 provides a typical example of such Sioux attacks. That year the Sioux surprised a lone Palani trapping eagles. The Sioux massacred this man while he was huddled inside his eagle-trapping pit. The act required a commensurate Arikara response. The following year they retaliated by sneaking into a Sioux encampment, opening the door to one of the lodges, and shooting a man who was sleeping inside.[25]

In 1903 Elk and Many Fox mentioned two Sioux attacks on Arikara eagle trappers. In Many Fox's account, the Sioux captured and tortured a young eagle trapper before he managed to escape and tell his people of the attack. In Elk's account, seven eagle trappers were besieged by the Sioux but successfully defended themselves with muzzle-loading guns. Though these stories may refer to later events, the Sioux method of attacking isolated (groups of) Arikaras is obvious. Unlike the Sioux winter counts, in these tales the Arikaras emerge victorious.[26]

Cycles of revenge succeeded each other in rapid order, but only a handful of these were recorded. In 1730–31, for example, the Arikaras killed eighteen Sioux hunters in retaliation for the murder of a group of Arikaras the year before.[27]

Though raids (quick and small-scale attacks into enemy territory) and opportunistic attacks were most common, on occasion both sides also staged attacks against entire towns. In 1704–5, for example, a party of Palanis (probably Arikaras) attacked a Sioux camp. According to the Battiste Good count, the Sioux killed fifteen of the attackers, but High Hawk's winter count states that those killed were Sioux.[28] In 1754–55, Sioux and Arikaras faced off on opposite sides of a stream. Apart from exchanging insults, the Arikaras shot arrows into a Dakhota village and succeeded in killing one man. According to High Hawk, however, this occurred during an attack on an Arikara town.[29]

In this back and forth, the Arikaras were at a disadvantage. Their towns were fixed in the same location except when people went out on their annual summer hunts. In contrast, the Sioux moved camp throughout the year, except for winter, when they sought shelter in river valleys or other sites to protect themselves against the elements. Still, the Sioux tactic also carried great risks: when Sioux were caught, the Arikaras showed no mercy. Likewise, Arikara strikes against Sioux camps sometimes failed and the results could be equally fatal. In the winter of 1726–27, for example, while attacking a Sioux encampment, two Arikaras—bravely or foolishly—ran among the Sioux lodges and died in a rain of arrows.[30]

The Sioux presence forced the Arikaras to bolster town defenses. They began to build their lodges closer together and to surround their towns with palisades and defensive ditches. These palisades lacked bastions but left enough space for defenders to shoot arrows or fire guns between the timbers. These defenses were generally sufficient to keep the Sioux at bay, but they did not protect Arikaras who went out to hunt for deer, antelope, elk, and lone buffalo.[31]

Sometimes the attacks were directed not at the Arikara people but at their horses. When they had enough items to trade, the Sioux would exchange these for horses and corn. However, when trade goods were scarce, the Sioux would take horses by other means. The winter of 1736–37 went into the records as the year the Sioux brought home Palani horses. In 1764–65, they stole horses from Arikaras on the winter hunt. In 1766–67, the Battiste Good winter count reported that the Lakhotas had captured sixty Assiniboine horses, including one spotted horse, but gave the pictorial corn symbol of the Arikaras to reveal the true source of the animals.[32]

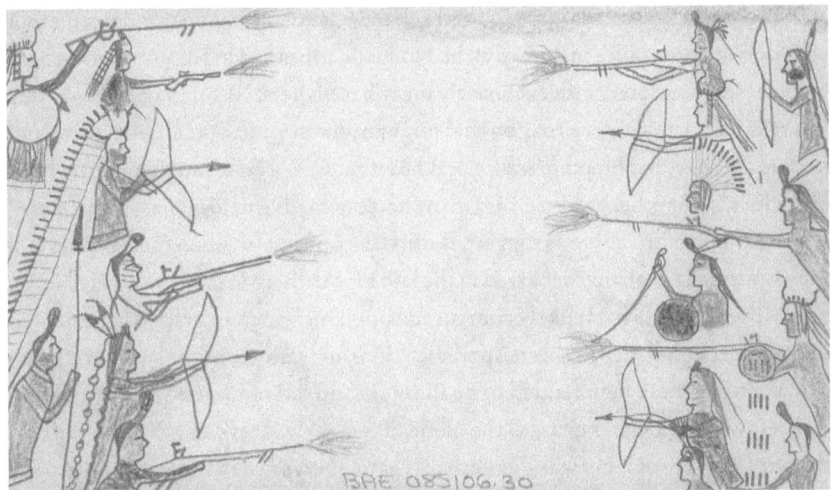

Arikara ledger drawing showing the impact of firearms on military tactics. In this case, traditional weapons and firearms are integrated into new line formations. National Anthropological Archives, Smithsonian Institution, MS 154064B #08510630.

Perhaps to pressure the Arikaras into submission, the Sicangu Lakhotas established a settlement in the Big Bend of the Missouri River. From here they controlled all traffic upstream, especially of French fur traders. This was also a convenient and highly defensible base from which to raid the Arikaras for food, horses, and captives.[33]

MEETING THE NEESIKÚSU' (FRENCH)

In the 1700s access to European trade goods became vital to Plains Indian nations in order for them to maintain independence and to avoid being swept away by rival tribes. Metal tools (including armor), guns, and horses were changing the geopolitical situation along the Missouri River. The source for horses lay in the Southwest in the Spanish trade center at Santa Fe. Guns and metal tools, meanwhile, were supplied primarily by Anglo-French traders of the Hudson's Bay Company (established 1670) and later the Northwest Company (established 1779). At first these items trickled into the central plains, but by the mid- to late 1700s, the gun and horse "frontiers" had converged on the Missouri River, where the towns of the Arikaras, Mandans, and Hidatsas served as markets and these items changed hands between local and visiting tribes. Here the Cheyennes and other southern nations brought horses, while the northern nations, especially the Lakhotas, brought guns.[34]

Corn was a vital commodity in this exchange. It not only served as currency but was of great importance in its own right. Nomadic tribes needed its nutrients to fight off diseases associated with exclusively meat-based diets. "Protein poisoning" due to a reliance on meat—a situation that might occur in winter—caused nausea and fatigue and lowered blood pressure and heart rates. Without supplementing their diet with corn or other garden crops, many horse nomads would not last the winter.[35]

As Arikara oral traditions suggest, the first encounters between the Arikaras and the sahništaaká probably occurred in the late 1600s. These first visitors were Neesikúsu' (Frenchmen), most likely coureurs de bois. Such encounters, undocumented in French colonial records, were sporadic. Their appearance in the sources is often by chance, as these men tended to be illiterate and did not leave any documentation. However, by sheer chance, the name of one early Neesikúsu' has survived in the annals of history. He was Pennesha Gegare. He was not a fur trader but rather a deserter from either Fort Chartres or a French garrison near Cahokia, Illinois. Traveling up the Missouri River, he reportedly settled among the Pawnees and the Arikaras. He traveled all over the territory and visited the Mandans as well. Fur traders hired him as an interpreter and guide on various occasions. There may have been other Neesikúsu' as well. However, unlike Gegare, who was at least mentioned in the writings of Peter Pond and Jonathan Carver, these unnamed men slipped through the cracks of history.[36]

French colonial records provide only limited insights into eighteenth-century Arikara history. Still, this book would not be complete without an overview of the different sources and what they tell us about the Arikara world.

In 1703 French cartographer Guillaume De L'isle published a map that listed four possible Arikara towns. The source of De L'isle's information is unknown, for it is not until 1714 that the Arikaras are specifically mentioned in colonial records. That year Etienne de Veniard, sieur de Bourgmont, explored the lower part of the Missouri River and obtained information about the Arikaras from other tribes. According to Bourgmont, there were two towns of the "Aricaras" on the left bank of the Missouri and forty more towns of the "Caricaras" farther north on both sides of the river. These tribes were probably Arikaras who spoke slightly different dialects. These Indians traded in furs and had met Frenchmen, Bourgmont reported. "They are very numerous," he added. Considering their great numbers, Bourgmont assumed that they had to live in one of the "most beautiful countries to be seen."[37]

Based on the reports by Bourgmont and others, cartographer De L'isle redrew the map of Louisiana in 1718. It showed the location of the Arikara towns. Three or possibly four "Aricara" towns are located on what may be the James River. Another

"40 Villages des Panis," also Arikara, are located on the Missouri River between the Big Bend and the mouth of the Cheyenne River. A "Chemin des Voyageurs" ("Trader's Road") runs from the Mississippi River to the villages of the Iowas and Omahas on the Big Sioux and Rock Rivers, just downstream of the Arikaras. Perhaps the Arikaras kept up a regular trade with Frenchmen coming from this direction. Above the Arikara towns, the map bears a notation that translates, "The French have not ascended the Missouri River beyond this point." This suggests that traders had indeed traveled as far as the Arikara towns by the early 1700s.[38]

In 1719 Jean Baptiste Bénard de La Harpe learned from the Wichitas that the Arikaras were numerous, inhabited seven towns, and formed part of forty-five towns of Pawnees. They also fought a "cruel war" with neighboring tribes such as the Canecy, Padoucas, and Panis. The exact identity of these tribes has never been established satisfactorily.[39]

In 1723, while staying with the Osages, French mining engineer Philippe de La Renaudière reported that the Arikaras lived ten leagues from the Omahas, with whom they were allied.[40] Eleven years later, in 1734, Jean Baptiste Lemoyne, sieur de Bienville, reported that a Frenchman who resided with the "Panimahas" (probably Skiri Pawnees) went north with them to visit the Arikaras on the upper Missouri. This man reported that the Arikaras had until then not yet met the French and that there were several rich silver mines in the area. Although Bienville said that two other voyageurs would leave with this man to verify the report, there is no account of a follow-up expedition.[41]

Taking a different route, Pierre Gaultier de Varennes, sieur de la Vérendrye approached the Missouri River country from Canada in search of a passage to the Pacific coast. In 1738 Vérendrye visited the Mandans near present-day Bismarck, North Dakota. They informed him that at a day's journey from the fifth and southernmost Mandan town lived the Panaux or Pananas, and beyond these lived the Pananis. Both these tribes were almost certainly Arikaras. They lived in several heavily fortified towns and occupied a large territory. Although previously the Mandans and the Pananas and Pananis had been allies, the peace had broken down four years earlier. In the war that followed, the Mandans were at a severe disadvantage because the Pananas and Pananis had horses while they had none. A long way beyond the Pananas and Pananis lived the Spanish, who traded horses to Indians. But it took men a whole summer to make the journey to Santa Fe, and because of the war with the Pananas and Pananis, the Mandans did not dare to venture far from their towns. This was all that Vérendrye was able to learn about the Arikaras at this time.[42]

The first officially documented contact between an Arikara group and whites dates to 1743. That year La Vérendrye's sons, Francois and Louis-Joseph, met an Arikara band they called "Little Cherry People." In 1742 the brothers left Canada and traveled to the Mandan towns before turning west. They encountered various tribes, including the Beaux Hommes ("Beautiful Men"), Petits Renards ("Little Foxes"), Pioya, Gens des Cheveaux ("Horse People"), Gens de la Belle Riviere ("People of the Beautiful River"), and Gens de l'Arc ("Bow People"). They joined the last tribe on a military expedition against the Gens du Serpent ("Snake People"). The Snake People were a powerful nation, reportedly responsible for the destruction of seventeen enemy towns, in which they killed all inhabitants except for the young women, who were carried off to be sold as slaves in exchange for horses and merchandise.[43]

Unfortunately, the exact identity of these tribes remains uncertain. Some scholars believe that the People of the Beautiful River and the Bow People may have been Arikaras. After all, at this time the Arikaras were quite populous and claimed much of the area through which the Vérendryes were traveling. Perhaps the People of the Beautiful River were Arikaras on their winter hunt. Based on the brothers' report that the Bow People lived in "forts" and cultivated corn, they must have been either Arikaras or Pawnees. According to the brothers, they were also "the only tribe sufficiently brave not to stand in dread of the *Gens du Serpent*," who may have been Padoucas (Plains Apaches). In fact, the Arikaras caused the latter "to be afraid of them through the wisdom and skillful leadership of the chief who is at their head." The Arikaras also had many horses and had contacted the Spanish. The chief even spoke a few words of Spanish.[44]

Traveling with a war party of the Bow People, the Vérendrye brothers came in sight of a mountain range on New Year's Day 1743. Twelve days later, January 12, they reached the mountains. Scholars have suggested these were either the Bighorn Mountains, the Rocky Mountains, or the Black Hills. The brothers did not get to climb the hills to see the "western sea" as they had hoped. The scouts of the war party had discovered an abandoned camp of the Snake People. Afraid that the Snake Indians had made their escape and were now on their way to attack their own towns, the Bow People quickly turned around to intercept them. Unwilling to remain behind in hostile territory, the Vérendryes accompanied them. They traveled east-southeast toward the Missouri River.[45]

In early March the Vérendryes learned that the Gens de la Petite Cerise ("Little Cherry People") lived in a town nearby. These were friends of the Bow People and almost certainly an Arikara band. Eager to visit this group, the explorers bid good-bye to the Bow People, and on March 15 they arrived among the Little Cherry People, who were just returning from their winter quarters and on their way to their fortified town on the Missouri River, near present-day Pierre, South Dakota. The brothers found a Spaniard who lived with this Arikara group and who spoke the language. This man informed them that the nearest Spanish settlement was at least twenty day away by horseback. The Spanish traded horses to the Indians but refused to give them guns and powder. The brothers also learned of another Frenchman who had lived with the Arikaras for years—probably Pennesha Gegare.[46]

To leave a record of their visit for other Frenchmen, the brothers buried a lead tablet with a Latin inscription near the town. They erected a pile of rocks over the buried tablet, telling the Arikaras that they had erected these stones "in memory of the fact that we had come upon their land." By a twist of fortune, this lead tablet was discovered near Pierre in 1913. It read, "In the twenty-sixth year of the reign of Louis XV, the most illustrious Lord, the Lord Marquis of Beauharnois being Viceroy, 1741, Peter Gaultier De La Verendrye placed this." A crude engraving on the back of the tablet marked the date (March 30, 1743) as well as two names, possibly of the men accompanying the brothers: "A. Miotte and Louy La Londette" (or Laudette).[47]

In April the brothers left the Arikaras to go back north. "I prepared to leave and made several presents to the chiefs of the tribe, who had not ceased to take good care of us and treat us well, and also to some of the most important of our good friends," wrote Louis-Joseph in his journal. Three Arikara guides accompanied the expedition. Louis-Joseph also commented, "I assured the chief of the tribe that I would take very special care of the three youths he was letting us have as guides, and that, although the Mandan were their enemies, there would be nothing to fear when they were with us."[48]

The expedition set out on April 2. Apparently, the brothers had made a favorable impression, because their departure was "much regretted by the whole tribe [who] begged us earnestly to come again and see them."[49] Undoubtedly, the Arikaras' desired to see the Canadians again for it carried the promise of access to trade goods vital for the defense and the prosperity of the people.

Following this historic meeting, many years passed before another detailed description of the Arikaras was written down. Only a handful of references to the Arikaras survived in between. In 1758 Louisiana governor Louis Billouart de Kerlerec mentioned that the Arikaras were more numerous than the Omahas. Kerlerec based this statement on information provided by Arikara "slaves."[50] Nearly thirty years later, in 1785, Governor General Esteban Rodriguez Miró reported that there were seven Arikara towns below the Cheyenne River.[51]

As fragmentary and confusing as these sources are, several important conclusions can be drawn from them. First, despite Bienville's report, it is clear that the Arikaras had met white people long before the first documented visit in 1743. Indeed, they had established relations with both the French and the Spanish and may have on occasion visited New Mexico. Second, the heart of Arikara territory was in central South Dakota, roughly between the White and Cheyenne Rivers. Third, the Arikaras were a strong, healthy, and numerous people. Fourth, their division along dialectal lines shows that their towns were semiautonomous and that the Arikara tribal political structure was more confederated rather than centralized. The Awaáhu may have been acknowledged as leaders, but this did not mean that their authority was definitive. Fifth, the number of towns mentioned changes over time. Perhaps this was the result of misinformation or mistranslation, but it is also possible that larger towns broke up while smaller ones coalesced. Finally, the Arikaras were so powerful that not even the dreaded Snake Indians were able to intimidate them. They also fought the Padoucas, as mentioned by La Harpe, who periodically captured Arikaras for slave markets in New Mexico. On occasion at least some Arikara towns were at war with the Mandans. At the same time, sources state, the Arikaras had formed alliances with the Omahas and (Skiri) Pawnees.[52]

The above facts indicate that the plains were in a state of change. Wars with enemy tribes, slave raids, and political divisions and realignments (perhaps as a result of disagreements on what diplomatic course to pursue) put pressures on the Arikara nation. Their towns became crowded as the people huddled together for defensive purposes. Despite these pressures, the Arikaras held on to the way of life taught by Mother Corn. However, as they indicated to the Vérendrye brothers, they hoped to count the Neesikúsu' among their friends. They wished the brothers would speedily return, undoubtedly loaded with precious goods like muskets and powder.

WAR AMONG THE SAHNIŠTAAKÁ

As inconspicuous as the aforementioned European intrusions may seem, they were of great consequence. Unlikely as it may have looked at the time, the fate of Native nations would be determined to a great extent in the halls of power in Paris, London, and Madrid. The European trade was indispensable to the Indians of America. Tribes competed with one another for access. The Sioux enjoyed a major strategic advantage over the Arikaras in this regard. They dominated the territory between the Great Lakes and the northern plains. They forced rival nations, such as the Assiniboines, deeper into Canada and forced sedentary nations, such as the

Arikaras, Mandans, Hidatsas, Omahas, and Poncas, to consolidate into ever smaller settlements. However, changing geopolitical tides caused temporary disruptions in this arrangement. For the Lakhotas especially, this moment arrived with the French and Indian War (1754–63).

The French and Indian War sent violent ripple effects across the eastern half of the continent. The war rekindled old rivalries, started new ones, and once again set in motion waves of refugees. After the fall of Montreal (1760), the Sioux were cut off from the French trade and unable to keep up the pressure on the Arikaras or even provide for themselves. The situation became so dire that soon some bands were starving. Two Oglala bands arrived among the Arikaras and begged for corn. The Arikaras allowed them to settle on the east bank of the Missouri River. Over the following months there was much visiting back and forth, resulting in a number of intertribal marriages. The close association of these Oglala bands with the Arikaras caused a split between the Oglalas that resulted into a civil war between 1763 and 1765, after which the factions friendly to the Arikaras reunited with the main group and apparently resumed raiding the Arikaras.[53]

Despite these problems, or perhaps because of them, other Lakhota bands continued their assault on the Arikaras. In 1762, for example, Lakhotas killed six Arikaras. A few years later, they killed four more Arikaras who had come to attack them, possibly in retaliation for the deaths of their comrades in 1762.[54] In 1773–74, Lakhotas murdered two Palani boys who were playing in the snow. Though the murder of children in war revolts modern-day sensibilities, the Lakhotas (and the Arikaras for that matter) nonetheless viewed these killings as acts of bravery because they required exposing oneself in the heart of enemy territory. Naturally, the act required a response. The next year, the Arikaras struck back by attacking a Lakhota encampment. The winter counts do not specify if the strike was successful.[55]

Lakhota winter counts mention a fateful event in 1775–76 that would have dire consequences for the Arikaras. That year a Lakhota named Standing Bull reportedly discovered the Black Hills.[56] The find signaled the moment when the Lakhotas now surrounded all of Arikara territory, in essence reducing the Arikaras to an enclave on the Missouri River. Relinquishing the Black Hills meant that the Arikaras would be cut off from the place of refuge offered by Mother Corn and Neešaanu. From hence on, the Black Hills lived on merely in the shape of the ceremonial Grandfather Rock erected during the Mother Corn ceremony.[57]

Even without diseases, the seasons could be hard on people. Droughts diminished crops; plagues of ravenous larvae and grasshoppers destroyed plants; game animals became scarce in particularly long and harsh winters, resulting in people running out of meat; blizzards killed horse herds; frozen soil did not provide enough feed for horses. The winter of 1777–78 was particularly harsh. Among the Lakhotas, this year was remembered as the winter when the Man Who Has No Skin on His Penis froze to death after a fight with the Palanis, who mocked his frozen body.[58]

But worse than harsh winters, parchingly hot summers, or even the troublesome Sioux were episodic visits by mysterious and deadly maladies. Our knowledge of these epidemics is fragmentary, but some scholars believe that smallpox visited the Missouri River region on at least two occasions in the mid-1700s. Sioux winter counts list other epidemics as well. The year 1734–35 went on record as the "used them up with belly ache winter." The exact germ and the mortality it caused are unclear. The infectious pathogen could have been the cholera bacteria or a parasite that causes dysentery, but there are a host of other germs that may have been responsible. During the French and Indian War, smallpox struck several Native American communities in the eastern part of the continent. The presence of the disease inspired British general Jeffrey Amherst to suggest the use of the virus for biological warfare during Pontiac's War (1763). Smallpox may have visited the Missouri River as well. Then, in 1776–77, tragedy struck again. A mysterious ailment affected pregnant women. That year the Rosebud count stated that many of these women had died, suggesting that they may have succumbed to puerperal fever.[59] Although there is no conclusive evidence that these infections reached the middle and upper Missouri River at this time, the existing intertribal trade network and the fact that the Arikara towns were important centers of trade made transmission here more likely than not.

Despite the whims of nature, the Sioux threat, and the occasional visitations by infectious diseases, the Arikaras nevertheless managed to stand their ground and maintain their position on the middle Missouri. Although the Lakhotas now claimed much of the land between the Missouri River and the Black Hills, they continued to consider the Arikaras as mighty opponents who had to be treated with caution.

5 BITTER YEARS

THE 1781 SMALLPOX EPIDEMIC AND ITS CONSEQUENCES

THE "DIVINE" WOMAN OF THE ARIKARAS

Lakhota winter counts recorded a curious incident in 1798. The Flame winter count stated, "A Ree woman is killed by a Dakota while gathering 'pomme blanche,' a root used for food." On its own, this event was hardly extraordinary. Lakhota and Dakhota raiders frequently ambushed women working in their gardens or out gathering roots, plants, or berries. But this woman, other counts state, was special. "Took the God Woman captive winter," the Battiste Good count reported. "Captured a holy woman gathering turnips," the Rosebud count added. The No Ears count described this event even more cryptically: "Found a woman the great mystery."[1]

Who was this mysterious Arikara "God Woman"? What made her special? Was she killed as the Flame count stated or merely captured and released as other counts stated?

Arikara oral traditions shed light on this incident. In 1903 Hawk sat down with Pawnee ethnographer James Murie and told the following story. One time, Hawk said, the people had plenty of corn but no meat. Game was scarce and they craved meat. So they offered smoke to Mother Corn, and she journeyed from the east to visit the people. When she arrived, she led the people into the holy lodge to speak to them. She was attractive but mysterious. She would eat only the meat of chickens, ducks, and other birds. She instructed some women to bring her moccasins. She placed a pair on her feet and began to walk. After only twenty paces, the moccasins were worn out and she put on another pair. She did this four times, and each time the moccasins wore out. "Her walk around the place meant that she had walked a long way off in the west, and that the way was very hard," Hawk explained. Then she told the people that she had seen the buffalo and they would be there in four days. Indeed, on the fourth day the buffalo appeared. The men went out and killed many animals. Afterward they celebrated and honored Mother Corn. A few days later the hunters went out again. Mother Corn stayed in town. Suddenly enemies attacked. The remaining men in town fought hard but were pushed out by the enemies, who captured and killed Mother Corn inside the holy lodge. After the enemies left, the grief-stricken Arikaras buried her. Later the buffalo hunters returned and learned what had happened. They cried and mourned for Mother Corn. Though she had been killed, her power was still there, because from her grave "grass, weeds, bushes, trees" and other vegetation sprang up.[2]

Mother Corn always returned in moments of crisis to aid the Arikaras. She came when they were hungry. She helped when diseases struck their towns. And, finally, she sacrificed herself in battle against enemies. Though on this occasion she was killed, she had provided the people with meat, and from her grave sprang new and lush vegetation, filled with roots, berries, nuts, and seeds. Arikara oral tradition provides details of this event, but Lakhota winter counts provide the year it occurred.

Mother Corn's sacrifice came at a time of great uncertainty for the Arikaras. Less than two decades earlier, a terrible smallpox epidemic had laid waste to many of their towns. The proud Arikara nation, which once consisted of as many as forty towns, had been reduced to just a handful of settlements where the survivors tried to adapt as best they could. Though the Sioux had suffered losses as well, their fluid social organization and nomadic ways had allowed many to escape the dreaded disease. They now took advantage of the demographic and military vacuum created by the pox. Seeking to monopolize the buffalo hunting grounds, they periodically besieged the remaining Arikara towns, where shocked survivors gathered and tried to adjust to the new situation. But there was no respite. Given the opportunity, Sioux warriors killed Arikaras who ventured too far from home as part of a larger Sioux strategy to control the central plains. Then, when they needed horses or corn, the Sioux temporarily made peace with the Arikaras. Some contemporary observers characterized these trade visits as "friendly raiding expeditions."

This chapter details the devastating blow dealt by the 1781 epidemic and subsequent attempts by the Arikaras to salvage what they could of their tribal autonomy. The epidemic left the Arikaras weakened and disheartened. Survivors were divided on how to proceed. Political rivalries ensued as chiefs juggled for power while the survivors formed new towns. Envy and factionalism resulted as the chiefs argued on how to handle the Sioux threat.

NASAČIRAÁNU: "WATER SUSPENDED IN PLACE" (SMALLPOX)

Europeans introduced a slew of diseases into America: chickenpox, bubonic plague, yellow fever, whooping cough, cholera, mumps, malaria, diphtheria, typhus, influenza, measles, and smallpox. Sometimes two or more diseases struck at the same time, increasing mortality by an unknown factor. Occasionally epidemics followed each other so fast that populations did not have enough time to recover.[3] In fact, it would be more accurate to say that there was "an epidemic of epidemics" in the eighteenth century.[4]

Like most Native nations, the Arikaras did not escape the ravages of diseases introduced by Europeans. It is hard to estimate the extent of the mortality, but it is possible that the Arikaras had suffered a population decline up to 90 percent by 1781. The results were devastating not only demographically but also politically, socially, psychologically, and militarily.

Scholars have identified several epidemics that may have affected the Arikaras between 1750 and 1781. One epidemic, either smallpox or measles, struck around 1750–52. Influenza spread to the Arikaras in 1761. It was followed by yet another smallpox or measles epidemic between 1762 and 1766. Although it is uncertain how these diseases reached Arikara settlements, it seems likely that germs traveled along trade routes that connected the Arikaras to the various corners of the continent. The most devastating of the epidemics was the smallpox outbreak of 1780–81.[5]

The pathology of smallpox tells a story of tremendous suffering. The first symptoms include a high fever, vomiting, and head- and body aches so severe that the patient is entirely incapacitated for several days. Some patients die from complications, stress, and pain during this early stage. Those who survive the early days soon develop a rash, and sores appear in the mouth. When these sores break, the virus spreads to the throat and nasal passages. Soon the rash spreads to the skin, especially the face, soles of the feet, palms of the hands, forearms, neck, legs, and back. Patients in whom the rash turns inward often die early, bleeding from the gums, eyes, and nose. On the third day the rash turns into pustules: dimpled bumps filled with a thick fluid. These bumps become hard and round. Four days later, they begin to form crusts and then scabs. Movement can cause the scabs to break, increasing the danger of secondary bacterial infections with potentially fatal consequences. In some cases the sores and scabs run together into a single oozing mass encrusting the entire body, making even the slightest movement extremely painful. Few victims survive this form of the disease. For those fortunate to survive, the fever subsides and the scabs begin to fall off after nearly two weeks of intense suffering. Patients remain contagious until the last scab falls off. The scabs leave pitted scars on the face and skin, disfiguring victims for the remainder of their lives.[6]

Among Native Americans, other factors increased the mortality rate of smallpox. People tended to be more vulnerable in late winter and early spring, when vitamin and protein deficiencies weakened the body's resistance. Epidemics also incapacitated entire village populations, preventing men from hunting and women from tending fields. Starvation further weakened a person's resistance. During an epidemic, there were not enough healthy people to look after the sick, cook, light fires, fetch water, or bury the dead. Secondary infections, such as colds and pneumonia, were common complications, further reducing a victim's chances for survival.[7] Writing about New England tribes in 1634, William Bradford described people crawling on hands and knees to get water and dying along the way. The stench of sickness and the unburied dead penetrated whole villages, according to Bradford.[8]

Unlike nomadic tribes, whose more fluid social structure allowed camps to break up into smaller groups at the first sign of an infectious disease, horticultural tribes like the Arikaras were particularly vulnerable to crowd-type diseases. As centers of trade, their towns attracted peoples from surrounding areas, who sometimes carried germs with them. Furthermore, Arikara families lived in close proximity to each other and often shared food and cooking utensils. The entire family was involved in the care of sick relatives. The distribution of the deceased's belongings through giveaways spread infections further. In addition, because the towns were built more compactly after the Sioux invasions, infectious diseases spread more rapidly through towns.

Indeed, the conflict with the Sioux created conditions that made the Arikaras more vulnerable to infections. The Sioux presence not only forced the Arikaras to live in more crowded (and thus unsanitary) conditions, but it also prevented them from breaking up into smaller bands in search of sanctuary elsewhere. The Black Hills, which previously had provided shelter, were now firmly under Lakhota control.

The plagues that devastated the Arikaras between 1750 and 1781 may have resulted in a population decline of almost 90 percent. One reason is that the diseases disproportionately affected the young, who were the future reproductive group. A succession of diseases had a snowball effect upon the reproductive capacities of the people. French fur trader Jean Baptiste Truteau, who visited the Arikaras in the mid-1790s, wrote that before the epidemics, the Arikaras had been able to muster about four thousand warriors; the disaster had reduced their fighting strength to a mere five hundred.⁹

The Arikaras called smallpox *nasačiraánu'*: "water suspended in place." The name referred to the pustules that manifested themselves at the height of infection.

At first glance, no accounts of the devastating epidemics appear to have survived in Arikara oral tradition. One could ascribe this to a case of "collective amnesia" caused by the traumatic impact of these events. Although that's possible, stories told by Two Hawks, Bear's Teeth, and Morsette show that Arikara traditions do offer clues. In these stories, diseases often appear in symbolic form: as whirlwinds, snakes, dogs, or bears.¹⁰ The use of such metaphors shows that the suffering caused by the epidemics was so dramatic that it could only be described in cosmological terms. For Arikaras, such disasters could only be explained as punishments for offenses against the supernatural: taboo violation, witchcraft, religious declension, or failure to observe and properly treat sacred things.

After the 1781 epidemic, surviving Arikaras gathered in a handful of towns where they tried to rebuild their lives. The process proved to be extremely difficult. The old town system had been based on the bundle complex, which had provided each group with a sense of community and identity. The new towns threw together people of diverse backgrounds and traditions. Many of the survivors spoke different dialects, causing a confusion of tongues. Worse, families from different towns competed with each other for political control. When French fur trader Pierre-Antoine Tabeau, a contemporary of Meriwether Lewis and William Clark, visited the Arikaras in 1804, he counted no less than "forty-two chiefs of the first rank." Some of these governed only the two or three families left from their original town, but they nevertheless insisted on their status as independent chiefs.¹¹ The social and political divisions weakened the Arikaras militarily, who had already suffered from the loss of so many people.

Arikara decline benefited the Sioux. During the latter half of the eighteenth century, the Sioux stepped up the pressure and began to push the Arikaras slowly northward. By 1750, shortly after the first series of epidemics, the Arikaras had been forced to abandon most of their settlements in the area of the Big Bend of the Missouri River. They now occupied the territory on the west bank of the Missouri River between the Bad and Cheyenne Rivers and both banks of the Missouri between the Moreau and Grand Rivers.¹²

To make matters worse, the Arikaras lost their Cheyenne allies. In the late 1700s the sedentary Cheyennes abandoned their settlements on the Missouri River to join their nomadic relatives near the Black Hills. Perhaps these Cheyennes left to escape the epidemics. Sioux aggression and the attractions offered by the southwestern horse trade may have also been factors in their decision. Although the Cheyennes continued to visit the Arikaras to trade, these visits were too brief to provide permanent protection against the Sioux.[13]

SAKHUÚNU': FOOLISH BOYS

In 1903 Two Hawks related an old Arikara oral tradition of two "foolish boys" who killed a mysterious snake and so brought great misfortune upon the people. While out on the tribal buffalo hunt one summer, Two Hawks said, the people came across a pretty little snake. The old people told the others to make presents of meat and moccasins to the snake. When two foolish boys saw the snake coiled on top of the pile of presents, they became angry. "We are poor," they said. "We are living with these people and they do not give us anything . . . and here they have given these things to this little snake." In their anger they killed the snake. As soon as the people learned the two foolish boys had killed the snake, they returned home. They climbed their arbors and roofs and in the distance saw snakes of all kinds descending on the town. The people prepared to fight the snakes. They were ready to die, for they knew what they had done. They killed many snakes with clubs, but the snakes also killed many Arikaras. The two foolish boys fought bravely, but the snakes bit one of them all over, thus killing him. After a while the snakes left, Two Hawks said, but not until they had killed many people, and all because the foolish boys had killed the young snake.[14]

A few years later, Bear's Teeth told a very similar story to anthropologist Robert Lowie. In Bear's Teeth's account, it becomes clear that the two foolish boys were in fact *sakhuúnu'*, "contrary" warriors who did the opposite of what they were told to do. Instead of leaving the snake alone, they killed it. Soon afterward snakes attacked the town. "All the people fled to the tops of their corn scaffolds and the roofs of their earth lodges," Bear's Teeth said. "The snakes crawled up, and the people tried to push them down with sticks, but many of them were bitten. The *sakhuúnu'* shot their arrows at the snakes, but were bitten in their shins. After a while they dropped dead. Then all the snakes, apparently knowing that they had killed their enemies, departed."[15]

A version of the story told by Alfred Morsette in the 1970s adds more details and presents a different ending. When the people returned home after the two sakhuúnu' had killed the snake, they hurriedly built a palisade to defend their town.

"The snakes," they said, "are coming to attack." When the snakes appeared, the two boys went outside the palisade and began to shoot the snakes with arrows. They killed many. But there were so many snakes that the boys could not stop them. The snakes started coming over the palisade and began to bite the people. Whenever someone was bitten, they died. The snakes even entered earth lodges where women and children were hiding. They came through the smoke holes and cracks in the walls. Innumerable people were killed. When the two boys were bitten, they went inside the medicine lodge to be restored. "Then many people, the poor things, died as each one was crying," Morsette said. "Their sounds ceased after they died, when the snakes did away with our people." The two boys retreated to a drying scaffold and from there clubbed many snakes to death. Dead snakes piled up around them. The snakes became afraid and retreated, for they could not kill the foolish boys. After the battle was over, the two boys went to the medicine lodge and restored the Arikara people to life, for they were holy boys. "They made the village alive again," Morsette said. "Then they also dug holes for burying the dead snakes." Afterward the two boys told the people to pack up their belongings and move to a different location. And so the people did.[16]

According to linguist Douglas R. Parks, who obtained the story from Morsette, the tale of the two foolish boys was a warning to Arikaras to treat holy or mysterious beings, such as the snake in this story, with respect. "[The] story illustrates the consequences of antisocial behavior, particularly a disregard for the holy," Parks wrote. Failure to treat holy things respectfully would invoke their wrath.

Parks did not realize that a historical event lay at the heart of the tale. Alternative interpretations allow us to make this link. One theory is that the snakes are an allegory on smallpox. Smallpox also (seemingly) struck suddenly and killed many people. Like snakebites, smallpox left circular scars on the skin of survivors. In this hypothesis, disaster descended on the town because the people had committed a sin, similar to what happened with Whirlwind in the creation story.

But there is another explanation. The snakes more likely represented an enemy tribe. Substitute the word "snake" with "Sioux" or "Padouca" and the story starts to sound more plausible. In this scenario the snakes were a nation with whom the Arikaras had been at peace or with whom they traded (hence the pile of gifts), until the two boys so foolishly killed one of them.

If the story relates to both an infectious disease and an enemy tribe at the same time, then it can only refer to an event after the year 1781. That year, a smallpox epidemic practically coincided with a Sioux offensive against the Arikaras. Both smallpox and Sioux attacks laid entire Arikara towns to waste. Indeed, to the

Arikaras, the two events were practically inseparable: smallpox paved the way for Sioux imperial expansion.

There is compelling archaeological evidence for this hypothesis. A few years before Parks obtained Morsette's story, archaeologists discovered evidence of a terrible massacre in an Arikara site in Walworth County, South Dakota. Situated in north-central South Dakota between the Grand and Moreau Rivers, the town had been occupied between 1750 and 1785 and was located on a high terrace on the east bank of the Missouri River. It was a strongly fortified settlement that included some twenty-nine lodges. Two defensive ditches surrounded the town. A nearby cemetery showed increased death rates among the people, probably as a result of infectious diseases. While excavating three lodges, the archaeologists found the remains of seventy-one people. One lodge contained the skeletons of no fewer than forty-four people. Their bodies were found in all positions. Some had been left where they had died. Others had been thrown together on a heap. At first the archaeologists believed these were the victims of a smallpox epidemic. Skeletal analysis, however, revealed that they had been massacred. Some bones had musket balls or copper arrow points lodged in them. Cut marks on skulls revealed that at least fourteen people, including children as young as four or five, had been scalped. Many corpses had been mutilated. Some victims had been decapitated judging from the number of missing skulls. The faces and skulls of many others had been crushed. Hands, arms, and legs had been removed from several victims. Most of the bones were charred by fire, signifying that the town was torched after the massacre. Not surprisingly, the survivors abandoned the town after the tragedy.[17]

Although the identity of the attackers cannot be established with absolute certainty, only the Sioux were strong enough to launch an attack of this magnitude against a heavily fortified Arikara town. This was not the usual hit-and-run attack but an all-out frontal attack. Searching for a cause of the war, researchers discovered that the number of young victims was relatively small. Based on this finding, they concluded that the purpose of the attack was to capture children under the age of five. Clearly the attackers were trying to replenish their own numbers and replace loved ones lost to smallpox or other diseases. It was desperation in addition to geopolitical considerations that drove the Lakhotas to attack the town.[18]

Equally desperate was the Arikara response. Numerically devastated by smallpox and abandoned by the Cheyennes, they sought peace and an alliance with the Mandans. Both nations had suffered terribly from the ravages of the pox and the insults of the Sioux. In 1783–84, they retaliated. That year they launched a grand military expedition and charged an Oglala Lakhota camp. The attack failed spectacularly.

THE 1781 SMALLPOX EPIDEMIC AND ITS CONSEQUENCES   95

The Oglalas drove the Mandans and Arikaras back and killed twenty-five of the attackers in the process. The survivors returned home to lick their wounds. The alliance they had forged had suffered a fatal crack.[19]

The failed attack revealed that the Arikaras were no longer a formidable military power on the plains. Now the Lakhotas reigned supreme, and they were determined to make the most of their newfound supremacy. The era of the sedentary tribes was about to be eclipsed by that of the horse nomads.

CHAOS AND REALIGNMENT

When he destroyed the giants in the Arikara creation story, Neešaanu returned the world to the chaos of primeval times before creating it anew. Likewise, the Arikaras had to rebuild their world after the smallpox epidemic of 1781. As always, they relied on the teachings of Mother Corn. It was a difficult process that was complicated by the presence of the Sioux. The Lakhotas, especially, were determined to establish a new order on their terms.

Once abused by the Ojibwas and other neighbors in their original homelands, the Lakhotas in turn became abusers in their quest to establish supremacy on the central plains. In the early 1700s, they had been refugees seeking to conquer a territory of their own; by the 1800s, the Lakhotas had become colonizers. They expected the Arikaras to pay tribute, either in corn or blood.

The new order imposed by the Lakhotas was a very different one from the world the Arikaras had known. The Lakhotas held the sedentary tribes in a tight grip. The Arikaras were on the front lines of the Lakhota imperialist project. Still, despite Lakhota pressure, the Arikaras bent but did not break. As best as they could, they maintained their autonomy and continued to resist.

On both sides there were occasionally voices of reconciliation. Among the Arikaras, some factions called for accommodation of—perhaps even association with—the Lakhotas. Likewise, some Lakhotas advocated peace with the Arikaras. In the end, nationalists on both sides carried the day. Among the Arikaras they prevailed because young and ambitious Lakhotas, eager to make a name for themselves as warriors, continued to harass Arikaras, whom they viewed as convenient targets. As a result of such provocations, peace factions among the Arikaras never held sway for long.

Lakhota "policy" (for lack of a better term) contained both carrots and sticks. They could be generous when it suited their interests, especially when they needed corn or other trade goods. Generally, however, they were more comfortable yielding the stick. And even their generosity came with conditions.

The Arikaras did not submit without a fight. In 1786–87, they killed the Hunkpapa chief Iron Shield, a warrior of repute among his people. The exact circumstances in which he was killed are unclear. Though sometimes experienced warriors were excellent peacemakers, it appears that Iron Shield rode against the Arikaras in war rather than as an emissary of peace.[20] Two years later, the Arikaras killed an Oglala warrior named Last Badger. He was a *heyoka*, or "contrary," a fierce warrior who did the opposite of what he stated he would do. Heyokas had great sacred powers. In this case, that power did not prove sufficient. As with Iron Shield, the exact circumstances of Last Badger's death are unclear, but it is unlikely he had come with peaceful intentions.[21]

Not only did the death count grow in these years; the number of people who survived mutilation by the Sioux also proliferated. These "scalped ones" (both men and women) were lamentable individuals. Apart from the physical scars they carried as a result of losing their scalps, hands, or other limbs, they were scorned by the people back home, who believed they were potentially harmful spirits. Scalped peoples were condemned to live a life of loneliness, far removed from loved ones. Arikara lore abounds with stories of scalped men who sometimes kidnapped women and held them captive for companionship.[22]

The Sioux threat strained Arikara leadership. The surviving Arikara towns were composites of different groups that sometimes spoke very different dialects. Forced to band together after the 1781 epidemic, leaders from different factions competed with one another for tribal leadership. Sometimes factions broke away. By 1790, under Sicangu and Oglala pressure, the Arikaras had retreated into two consolidated towns on the Cheyenne River. A few years later, after they moved to the Grand River, they were divided into three towns.[23]

Apart from carrots and sticks, the Lakhotas also engaged a "divide and control" policy to prevent the sedentary nations from forming alliances against them. In 1791–92, for example, they made peace with the Mandans to drive a wedge between the Arikaras and Hidatsas. Usually such peace agreements did not last long. After the 1791–92 peace had served its purpose, the Lakhotas resumed raiding the Mandans at their convenience. Indeed, just before they resumed warfare with the Mandans, the Lakhotas approached the Arikaras for peace.[24] This peace was formalized in 1792–93 when the Arikaras and Sioux met together in camp for talks. The following year, however, hostilities between these two sides resumed. That year the Arikaras killed Thin Face, a "noted Dakota chief," and another prominent Sioux man named Bear's Ears. As they returned to war with the Arikaras, the Sioux once again sent emissaries to the Mandans to negotiate a truce that would allow them to move more securely against the Arikaras.[25]

The Arikara piireeškáni', or adoption ceremony—sometimes called the calumet or peace pipe ceremony. The purpose of the ceremony was to establish kinship relations with other nationalities. National Anthropological Archives, Smithsonian Institution, MS 154064A #08510516.

Cycles of war and peace followed each other in rapid succession. Sedentary nations like the Arikaras, Mandans, and Hidatsas bore the brunt of the suffering. It is in this confusing situation that St. Louis fur traders, now operating under the Spanish flag, resumed business on the upper Missouri. They found the Arikara nation anxious to resume trade relations but also contentious over the Sioux threat.

NEW SPAIN AND CHIEFS LEFT HANDED AND CRAZY BEAR

While the Arikaras tried to cope with the social, political, and emotional consequences of the 1781 epidemic, French fur traders were dealt a disaster of their own. In 1763 Britain defeated France in the French and Indian War, forcing the French to relinquish Canada to the British while Spain acquired the province of Louisiana west of the Mississippi River. Numerous French fur traders suddenly found themselves subjects of the Spanish crown.

Concerned more with protecting its internal provinces, Spain at first showed little interest in trade with the distant tribes of the upper Missouri. Spanish mercantilism also hampered exploration. Corruption, bureaucratic delays, discrimination against French traders in favor of Spanish ones, expensive licenses, and the Spanish policy forbidding gun sales to Indian tribes frustrated merchants and businessmen in St. Louis, founded at the confluence of the Missouri and Mississippi Rivers by French fur traders in 1764. Warfare between the Sioux, Poncas, Omahas, and Arikaras may also have discouraged coureurs de bois from trading upriver after 1764.

One of the few references to the Arikaras in Spanish government documents dates to 1785, when Esteban Míro, governor general of Spanish Louisiana, reported that the Arikaras lived ninety leagues upstream of the mouth of the Niobrara River. Here they had seven towns and some nine hundred warriors. It is impossible to say how accurate this report is.[26]

Still, formal Spanish exploration of the upper Missouri River began in the late 1780s. In 1787 Don Andres Fagot la Garciniere of St. Louis sent twenty-three-year-old Joseph Garreau to hunt and trap on the Missouri River. Although Garreau would later play an important role in Arikara history, it is uncertain whether he actually completed the trip this time.

The voyage that really sparked Spanish interest in the upper Missouri country occurred in 1790. That year Jacques d'Eglise received permission to ascend the Missouri to search for tribes with whom formal trade had not been established. D'Eglise passed the Arikara towns but left no record of his visit there. Eventually, d'Eglise reached the Mandan settlements, where he discovered that traders from the Hudson's Bay Company and the Northwest Company frequently visited the Mandans to trade guns and other objects. When d'Eglise reported this discovery upon his return to St. Louis in 1792, the Spanish authorities responded with alarm. The appearance of Canadian traders on territory claimed (but not occupied) by Spain required action. Lieutenant Governor Zenon Trudeau immediately alerted the governor's office in New Orleans. He also granted d'Eglise permission for another expedition to the Mandans.

In the spring of 1793, d'Eglise set out from St. Louis once again. This time he was accompanied by Joseph Garreau. Both men commanded a pirogue equipped with oarsmen and merchandise valued at more than two thousand *pesos fuertes*, paid for by St. Louis creditors. Their plan was to sail to the Mandan towns. They never completed the journey. D'Eglise later reported that one thousand leagues from their destination they were stopped by Arikaras and Sioux. Here Garreau "squandered" the articles entrusted to him to the Arikaras. Rather than returning to St. Louis and face his creditors, Garreau decided to stay with the Arikaras. D'Eglise, meanwhile, hurried back to St. Louis.

Thus began the lifelong association between Joseph Garreau and the Arikaras. Garreau became one of the most colorful figures in Arikara history. In many ways he embodied all the character traits of the coureurs de bois: adventurous, independent, a little dishonest, and above all highly ambitious. We know little of his early years. He was probably born in St. Charles County, Missouri, in 1764 and spent most of his youth in St. Genevieve and St. Louis. As a teenager he may have accompanied traders on their journeys and so learned about the Missouri River and the Indian nations living there. He was an experienced voyageur when he was hired to hunt and trap up the Missouri in 1787. It is possible that Garreau first met the Arikaras on this trip. At this time he may even have developed a friendship with chief Le Gauche ("Left-Handed"). Perhaps this explains his peculiar behavior in 1793, when he "squandered away" d'Eglise's goods. Apart from avoiding his creditors, there may have been other reasons for him to stay with the Arikaras. Love may have been one of them because after joining the Arikaras, he married the sister of Chief Left Handed. It may not have been an entirely romantic affair, however. Through this marriage, Garreau entered the Arikara "aristocracy," a position he would never have been able to attain in French or Spanish society. Chief Left Handed, meanwhile, may have found an associate who spoke the language of the whites and knew their ways. Whatever the reason, Garreau remained with the Arikaras for the rest of his life. He adopted his wife's children from a previous marriage and named them Pierre and Antoine. He learned the Arikara language and served as an adviser and interpreter for the Arikara chiefs. Although later fur traders claimed that Garreau's "bad example" prejudiced the Arikaras against the whites and made them less friendly, it is more likely that Garreau had a positive influence on the Arikaras by warning them of the possible motivations of the traders.[27]

The Arikaras needed Garreau's help. They were disorganized after the epidemics and at war with the Yanktons and Yanktonais and several Lakhota bands as well. Under Sioux pressure, the Poncas and Omahas, former Arikara allies, were now also at war with the Arikaras.

In 1794 the Arikaras occupied two towns. One of these was located on the Bad River (near present-day Pierre, South Dakota). It was led by l'Ours Foux, "Crazy Bear" or "Foolish Bear." A second town of comparable size was located on the Cheyenne River. The name of its chief is lost to history, but he could have been Left Handed. Both towns consisted of survivors of the 1781 epidemic. Apparently there were many tensions as rival chiefs sought to impose their authority on others. This crisis of authority further weakened the Arikaras. It also made it more difficult for the chiefs to control ambitious young warriors.[28]

In 1794 the Sioux marched against Crazy Bear's town on the Bad River. The Sioux force must have been considerable because Crazy Bear decided to abandon the town even though the corn had not yet been harvested. The Sioux subsequently ransacked the town and burned down some lodges. Crazy Bear, meanwhile, led his people to the Arikara town on the Cheyenne River. There Crazy Bear's people erected a new settlement just below the existing town.[29]

The new situation only increased tensions among the Arikaras. In the spring of 1795, two rival faction leaders, reportedly jealous of Crazy Bear and the other town chief, separated from the tribe and took their followers with them. One of these chiefs led his people south to live with the Skiri Pawnees. The other went north and established a town near the Mandans.[30] This northern group settled at a place called the Painted Woods, so named because the Yanktonai Sioux and Mandans decorated the trees there with bright paint to signal their military achievements after a terrible war between them.[31] Apart from jealousy, political reasons may also have motivated these dissident chiefs. Perhaps each sought security through an alliance with the Skiris or the Mandans. In any event, Crazy Bear and the other town chiefs were not prepared to give up their territory in central South Dakota. There were now in effect four Arikara towns: one with the Mandans at Painted Woods, one with the Skiri Pawnees, and two on the Cheyenne River. It would take a tremendous effort, accomplished by a hero named Young Eagle, to eventually reunite the people.

Meanwhile, merchants in St. Louis formed the Company of Explorers of the Upper Missouri to open up trade relations with tribes in this area. Spanish authorities supported the company to strengthen Spain's claims to the region. The new company was to explore the Missouri River, establish Spanish dominion and trade among the Indian tribes in the area, evict British traders trespassing on Spanish soil, and search for a path to the Pacific Ocean. In 1794 the company sent its first expedition upstream. It was led by Jean Baptiste Truteau, who was ordered to establish a trading post among the Mandans. Truteau wrote a detailed account of the trip and his yearlong stay among the Arikaras. His journal is invaluable because it offers insights into the political complexity on the plains.[32]

While traveling up the Missouri River, Truteau ran into a Lakhota and Yankton hunting party. These Sioux were very suspicious of traders ascending the Missouri after the bad treatment they had received at the Arikara towns by Garreau and a certain Lauson, who had shot at them. The Sioux also informed Truteau of the attack against Crazy Bear's town. When Truteau stated the purpose of his mission, the Sioux responded that they did not recognize the Spanish "father" as their chief and were angry at the Frenchmen for carrying guns and ammunition to the Arikaras. The Sioux blamed Garreau and other Frenchmen like him for "always speaking ill against them" and for urging the Arikaras "to kill them when they went to parley in order to obtain tobacco."[33]

After resuming his journey in the spring of 1795, Truteau met an Arikara war party on its way to the Poncas. Despite Truteau's pleas not to make war on the Poncas in order to keep traffic on the Missouri River possible, the Arikaras continued on their expedition. Two weeks later, on May 15, Truteau finally arrived at the Arikara towns below the mouth of the Cheyenne River. Here he found Jacques d'Eglise but not Joseph Garreau.[34]

It is unclear where Garreau was at this time. Perhaps he had gone north to the Mandans to avoid being arrested by Truteau. It is more likely, however, that the chiefs had sent him on a diplomatic mission. Perhaps he was sent to the Mandans to persuade the dissident Arikaras there to come back, seek peace and a military alliance with the Mandans, or encourage Canadian traders to supply the Arikaras with guns and ammunition. The other possibility was that he was sent south for a similar diplomatic mission among the Skiri Pawnees.

The Arikaras welcomed Truteau. Undoubtedly, they hoped he would provide them with guns and powder. Crazy Bear invited Truteau into his lodge and allowed him to stay there for the duration of his visit. Truteau noticed that both Arikara towns were roughly the same size, each containing twenty-five to thirty earth lodges and between two hundred and three hundred people. Nearby was a camp of sixty lodges of friendly Oglala Sioux, which again illustrates the complexity of Arikara–Sioux relations at this time.[35]

On May 16, 1795, a Cheyenne band arrived at the Arikara town to trade. Seizing the opportunity, Truteau called a council of the chiefs of the tribes. Two days later they gathered at Crazy Bear's lodge. Apart from Crazy Bear, the head chief of the other Arikara town and the head chiefs of the Cheyennes and the Oglalas were present. Truteau gave each chief a peace medal depicting King Charles IV of Spain, a Spanish flag, and small quantities of tobacco and gun powder. He announced that they were now children of the king of Spain and that their father wished them to be at peace with all the other nations in his territory. The king also wanted them to treat the white people well and trade beaver pelts and other furs with them.[36]

Crazy Bear and the other Arikara chief responded that they "would not cause trouble on the routes of the white men" and that they would try to prevent their young men from going on war expeditions. However, they stated that it was impossible to maintain peace with the Sioux nations that lived east of the Missouri. They were treacherous and had "bad hearts." They came to the Arikara towns pledging peace but then betrayed and killed the Arikaras.[37]

Truteau noted that the Arikaras were of a "rather gentle nature" and treated whites with respect. They formerly had called all white people "spirits" because of the powerful objects they carried and sacrificed small morsels of food into the fire during feasts in honor of the whites. But through their interaction with the friendly Sioux and the Skiri Pawnees, they changed their opinion of white people. "Now they think of us simply in connection with the merchandise that we bring them [and] that is so necessary to them." Especially desirable were firearms, "which protects them from so many formidable enemies who often used to steal their women and children."[38]

The Arikaras remained divided over peace with the Mandans. The problem was highlighted when, on June 12, an enemy party stole some horses from the upper town. Because the trail came from the north, the Arikaras suspected that the horse thieves were Mandan. The young men immediately called for war, but Truteau persuaded the chiefs to stop them. With the chiefs' approval, he wrote the Canadians among the Mandans to return the horses and make peace. But the young men were not easy to placate. When another war party was ready to ride out against the Mandans, Truteau called another emergency meeting of the chiefs. Crazy Bear harangued the young men "with great severity" and warned them that he was going to send Truteau back to St. Louis with his gunpowder and merchandise. Truteau then suggested that Crazy Bear go to the Mandan town with the chiefs to make peace. The chiefs instead asked some visiting Cheyennes to carry the message to the Mandans. Truteau gave the Cheyennes extra tobacco to extend the invitation to the Cayouas (Kiowas), Caminanbiches (Arapahos), and Pitapahatos (an unidentified tribe).[39]

On July 14, the messengers carrying Truteau's letter to the Mandans returned. They brought news that the Mandans and Hidatsas were glad to accept the peace offer but could not return the stolen horses because they had been stolen by some Arikara men who had taken refuge with the Mandans. They had taken the horses in retaliation for horses that had been stolen from them by the lower-river Arikaras at the time of their separation. This news did not satisfy the men of the upper town, and Truteau deemed it necessary to give the men whose horses had been stolen a number of gifts to preserve the peace.[40]

Several Sioux groups arrived later that summer. On July 20, a Minneconjou Sioux camp of eighty lodges arrived and joined the sedentary Oglalas. They came to trade guns, clothes, hats, kettles, cloth, and other merchandise for horses. According to Truteau, the Arikaras tolerated them out of fear, hoping to avoid making enemies among them. However, after the trading season was over, the Minneconjous moved across the river, stole Arikara horses, and murdered some Arikaras.[41]

Two weeks later, on August 2, a Saone Sioux camp of 120 lodges and another 50 lodges of Yanktonais arrived. They stayed for a few days to trade for corn, tobacco, and horses with the Arikaras and then returned east to their campgrounds on the upper Minnesota River.[42]

Later that August, two Cheyenne bands approached the Arikara settlements. Crazy Bear, Truteau, and the unnamed chief of the other town rode out to meet them. The Cheyennes told them that the Arapahos, Kiowas, and Pitapahatos did not dare to come in on account of the Sioux. The Cheyennes also refused to smoke the pipe with the Sioux and announced that they would not come until the Sioux had left the Arikara towns.[43]

The refusal of the Cheyennes to smoke the pipe with the Sioux created a dangerous situation. When a few Sioux stole some Cheyenne horses, the Cheyennes demanded these be returned immediately. They said they were not afraid to fight the Sioux but refrained from going to war only because Truteau had urged them to maintain peace. The horses were returned to them, thus narrowly preventing a major conflict. Still, when the Sioux left the area several days later, they were angry at the Arikaras and the Cheyennes and shouted that it was in consideration of Truteau that they had not killed anyone.[44]

The Arikara and Cheyenne chiefs conducted the piireeškáni' ceremony. On this occasion, a Cheyenne chief presented Truteau with a set of richly decorated buckskin clothes. Crazy Bear presented a lone Arapaho chief who had accompanied the Cheyennes with a beautifully decorated calumet. Undoubtedly, the gesture was intended to win over the sympathy of the Arapahos and solidify their friendship with the Arikara people. The Cheyennes stayed for a week, during which there was lively trade. On September 13, the Cheyennes left again "after many dances and presents having been made on both sides."[45]

Despite his efforts, Truteau had underestimated the difficulty of maintaining peace between the Arikaras and the Sioux. In mid-September, a group of Oglalas killed three Arikara men after Truteau had urged the Arikaras to trap beaver and go out to hunt. This attack caused much consternation among the Arikaras, who held Truteau responsible for the disaster. The incident also caused more pressure on the chiefs. Some people wished to go to the Mandans. Others called upon the chiefs to move the towns to better lands forty or fifty leagues upriver. In both cases the continuous threat posed by the Sioux was an important consideration. The chiefs, however, refused to move.[46]

In early December, the Oglala band that had attacked the Arikara hunters in September established a winter camp only a few miles from the Arikara towns.

Carrying the pipe, these Oglalas promised to return the stolen horses and provide guns and beaver furs in compensation for the three men they had killed. Crazy Bear accepted the pipe and prepared for the piireeškáni' ceremony. Then things turned terribly wrong. After conducting the ceremony, giving presents to the visitors, and treating them to a feast, Crazy Bear received news from the chief of the upper town that some Oglala men had killed one Arikara and wounded another. Crazy Bear and his advisers were enraged. These Oglalas had killed three men in the spring, they said, and three more in September. "[W]e forget everything," said the chiefs, but "they enter with the calumet through one door and kill us at the other."[47]

That night, young men from both Arikara towns attacked the Oglala camp and killed two men and three women. When the Oglalas vowed to return the next day, the Arikaras appealed to Truteau for help. Only at Crazy Bear's urgent request did Truteau sell them a sack of gunpowder and some balls. The next day, December 13, the Oglalas and Arikaras battled in the flat country near the town. The battle ended inconclusively, but the Oglalas withdrew to their winter camp five or six leagues below, within striking range of Crazy Bear's town. Most of the sedentary Oglalas, who had been friendly to the Arikaras, joined them there. Only a small group of these Oglalas remained with the Arikaras to fight their own people. The Saone and Minneconjou bands further north pledged to remain neutral, but the Arikaras suspected that young men from these bands had joined the hostile Oglalas.[48]

On December 21, another battle took place after the Oglalas crossed the ice to attack the town. The Arikaras went out to meet them and fought for several hours. The fight again ended in a draw, with both sides suffering similar losses. On December 30, the Oglalas lured a group of impatient young Arikara warriors into an ambush and killed and scalped five of them.[49] Several Sioux winter counts mention these battles. According to one, the Arikaras killed Ité Číkʼala ("Little Face") while others refer to an incident in which the Oglalas erected the frozen body of an Arikara warrior and placed a paunch of frozen water in his hands.[50]

The disaster of December 30 caused much consternation among the Arikaras. Many again wanted to abandon the towns and withdraw to the Mandans. Others urged people to join the Cheyennes. A third group advocated joining the Skiri Pawnees. Every day, Crazy Bear and the other headmen called upon Truteau to trade powder and balls so they could defend their people. Truteau's refusal to trade anything other than beaver pelts frustrated them deeply.[51]

In February 1796, a group of fifty or sixty Skiri Pawnees arrived at the town. They too admonished Truteau for his refusal to help the Arikaras. By the end of the month, Truteau found himself virtually alone. Only Crazy Bear remained loyal to him. Although fearing for his life, Truteau stubbornly refused to supply powder and balls to the Arikaras. "I spend the nights meditating and searching for some means to escape from the peril in which I am," he wrote in his journal. "I find none."[52]

On March 20, the crisis reached a climax. That day an Arikara messenger arrived from the Mandan towns announcing that the Mandans had received a great deal of guns, balls, and powder from British and Assiniboine traders at lower prices than Truteau was willing to offer. The Mandans also invited the Arikaras to join them and the Hidatsas in north. Upon hearing this news, the chief of the upper town ordered his people to depart for the Mandans. Under pressure from people in his own town, Crazy Bear gave Truteau "no more than four days; that at the end of this time I must trade either under coercion or in good friendship." When Truteau continued to resist, the Arikaras forced him to trade. Then, on April 1, they left. His mission an utter failure, Truteau gathered his supplies and left for St. Louis, where he arrived on June 4.[53]

It is unclear where the Arikaras went after abandoning the Cheyenne River settlements. It is possible that they moved north and joined the other Arikaras near the Mandan towns. However, it is also possible that they accompanied the Pawnees to the Skiri towns in Nebraska. The pattern of Arikara bands seeking refuge among the Skiris would be repeated in later times.

A few months later, in August 1796, an expedition led by Welshman John Evans arrived at the northern Arikara settlement, some ten leagues (about twenty-seven miles) below the Mandan town. These Arikaras stopped Evans because they were in dire need of goods. Evans eventually persuaded the Arikaras to let him continue to the Mandans, but not until he had provided them with supplies.[54]

Around the same time Truteau and Evans struggled with the Arikaras, French visitor Georges-Henri Victor Collot (1750–1805) traveled North America and left a short description of the Arikaras as well as a map of the Missouri River country listing the abandoned Arikara towns. The source for Collot's information is unclear, but his map throws more light on the confusing geopolitical situation facing the Arikara people.[55] In his description, Collot wrote that one band of Oconomas (Oglalas), formerly allies of the Arikaras, had lived on the Little Missouri River but had been driven away from there. The Arikaras were divided into two towns short distances from each other, but they had abandoned these towns to live near the Mandans. Formerly numerous, the Arikaras had once occupied thirty-two towns, now destroyed in part by the Sioux. "The small-pox has also made such ravages in this nation," Collot concluded, "that they are reduced to five hundred warriors at most."[56]

Collot reported that the "Titons" (Lakhotas) were divided into four great nomadic divisions that traveled on both sides of the Missouri River: "[They] are accustomed to frequent the Chaguiennes and the Ricaras, and sometimes the Mandanes; from the two first nations, they purchase horses, beaver skins, and dresses suitable to their customs, and deal with latter for Indian corn and tobacco."[57]

Most curious, however, is Collot's listing of a mysterious "Richaare Nation" living in tipis along the western stretches of the White River. Collot did not describe the Indians who camped on this river, but they were possibly Arikaras who had left towns on the Missouri River in 1796. The fact that Collot put the "Arricaras" and "Richaare" next to each other in his list of nations inhabiting the Missouri country supports that conclusion, but it is also possible that this was a branch of Lakhotas friendly to the Arikaras. In any case, the landscape along the White River was rather bleak according to Collot: "Neither trees nor herb, except wild thyme [sage], are to be seen; and of animals, only the rabbit and the small meadow dog." The water of the river, Collot wrote, was "as white as lime water, running through a country the soil of which is pure chalk. This river is not large, or navigable for any kind of vessels."[58]

YOUNG EAGLE AND YELLOW CALF REUNITE THE ARIKARA PEOPLE

In 1903 Yellow Bull told the story of a remarkable young man named Young Eagle. It was an old story, Yellow Bull said. It took place at a time when the Arikaras were divided into two camps—a northern and a southern group.[59]

Though the Arikara nation split up and reunited on several occasions in history, Yellow Bull's account probably refers to the mid-1790s, after the Arikaras under Crazy Bear and the unnamed chief left the Bad River towns. One group moved north to live among the Mandans, while the other went south to live with the Skiri Pawnees. According to Yellow Bull's tale, it was Young Eagle who eventually brought the two groups back together.

Young Eagle lived in the southern town, where his father, Black Sun, was an important chief. At this time, young men from both camps visited each other on occasion. During one of these visits, Young Eagle learned of Yellow Calf, the daughter of a northern chief. In turn, Yellow Calf heard of a handsome chief's son in the southern camp. Young Eagle and Yellow Calf simultaneously started on a journey to meet each other. They met on top of a high hill between the two towns and fell in love. Young Eagle followed Yellow Calf to her northern home. Yellow Calf took him to her lodge and they spent the night together. The next morning, Yellow Calf's parents discovered that their daughter had married the strange boy.

One day Young Eagle joined a war expedition. During the mission, Young Eagle transformed himself into an eagle and soared up into the skies in advance of his fellow warriors. When the war party caught up with him, Young Eagle, now on foot, drove a large herd of ponies before him. He distributed the ponies among the men, went back to the enemy camp, and brought back scalps. When the warriors finally came home, the people honored Young Eagle for his brave deeds. He became a great warrior among his wife's people.

Later, Young Eagle and Yellow Calf set out to visit his southern relatives. He brought along ponies, scalps, and other spoils. Black Sun proudly displayed his son's gifts to the people of the southern town. The soldiers in the southern camp discussed among themselves and decided that Young Eagle should lead the southern people to Yellow Calf's town. "So the people of the other village went north," Yellow Bull concluded in his account. "The north and the south tribes of the Arikara came together and became one tribe again."

Thanks to Yellow Bull's story, we now know the name of the second chief at the Bad River towns: Šakuúnukatít ("Black Sun"). Admittedly, this is speculation, but the fact remains that by 1804 the Arikara people had once again united, though they still occupied separate towns. Yellow Bull also provides us with the name of the boy hero responsible for this reunification: Neetahkaasiháni' ("Young Eagle"). The story echoed a familiar Arikara theme in which a boy and a girl of opposing towns or people come together in marriage. Indeed, uniting or solidifying tribal relations through marriage was common practice throughout Native North America, as it was among the Arikaras.

But marriages were not always a guarantee of enduring peace. The Sioux were notorious for breaking peace agreements thus forged. Arikara oral traditions recall one particular case in which a young Sioux woman married a powerful Arikara soldier in order to steal his secrets. According to White Bear, who told the story in 1903, the name of the Arikara warrior was Pretty Voice. He had obtained power from Elk, which made him successful not only on the battlefield but in the ways of romance as well. His power to mesmerize women prompted jealous Arikaras to try to kill him, but armed with a magic whistle, Pretty Voice was invulnerable to their bullets and arrows. One day the Sioux attacked the town where Pretty Voice lived. Armed only with his magic whistle, Pretty Voice held off the enemy. When the Sioux saw they could not kill him, they retreated. They gave up the fight but decided to come on a friendly visit instead. During this visit, Pretty Voice met a Sioux girl, who moved in with him. After a while, the girl began to question Pretty Voice about his great power and asked if it could be destroyed. Pretty Voice told her that he could be killed with arrows and bullets that had been smudged with the smoke of burned elk hair and elk horn shavings. Soon thereafter, the Sioux girl deserted her husband and informed her people how to kill Pretty Voice. The Sioux immediately took to the field again to engage Pretty Voice in battle. Although he managed to kill many Sioux before he fell, Pretty Voice soon "looked like a porcupine tail with arrows." The Sioux scalped him and cut up his corpse. According to White Bear, Pretty Voice could have been restored back to life if his mother had thrown the pieces of his body into a stream nearby, as he had instructed her to do. But jealous Arikaras prevented her from doing so. Instead they burned his body to prevent him from ever returning again.[60]

The story not only warned young Arikara men not to pursue the wives of married men (which would endanger the peace in town) but also contained a warning that the Sioux could not be trusted. Not even the bonds of marriage, White Bear's story indicates, were sacred to them.

RETREAT AND REORIENTATION

For most of the eighteenth century, the Arikaras had been able to hold off the Sioux and maintain their independence. Indeed, they had thrived. Their towns were attractive centers of trade where corn, metal tools, guns, and horses changed hands. Their lifestyle was so successful that many first-wave immigrant nations (such as the Omahas) adopted semisedentary horticulturalism as well. Even some second-wave immigrants, such as the Cheyennes and a few Oglala groups, experimented with the horticultural way of life of the Arikaras. Corn was the glue that held Arikara culture together and allowed their towns to thrive. Although they sometimes suffered from slave raids and occasional pinprick attacks—first by the Padoucas and later by the Sioux—the period between 1650 and 1750 was one of consolidation for the Arikaras.

The 1781 epidemic changed everything. Apart from its demographic devastation, it caused a major political crisis in Arikara leadership. The Arikara confederation had always been based on semiautonomous towns. Each town had its own sacred bundle, spoke its own dialect, and had its own leaders. Though these leaders came together to discuss matters of foreign policy and mutual defense, there were occasional tensions. They could not, for example, agree on a united policy toward the Mandans. The 1781 smallpox epidemic now forced the survivors to gather into new towns, and the chiefs (and perhaps priests too) competed with one another for supremacy in their newly consolidated communities.

The epidemic also weakened the Arikaras militarily. They would never recover. Military weakness forced the Arikaras on occasion to seek support from the Mandans and Hidatsas, while on other occasions it compelled them to compromise with the Sioux. With a divided political leadership, the Arikaras could not decide what to do next: remain independent; join the Mandans, the Pawnees, or the Cheyennes; or become horse nomads themselves. Unable to reach a consensus, Arikara chiefs pursued different options. In the mid-1790s, some briefly joined the Skiri Pawnees while others joined the Mandans. But the pull of Mother Corn's power was always present. Even though on occasion towns separated, they always reunited later. Still, unable to hold off Sioux aggression, by the early 1800s, the Arikaras were in full-fledged retreat.

In the aftermath of the 1781 smallpox epidemic and devastations suffered from Sioux attacks, the Arikaras undoubtedly wondered why these horrors were thrust upon them. Had they violated the commands of the Great Chief Above? Had they neglected their ceremonial obligations? Why had the sacred powers forsaken them? Would the sacred powers come back or had they abandoned the people forever?

Mother Corn put these doubts to rest when she returned to the people in their moment of need. The mysterious "God Woman" who sacrificed herself at the hands of the Sioux in 1798 taught the people that not even death would prevent her from looking after them. Like Jesus, Mother Corn told the Arikaras to not fear violence or death as long as they kept their faith in the sacred powers.

6 MEETING THE LONG KNIVES, 1800–1823

> Then the soldiers came on the steamboat to fight, bringing cannon with them. They arrived. Then they began shelling the Arikaras. Then they leveled the village, killing and wounding many people.[1]
>
> —ALFRED MORSETTE SR., "THE KILLING OF WHITE HORSE'S SON"

ARIKARA ORAL TRADITION

In 1823 American soldiers under the command of Colonel Henry Leavenworth surrounded the Arikara towns on Cottonwood Creek, about five miles above the Grand River. They were supported by a contingent of American fur traders under command of Missouri Fur Company director Joshua Pilcher. Also present were nearly 750 Sioux. Together they marched to the Arikara towns under Chiefs Grey Eyes and Little Soldier. There they took up position. Leavenworth's hopes to intimidate the Arikaras into a settlement with a show of force were dashed when impatient Sioux warriors initiated the attack. Now forced to join in, Leavenworth's troops shelled the town.

One hundred and fifty years later, Alfred Morsette recounted what Arikara oral traditions told of this event. A young Arikara woman, Morsette said, tried to seek shelter when something landed nearby. It was a cannonball with a burning string sticking out of it. The young woman plucked the string from the ball and so diffused the bomb. Then she told the young men to do the same. Everywhere men began to pull the strings from bombs that landed in the town. As they did so, the men earned war honors for their deeds.

The siege lasted three tense days. Despite Arikara attempts to settle the dispute, Leavenworth's auxiliaries, the fur traders and the Sioux, pushed the colonel for more aggressive action and even extermination of the Arikaras. Leavenworth refrained.

Then, on the morning of August 13, the besieging forces learned that the Arikaras had vanished mysteriously from the town overnight. According to Arikara oral traditions, a mysterious dog appeared and showed the people how to escape by transforming them into animals that could crawl through a tunnel underground. As in the Arikara creation story, dogs assisted the people while Mother Earth provided safety and shelter, allowing the people to avoid destruction.[2]

The peculiar fact is that Chief Grey Eyes was one of the chiefs who had warmly received Captains Lewis and Clark among his people in 1804. Less than two decades later, one of Leavenworth's cannonballs took off Grey Eyes's head during the bombardment. What had caused such a dramatic turn of events?

In 1804 Grey Eyes had reluctantly accepted American paternalism in return for US support against the Sioux. Hence he welcomed Lewis and Clark, supported their attempts to forge peace, and sent another chief, Eagle Feather (also known as Too Né), to Washington to solidify ties with the United States.

Peace with the United States fell apart quickly. Eagle Feather died in Washington and instead of offering protection, the United States began to pursue purely selfish interests. American fur traders, especially, cared little for Arikara well-being and favored the Sioux more than the Arikaras. Arikara frustrations led to conflict with the United States in 1807 and to all-out war in 1823.

Self-preservation determined Arikara actions, but the United States regarded the Arikaras as aggressive and hostile. The events between 1804 and 1823 would poison US attitudes toward the Arikaras for decades to come.

ON THE GRAND RIVER

After war with the Sioux broke out in 1796, a significant portion of the Arikara tribe settled near the existing Arikara "refugee camp" below the Mandans. The newcomers established two towns at short distances from each other. One town was located on top of a hill; the other was located in the valley. These towns were occupied until 1799, when war with the Mandans and Hidatsas forced the Arikaras to move to the Grand River, where they established new towns.[3] Here they were vulnerable to Sioux attacks. Apart from the Arikara "God Woman," the Sioux killed several Arikaras who ventured too far from town between 1798 and 1800.[4]

We do not hear more about the Arikaras until fur traders contacted them again in 1804. That year, the Arikaras lived in three towns above the Grand River in north-central South Dakota, some 130 miles below the Mandans and Hidatsas.[5] One town, under Chief Kaakaawiisisa ("Crow Going Across"), was located on an island in the Missouri River. It consisted of sixty lodges. The gardens where the people cultivated their crops covered the entire island. Recently a group of Arikaras under Chief KaakaawiitA ("Man Crow") had joined them on the island.

Two other Arikara towns were located a short distance upstream on the west bank of the Missouri. A small creek separated these two towns. The first town consisted of sixty to seventy lodges under Chiefs Grey Eyes and PakUs ("Hay" or "Straw"). The next town, across the creek, was led by Chief Pi'a'hiitu' ("Eagle Feather" or Too Né). This town was composed of possibly nine different Arikara groups, each speaking its own dialect.[6] The name of chief Crazy Bear does not return in the historical record.

Arikara society was divided as a result of warfare with the Sioux. The chiefs disagreed on a common policy toward the Sioux and Mandans. Some chiefs called for war against the Mandans and advocated an alliance with the Sioux, but others rejected this proposal. To make matters worse, several chiefs were engaged in a struggle for supremacy. Soon after arriving on the island town, for example, Chief Man Crow challenged Chief Crow Going Across's authority.

It was in these volatile circumstances that the United States entered Arikara history. When Lewis and Clark arrived in November 1804, they came as agents of empire. They sought to impress the Arikaras with the power of the United States, bring them into the American trade network, impose peace on the region, and simplify diplomacy by appointing a single head chief for all Arikaras. Although the Arikaras accepted the presents offered to them by their American "father," they did not surrender to US hegemony. Despite their divisions, they remained fiercely independent.

"INSUBORDINATION AND DISCORD REIGN HERE STILL MORE THAN AMONG THE SIOUX"

On May 24, 1804, St. Louis fur trader Pierre Antoine Tabeau arrived at the island town of Chief Crow Going Across.[7] Most of the Arikaras were on their annual summer buffalo hunt, but a few families had remained behind.[8] After the people returned from the hunt, Tabeau learned that they had suffered tremendously from diseases and enemy attacks. "Of the eighteen large villages," he wrote, "the Ricaras are reduced to three very mediocre ones." There were no more than five hundred warriors, and the people and chiefs were hopelessly divided. Tabeau counted ten different bands and "forty-two chiefs of the first rank." Jealousy reigned among the chiefs, for when Tabeau overlooked some, he was "bitterly reproached afterwards." Some chiefs commanded only two or three families, but these still distinguished themselves by their bundles and the chief's pride.[9]

Table 3
Arikara Bands and Chiefs Listed by Tabeau

Tabeau listed the ten largest Arikara bands and their head chiefs. They were, in order of size (largest to smallest):

Tribe/Band	Translation	Chief	Translation
1. Rhtarahe	Concave Foot	Pacosse	The Straw
2. Sawa-haini	(unidentified)	Kakawissassa	The Crow Going Across
3. Waho-erha	Sides of Head Shaved	Piahito	The Eagle Feather
4. Awahaux	Left Behind	Kaydjai	The Chief Robe
5. Toucatacaux	Village against a Hill	Laitacas-taga	The White [Golden] Eagle
6. Touno-catacaux	Village on Creek Bank	Kaka-nechane	The Chief Crow
7. Laocata	By the Water	Tailala	The Gourd Rattle
8. Tchinantacaux	Ash Wood on Hill	Rha-nechane	The Chief Dog
9. Toucoustahane	Buffalo Sod Village	Tchiri-Tiranihau	Great Wolf/Many Wolves
10. Narh-karicas	Tree with Branch Sticking Out	Kakawita	The Male Crow

Source: Abel, *Tabeau's Narrative,* 125.

Note: Tabeau does not list chief Grey Eyes, reportedly the leading chief. Perhaps he was the same as Kaydjai of the leading Awaáhu band, but any attempt to link Grey Eyes to the names above is speculative.

Each group spoke its own dialect, which led to a "confusion of tongues."[10] Worse were the rivalries between chiefs. Not even the chief of the Awaáhu band was able to forge a consensus. "Insubordination and discord reign here still more than among the Sioux," Tabeau reported. The result was that the Arikara nation was "infinitely more unhappy, as much by its internal and destructive quarrels, as by the number of enemies that it makes."[11]

Man Crow invited Tabeau into his lodge for the duration of his stay. He was chief of one of the smaller bands but respected among the Arikaras for his bravery and his knowledge of medicines. He was proud, fierce, thoughtful, and patient but could also be ruthless when necessary. Several years earlier, probably in revenge, he had killed the brother of a Brulé Sioux chief during a truce. The murder sparked a new round of retaliations but also confirmed his reputation as a fearless man. Man Crow's lodge was one of the largest in the town. It was 108 feet in circumference and housed no less than four families. Man Crow's status ensured Tabeau's safety to conduct his business.[12]

Tabeau recorded his observations in a journal. The Arikara country was healthy, he wrote. Except when epidemic infections visited their towns, the Arikaras were rarely sick. They believed diseases were "either the result of the vengeance of some angry spirit or a succession of evil deeds of a magician." Arikara men were well built and active and excelled in sports. Among the other nations, they enjoyed a reputation as excellent runners and were considered the best swimmers in the world. The men dressed simply: moccasins, antelope leggings, a breechcloth, and a robe. Arikara women were hardworking. They had a "superior way of dressing the skins of the antelope and make of them a pliable leather which they use for fine garments for the two sexes."[13]

Tabeau remarked that the Arikaras raised "a considerable amount of maize and other crops," fished for catfish, and gathered a great variety of fruits. Nevertheless, at the end of the winter season their supplies were often exhausted, and natural disasters sometimes brought them to the brink of starvation. An unexpected flood in 1803 had destroyed their crops, forcing them to spend the rest of the year wandering around in search of buffalo before returning the next year to plant a new crop.[14]

In August 1804, more than fifteen hundred Sioux, Cheyennes, Padoucas, and Arapahos set up camp nearby to trade with the Arikaras. Although usually at war with each other, the Sioux and Cheyennes concluded a temporary truce. Still, to prevent hostilities, the Sioux built their camp on the east bank of the Missouri, while the Cheyennes camped on the west bank next to the Arikara towns. The Cheyennes had come to exchange horses, prairie turnip flour, and buffalo meat for corn, tobacco, and beautifully decorated deer- and antelope-skin garments. Here they also purchased guns and ammunition, which the Arikaras had obtained from the Sioux. While the Cheyennes were nearby, the Arikaras were relatively safe from Sioux harassment. After concluding their trade, the Cheyennes departed for the Black Hills.[15]

Arikara relations with the Sioux were as complex as ever. One Oglala band still had many relatives among the Arikaras. For now, Chief Sitting Bear's Yanktonais camp of five hundred warriors was also peaceful.[16]

Arikara relations with the other Sioux bands were strained. According to Tabeau, these Sioux saw in the Arikaras "a certain kind of serf, who cultivates for them and who, as they say, takes for them, the place of women."[17] In reality, both sides depended on each other. The Sioux, for their part, relied on the Arikaras for horses and corn.

As always, the Sioux worried about a possible military alliance between the Arikaras, Mandans, and Hidatsas. To prevent such an alliance from materializing, the Sioux sent spies to the different towns and pressured factions there into war with one another. The factional nature of Arikara politics played right into Sioux hands. In August 1804, the Arikara chiefs agreed to make peace with the Mandans, but because of Sioux pressure, their proposal was rejected by The Gourd Rattle, chief of the Laocata village. Shortly thereafter, a Laocata war party stole some Mandan horses, ensuring that hostilities continued.[18]

To be fair, some Arikaras opposed an alliance with the Mandans and Hidatsas because they prevented Canadian traders from trading with the Arikaras. In response, the Arikaras prevented St. Louis–based traders from traveling upriver to the Mandans and Hidatsas. Because of the Mandan–Hidatsa blockade, however, the Arikaras remained dependent on trade with the Sioux.[19]

The tensions between the Arikaras and the Sioux presented Tabeau with a predicament. He did not want to offend his hosts, but he had come to make a profit, and trade with the Sioux was more lucrative. Frictions between Tabeau and the Arikara chiefs soon became apparent. The issue was the price Tabeau charged for his goods. During a first meeting with the chiefs, on August 18, 1804, Chief Hay demanded that Tabeau lower the price of knives, cloth, balls, and powder. When Tabeau refused, Hay ordered him to leave town. Tabeau calmed matters with some small presents, but the quarrel over prices continued. Hoping to break Tabeau's stubbornness, the chiefs forbade anyone to trade with him at the risk of punishment. When Joseph Garreau arrived from one of the upper towns to trade with Tabeau, the chiefs threatened to kill his horses.[20]

To improve relations, Tabeau invited the chiefs to another meeting. Garreau acted as interpreter. The chiefs were pleased with the feast and the presents Tabeau offered them, and they allowed him to remain. They did not, however, permit him to continue his journey to the Mandans. The issue of prices lingered. By the time Lewis and Clark arrived among the Arikaras, in October 1804, Tabeau had not made much progress.[21]

LEWIS AND CLARK AMONG THE ARIKARAS

When they began their journey to the Pacific Northwest, Lewis and Clark received instructions from President Thomas Jefferson to search for a passage to the Pacific Ocean, map the territory, describe the land and its plant and animal life, gather information on Indian nations, establish peace between tribes, investigate opportunities for trade, and above all inform the local tribes that they were now subjects of the "Great Father" in Washington. Although the expedition was named the Corps of Discovery, Lewis and Clark were really agents of empire.[22]

Their message was not received well by all nations. The Lakhotas rejected American hegemony, and they did not want the Americans to trade directly with the Arikaras. Although the Lakhotas allowed Lewis and Clark to continue their journey, the United States had gotten off to a bad start with one of the most powerful Plains Indian nations.[23]

On October 8, 1804, Lewis and Clark arrived at the island town of Chief Crow Going Across. Many people came out to see the visitors. Lewis entered the town and invited Crow Going Across and Man Crow to a council the next day. Lewis sent out messengers to the chiefs of the two upper towns as well. Tabeau's associate Joseph Gravelines agreed to act as interpreter.[24]

The next day the meeting was canceled due to bad weather. The explorers used the time to gather information about the Arikaras from Tabeau. But because of Tabeau's flawed understanding of Arikara politics as well as their own prejudices, Lewis and Clark completely misjudged Arikara domestic and diplomatic affairs. This cultural distance became clear during various council meetings in subsequent days.[25]

On Wednesday, October 10, Lewis and Clark dressed in their best uniforms and raised the American flag to welcome the chiefs. To their surprise, only Crow Going Across, Man Crow, and some of the other chiefs of the lower town showed up. Tabeau explained that Hay and Eagle Feather preferred to stay home because they had heard that the explorers intended to make Crow Going Across head chief of the entire nation. Such a decision was especially hard to swallow for Hay and the headmen of the upper town, who regarded Chief Grey Eyes, who was currently traveling, as their principal chief. In his journal, Clark wrote, "We have every reason to believe that a jellousy exists between the Villages for fear of our makeing the 1st Cheif from the lower Village." It is also possible that the chiefs objected to non-Arikaras appointing head chiefs without going through the proper procedure established by Neešaanu' and Mother Corn. Around noon, the explorers dispatched Joseph Gravelines to urge Hay and Eagle Feather to join the council after all. The two chiefs arrived an hour later.[26]

The chiefs were baffled when the explorers offered liquor to them. Refusing the drink, they expressed their disappointment that "their father should present to them a liquor which would make them fools."[27] Then Lewis read a standard speech declaring that the Arikaras were now children of the Great Father in Washington. He said they wished the Arikaras would make peace with the Mandans and Hidatsas and that they wanted to trade with the Arikaras for beaver skins. He then invited the chiefs to visit the Great Father in person.

After concluding the speech, the explorers opened a bale containing presents for the Arikaras. They committed another error when they handed out the peace medals. They presented Crow Going Across with the largest peace medal, in effect recognizing him as head chief of the Arikara nation. They gave a medal of the middle size to Hay and presented Eagle Feather with a medal for a chief of the third rank. Hay and Eagle Feather reluctantly accepted the medals. Each chief also received an American flag, a red coat, a cocked hat, feathers, and some paint. At the end of the conference, Lewis demonstrated his airgun to impress the Arikaras with American technological ingenuity. The chiefs promised to return the next day with their response.[28]

That afternoon members of the expedition visited the island town. They were impressed with the appearance and friendliness the people who welcomed them. "They have [received] us in the most friendly manner," wrote Sergeant John Ordway. "[They] gave us corn & beans dryed pumkins & Squasshes [and] Some of their women are verry handsome & clean." Patrick Gass added, "They are the most cleanly Indians I have ever seen on the voyage, as well as the most friendly and industrious."[29]

The Arikaras were especially impressed with York, William Clark's slave. "Those Indians wer much astonished at my Servent," Clark wrote in his journal: "They never Saw a black man before, all flocked around him & examind. Him from top to toe." Associating York's dark-colored skin with victory and power, the Arikaras believed he was superior to Lewis and Clark's pale-skinned companions. Clark later complained that the attention heaped on his slave made York less subservient.[30]

The Americans also attracted the attention of Arikara females. "Their womin [are] verry fond of carressing our men," wrote Clark on October 15, implying that there was considerable sexual intercourse between Arikara women and members of the expedition. As mentioned earlier, sex was one way to transfer spiritual power from one individual to another. Such exchanges, however, would have been conducted only by the lowest-ranking members of Arikara society.[31]

On October 11, chief Crow Going Across responded to Lewis's speech. He said he was happy to see the captains and that he wished for peace with the Mandans. He added that his people would make buffalo robes to trade with the Americans.[32]

The next day, Chief Hay made his reply. Like Crow Going Across, he was glad to see the Americans. He hoped that the Great Father would take pity on his people, trade with them, and protect them. He promised to keep the Missouri River open to traders and wished for a speedy return of the expedition. He also wished that the Mandans would open the road to allow Canadian traders to come down. Hay also presented the captains with a pair of beaded leggings and a decorated buffalo robe, and the people of the town gave the explorers seven bushels of corn and some tobacco.[33]

Eagle Feather spoke later that day. He would go to Washington to see the Great Father, but he complained bitterly that the Sioux were treacherous and had bad hearts. He promised he would join the captains to make peace with the Mandans and expressed his hope that after visiting Washington he could bring back knives, powder, and balls for his people.[34]

Although Eagle Feather wished to see his "grandfather," he also wished to "return quicke for fear of my people being uneasy," adding that "my Children are Small & perhaps will be uneasy [until] I may be Safe." It is unlikely that Lewis and Clark understood the significance of these words. As later events proved, Eagle Feather's unfortunate death while visiting Washington would infuriate the Arikaras.

Eagle Feather's people provided Lewis and Clark with more corn, beans, and squash. After presenting the chiefs with more gifts, Lewis and Clark and Eagle Feather bid good-bye to Crow Going Across and Hay and sailed for the Mandan towns. Joseph Gravelines accompanied them as interpreter.[35]

PEACE WITH THE MANDANS

Despite the scientific component of their mission, Lewis and Clark did not pay much attention to Eagle Feather's stories about the country they traveled through. Eagle Feather recounted the story of the sacred Standing Rock and other "Treditions about Turtles, Snakes, &. and the power of a perticular rock or Cave on the next river which informs of everr thing." Clark did not believe Eagle Feather's comments were worth recording. He could not appreciate that the world of the Arikaras was inhabited by mysterious forces.[36]

At Knife River, the expedition arrived at the Mandan town. Among the chiefs was an Arikara who had been adopted by the Mandans. This man, named It's a White Cloud (Clark recorded his name as The Coal), may have been the reason the Arikaras had sought refuge near the Mandans in the 1790s. He was a rival of Chief Black Cat, considered by the captains to be the head chief of the Mandans.[37]

On Monday, October 29, Eagle Feather and the captains met the Mandan and Hidatsa chiefs in council for the first time. Among the chiefs in attendance were Sheheke ("White Coyote"), Little Raven, and Black Cat. Before distributing peace medals and other gifts, Lewis gave his usual speech. He also introduced Eagle Feather, who had come to make peace with them.[38]

Over the next few days, Eagle Feather visited the chiefs. Chief Black Cat said that peace with the surrounding tribes would give great satisfaction to the entire nation. The men could now hunt without fear, the women could work in the fields without looking every moment for the enemy, and all could safely take off their moccasins at night. They accepted the peace offer of the Arikaras and agreed to send one chief and several soldiers with Eagle Feather to smoke the calumet at the Arikara towns. Other chiefs echoed Black Cat's desire for peace with the Arikaras, but they also reminded Eagle Feather that the Arikaras had massacred a peace delegation once before, which had led to the current state of war between the two sides. One chief, Big Man Cheyenne, told Eagle Feather that he did not believe the peace would last because the Arikaras were liars and their hearts were bad. He only agreed to peace because Lewis and Clark had asked him to do so.[39]

On Friday, November 2, 1804, Eagle Feather set out for home accompanied by one Mandan chief and several Mandan soldiers.[40] They arrived a few days later and met the chiefs of all ten Arikara bands. Nine chiefs agreed to make peace with the Mandans. Only one chief, The Gourd Rattle of the Laocata band, rejected the pipe. Tabeau believed that The Gourd Rattle merely wished to demonstrate his independence, but his ties to the Sioux may also have been a factor. The Gourd Rattle's rejection angered the other chiefs, who "threatened to cut off the Laocata from the Ricara body to join themselves to the Mandanes in order to destroy them." Faced with this threat, The Gourd Rattle gave up his resistance.[41]

Agreeing to peace was one thing; maintaining it was another. The Sioux were determined to drive a wedge in the Arikara–Mandan alliance. An Oglala band that had been camping near the Arikaras since October 22 learned about the peace negotiations and immediately prepared for war against the Mandans. They called upon the Arikaras to join them, and undoubtedly some Laocatas answered their call. On November 30 they attacked a small Mandan hunting party, killing one man, wounding two others, and capturing nine horses. They also killed four men in a Hidatsa hunting party. The Mandan chiefs were angry at this violation of the peace agreement and complained to Lewis and Clark, who were spending the winter at nearby Fort Mandan. The Arikaras "have not opened their ears to your good Councils but have Spuilt our blood," they said. They sent away two Arikara visitors because they feared their lives were in danger from relatives of the slain man. Clark cautioned restraint. He explained that most of the Arikaras followed their counsel but that a few bad Arikaras had been led astray by the Sioux. Clark told the chiefs, "You know that the Ricarees, are Dependant on the Sceaux for their guns, powder, & Ball, and it was policy in them to keep on as good terms as possible with the Siaux untill they had Some other means of getting those articles." Clark's appeals had effect, because the Mandan chiefs prevented their young men from going to war against the Arikaras. For now, war had been averted.[42]

In February 1805, Chief Man Crow wanted to visit the Mandans to reassure them that the Arikaras would observe the peace.[43] The situation at the Arikara towns was dire. In mid-March they ran out of ammunition; they were unable to hunt or defend themselves. Chief Crow Going Across visited Tabeau and demanded that he should trade for powder and ball at an affordable price. Tabeau made some concessions, but when the powder ran out a few days later, he refused to trade again. Now even Chief Man Crow grew tired of him. With Man Crow about to leave for the Mandans, in early April, Tabeau's situation became almost unbearable. The pressure on him to trade was tremendous.[44]

The Arikaras could not understand why Tabeau refused to trade powder and balls when they were in such desperate need of these articles. To them, trade was a social contract by which items changed hands, and kinship relationships and obligations were strengthened as well. Tabeau's stubborn refusal to share with his Arikara "brothers" puzzled and irritated them. "You are foolish," one Arikara chief said to him. "Why do you wish to make all this powder and these balls since you do not hunt?" He answered his own question: "It is only your wicked heart that prevents you from giving them to us. Do you not see that the village has none? I will give you a robe myself, when you want it, but you already have more robes than are necessary to cover you."[45]

Man Crow's council with the Mandans and Hidatsas was unsuccessful. He had been sent by his people to find out how the Mandans and Hidatsas felt about the Arikaras settling near them, but the Mandan chiefs were unwilling to travel to the Arikara towns, as was custom, to smoke the calumet. They feared for their safety while the Sioux were camped nearby. Some may have been suspicious of The Gourd Rattle and the Laocatas. In any event, distrust between the Mandans and the Arikaras remained deep. With Lewis and Clark gone, hostilities between the two tribes would soon resume.[46]

EAGLE FEATHER IN WASHINGTON CITY

While Man Crow was negotiating with the Mandans, Lewis and Clark prepared a barge to take Eagle Feather to Washington. The barge, commanded by Corporal Richard Warfington, also contained numerous objects the expedition had collected during the journey.[47] Among these objects were some Arikara "snap beans." These beans were forwarded to Thomas Jefferson, who planted them in his garden at Monticello. Jefferson wrote that the "Ricara bean is one of the most excellent we have had." Impressed with Arikara bean stock, Jefferson added that he had "cultivated them plentifully for the table two years" and had "found one kind only superior to them."[48]

Apart from Eagle Feather and interpreter Joseph Gravelines, trader Tabeau also boarded Corporal Warfington's barge.[49] As they descended the river, Ponca, Sioux, Omaha, Otoe, and Missouria chiefs also joined them.

The journey was hard on Eagle Feather. In September, while staying in St. Louis, Eagle Feather and several Otoe chiefs fell sick. They were so "sorely afflicted, that their Lives were despaired of." They were too weak to travel on horseback and were forced to stay behind as the remainder of the delegation continued toward Washington. Eagle Feather and the Otoe chiefs wished to return to their homes to recuperate. However, when they reached Kaw territory, the Kaws turned them back to St. Louis. Eagle Feather's health improved somewhat, allowing him to resume his journey to Washington.

Impressed with Eagle Feather's knowledge of the geography and peoples of the region, Louisiana territorial governor James Wilkinson advised Jefferson that Eagle Feather's "influence over the Nations of the Upper Missouri" might make him "an important Instrument of Humanity & of policy." Wilkinson added that in his opinion, Eagle Feather should be returned to his people as soon as possible after his visit to Washington "without regard to the other Deputies, & sent up to his Nation by a Military Escort loaded with presents."[50]

Although still weak, Eagle Feather reached Washington in 1806. It is uncertain if he ever met Jefferson there, but he probably visited with Secretary of War Henry

Dearborn. He received a number of gifts, including a used blue military coat with large gold epaulets, a flannel shirt, light-colored pantaloons, and shoes. He wore rings in his ears and a blue cotton handkerchief around his head, tied with a buckle in the front. He carried with him a letter of recommendation from Lewis and Clark as well as a map he had drawn of the Arikara country. Apart from the names of the different Indian nations on the Missouri, the map included depictions of Arikara sacred sites as well as Nuutawáčeš, the mysterious horned water serpent living in the Missouri River, to whom Arikara war parties made sacrifices of tobacco or meat when they wished to cross.[51] Eagle Feather also drew a picture of the president's mansion, "beyond which he had drawn a gun, a sword, powder, ball & tobacco as the presents he expected."[52]

Eagle Feather also visited Boston and Philadelphia and made a favorable impression on government officials there. But his health continued to be of concern. Dearborn wrote, "The Ricardi Chief is an interesting character;—and we shall not fail of sending him away particularly satisfied. I most ardently hope, he will return home in safety."[53]

Eagle Feather fell ill once again and died of pneumonia on April 7, 1806. It is unclear what happened to his remains,[54] but his death caused much consternation in Washington. Dearborn suggested sending Gravelines and a Pawnee Indian to the Arikaras to inform them of Eagle Feather's death. Dearborn also suggested forwarding the chief's medal, clothes, and other possessions to his son. In addition, he thought it advisable "to send presents to his wives and children, to the amount of, from two to three hundred Dollars" and "100 lbs. of Powder and a corresponding quantity of Lead, to be distributed to the Chiefs of the Ricaras and Mandanes &c."[55]

"HERE IS MY COUNTRY": EAGLE FEATHER'S MAP

Long believed to have been lost or destroyed, one of Eagle Feather's maps was fortuitously rediscovered in the Bibliothèque Nationale de France in Paris.[56] Eagle Feather had drawn the map at the request of William Clark and territorial governor James Wilkinson, who were interested in the location of different Indian nations in the region. Eagle Feather, however, used his map to demonstrate the extent of Arikara territorial sovereignty. In doing so he challenged US notions that defined Arikara territory much more narrowly. "Here," he told the white people he met, "is my country." The map showed the extent of Eagle Feather's travels. He had traveled as far south as Santa Fe, New Mexico. If the United States ever wished to go to war with the Spaniards, Eagle Feather told Governor Wilkinson, he could tell them how to get there. To the north, Eagle Feather's map ended at Fort Assiniboine, a Northwest Company trading post in Canada. White settlements, then, marked the northern and southern borders of Eagle Feather's map. Undoubtedly, by traveling all the way to Washington, Eagle Feather hoped to broaden his geographical and cultural understanding of the eastern world as well. He was for all intents and purposes the Arikara equivalent to Lewis and Clark, except that his journey of discovery led him east instead of west.

Eagle Feather's map is an extraordinary ethnohistorical source. It not only shows familiar geographic features such as mountains and streams but also provides insights into the spiritual landscape of the Arikaras. The map showed the lake into which fifty-six Arikaras had disappeared when a mysterious turtle carried them off into the deep. Another lake contained a horned animal: Cut Nose, the monstrous "buffalo" from Arikara oral tradition. A third lake had rocks that had moved to the bottom. The map also showed the now famous Standing Rock, which depicted a petrified woman and her dog; a "pyramid" where Indian men went to catch eagles; a strange cave "where crows gather in abundance" on the east bank of the Missouri River; and "Medicine Rock," which served as an oracle, allowing visitors to foresee the future. At the heart of Eagle Feather's world, however, was Tswaarúxti', the Mysterious River, where the three Arikara towns were situated. It meanders through Eagle Feather's map like a giant aorta.[57]

Eagle Feather also listed the different Indian nations he was familiar with. Most of these, such as the Pawnees, Missourias, Omahas, Cheyennes, Kiowas, and Kiowa Apaches, are known to scholars today, but there were others whose identity remains uncertain, including the "Ounnissiou or the Rattlesnakes," the Towassas, the Tieracos ("Foxes"), and others.

Beyond the Mandans, Hidatsas, and an enigmatic group called the Whistlers lived the Assiniboines, Crees, Atsinas, and Blackfeet. To the northwest were the Crows as well as a Cheyenne band. Beyond the Rocky Mountains were various other nations, including the Ris—probably the Niitaxkstaáwo ("They Who Went after Sinew")—a mysterious Arikara band that had separated from the main body earlier and whose fate is unknown. Here also lived the "Skin People," the "People who carry on their heads," the "Beaver people," and a group called Chicacha. Beyond the Rocky Mountains, the Aliatan ("Snake People") lived.

Interestingly, Eagle Feather continued to locate the Sioux as properly belonging east of the Missouri River. Apart from a generic-sounding "Sioux village," he listed the "Richara Sioux," the "Tacohoua Sioux," the "Sahoini Sioux" (Saones), and the "Ottowa Sioux." The Richara Sioux, an Oglala band, were probably so-named

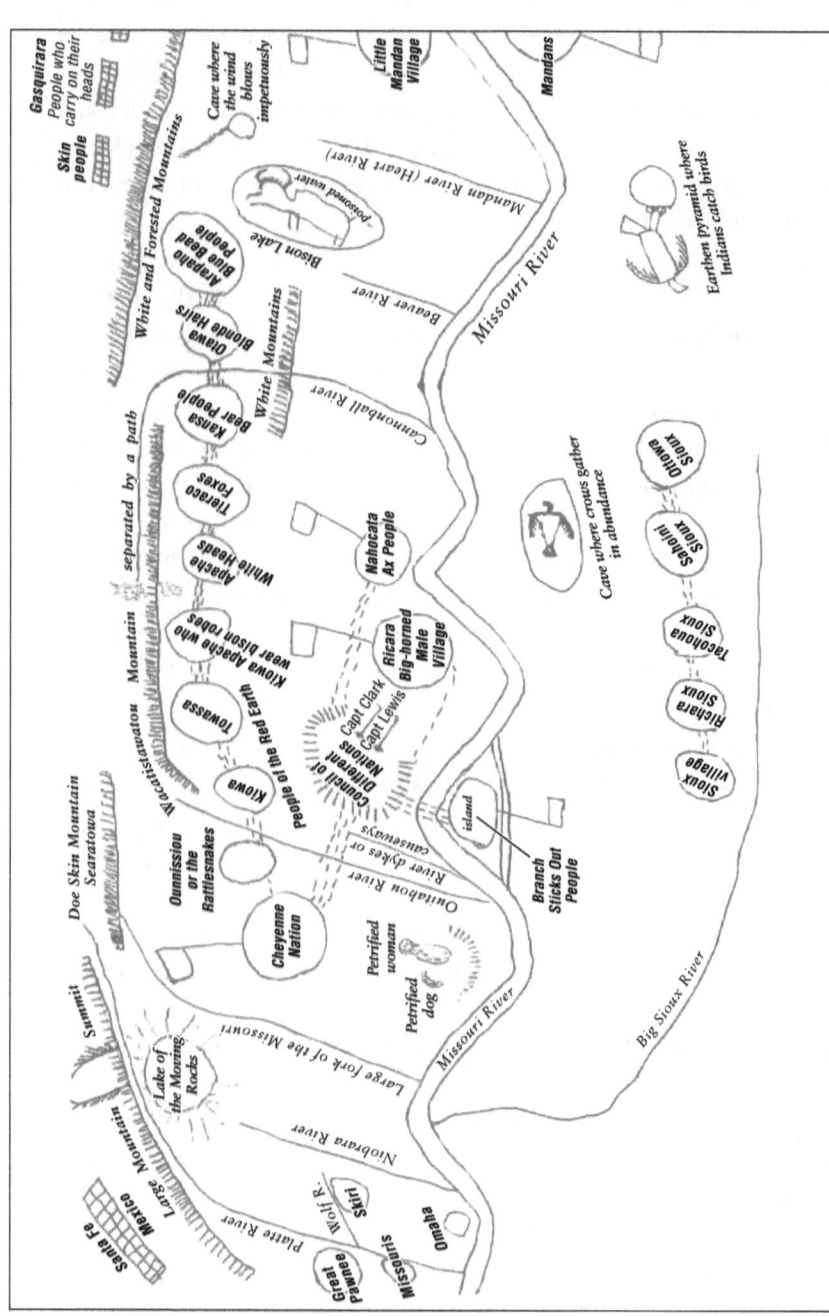

Too Né's map, circa 1806, part 1
Adaptation of a map of the Arikara heartland drawn by Too Né ("Eagle Feather") around 1806, including neighboring nations (circles), distant nations and Euro-American settlements (boxes), geographical features (streams, lakes, mountains, and the Missouri River), as well as a number of sacred sites. Rather than providing topographical accuracy, the map reflects Arikara geopolitical realities and sacred geography.

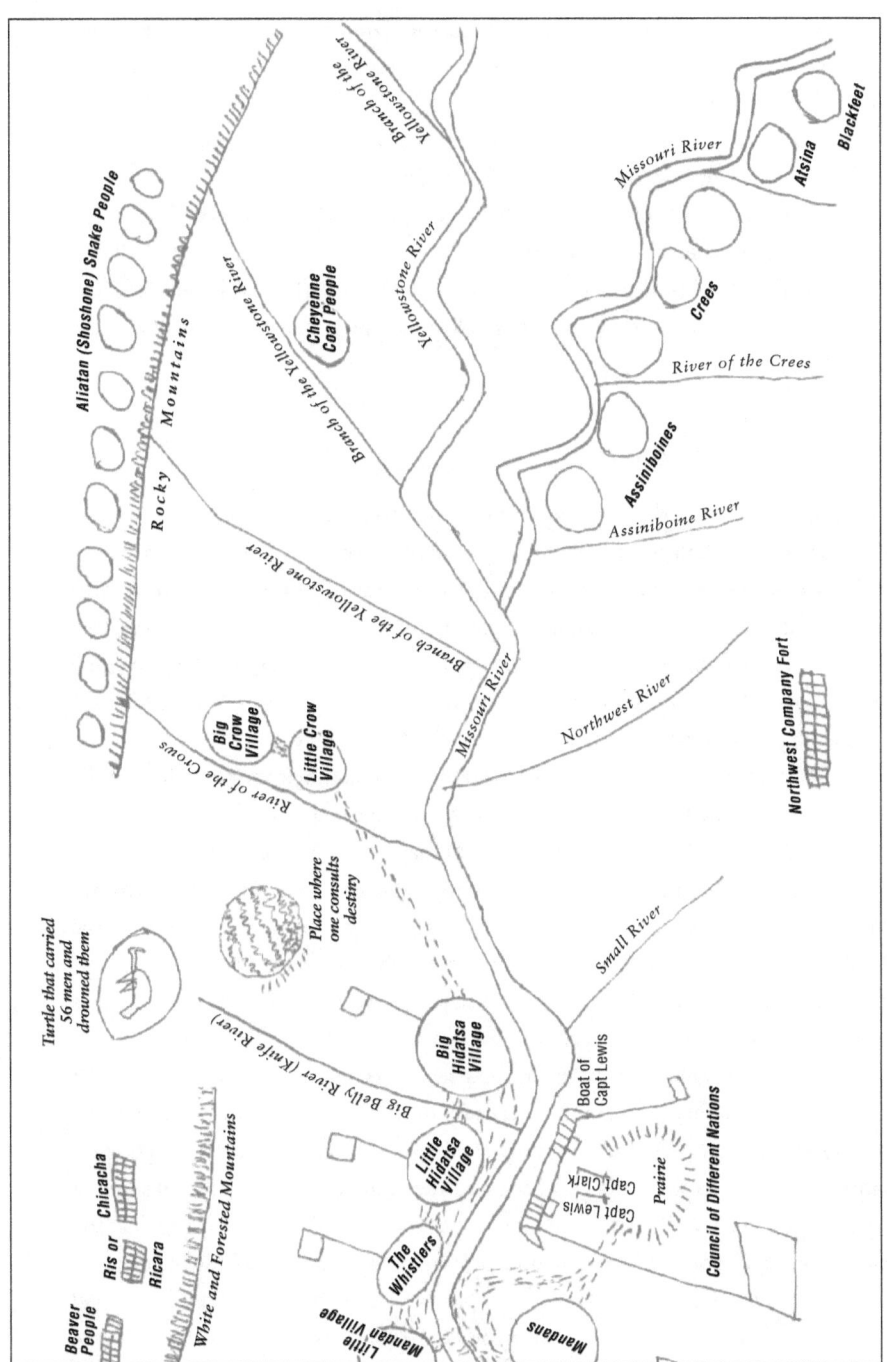

Too Né's Map, circa 1806, part 2

because of their ties with the Arikara nation. The "Ounnissiou or the Rattlesnakes" who dwelled west of the Missouri River, could possibly be a western Sioux band, but this is uncertain.

While the map is an invaluable ethnohistorical artifact and an object of special meaning to present-day Arikaras, President Jefferson apparently thought it was not worthy of saving. He viewed it as a curiosity and gave it to one of his staff members, who eventually gifted it to French diplomat Jean-Guillaume Hyde de Neuville. In 1905 descendants of de Neuville donated the map to the National Library of France, where it remains today as a rare and priceless example of early Native American mapmaking.[58]

LEWIS AND CLARK RETURN

News of Eagle Feather's death had not yet reached the Arikaras when Lewis and Clark arrived on their return trip in August 1806. By this time, hostilities between the Arikaras and the Mandans and Hidatsas had resumed. The war started when some Arikaras stole a number of Mandan horses. In retaliation, the Mandans killed two Arikaras. In an attempt to restore the peace, Lewis and Clark urged Mandan Chief White Coyote (also known as Big White) to accompany them to the Arikara towns.[59]

On August 21, 1806, the Arikara chiefs met Lewis, Clark, and White Coyote in council. This time, Grey Eyes, recognized by many as the prominent chief of the nation, was present. Clark described him in his journal as a man of about thirty-two years of age. Chief Crow Going Across, who had accepted the large peace medal from the captains during Grey Eyes's absence, informed Clark that Grey Eyes was the head chief who spoke for his nation. Grey Eyes explained that the war with the Mandans had been started by some young men who would not listen to the chiefs and had joined the Sioux. These young men had now been driven from the towns. He assured White Coyote that his people wanted peace and told Clark that he wished to visit Washington to get support in their struggles against the Sioux, though he worried for his safety because the journey would lead him through enemy territory. Grey Eyes also expressed concern for Eagle Feather, who had been gone for more than a year now. At the conclusion of the council, Clark suggested that the Arikaras, Mandans, Hidatsas, and Cheyennes form a military alliance against the Sioux. White Coyote and the Arikara chiefs then smoked to conclude the peace.[60]

But looks were deceiving. Things were not well in the Arikara nation. They had not received any traders from St. Louis, and their supplies of powder and ball were almost exhausted. One of the chiefs, possibly Hay, had lost his nephew in a fight with the Sioux. He had cut his hair and "disfigured himself" in mourning. That evening, Grey Eyes told Clark that none of the chiefs would go to see the Great Father until Eagle Feather had returned. Clark gave Grey Eyes a nice ribbon on which to suspend his peace medal, as well as a shell he had received from the Snake (Shoshone) Indians.

When the captains arrived at the island town later that afternoon, they met Man Crow, who, upon seeing White Coyote, "spoke to the Mandan Chief in a loud and thretening tone." Sensing danger, Clark cautioned Man Crow that they would defend White Coyote with their lives. Man Crow invited them all into his lodge for a council. He explained that the Sioux were the cause of all the problems. The talks ended on friendly terms.[61]

Still, the Arikaras remained suspicious of the captains. When Clark visited Crow Going Across, Man Crow, and interpreter Joseph Garreau at the island town the next day, the chiefs repeated that they would not go to see the Great Father until Eagle Feather had returned safely. They also desired to stay to prevent the young men from going to war with the Mandans and Hidatsas. Finally, they promised to sever their ties with the Sioux after one more trading session to obtain guns and powder. Anxious to return to St. Louis, Clark and the other members of the expedition hastily bid them good-bye and resumed their journey.[62]

WAR WITH THE UNITED STATES

A few weeks after their departure from the Arikaras, Lewis and Clark met Joseph Gravelines on his return to the Arikara towns. He had a letter from President Jefferson announcing Eagle Feather's passing.[63] "My friends & children of the Ricara nation," Jefferson wrote. "It gave me a great pleasure to see your beloved chief arrive here on a visit to his white brothers of the United States of America."[64] Jefferson assured the Arikaras that Eagle Feather had "found nothing but kindness & good will wherever he passed." Regrettably, Eagle Feather had fallen ill and despite medical attention had passed away. "We buried him among our own deceased friends & relatives [and] shed many tears over his grave, and we now mingle our afflictions with yours on the loss of this beloved chief. But death must happen to all men; and his time was come."[65]

Despite Jefferson's soothing words, the news of Eagle Feather's death infuriated the Arikaras. They unleashed their anger at Gravelines, who barely escaped with his life.[66] Eagle Feather's death strained Arikara relations with American traders too. In revenge, the Arikaras molested American traders who passed their towns.

In June 1807, they attacked Joseph Dickson. The American trapper and hunter narrowly escaped with his life.[67] That same month they plundered trader Charles Courtin of his merchandise.[68]

An Arikara war party also stopped St. Louis trader Manuel Lisa. Seeing that Lisa's outfit was well armed, they agreed to trade with him instead. As women appeared with sacks of corn to trade, a young warrior slashed the sacks with a knife, spilling the contents to the ground. Taking this as a bad sign, Lisa ordered his men to arms. As the crews pointed small boat-mounted cannons toward the shore, the Arikaras retreated in confusion. They soon returned to invite Lisa for a council. After smoking with the chiefs, Lisa distributed presents, traded guns and ammunition, and received permission to continue his journey.[69]

In September 1807, an American expedition under command of US Navy ensign Nathaniel Pryor, a former member of the Corps of Discovery, approached the Arikara towns on the Grand River. Pryor had been instructed by Jefferson to escort Mandan chief White Coyote home. A group of traders under Pierre Chouteau from St. Louis also accompanied Pryor in order to trade with the Mandans. When Pryor and Chouteau arrived at the Arikara towns on September 9, the Arikaras stopped them. Pryor explained the purpose of his mission during his council with the chiefs. Although Chief Grey Eyes accepted a peace medal, Pryor noticed that the Arikaras were not particularly friendly. Nevertheless, the chiefs gave him permission to move on. Later that day, however, Grey Eyes's warriors gathered on the shore where Pryor's boats passed. They told him he could not proceed until he had traded with them. In the exchange that followed, the Arikaras became very agitated. Chief Grey Eyes threw away his medal and a fight ensued. Three of Chouteau's men were killed and nine others were wounded. The survivors scrambled into their boats and escaped downstream. Several days later, they arrived in St. Louis.[70]

Pryor blamed Manuel Lisa for the incident, claiming that Lisa had told the Arikaras that Pryor's party would trade with them. The fact is that the Arikaras not only blamed the Americans for Eagle Feather's death but also believed the United States was siding against them in their war with the Mandans. The presence of Chief White Coyote among the soldiers and the number of goods the traders intended to take to the Mandans confirmed their suspicions.[71]

The attack on Pryor's party troubled relations between the Arikaras and the United States. On August 24, 1808, Jefferson wrote to Meriwether Lewis, now governor of the territory of Louisiana, that he considered "a severe punishment of the Ricaras indispensable."[72] Lewis, however, had already persuaded the War Department to pay $7,000 to the newly organized Missouri Fur Company to escort

White Coyote back to his people.[73] Pierre Chouteau and Manuel Lisa would lead the mission. This time 350 well-armed men would accompany them. Lewis authorized Chouteau to recruit warriors from other Indian nations as well.

Lewis's instructions to Chouteau contained a disturbing order. Apart from demanding the unconditional surrender and execution of Arikaras responsible for killing Pryor's men, Lewis demanded that if the guilty men could not be ascertained, the Arikaras should deliver four men who would be "shot in the presence of the nation." In addition, the Arikaras should present horses to any Indian auxiliaries that Chouteau recruited. Should the Arikaras refuse, Chouteau was at liberty to incite the Mandans, Hidatsas, and any other tribe against the Arikaras, for "it is the wish of their Great father, that [the Arikaras] should be driven out of the Country or distroyed." What Lewis called for was nothing less than genocide.[74]

White Coyote, Chouteau, Lisa, and their small army of traders set out from St. Louis in thirteen barges in May 1809. Along the way Chouteau tried to enlist three hundred Sioux warriors, but surprisingly, only six Sioux chiefs agreed to come along. When Chouteau and Lisa arrived at the Arikara towns on September 12, they found a Mandan peace delegation already there.[75]

The Arikara chiefs were much alarmed by the sudden appearance of Chouteau and Lisa's men. Grey Eyes and the other chiefs refused to approach Chouteau until an exchange of hostages was agreed upon. In the council that followed, the chiefs explained why they had attacked Pryor's party. They said a Frenchman who resided among them had told them that the goods in Pryor's barges were presents from their Great Father. But when Pryor kept the goods and handed out only medals, they attacked the command in anger. Chouteau demanded that this Frenchman be delivered to him, but when the chiefs said that he was now living with another tribe, Chouteau let the matter rest.[76]

The Mandan and Sioux chiefs urged Chouteau not to make war against the Arikaras. Chouteau agreed. As a trader, he had little to gain from a renewed outbreak of hostilities. Wisely, he ignored Lewis's instructions to execute Arikara hostages in retaliation for the attack on Pryor's party. Instead, Chouteau and Lisa agreed to a peace with the Arikaras.[77]

Chouteau and Lisa stayed at the Arikara towns for two days. During this time, the men of the expedition mingled with the people and visited their lodges. One member, expedition surgeon Thomas James, wrote that their cornfields were well fenced "and better cultivated than many farms on the frontiers of the United States."[78] At the end of the visit, Chouteau and Lisa resumed their journey to the Mandans, where they returned Chief White Coyote safely to his family.[79]

Although the Arikaras were now again at peace with the United States, the attack on Pryor's party received much attention in newspapers all over the country. The reports depicted the Arikaras as a menace to traders and US interests. This reputation was largely undeserved. Traders' reports show that the Sioux were generally more troublesome than the Arikaras.[80] In any case, both the Arikaras and the Sioux were simply protecting their own interests. The Arikaras preferred to be at peace with the traders, but they would, if necessary, take up arms if their interests and security were at stake.

Louisiana territorial governor Meriwether Lewis, however, refused to issue licenses to traders wishing to do business with the Arikaras, thus ensuring further bad blood between the Arikaras and whites. It appears, however, that traders such as Manuel Lisa had little intention of following Lewis's 1809 order and traded with the Arikaras if expedient.[81]

THE ARIKARAS AND AMERICAN FUR TRADERS

Although the Arikaras narrowly dodged a war of extermination with the United States, problems continued to plague them. War resumed with the Sioux, forcing Crow Going Across and Man Crow to abandon the island town. They most likely joined the two upper towns, but it is also possible that they joined the Pawnees to escape the Sioux threat. Such a move was not unprecedented; nor would it be the last time Arikara bands joined their Pawnee relatives. They may have also joined the Mandans and Hidatsas on the Knife River, because at this time the three tribes were at peace and had formed a military alliance against the Sioux. The two upper Arikara towns remained on the Grand River, however. Grey Eyes was chief of the first town. Left Handed was now the principal chief of the other town, with Big Man as second chief. The towns had a combined population of about two thousand, including five hundred warriors. There were about 150 to 160 lodges in total. A nine-foot-high palisade made from cedar logs surrounded the towns.[82]

The Lewis and Clark expedition precipitated a rush of American traders into the upper Missouri country. The Missouri Fur Company, led by Lisa and the Chouteau brothers, in 1811 prepared to travel to the rich trapping grounds along the Yellowstone River. At the same time New York businessman John Jacob Astor, founder of the American Fur Company, sent an overland expedition under Wilson P. Hunt to establish trading posts among the tribes of the Pacific Northwest. The two expeditions met on the Missouri River and decided to travel together for mutual security.[83]

Well below the Cheyenne River, Lisa and Hunt spotted an Arikara war party of three hundred men. The appearance of the warriors impressed the Americans.

One member of the expedition commented that many were over six feet tall and "more robust" than the Sioux. Particularly remarkable was an Arikara warrior whose arms and chest were covered with scars, apparently inflicted upon himself in his grief for his father's death. That evening, the Arikaras honored the traders with a dance.[84] Desperately in need of arms and ammunition, the Arikaras aborted their expedition to meet the traders at the Grand River towns.

When Lisa and Hunt arrived there ten days later, Left Handed, Big Man, and interpreter Joseph Garreau welcomed them in council. After all smoked the pipe, Left Handed said that his people were glad to see that the Americans had arrived, but he informed them that the Arikaras would allow them to continue only if they traded with them first.[85]

Chief Grey Eyes agreed to provide Hunt with horses. He told Hunt that they could easily replace the horses through trade or stealing. In the days following the council, the chiefs set the price for a buffalo robe at twenty loads of ball and powder. The Arikaras brought robes to Lisa and horses to Hunt. Carbines, ammunition, axes, and knives were especially in demand "as another expedition against the Sioux was meditated."[86]

While the Arikaras and Americans traded, two expedition members, John Bradbury and Henry Marie Brackenridge, explored the towns. They noticed that the Arikaras protected their gardens against birds with scarecrows made from discarded buffalo robes attached to long poles. A buffalo hipbone represented the head. "I have not seen, even in the United States, any crop of Indian corn in finer order, or better managed than the corn about these villages," wrote Bradbury, a professional botanist, in his journal.[87]

Because of the war with the Sioux, the Arikaras were on high alert. Many of the warriors were dressed and ready for war. Some warriors wore fox tails on the heels of their moccasins, a sign that they had killed an enemy in hostile territory. Their weapons consisted of guns, war clubs, spears, bows, and lances. There were numerous warrior societies, of which the Young Dog Society was among the fiercest. Warfare took a heavy toll among the men of the tribe, and because of the shortage of males, many men looked after four or five wives each.[88]

There were many encounters with enemy war parties that summer. On June 15 the Arikaras battled Sioux attackers while the women, children, and old men cheered them on from lodge roofs. Over the following days, Arikara war parties returned from expeditions. Upon arrival the warriors were conducted to the medicine lodge, where they were questioned by the chiefs. One war party brought back horses from a raid against the Snake Indians. Camp criers spread the cheerful news to the people.[89]

On July 10, a large Arikara war party under Chief Grey Eyes returned. It carried many Sioux scalps and received a grand welcome in the town. The entire procession was nearly a quarter of a mile long. Many warriors had painted red hand marks over their mouths with vermillion to signify that they had figuratively "tasted the life blood of the enemy." Old men who could barely walk rubbed their hands over the warriors. Women sang songs. The wounded were brought to the medicine lodge, which served as a temporary hospital.[90]

Despite the loss of several warriors, the battle was hailed as a tremendous victory. Bradbury explained that Grey Eyes's warriors had "driven away an enemy, who had for two or three weeks been hovering round, and threatened us all with starvation."[91] Because of the Sioux threat, the Arikaras had not yet been able to go on their annual buffalo hunt. That evening six hundred people gathered in the medicine lodge for a great dance. Several women dressed as warriors and performed the scalp dance. The spirit of tribal identity and pride left a great impression on Brackenridge. In his journal, he noted, "How much superior does this little independent tribe appear, to the rich, but mean and spiritless province or colony, where nothing but individual interests are felt!"[92]

"TERRIBLE DEEDS WHICH I WILL NOT DESCRIBE WITH MY PEN": FORT MANUEL, 1812–1813

Ball and powder were responsible for Arikara military successes that summer. Not surprisingly, the Arikaras cheered Manuel Lisa's plan to establish a permanent trading post in the area. Access to trade goods was more important than ever.

But the political situation quickly deteriorated. In 1812 the Sioux succeeded in driving a wedge in the Arikara–Mandan–Hidatsa alliance by forcing some Hidatsa bands to switch sides. War with the Hidatsas seemed imminent.[93]

The prospect of war caused old rivalries and jealousies between the chiefs to reappear. Some chiefs wished to patch things up with the Hidatsas. Others called for war. It is possible that Sioux schemers tried to persuade some of the chiefs to side with them against the Hidatsas. Young and ambitious men seeking to increase their social status were particularly receptive to such arguments. An alliance with the Sioux appeared logical for another reason. Unlike the Mandans and Hidatsas, who had access to a steady supply of guns and powder from traders operating from Canada, the Arikaras still largely depended on the Sioux for guns and ammunition.

Faced with this new geopolitical reality, Arikara tribal unity soon broke down. Once again the chiefs found themselves embroiled in a struggle for control of the nation. Among the main players in this struggle were Left Handed, Grey Eyes, Elk's Tongue, Big Man, and Eagle Feather, the son of Too Né, who had adopted his father's name after learning of his death.[94]

When Lisa returned at the Arikara towns and called a council in August 1812, several chiefs refused to appear because "jealousy reigned among them." Those in attendance were upset when they learned that Lisa was going to build his fort twelve miles north of the Arikara settlements.[95] Left Handed and Eagle Feather accompanied Lisa to the new site, possibly to make certain that he would not go too far. They chose a location just above the mouth of what was later called Hunkpapa Creek, in present day Corson County, South Dakota.[96] While Lisa built Fort Manuel, Arikara war expeditions moved against the Hidatsas and Sioux.[97]

In November Lisa successfully brokered a peace between the Arikaras and the Hidatsas but failed to do the same with the Sioux.[98] A council between Left Handed and several Saone chiefs at Lisa's camp in September broke down when one Sioux warrior, apparently drunk on whiskey, caused a disturbance. In late November, a Saone Sioux band of 150 lodges arrived at the Arikara towns to trade. However, when the Saone chiefs decided to move their camp between the Arikaras and Fort Manuel, the Arikara chiefs were angry because this cut them off not only from Lisa's post but also from the buffalo herds that were presently roaming in that area. In January 1813, war began in earnest after some Sioux murdered an Arikara man. Arikara women and children sought refuge in Lisa's fort. On February 7, post clerk John Luttig counted sixty-five Arikara people, mostly women and children. On February 11, a Sioux war party ambushed a small Arikara party, killing a man and a woman and taking a child captive. Among the missing was chief Left Handed's blind son. The Arikaras feared for his life, but he was found the next day hiding in a bush. Two days after the attack, on February 13, Chief Eagle Feather and fifty or sixty people arrived from the town to give the two victims a proper burial.[99]

The war threatened Lisa's profits. Traveling the country to trap for beaver or to visit tribes to trade became too dangerous. On February 22, the Sioux attacked Fort Manuel but were repelled by swivel guns. However, they killed and mutilated *engagé* Louis Archambeau. Apart from twenty-nine arrows in his body, his head had been crushed and his brains scattered about. His nose and ears had been cut off and his teeth knocked out. According to Luttig, the Sioux had done several "more terrible Deeds which I will not express with my Pen."[100]

Although the sources do not explain why the Sioux opposed Fort Manuel, it seems likely that they wanted to prevent the Arikaras from having direct access to the white man's guns. They also believed the traders were detrimental to their divide-and-conquer policy toward the Arikaras and Hidatsas. In any case, their attacks unnerved the traders. On February 26, Luttig wrote in his journal that "[we] are like Prisoners in Deserts to expect every moment our fate." Rather than awaiting another attack, Lisa decided to abandon the post and return to St. Louis, where they arrived in May 1813.[101]

Once again the Arikaras were cut off from essential supplies of guns and powder.

PRELUDE TO THE ARIKARA WAR OF 1823

The Arikaras were blocked from the St. Louis fur trade for nine long years. As long as the Sioux remained determined to prevent traders from trading directly with the Arikaras, St. Louis businessmen were unwilling to invest in new trading expeditions, especially since the Arikaras did not have beaver skins to warrant such a risky investment. The War of 1812 also deterred investors, who feared that Canadian traders might attack and rob American traders of their precious cargo. Finally, the financial panic of 1819 caused the collapse of numerous banks upon which traders depended for credit to finance their expeditions.[102]

The period between 1813 and 1822 was full of hardship for the Arikaras. They were now at the mercy of the Sioux for firearms and ammunition. Although the lack of a trader living among them was frustrating, the fact that traders continued to supply the Sioux angered the Arikaras beyond measure. In their frustration, Arikara war parties attacked two distant Missouri Fur Company posts serving the Sioux in the Big Bend of the Missouri River in 1820.[103]

Not until 1822 did two trading expeditions reach the Arikaras. The first was led by Joshua Pilcher, who had succeeded Manuel Lisa as director of the Missouri Fur Company. The Arikaras welcomed him cordially. The chiefs assured Pilcher that they wanted good relations with the traders and promised not to attack whites in the future. They even allowed Pilcher to continue to the Mandans and the Hidatsas. However, on his return journey later that year, Pilcher eluded what he believed was an Arikara plot to rob his boat. The second expedition that reached the Arikaras was led by William Ashley and Andrew Henry. They too received a cordial welcome from the chiefs. Unfortunately, they had few goods to trade. Ashley explained that his outfit was on the way to the Rocky Mountains to trap beaver. He merely wished to trade for horses but promised to return the next year from St. Louis to trade with the Arikaras. Although the prospect of traders visiting them pleased the chiefs, they were very concerned about traders building posts farther north, where they could supply the Sioux, Assiniboines, Crows, and other potential enemies.[104]

Once again the Arikara chiefs were divided on how to deal with the traders. The Bear and Little Soldier were conciliatory. They believed that good relations with the traders were essential, even if the traders were supplying enemies with firearms. Grey Eyes, however, took a hard-line position: traders wishing to do business with the Arikaras were welcome, but those wishing to trade or caught trading with enemies of the Arikaras would be stopped and have their goods confiscated.[105]

In March 1823, Grey Eyes put his policy into effect. That month an Arikara war party met a few Missouri Fur Company traders accompanied by some Sioux. When the traders refused to surrender the Sioux, the warriors beat them severely and took off with the furs and hides. A few days later, another Arikara war party attacked Cedar Fort, a Missouri Fur Company trading post on the White River that supplied the Sioux. The attack failed. Two Arikaras were killed and several others were wounded. One of the dead was a son of Chief Grey Eyes.[106]

Grey Eyes was still in mourning when William Ashley arrived with ninety trappers a few weeks later. Ashley was on his way to resupply Fort Henry at the confluence of the Missouri and Yellowstone Rivers. On May 30, Grey Eyes, The Bear, Little Soldier, and the other chiefs welcomed Ashley, but upon learning that Ashley once again merely wished to buy some horses, Grey Eyes became angry. Little Soldier warned Ashley that Grey Eyes's warriors might attack. Ashley ordered his men back to the boats, but on the night of June 1, two of his men, Edward Rose and Aaron Stephens, snuck into the town in search of female company. What happened next is unclear, but on the morning of June 2, Stephens was killed in a dispute. Rose escaped to warn Ashley's men. His warning came almost too late. At dawn Grey Eyes's warriors attacked. In the fight, they killed twelve men and wounded eleven others.[107]

THE ARIKARA WAR OF 1823

Ashley and the survivors fled downstream and alerted Indian agent Benjamin O'Fallon, who appealed to Colonel Henry Leavenworth of the Sixth US Infantry Regiment at Fort Atkinson, Nebraska, for military assistance. Leavenworth immediately began preparations for a campaign against the Arikaras.[108]

Leavenworth had only recently been appointed commander at Fort Atkinson. Though a capable officer, he had little experience with Indian warfare and was unfamiliar with the nations west of the Mississippi. He was also caught in an ambiguous Indian policy: as commander, he had to protect American fur traders while, simultaneously, being ordered to "gain the confidence and friendship of all the Indian tribes." Leavenworth was instructed to negotiate with the tribes whenever possible and use force only as a last resort. He gathered six companies of the Sixth Regiment and several cannons, and boarded three keelboats on June 22, 1823.[109]

Agent O'Fallon, meanwhile, appointed Joshua Pilcher as special subagent of Indian affairs to assist Colonel Leavenworth. Pilcher knew the Missouri River and the tribes along it well. As subagent of Indian affairs, he was supposed to look out for the welfare of the Indian tribes under his charge, but he was also director of the Missouri Fur Company, whose traders had been attacked by Arikaras in earlier raids. As director of the fur company, he believed that a serious punishment of the Arikaras was absolutely necessary. This conflict of interests was illustrative of the entanglement of the fur trade in western politics. As events soon proved, Pilcher was more interested in what was best for his company than in seeking a peaceful resolution of the conflict. While Leavenworth prepared for the expedition, Pilcher gathered forty heavily armed men from his company and joined the troops.[110]

On July 19, the expedition arrived at Cedar Fort, where they met William Ashley and his men. Anxious to punish the Arikaras for the attack on June 2, Ashley joined the campaign with about eighty men. Along the way, Pilcher recruited 750 Sioux, who "cheerfully consented" to march against the Arikaras. The entire force now consisted of more than eleven hundred men. On August 8, they passed the Grand River. The Sioux advance force shielded the troops from view. Undoubtedly, the Arikaras had already discovered the Sioux, but they were not concerned because the trading season was about to begin. They felt safe in their well-stockaded towns.[111]

On August 9, the expedition came in sight of the Arikara towns. Leavenworth's troops immediately surrounded the twin towns, but the colonel was unable to restrain the Sioux auxiliaries, who rushed to attack before the artillery had been brought into position. When the Arikaras heard the Sioux war cry, their warriors spilled from the towns to rebuke the attack. They not only held their ground but drove the Sioux back.[112]

The sudden outbreak of hostilities posed a problem for Leavenworth. He had hoped to settle the conflict with the Arikaras with a show of force. Now that blood had been shed, he could do little but drive his soldiers forward to assist the Sioux. When the Arikaras saw the soldiers, they turned back, temporarily exposing themselves to Sioux fire. Ten Arikara warriors were killed in the retreat. While Leavenworth put the cannons in place, the Sioux mutilated the corpses of the fallen warriors. "We saw three or four with their heads, arms, hands, feet, and legs cut off," wrote Leavenworth later in his report: "Several Sioux were dragging about in great triumph the hands, feet, legs, or arms of the slain Arickarees by means of a long string or cord." As darkness began to fall, Leavenworth's artillery was in position.[113]

The next day, the artillery bombarded the towns. Leavenworth decided to concentrate his efforts on the lower town, which had led the attacks against Ashley's men. One of the first shots killed Chief Grey Eyes. A cannonball took off his head as he peeked over the palisade to assess the situation. His death demoralized the people of the lower town. While the warriors looked about for leadership, the bombardment continued. The grapeshot-filled bombs caused much destruction. Some Arikara warriors earned war honors by running up to the shells to defuse them before they could explode. Leavenworth later estimated that fifty Arikaras perished in the attack, but this was an exaggeration. Despite the bombardment, the Arikaras would not surrender. The warriors took up positions at various locations to prevent a direct assault on the palisade. The women, meanwhile, gathered food and supplies from caches in event of a retreat.[114]

Leavenworth became increasingly frustrated with his Sioux auxiliaries. While his artillery shelled the towns, the Sioux entered the Arikara cornfields to plunder the crops. They were disgusted by Leavenworth's refusal to attack the town and utterly unimpressed by the bombardment. Many started deserting the battlefield. Leavenworth later observed an Arikara who had come out to talk with the Sioux. Fearing that the Sioux might join the Arikaras against the troops, Leavenworth and Pilcher rode toward them to investigate. The Arikara negotiator said they wanted the troops to stop firing on them. The chiefs were willing to make peace. Leavenworth promised that the chiefs would not be harmed if they came out to talk.[115]

Shortly thereafter, the chiefs and headman came out carrying several buffalo robes as gifts. They told Leavenworth to "do with us as you please, but do not fire any more guns at us, we are all in tears." Leavenworth agreed to stop the attack if the chiefs agreed to compensate Ashley and if they promised never to take up arms against the traders again. He also demanded that five chiefs stay behind while the others collected the guns and horses as payment to Ashley. The chiefs agreed and the peace pipe was lighted. However, when it was Pilcher's turn to smoke, he rejected the pipe and refused to shake hands. Walking back and forth in agitation, he told the chiefs he would not accept peace. This announcement had a "very unfavorable effect upon the Indians," Leavenworth reported, "especially as his Interpreter (one Collin Campbell) had told the Indians that Mr. Pilcher was the chief of our expedition."[116]

As they escorted the five hostages to Leavenworth's camp, Campbell and Pilcher continued their threats. The sight of a dead Arikara warrior, his body riddled with

Sioux arrows, alarmed them, and they refused to continue. Thereupon Campbell and several other traders drew their guns and fired. Remarkably, nobody was hurt in the exchange. After calm had been restored, Leavenworth allowed the Arikara chiefs to return to their town.[117]

The next day, August 11, Chief Little Soldier emerged from the town to speak with Leavenworth. He asked Leavenworth why the white people fired upon them so soon after smoking and making peace. He said his people worried that the troops would kill them when they surrendered. He then invited Leavenworth to send some of his officers and soldiers to visit the chiefs in the towns. Leavenworth promised Little Soldier that his people would not be harmed and agreed to send officers to meet with the chiefs inside the town. Little Soldier escorted the delegation to the ceremonial lodge. The Arikara warriors seated themselves around the officers. The warriors "appeared very melancholy," for they had just buried their dead, "many of whom had layed exposed two days." Little Soldier explained that his young men were frightened because they had been "flogged with whips [the cannons] of which they had heretofore no knowledge and such as they supposed the Great Spirit alone had power to punish them with." Little Soldier promised he would meet with Leavenworth, and he generously offered to provide food for the hungry soldiers.[118]

Later that afternoon, the chiefs signed a treaty Leavenworth had drafted. In it they promised to compensate Ashley, refrain from obstructing river traffic in the future, and behave friendly toward the whites. After signing the treaty, the Arikaras buried their dead, welcomed the soldiers into town, and supplied them with corn and vegetables.[119]

Pilcher, who objected to the treaty, later claimed that it had not been signed by the principal chiefs but by minor chiefs, making it a worthless document. However, after making a brief inquiry, Leavenworth was satisfied that the treaty had been signed by "every chief and principal man of both villages . . . except one who had always been considered as the first soldier of the late chief Grey Eyes and [who] was now considered no better than a dog."[120]

The affair did not end there. The next day, the Arikaras were able give Ashley only three rifles, one horse, and sixteen buffalo robes. This confirmed that the Arikaras were poor and strapped for goods, but they were told that this was not enough—they had to bring more or else the soldiers would resume the attack. The chiefs returned to the town very much alarmed.[121]

Late that afternoon, Little Soldier returned to speak with Leavenworth. He was in great distress. He explained that it was impossible to do any more for Ashley because the Sioux had stolen many of their horses and bombs had killed the rest.

Furthermore, the people of the upper town refused to surrender their horses for the mischief done by Chief Grey Eyes and the warriors of the lower town. If the soldiers intended to resume the attack, Little Soldier asked to remain with the troops. In his desperation, he even told the army where to place its artillery to do maximum damage. Though Little Soldier's actions appear treasonous, he actually bought time so that his people could plan their escape. In fact, he asked Leavenworth to postpone the attack until the next day so he could have time to bring out his family.[122]

Edward Rose escorted Little Soldier back to his town. Rose later returned with a handful of buffalo robes and said that the Arikaras had no more to give. He also stated that the Arikaras were preparing to escape. Leavenworth, believing that the Arikaras had been humbled sufficiently, sent Rose back to the towns to inform the chiefs that he was satisfied and that they would not be attacked.[123]

However, the next day, August 13, the soldiers discovered that the Arikaras had abandoned their towns during the night. In his report, Leavenworth did not explain how the Arikaras were able to get away. Perhaps he could not. Arikara oral tradition states that while the town was surrounded by the troops, a mysterious dog appeared to help the people. In a remarkable parallel to the Arikara creation account, the dog showed the Arikaras how to change themselves into animals and directed them to go through a hole in the ground to elude the troops.[124]

Shortly after the mysterious disappearance of the Arikaras, the troops and Pilcher's men prepared to return to their various stations. On August 15, several of Pilcher's men set fire to the towns. Pilcher's actions infuriated Leavenworth. In his report, he complained that it would be impossible for the army to preserve peace with the Indians "if traders or citizens can with impunity burn the villages and towns of Indians whenever they choose to do so." Now, Leavenworth believed, the Arikaras would surely retaliate. Pilcher, meanwhile, criticized Leavenworth for having mishandled the war. He claimed that the army had lost the respect of the Sioux and other Plains Indian nations because only swift and severe punishment impressed Indians.[125]

While Leavenworth and Pilcher hurled insults at each other in newspapers, the Arikaras broke up into several groups. One group, under Chief Elk's Tongue, set up camp near the Mandans. Still angry at the destruction of their towns during the war, they launched several attacks against American traders. On August 20 they killed two men and wounded two others belonging to William Ashley's outfit near the mouth of the Yellowstone River.[126] In October, near the Mandan towns, they attacked and killed four traders coming upriver by boat. Among the dead was Antoine Citoleux, who had been with the trader's militia during Leavenworth's attack.[127] A few days later, Arikara warriors under Bloody Hands (also known as Little Hawk with the Bloody Hands) attacked Tilton's Fort of the Columbia Fur Company. Later that winter, they also killed a resident trader there. In December, the Arikaras attacked three traders returning from the Rocky Mountains. Although the three men escaped, they lost their cargo.[128]

Other Arikara bands fled southward and joined the Pawnees. One group found refuge among the Skiri Pawnees on the Loup River in present-day Nebraska. Another group moved to the confluence of the North Platte and Laramie Rivers in present-day Wyoming. In April 1824, these Arikaras attacked five fur traders descending the North Platte River in bull boats. Two of the traders were killed and the others escaped with their lives. According to some sources, the attackers belonged to Elk's Tongue's band. If so, Elk's Tongue must have abandoned his town near the Mandans. It is possible that the Mandans and Hidatsas forced him to leave because they were fearful that the Arikara attacks against traders might prompt the army to launch another punitive expedition.[129]

In the months following the Arikara War, panicked reports told the authorities of supposed Arikara depredations and hostile movements. Many of these reports were exaggerated or patently false. In April 1824, for example, Colonel Josiah Snelling at Fort Anthony (later called Fort Snelling), Minnesota, relayed messages from two traders. According to their reports, the Arikaras had persuaded the upper Sioux tribes and the Mandans to join in an all-out war against the United States. Snelling put little confidence in the messages of these men, one of whom belonged to Joshua Pilcher's outfit. Snelling's skepticism proved correct. In fact, it seems that Pilcher circulated many false reports along the upper Missouri to blame the Arikaras for every misfortune that occurred in the region and so place himself in the most favorable light possible while his feud with Leavenworth continued.[130]

A POISONED RELATIONSHIP

The Arikara War was the culmination of two decades of botched US diplomacy. Starting with Thomas Jefferson, the United States underestimated the complexity of intertribal relations on the plains. Jefferson's attempt to impose peace on the Indians of this region was naive. Peace medals and other gifts meant little if the promises for protection and leadership were not backed up by action by the Great Father. Instead, the government pursued policies designed to strengthen American interests rather than seek common ground. Worse, the government confused the interests of trading companies with national interests and even surrendered diplomatic responsibility to fur traders like Clark, O'Fallon, and Pilcher. Thus American policies toward the Indians were largely shaped by men who had personal financial interests in the region.[131]

Single-handedly, Pilcher did more to poison US–Arikara relations than any other individual over subsequent decades. Pilcher blamed the Arikaras for the Missouri Fur Company's demise. He railed against the Arikaras, even after he became superintendent of Indian affairs for the Upper Missouri Agency, a position in which he was also supposed to represent the interests of the Indians and that he held from 1838 until his death in 1843. He created the image of the Arikaras as a dangerous and warlike nation. In reality, Pilcher himself was responsible for the hatred between the Arikaras and the traders. He tried to bypass the Arikara trade network, thus putting the Arikaras at a disadvantage against their enemies. In 1823 he enlisted the Sioux to accompany Leavenworth's expedition, and throughout the campaign he called for genocidal action against the Arikaras. He sabotaged Leavenworth's attempt to bring the Arikaras to terms by a show of force. After the Arikaras escaped, Pilcher's men burned their towns, thus ensuring the continued hostility of the Arikaras to white traders. Historians have been too kind to Pilcher, portraying him as an indefatigable frontiersman, a man of great entrepreneurial spirit, when in fact he was an unscrupulous and blatantly selfish opportunist who would not hesitate to betray Indians—or even friends—if they stood in his way.[132]

Long before Pilcher, Meriwether Lewis had displayed similar attitudes toward Indians who defied US supremacy. Lewis's 1807 order authorizing the extermination of the Arikaras is a blotch on US–Indian relations. In Lewis's case, however, his disgraceful order could have been an early sign of mental illness, which might have led to his later suicide. Though Lewis's and Pilcher's genocidal tendencies did not take fruition, their characterization of the Arikaras as implacable foes of the sahništaaká would prevail for decades.

7 THE FUR TRADE ERA, 1824-1864

> They swear vengeance against all the Whites, as they say the small pox was brought here by the [steamboat].
>
> —FRANCIS A. CHARDON, FUR TRADER AT FORT CLARK, 1837

Sometimes history rhymes. Events between 1824 and 1864 sound eerily familiar: harassment by the Sioux; an indifferent Great Father in Washington; tensions with traders; a series of new epidemics; internal divisions.

Under these pressures, Arikara society started to drift. For a while the Arikaras adopted a seminomadic lifestyle near the Black Hills. Here they hunted buffalo and raided white traders. Later they sought shelter among the Skiri Pawnees. Depletion of the buffalo herds, competition with other tribes, difficulty of accessing horses, tensions with the Skiri Pawnees, and, above all, the strength of their tradition eventually forced the Arikaras back to the upper Missouri, where in 1837 they resumed the semisedentary lifestyle first taught by Mother Corn. But as they returned to old ways, old problems returned as well.

"TOUCHING THE PEN": THE TREATY OF 1825

In the months following the Leavenworth affair, the Arikaras returned to their towns on Cottonwood Creek. They rebuilt their lodges and planted new gardens. Bloody Hands emerged as the leading chief, together with a new generation of headmen, including Little Bear, Skunk, Fool Chief, The Chief Who Is Afraid, and Bad Bear.[1] Other chiefs, such as Eagle Feather, disappeared from the historical record.

The Arikara War had consequences in Washington as well. Alarmed by the event, Congress pursued a more diplomatic course. For this purpose, it established the Indian Office in 1824. Apart from negotiating removal treaties with eastern tribes, its primary mission was to maintain peace with the nations in the west. Ironically, because Congress believed that only the army could enforce peace, the Indian Office became part of the War Department.

In May 1824, President James Monroe directed Brigadier General Henry Atkinson and Indian agent Benjamin O'Fallon to negotiate peace and trade treaties with the tribes on the Missouri River. Atkinson was anxious to restore the reputation of the US Army. On May 16, 1825, Atkinson, O'Fallon, and 475 soldiers of the First and Sixth Infantry Regiments, under the command of Colonel Leavenworth, left Fort Atkinson aboard of eight human-powered wheel boats. In addition to supplies for the troops, the boats also carried gifts for the tribes.[2]

Moving up the Missouri, Atkinson and O'Fallon signed treaties with the Poncas, Yanktons, Yanktonnais, Cheyennes, and several Lakhota groups. In these treaties, the tribes recognized that they resided within US boundaries, accepted the government's supremacy and right to regulate all trade, promised to protect US traders and other authorized personnel, promised to capture foreigners and hand them over to the government, agreed to surrender Indians who had harmed white people to US courts for trial (while the government pledged to punish white people who harmed Indians), and agreed not to sell guns and ammunition to nations that were at war with the United States. In return, the government promised to protect the Indians and to extend occasional "benefits and acts of kindness" to them.[3]

On July 15, Atkinson's expedition passed the Grand River and went into camp a mile below the Arikara towns. Here they met Hunkpapas under Chief Little White Bear who had been trading with the Arikaras.[4]

On July 16, Atkinson and O'Fallon met the Hunkpapas in council and concluded a treaty with them. That same day, Bloody Hands and the other chiefs invited the commissioners to a visit. Atkinson declined, but O'Fallon accepted. While the chiefs listened silently, O'Fallon admonished them for past attacks against US traders. The chiefs presented O'Fallon with seven horses, a pile of buffalo meat, and some pottery as tokens of goodwill and agreed to meet in council the next day.[5]

At daybreak on Sunday, July 17, a strange group of Indians appeared in the distance. Their sudden appearance caused some alarm among the Arikaras, but they turned out to be a party of Skiri Pawnees under Knife Chief.[6] The purpose of the Skiri visit was not recorded, but it is possible they invited the Arikaras to join them on

Stán-au-pat ("Bloody Hands") portrait by George Catlin, circa 1832. Bloody Hands emerged as the leading chief after the 1823 war, in which Chief Grey Eyes was killed. His shirt is heavily decorated with scalp locks (sometimes horsehair was substituted for human hair) and depictions of battle scenes. Courtesy Smithsonian American Art Museum, SAAM-1985.66.123.

the Loup River in Nebraska. Like the Arikaras, the Skiris were engaged in a mortal struggle with the Sioux, who had vowed to exterminate them. Perhaps Knife Chief hoped to forge a military alliance with the Arikaras to counter the Sioux threat.

On July 18, Bloody Hands and five other chiefs met with the commissioners. They were accompanied by the leading warriors of the tribe and one hundred spectators. Joseph Garreau and his sons, Pierre and Antoine, acted as interpreters. In his journal, Atkinson wrote that the chiefs "appear to be impressed with deep & full contrision for their offences & it is thought they will behave well in [the] future." The commissioners presented Bloody Hands with a medal, gave armbands to the other chiefs, and made a gift of tobacco. They quickly concluded a treaty of trade and friendship. It was virtually identical to the treaties signed with other tribes, but one more article was added. It stated that from then on "there shall be a firm and lasting peace between the United States and the Ricara tribe of Indians; and a friendly intercourse shall immediately take place between the parties." The treaties bore the marks of Bloody Hands, Little Bear, Skunk, Fool Chief, The Chief Who Is Afraid, and Bad Bear. Fourteen Arikara soldiers also signed. The Garreaus signed as witnesses. After concluding the treaty, the commission continued its journey.[7]

"THEY HAVE SWORN DEATH AND DESTRUCTION TO EVERY WHITE MAN WHO COMES IN THEIR WAY": FLOODS, DROUGHTS, AND SIOUX, 1825–1833

At first glance the treaty of 1825 signified a normalization of US–Arikara relations. But the US promises were barely worth the paper they were written on. Although the Arikaras largely followed the stipulations of the treaty, the government fell short of its promises. While it was quick to punish Arikaras for mistreating US citizens, it was much less resolute when it came to citizens who mistreated Arikaras. However, no issue was more frustrating and contentious to the Arikaras than the government's failure to provide protection against hostile Sioux bands. Although the treaty prohibited the Arikaras from supplying tribes that were at war with the United States, US traders continued to provide arms and ammunition to the Sioux without interference. The government's failure to adhere to its treaty obligations soon soured US–Arikara relations once again.

In the months after the treaty, Sioux war parties stole horses and attacked lone Arikara men and women caught a short distance from their towns. Such attacks triggered retaliation by the Arikaras. The cycle of war was interrupted only by ceasefires during the trading season. In 1831 a great battle between the Arikaras and Sioux resulted in great bloodshed. According to some reports, this bloody affair contributed to the decision by Bloody Hands and the other chiefs to abandon the region the following year.[8]

Arikara relations with the fur traders also remained poor. Although the American Fur Company (AFC) constructed a series of posts along the Missouri River to trade with the Crees and Assiniboines (Fort Union), Mandans and Hidatsas (Fort Clark), and Sioux (Fort Pierre), no such post was built near the Arikara settlements on Cottonwood Creek.[9] In fact, except for sporadic encounters, traders usually avoided the Arikaras altogether, effectively boycotting them while supplying surrounding tribes with goods.[10] Consequently, the Arikaras either had to rely on Sioux middlemen or rob traders passing their towns. In 1830 Arikara warriors reportedly killed three traders on their way to the Mandans and carried off four horses loaded with goods.

Later that fall, they intercepted a group of traders under Kenneth McKenzie and confiscated all their horses. AFC traders began calling the Arikaras "river pirates."[11]

This reputation was not entirely deserved. In 1831, fur trader David D. Mitchell spent a few days among the Arikaras and found them friendly and hospitable. Mitchell even attended the sleight of hand performances of Arikara doctors in the medicine lodge ceremony. He was baffled when doctors brought small clay figurines to life. "I failed altogether to detect the mysterious agency by which inanimate images of clay were to all appearance suddenly endowed with the action, energy and feeling of living beings," Mitchell wrote.[12] Despite such brief interludes, Arikara–trader relations remained strained.

The Arikaras received little sympathy from Indian agents. Agents were political appointees who lacked experience with Native Americans. They did not live among the Indians but stayed in or near St. Louis. At best they traveled up the Missouri once a year to deliver annuities or presents. Most agents relied on traders' reports in their communications with the Indian Office in Washington. The close connection between agents and traders is further illustrated by the fact that agents relied on the companies for interpreters, the purchase of annuity goods, and steamboats for transportation of annuities up the river. Not surprisingly, agents often represented the interests of traders rather than those of the Indians under their charge. A good example was Agent John F. A. Sanford. "I wish likewise that the Govt would take some measures to punish the Arickaras for the murder of our citizens," Sanford wrote in 1830. "Your attention to this matter will confer a particular favor upon our traders and secure their lasting friendship and who will stand by you in the time of need."[13]

Travelers avoided the Arikaras. In 1832 artist George Catlin was relieved when the steamboat he had boarded did not stop at the Arikara towns, because he had been told that the Arikaras had "sworn death and destruction to every white man who comes in their way."[14] Catlin continued to the Mandans, where he met Chief Bloody Hands and several other Arikara leaders on a peace mission to the Mandans and Hidatsas. Catlin seized the opportunity to paint Bloody Hands and could not to resist the temptation to present him holding a scalping knife and sporting a fierce snarl. Catlin also painted portraits of Bloody Hands's wife The Twin and his twelve-year-old daughter, Sweet-Scented Grass. During his stay among the Mandans, Catlin was also a guest of He Who Strikes, who treated him with the utmost consideration and friendliness. Catlin drew a portrait of He Who Strikes in his robe.[15]

It is unclear whether Bloody Hands's peace mission to the Mandans and Hidatsas was successful since by the following year, the Arikaras had abandoned their towns on the Grand River. When German scientist-explorer Prince Maximilian von Wied-Neuwied ascended the Missouri River in 1833, he learned that the Sioux threat, fear of punishment by US traders, and a severe drought had caused Arikaras to move south. Maximilian estimated the total size of the Arikara tribe at four thousand, including five hundred to six hundred warriors.[16]

At the Mandan towns, Maximilian met Joseph Garreau and trader David LaChapelle, who was married to an Arikara woman, as well as several Arikaras who had married into the Mandan tribe, including a warrior named Pachtüwa-Chtä.[17] Maximilian also obtained a list of Arikara chiefs that included Bloody Hands, Old (Man) Head, and White Horse of the upper Arikara town, and Mad Chief, White Rabbit, and Bad Brave of the lower town.[18] We know little else of these men.

EXILE, 1832–1837

As Prince Maximilian noted, the Arikaras had abandoned their towns on Cottonwood Creek after a series of calamities in 1832. After considerable debate, the chiefs agreed to move south to live with the Skiri Pawnees. Instead of descending the Missouri River, which would lead them through the heart of Sioux territory, they first followed the Grand River to the Black Hills.

Because they were now entirely cut off from trade with the whites, and without surplus supplies of corn, the Arikaras obtained what little goods they could find by raiding white traders. From their camp near the Black Hills they sent out warriors in search of guns and horses. Their war parties were reported as far south as the Santa Fe Trail and into the Rocky Mountains. One party stole a number of horses from trappers belonging to Henry Fraeb's outfit.[19] Another group traveled to Crow country, where they stole horses and killed men belonging to a party of traders under Johnson Gardener. One of the men killed was Edward Rose, who had lived with the Arikaras in the 1820s but had joined Leavenworth's hated 1823 expedition. Gardener avenged his comrades by burning two Arikara captives to death. Gardener himself was later killed by Arikaras in retaliation.[20]

These attacks enraged the traders. Arikara war parties effectively cut off the trail along the North Platte River into the Rocky Mountains. Unable to attack the Arikaras directly, the traders turned their frustration against Antoine Garreau, lynching him near Bellevue, Nebraska, in June 1835. These traders also threatened to kill David LaChappelle, who had married into the Arikara tribe and frequently worked as an interpreter.[21]

In the spring of 1833, Bloody Hands moved his people to the North Platte River, from where they contacted the Skiri Pawnees.[22] The Skiris lived on the Loup River in present-day central Nebraska. Skiri chief Big Axe was happy to see them because his people needed help in their war against the Cheyennes, Arapahos, and Sioux. He hoped the Arikaras would provide military assistance, but there was no suitable place for the construction of a new earth lodge town. Furthermore, it was too late to clear the land for their gardens. So the Arikaras set up a temporary camp nearby. Forced by these circumstances, they adopted a seminomadic existence. Living in tipis, they spent most of their time in search of buffalo. Samuel Allis, a Presbyterian missionary to the Pawnees, estimated the number of Arikaras at twenty-two hundred.[23]

Although relations with the Skiris were generally good, those with the South Band Pawnees were more problematic. The Skiris and South Band Pawnees were at odds with each other. Perhaps this was another reason the Skiris invited the Arikaras to join them. In the past the Skiris had battled the Chaui Pawnees for supremacy in the tribe, and tensions between the two bands continued to linger. More recently, the Skiris had angered the South Band chiefs by stealing horses from the Wichitas, who were friendly with the South Bands. To complicate matters, in the spring of 1835 some young Arikara men stole some Kitkahahki horses. Arikara hunting expeditions to the Pawnee hunting grounds on the Republican River were another source of irritation among the South Band chiefs.[24]

The Lakhotas, Cheyennes, and Arapahos had vowed to "wipe out" (*kasóta* in Lakhota) the Pawnees. With this objective in mind, the Cheyennes carried their most sacred objects, the sacred arrows, into battle against the Pawnees in 1830, only to lose their medicine during the fight. In 1833, the year the Arikaras settled among them, the Skiris sacrificed a Cheyenne captive in the Morning Star ceremony. Through their close association with the Skiris, the Arikaras were pulled into the war with the Cheyennes.[25]

Genocidal warfare caused a spiritual crisis among the Pawnees. To many Skiris, it appeared that Morning Star, the powerful warrior-deity, had abandoned them. The demoralized Skiris found inspiration in Pahukatawa, the spirit of a man who had been killed and dismembered by enemies in the early 1830s. Pahukatawa had been brought back to life by the sacred powers. He inspired the Skiris to several battlefield victories against their enemies. During their time among the Skiris, the Arikaras learned about the deeds of Pahukatawa. Years later, after the Arikaras had returned to the upper Missouri River, Pahukatawa joined them there. Although he was a spirit, he fathered at least one child with an Arikara woman. This child was also named Pahukatawa. When visited by ethnologist George Bird Grinnell in the late 1880s, this man said that he had seen his father only once and described him as a man who had "feet like a wolf" and who wore a robe made of wolf skins. Interestingly, a cult of Pahukatawa never emerged among the Arikaras. They remained unequivocally committed to the worship of Mother Corn.[26]

In 1835, the Arikaras learned that a US military expedition under Colonel Henry Dodge was moving in their direction. Although the purpose of the expedition was to explore the Platte and Arkansas River valleys to identify suitable locations for military forts and to establish peace between tribes who were at war with each other, the arrival of the dragoons alarmed Chiefs Bloody Hands, Star,[27] and Two Bulls. They immediately prepared to move their people.[28]

While Bloody Hands led the Arikaras west, Star met with Dodge on June 28. Dodge convinced Star that his intentions were peaceful, and a few days later, Star and Captain John Gantt left with a message for Bloody Hands. While Dodge's dragoons lumbered forth, Chief Star and Captain Gantt caught up with Bloody Hands several days later.[29]

While marching along the Platte River, Dodge's troops stumbled upon an abandoned Arikara sun dance camp. The Arikaras had made an arbor of poles and brush. At the center of the circle was the sun dance pole. A red coat, two red blankets, a bear or buffalo skin, and a fine pair of leggings were attached to it. Also attached to the pole was a human finger, cut off near the second joint. There were traces of blood all around the interior of the lodge, where dancers, attached to the tree with thongs through pierced skin, had pulled themselves free in self-sacrifice or pulled buffalo skulls on strings attached to piercings on their shoulders. Two buffalo heads were arranged on one side of the lodge. They pointed toward the east, apparently to bring buffalo from the west. The meaning of the ceremony was lost on the troops. Lieutenant Gaines P. Kingsbury wrote that the Arikaras "frequently scarify their bodies, and inflict corporeal pain upon themselves, for the purpose of appeasing the anger of the Great Spirit, that he make them successful in their hunts, and against their enemies." Some soldiers rumored that the Arikaras had performed the dance to gather power for an upcoming war.[30]

The presence of an Arikara sun dance camp is surprising. It is unclear when the Arikaras adopted this ceremony. Perhaps they adopted it after observing the Mandan *okipa* ceremony. Perhaps they learned the ceremony from the Sioux during a period when these tribes were at peace. The Pawnees had a version of the sun dance called Young Dog's dance. What is striking about the sun dance is that it is not native to Arikara culture. Although the Arikaras studied non-Arikara traditions and incorporated them if they were compatible, they always maintained the integrity of the ceremonies taught to them by Mother Corn. Perhaps the adoption of the sun dance signaled a spiritual crisis of some sort. At the same time, one should not exaggerate this. Unable to support themselves with corn horticulture, the Arikaras emphasized ceremonies that were more closely associated with the buffalo hunt. Later events show that they had not abandoned the ceremonies taught by Mother Corn.[31]

On July 5, Bloody Hands, Star, and twenty-three other chiefs and warriors met with Colonel Dodge in council. The Arikaras wore their best clothes for the occasion: finely dressed antelope-skin shirts trimmed along the sides and neck, decorated with colored beads and long coarse hairs of different colors; white leggings and moccasins beautifully embroidered with beads. "They were the best looking tribe of Indians we had seen," wrote Kingsbury. Dodge welcomed the chiefs and told them the purpose of his mission. The Great Father in Washington wanted all his "red children" to be at peace. Dodge promised to ask the president to set aside land for the Arikaras near the Pawnees, where they could cultivate corn and raise cattle. He ended his speech by calling upon the chiefs to make peace with all the Cheyennes, Arapahos, and other nations on the plains and to live with them on land specially reserved for them.[32]

Bloody Hands explained that his people were in a desperate situation. They had no land and dwelled on the land of their Pawnee brothers. They were forced to hunt buffalo and cut trees, even though these belonged to the Pawnees. He thanked Dodge for helping them to arrange for a reservation. "We want land so that we can kill buffalo with [the Pawnees]," he said. "We would like to live upon land near the Pawnees, and have the privilege of hunting as well as them."[33]

Chief Two Bulls reiterated Bloody Hands's words. "If you take us and put us on a piece of ground, and tell us where it is," Two Bulls said, "next year you will find us there." Two Bulls especially liked the land south of the fork of the Platte River. He also called upon Dodge to send knives and other goods for hunting buffalo, and axes for cutting wood so they could make lodges. They would "kill buffalo, and sell their skins for axes and hoes, with which we can build lodges and raise corn."[34]

Speaking last, Chief Star said he was encouraged by Dodge's promise to help them secure a reservation in the area. "We were very poor, but now that you are to give us land, we will no longer be poor," he said. "My father," he added, "when you come next time, you will perhaps bring some hoes and axes for our [women]; they are now very poor, and have nothing."[35] Star's pleas for hoes indicates that the

Arikara chiefs were anxious to return to their old sedentary lifestyle. While the buffalo hunt might help them secure skins for the trade, it was their commitment to and love for Mother Corn that lay underneath their actions.

After concluding the council, both sides exchanged gifts. The next day, Bloody Hands and his followers returned to their camp while Dodge continued his journey to the Rocky Mountains.[36]

Back in their camp, Bloody Hands, Two Bulls, Star, and the Skiri chiefs, led by Big Axe, agreed to send a peace delegation to meet with Dodge and the Cheyennes and Arapahos, who were camping fifty miles east of Bent's Fort in southeastern Colorado. Because he was one of the most vocal advocates of peace, Chief Star was selected to head the Arikara delegation. Big Axe and the other Skiri chiefs joined him. A number of warriors went along for protection. The entire party consisted of about one hundred Skiris and thirty Arikaras.[37]

On August 15, Star's Arikara–Skiri peace delegation met with the Cheyennes. Dodge joined them the next day. He encouraged the tribes to make peace so that they could hunt together, their children would become friends forever, and all warfare would cease. The Cheyenne chiefs seemed "desirous of making a permanent peace with the Pawnees and Arickaras." They promised to meet the Pawnees on the Platte River the next winter to hunt with them. They also promised to bring about peace between the Arikaras and the Arapahos, who were close allies of the Cheyennes. In return for peace, the Cheyennes demanded the return of the sacred arrows from the Pawnees.[38]

Star and Big Axe's brother accepted the Cheyenne peace offer on behalf of the Arikaras and Pawnees. They gave the Cheyennes forty or fifty guns as peace gifts. But Big Axe's brother reminded the Cheyennes that this was the third or fourth time the Pawnees had come to make peace, and each time the Cheyennes had violated it. He refused to return the sacred arrows, stating that the year before they had given one of the arrows to Cheyenne chief White Thunder (the keeper of the sacred arrow bundle) in return for peace, but Cheyenne war parties had continued to attack them.[39]

Dodge was too optimistic when he reported to Washington that the council had been successful. A short time after the meeting, Walking Whirlwind, a renowned Cheyenne warrior, led a war party against the Pawnees. Leaving his camp on the Republican River on a foggy morning, he and his warriors blundered straight into a Pawnee encampment. They were soon surrounded and slain. The peace Dodge had triumphantly declared in his report ended prematurely.[40]

Pshán-shaw ("Sweet-Scented Grass"), twelve-year-old daughter of Chief Bloody Hands, with earth lodges in the background. Her dress, boots, and buffalo robe are painted with designs and decorated with quillwork or beadwork. Her parted hairline is painted red with vermillion. Her dress signifies her status as the daughter of one of the leading Arikara chiefs. Painted by George Catlin, circa 1832. Courtesy Smithsonian American Art Museum, SAAM-1985.66.125.

The land issue remained close on the minds of the Arikaras. Without a reservation of their own, they depended on the hospitality of their Skiri relatives. But their hunting expeditions caused frictions with the Pawnees. An incident in December 1835 illustrates the increasingly strained Skiri–Arikara relationship. That winter, the Skiris were unable to find any buffalo on account of the Arikaras, who camped between them and the buffalo herds. The Skiris sent soldiers to the Arikara camp, asking to join them in the hunt. For reasons not entirely clear, the Arikara chiefs refused. This decision irritated the Skiris. By 1836, the threat of war with the Pawnees loomed. To avoid violence, Bloody Hands once again decided to move.[41]

Arikara oral tradition remembers this event differently. According to the Arikaras, the Pawnees did not treat them well. If an Arikara man courted a Pawnee female, the Pawnees would whip him; the Arikaras would not harm a Pawnee man courting an Arikara girl. The Arikaras also helped the Pawnees when enemies attacked, but the Pawnees would not reciprocate if enemies attacked the Arikaras. Finally, the Pawnees would not let Arikaras join them chasing after buffalo, but they would insist on joining the hunt when buffalo appeared near the Arikara camp. Despite pleas from the Pawnees not to leave, the chiefs decided to seek their fortune on the open prairie.[42]

In 1836 the Arikaras left the Platte River. By September of that year they were near the Black Hills, from where they sent a delegation to the Mandans and Hidatsas near Fort Clark to discuss a possible return to the Missouri River. On September 10, 1836, the delegates arrived at Fort Clark, where they received a warm welcome from the Mandans and Hidatsas, who supported the return of the Arikaras. At this time the Hidatsas were at war with the Assiniboines, and Sioux war parties continued to harass both tribes. An alliance with the Arikaras would add some badly needed security.[43]

The next spring, 250 Arikara lodges arrived at Fort Clark. Most set up camp with the Mandans. Twenty lodges moved to the Hidatsas. Fur trader Francis A. Chardon hoisted the flag and saluted them with ten shots from the fort's four-pounder cannon. Perhaps this was also a warning that the traders were heavily armed.[44] To his surprise, Chardon discovered that the Arikaras were friendly and generous. He was also pleased when he learned that they had brought three thousand buffalo hides as well as one pack of beaver skins. The Arikara chiefs also kept a short leash on any young warrior who threatened traders.[45]

Chardon's reaction stood in contrast with newly appointed Indian agent William Fulkerson. Fulkerson was displeased at the sudden appearance of the Arikaras at Fort Clark. "I mentioned in my last report that the Arickarees were in the River Platte, and that I hoped they would not come back," Fulkerson wrote. Fulkerson did not believe peace between the Mandans and Arikaras would last. Already the Arikaras talked about constructing a new town some eighteen miles below the "Big Mandan Village." Based on what he had heard about their supposed hostile disposition, Fulkerson did not trust the Arikaras. "They make very fair promises and professions as to their friendly feelings towards the whites, and their disposition to maintain peacible relations with the neighboring tribes, but no reliance can be placed in them." Fulkerson described the Arikaras' expulsion from their towns by the Sioux, their sojourn with the Pawnees on the Platte River, and their subsequent nomadic existence. He urged the government to encourage the Arikaras to settle down in permanent towns "and to hold sufficient inducements for them in some measure to forsake their former wandering treacherous course of life and betake themselves at least in part to the cultivation of the earth." Clearly Fulkerson did not understand that corn horticulture had been the backbone of Arikara subsistence ever since Mother Corn had taught the people.[46]

Fulkerson's first encounter with the Arikaras was troubled. When he ascended the Missouri River to speak to the different nations, he failed to deliver promised annuities. The Arikaras were disgruntled. "The Arrickarees expressed more dissatisfaction than any other tribe; they had been informed that they should receive presents when the Boat should arrive, and could not repress their indignation when disappointed." Fulkerson admitted another reason why the Arikaras were particularly sensitive: "Only a few days before this disappointment they had heard of the murder of one of their tribe [Antoine Garreau] by some of the whites at the Council Bluffs, which inteligence was not calculated to soften the asperity of their feelings towards us." Hurriedly, Fulkerson called a council with the chiefs. He promised they would receive their gifts next time.[47]

"THEY DIE SO FAST THAT IT IS IMPOSSIBLE": THE 1837 SMALLPOX EPIDEMIC AT FORT CLARK

In June 1837, Fort Clark and the nearby town of Mih-tutta-hang-kusch were buzzing with activity. Arikara chiefs Bloody Hands, Two Bulls, and Star frequently visited the fort. Francis Chardon regularly attended councils in the town. The area was packed with people. There were horses and dogs everywhere. Every day, hunters brought in buffalo skins. Town and fort were also overrun with rats, which proliferated partly as a result human refuse. It built up because the town was so densely populated— perhaps overpopulated—to defend itself against Sioux attacks.[48]

Then tragedy struck. On Sunday, June 18, the steamboat *St. Peters* arrived at the fort. On board were Antoine Garreau's widowed wife, who told the chiefs details of her husband's death at the hands of the traders. Although most of the chiefs assured Chardon that they would remain peaceful, one chief "swore death and distruction if the [Indian] Agent did not pay him for one of his relations that was Killed by the Whites." The incident reminded all of the shaky relationship between traders and Arikaras.[49]

But the steamboat also carried something more serious than the details of Garreau's death. It carried the smallpox virus. How the virus came on board is not exactly clear. The fact remains that the steamer's captain was aware that the disease was on board when he arrived at the fort. Fearing a delay in schedule, he refused to quarantine the crew and passengers. Among the passengers were two Arikara women from Fort Pierre, who disembarked to visit relatives. Perhaps they were already infected, but it is also possible that the virus was carried ashore in blankets and other trade objects.[50]

Indian agent William Fulkerson quickly apportioned blame to the Arikaras when he claimed that the disease "was communicated here from a blanket, clearly stolen by a Rickaree from one of the hands of the steamboat *St. Peters* which arrived here this spring;—he was just recovering from it when the blanket was stolen." Fulkerson's accusation conveniently fit widespread prejudices against the Arikaras. Historians have since debunked this claim. Likewise, Indian agent Joshua Pilcher deflected responsibility to the Arikaras. Pilcher was on board the *St. Peters* when the infection was discovered. In a letter to William Clark, superintendent of Indian Affairs, Pilcher reported that the disease had first manifested itself in a mulatto employee of the fur company near Fort Leavenworth. Pilcher claimed to have suggested putting the sick man ashore, but apparently he did not put up much resistance when his suggestion—if he made it—was ignored. According to Pilcher, three Arikara women, who had lived among the Pawnees and wished to visit their relatives, subsequently contracted the disease. They had mostly recovered by the time the boat reached Fort Clark. Such deflections by Fulkerson and Pilcher conveniently masked the responsibility of the American Fur Company and the Indian agents themselves for preventing the spread of the infection upriver.[51]

The disease spread rapidly in the densely populated towns. The first recorded casualty, a young Mandan, died on July 14. Within a few days, the death rate climbed to twelve victims a day. All died suffering terribly. Horror gripped the towns. Those who could left, sometimes leaving the sick behind to die alone. "I keep no a/c [account] of the dead," wrote Chardon, "as they die so fast that it is impossible." Some Indians, either suffering from the disease or watching their loved ones suffer, committed suicide in despair. On August 20, two young Arikaras killed themselves. One stabbed himself with a knife, the other with an arrow. Another Arikara asked his mother to dig a grave for him. With the help of his father, he walked to the grave and lay down. Chardon and Garreau tried to persuade him to return home. He refused and toward evening he died. In their desperation, some resorted to murder and infanticide. A young Arikara who had contracted the disease struck his nineteen-year-old wife with a tomahawk before cutting his own throat. A young Mandan shot his suffering wife and then ripped open his own belly with his knife. Later, a grief-stricken Mandan woman, who had lost her husband a few days earlier, killed her two children and then hanged herself.[52]

In their desperation, some Mandans and Arikaras appealed to the powers by staging dances. Others made their own medicines. "Some [Arikaras] have made dreams, that they talked to the Sun, others to the Moon, [and] several articles has been sacrificed to them both," wrote Chardon. Some did survive. One Arikara, who was in such pain that he wished to die, began to rub his scabs until blood was running all over his body. He then rolled himself in ashes, "which almost burnt his soul out of his body." Two days later, his health was improving. One Indian "vaccinated" his child by rubbing some of his scabs on the child's arms—a risky operation that reportedly was successful. Among the surviving Arikaras were Bloody Hands, Two Bulls, White Horse, Wolf Chief, and Star. Although Star's daughter died of the disease, his son Rushing Bear, the future head chief of the Arikara tribe, was among the survivors as well.[53]

The extent of the suffering was indescribable. Chardon estimated that nearly seven out of eight Mandans had died. Among them were Chiefs Four Bears, Wolf Chief, and Long Fingers. He also estimated that half of the Arikaras and half of the Hidatsas had died. The smell of death was intolerable. On September 19, Chardon wrote, "The Number of deaths Cannot be less than 800." By this time the epidemic had begun to wind down.[54]

The survivors carried the scars of the disease on their arms, legs, and faces, and in their hearts. The emotional trauma of the epidemic cast a gloomy shadow on the survivors. Joshua Pilcher, hardly a friend of the Arikaras, described the traumatic effects of the infection on the survivors. "Most of those that survived," Pilcher wrote, "subsequently committed suicide, dispairing, I suppose at the loss of friends and the changes wrought by the disease in their persons; some by shooting, others by stabbing and some by throwing themselves from the high precipices above the Missouri."[55]

Many Arikaras blamed the traders for the disaster. "They swear vengeance against all the Whites, as they say the small pox was brought here by the S. B. [steamboat]," wrote Chardon in his journal. On June 28, an angry Mandan arrived at the fort intending to kill Chardon. On August 17, a young Arikara killed an employee at the fort. He then fled, pursued by Chardon and others. When he came to the place where one of his brothers had been interred, he stopped and announced that he wished to die there. Pierre Garreau, who was employed at Fort Clark, then shot and killed him. Chief Two Bulls later visited Chardon but would not say much about the incident. In fact, the Arikara chiefs threatened anyone who tried to harm the traders. It is significant to note that while the traders had denounced the Arikaras for so many problems in the past, the Arikara chiefs now proved to be their greatest protectors.[56]

Some Arikaras preferred death on the warpath over death by sickness. This way they would enter the afterworld as warriors. Another reason to go to war was to capture women and children to replace those who had died. Others went on the warpath to numb the grief caused by the death of a relative or loved one. These expeditions had the character of revenge parties. In a society in which diseases were considered of supernatural origin or witchcraft, it was only natural that revenge had to be exacted through the taking of enemy scalps. An Arikara and Mandan war party left Fort Clark on July 26 and killed seven Sioux men, women, and children who were camping at the mouth of the White River. But the Sioux they killed also had the disease, and shortly afterward several members of the war party fell ill. A war party consisting of Arikara and Hidatsa warriors fared even worse. They were defeated by a group of Saone Sioux. According to one report, nearly seventy of them were killed. It is possible, however, that many of them were too sick to defend themselves. If so, they may have passed on the disease to the Sioux, who accused the Arikaras of infecting them and again called for their extermination.[57]

The smallpox epidemic of 1837 was one of the most traumatic events in Arikara history. A troubling aspect of the tragedy is the US government's failure to prevent it. In 1832 Congress had passed the Indian Vaccination Act, which provided $12,000 in funding to vaccinate Indian peoples against the dreaded disease. Vaccination efforts began in 1833. Inexplicably, the upper Missouri nations were specifically excluded from the program. Some historians suggest that the Arikaras, Mandans, and Hidatsas were excluded because trade with them was less lucrative than it was with other tribes. Secretary of war Lewis Cass, who was in charge of the program, ordered that "hostile nations" and tribes that lived "beyond the pale of civilization" should not be included in the program. The Arikaras had been considered hostile since the War of 1823. Joshua Pilcher argued against any federal help for the Arikaras. Consequently, emergency vaccines never reached the Arikara settlements. They were used instead by Indian agent John Dougherty to inoculate the Yanktons, Santees, Otoes, and Omahas.[58]

The epidemic not only destroyed lives and scattered families, but it also impacted social organization. The dramatic loss of life forced the Arikaras—temporarily at least—to relax restrictions on marriages between blood relatives (consanguinity) for the purpose of increasing offspring.[59] Furthermore, as society leaders died, they carried the customs and secrets of their associations to the grave. As a result, some medicine, military, and charitable societies died out, which partly explains why different sources list different societies over time.[60]

RECOVERY AND ADJUSTMENT

During the epidemic, the Arikaras separated into several camps to escape the disease. Chief Star lived near Fort Clark. Wolf Chief and Bloody Hands moved their camps above the fort near the Hidatsas. Two Bulls and White Horse established a camp below the fort. After the epidemic subsided, the groups remained in their camps to hunt buffalo until the spring of 1838. In March 1838, all returned to Fort Clark.[61]

Now a period of recovery began. Adjustment was particularly difficult for the Mandans. They had suffered tremendous losses (nearly 90 percent) and were heavily outnumbered by the Arikaras. Feeling more at home with the Hidatsas, who spoke a language more familiar to them, some Mandans decided to move closer to the Hidatsas. They also charged that the Arikaras were stealing their women in an attempt to repopulate the tribe.[62]

Until their move to Fort Clark, the Arikaras had subsisted primarily on buffalo meat. Now they were ready to resume their old horticultural lifestyle. Some families moved into abandoned Mandan lodges. Others built new lodges of their own. Many continued to live in tipis. They also cleared the bottomlands of brush and trees and prepared the fields for planting. From their sacred bundles they collected corn seeds to plant the fields. By all appearances, the Arikaras had resumed the old familiar town pattern.

They also resumed warfare with the Sioux. A Sioux war party attacked on May 18, 1838, killing one man and wounding another. On June 7, the Arikaras captured a Sioux, who told them the Sioux planned to attack the Hidatsas. The Arikaras gave him two horses and warned the Hidatsas of the impending attack. When the Sioux attacked at dawn the next day, the Hidatsas were ready. They killed fourteen Sioux, whose bodies they placed in a heap and burned in sight of their friends. On June 21, a large Yankton war party attacked the fort and the town. After a four-hour battle, they withdrew. There were no losses on either side. Five days later the Sioux and the Arikaras fought another battle; several men were wounded. On July 1, there was yet another attack against the town. One Arikara and three Sioux were killed. After scalping the dead, the Arikaras burned the bodies of their enemies in sight of the Sioux.[63]

On July 12, an Assiniboine war party under He That Holds the Knife attacked the Hidatsas. Arikaras swam across the river to assist their neighbors. After a hard fight they reportedly killed sixty-four Assiniboines and took eight women captive. There were celebrations in the towns all night and into the next day. In his journal, trader Chardon wrote that the scalps were "flying in all direction." Men, women, and children joined in the festivities. Chardon purchased a twelve-year-old captive girl from an Arikara warrior. But the Sioux threat continued. The next day, Chardon almost lost his own scalp when he ran into a Sioux war party merely one mile from the fort.[64]

Meanwhile, administrative changes took place in the Upper Missouri Agency. Agent William N. Fulkerson resigned his position after it was discovered that he resided in St. Charles instead of being at his post. In his letter of resignation, Fulkerson justified his absence, claiming the agency was too small and insignificant, even more so after the smallpox disaster had further reduced the Indian nations under his jurisdiction. Though Fulkerson's departure was hardly a great loss to the Indian service, his replacement was none other than Joshua Pilcher, who cared even less for the three tribes—the Arikaras in particular.[65]

Indeed, Pilcher wasted no time in discrediting the Arikaras to his superiors. Still smarting from his failure as director of the Missouri Fur Company, Pilcher smeared the Arikaras in a series of letters to Superintendent William Clark. After reporting that affairs had never been more peaceful and tranquil in his jurisdiction, Pilcher added,

> I should perhaps except the Riccaras, who have very lately settled on the Missouri and in whom no confidence can ever be placed though they are at present altogether quiet and occupy the Mandan towns. They may trouble the traders, but this will give me no trouble, because if they will give these treacherous Indians the means of swaying their whole trade on the upper Missouri with a full knowledge of their character let them abide the consequences—I don't pretend to have any influence or control over them whatever.

In other words, Pilcher advised the traders that they could not count on his support if they ever decided to conduct business with the Arikaras.[66]

For the duration of Pilcher's tenure as Indian agent/superintendent, the Arikaras could not expect much support from the Indian Office. Pilcher consistently favored the Sioux bands under his care. The Arikaras, he believed, did not deserve any sympathy from the government.[67]

Despite Pilcher's obstructions, by the time of his death in 1843, the Arikaras appeared to have overcome the ravages of the 1837 epidemic. The only visible evidence of the epidemic, according to John James Audubon, who visited the area that year, was the "numerous small mounds on the prairies around the village [which are] still bare of vegetation." Generally, Audubon added, the Arikaras were a healthy and "fine noble looking race of men, above the average in height and stout, with lean sinewy limbs."[68]

The Arikara town at Fort Clark was small and compact. By 1862 it counted forty-eight lodges. The town was located on a cliff some forty to fifty feet high at a bend in the river. The side facing the plains was protected by a wooden stockade about ten to twelve feet high. The whole town covered about five acres. The houses were built close together and formed a labyrinth of narrow paths, which undoubtedly provided advantages against invading enemies. In the center of the town was a small plaza, where dances, ceremonies, and games occasionally took place. In the plaza was a large granite rock "spotted over with vermillion." Right next to it was a cedar pole, about seven feet high and three and a half inches in diameter. It had been stripped of its bark and ornamented with strips of red flannel.[69]

THE IMPACT OF THE FUR TRADE, 1837–1864

Until the 1860s, the trading post was the only permanent white establishment among the Arikaras. The fur companies transported government annuities to Fort Clark, acted as intermediaries between the tribes and the government, and provided the Arikaras with goods.

At Fort Clark and similar posts, people gathered from all ethnic backgrounds: Arikaras, Mandans, Hidatsas, French, English, Americans, Germans, Scots, Mexicans, and African Americans (either slave or free). As the owners of agricultural produce, Arikara women played a particularly important role. Fur company employees sometimes married Arikara women to strengthen diplomatic ties or simply for (sexual) companionship. Indian wives often served as mediators between traders and their nation. Some marriages were short-lived. For example, Francis Chardon married a string of Arikara women, most of whom left him after a short while because of his volatile and abusive temperament. Other unions were more harmonious.[70]

The fur and buffalo hide trade provided employment for some Arikaras as interpreters, hunters, scouts, and messengers. For example, Chief Star and his son Rushing Bear provided meat for traders during the 1837 and 1838 seasons. Arikara women also earned extra income by cooking and sewing for men at the post or loading and unloading boats.[71]

But the fur trade also caused disruptions. Steamboat crews chopped down trees for fuel, thus reducing natural habitats for a number of animals.[72] Worse was the depletion of beaver and buffalo populations. In 1847 the upper Missouri nations traded seventy-five thousand buffalo robes. A year later this number had climbed to 110,000 robes, excluding robes the tribes needed for its own use.[73] In 1853 Indian agent Alfred D. Vaughan estimated that nearly four hundred thousand buffalo were killed annually and said that herds had become significantly smaller.[74] By 1858 the

Kah-béck-a ("The Twin"), wife of Bloody Hands, painted by George Catlin, circa 1832. Her face and parted hairline are painted with vermillion. She wears brass rings, bracelets, and necklaces with large blue beads made by Arikara craftsmen. As producers of corn for trade, Arikara women were essential contributors to the Arikara economy. Courtesy Smithsonian American Art Museum, SAAM-1985.66.124.

trade went into a sharp decline. Agent Alexander H. Redfield reported that year that the trade was less than half of what it had been fifteen years earlier. "[The] buffalo in the whole country are decreasing at an alarming rate," Redfield wrote. He was also one of the first to call for the preservation of buffalo for the benefit of the Indian tribes who subsisted on them.[75]

Declining buffalo populations meant increased intertribal conflicts. By the 1860s, the buffalo herds had practically disappeared from Arikara territory, forcing hunters to travel greater distances. The Sioux threat made such expeditions extremely dangerous. To protect themselves, the Arikaras, Mandans, and Hidatsas went on joint summer hunts. On the 1859 hunt they were attacked by a large Sioux war party. After a terrible battle, thirty Sioux and ten Arikaras lay dead. When the Arikaras returned to the Missouri River, many wore their hair tied up in a knot in front in token of losses sustained in the battle.[76]

With the collapse of the buffalo hide trade, the Arikaras relied almost exclusively on horticulture for subsistence and trade. But crops were vulnerable to environmental pressures. Grasshoppers devoured crops in 1853, droughts and frost destroyed the yield in 1855, and a devastating hailstorm did the same in 1856.[77] Starvation, especially at the end of the winter season, became a reality. In the winter of 1865 some fifty people died of starvation.[78] The Arikara chiefs regularly appealed to the government for assistance, but annuities were insufficient and rarely arrived on time. The credit system at the trading post further increased Arikara dependency on the traders. Because the American Fur Company practically held a trade monopoly over the Arikaras, it charged inflated prices for goods. Occasionally "opposition companies" opened up for business, but they usually did not survive long against the AFC.

Alcohol was another curse of the fur trade. The chiefs objected to the sale of liquor. Despite a government ban, traders continued to sell liquor illegally. As the Arikaras descended deeper into poverty in the 1850s and 1860s, their resistance to alcohol gradually broke down. A visitor traveling up the Missouri River in 1862 reported large numbers of Arikaras, Mandans, and Hidatsas at Fort Berthold who "lined the bank and offered robes and women in exchange for whiskey."[79]

Diseases introduced by traders also plagued the Arikaras. A measles epidemic caused many deaths in 1846.[80] Cholera struck the tribe in 1851. The bacteria causing the disease had traveled on a steamboat that also carried Jesuit missionary Pierre-Jean DeSmet. Ironically, DeSmet may have used contaminated water to baptize some two hundred Arikara children. In all, about three hundred Arikaras died. "What a consolation," wrote DeSmet, "that by the sacrament [of baptism] I unlocked the gates of heaven to them!"[81] Sixty-three Arikaras perished in a smallpox epidemic in 1856. Among them were thirty children. Once again the disease had been carried on board a steamboat. The total Arikara population had now been reduced to eight hundred souls. Chief White Shield (possibly Bloody Hands's son and successor) and the other chiefs blamed the traders for the disaster. With great difficulty they prevented young men from committing violence against the traders. The Indian agent placated the chiefs with extra provisions intended for but rejected by the Sioux. Nevertheless, the next year a white trader named La Brune was killed by an Arikara who had lost his entire family in the epidemic.[82]

ARIKARA POLITICS AND DIPLOMACY, 1837–1864

After settling at Fort Clark, the Arikaras formed a military confederacy with the Mandans and Hidatsas against the Sioux. For several years the "earth lodge federation" held. Occasional quarrels between young men were resolved quickly by chiefs in the towns. Because of the alliance, warfare between the Arikaras and the Crows, who were close relatives of the Hidatsas, ceased.[83]

Exhausted natural resources and a desire to maintain their cultural identity led the Hidatsas to establish a new town upriver on the north bank of the Missouri in 1845. They called it Like-A-Fishhook. Many Mandans joined the Hidatsas at the new settlement, fifty miles north of Fort Clark. That same year, the AFC constructed Fort Berthold nearby. Not all Mandans joined their kinsmen at Like-A-Fishhook. Some remained with the Arikaras at Fort Clark. One small band of Mandans, the Nuptadi, who were on friendly terms with the Yankton Sioux, established a small town a few miles north of Fort Clark. These moves did not end the earth lodge federation but rendered it largely ineffective as a defensive alliance.[84]

In 1851 the US government invited the northern Plains tribes to attend a grand council near Fort Laramie. The primary purpose of the council was to secure safe passage for European migrants on the Oregon and California Trails. To police the migrant route, the government wished to build military posts along the trail. In return for their surrender of hunting grounds adjacent to the trail, the government promised to pay the Indians annuities. To stabilize the region, the government also wished to formalize boundaries between the tribes. The Arikaras were among the nations invited to attend.

In September 1851, Bear Chief and Grey Prairie Eagle traveled to Fort Laramie. They were accompanied by Nochk-pi-shi-toe-pish and She-oh-mant-ho, who formed the Mandan and Hidatsa delegation. For several weeks, Sioux, Assiniboines, Hidatsas, Crows, Shoshones, Cheyennes, Arapahos, and Arikaras camped together in a large circle. Indian affairs commissioner David D. Mitchell opened the talks, after which the delegates of each tribe responded.[85]

On September 8 it was Grey Prairie Eagle's turn to speak for the Arikaras. After shaking hands with the commissioners, he said he was glad to see everyone. "We come hungry for we are very poor and could find no buffalo," he said of the long journey, "but we found friends and they gave us something to eat." Then he expressed the wish of the Arikara people to please the Great Father. He concluded his short speech by saying that he hoped that the Great Father would send them more buffalo.

Perhaps he hoped the Great Father would keep white people from slaughtering anymore buffalo or else send cattle instead.[86]

On September 17, the treaty was signed. The tribes pledged to abstain from hostilities against one another. They also recognized the right of the US government to "establish roads, military and other posts, within their respective territories." The government in turn promised to protect the tribes against depredations by US citizens. In exchange for allowing the building of posts and roads in tribal hunting territories, the government promised to deliver to the tribes annuities of up to $50,000 for fifty years.[87]

The tribes also agreed to recognize tribal territories and boundaries. The territory of the Arikaras, Mandans, and Hidatsas comprised an enormous area that extended from the Missouri River to the Yellowstone River and into the Powder River and Black Hills country. Ironically, the territory included land that the three tribes had never used and was beyond their control. Also problematic was the fact that the territory did not include the Mandan and Hidatsa settlement of Like-A-Fishhook. The all-important issue, however, was whether the Sioux would abide by the treaty and refrain from attacking the three tribes.[88]

The prospects for peace turned when Congress unilaterally reduced the payment of annuities from fifty to ten years in 1852. The Arikaras, Mandans, and Hidatsas accepted the changes "without hesitation." Although the government's reconsideration of the treaty was disappointing to them, the three tribes still believed they had more to gain from the amended treaty than from no treaty at all.[89] Many Sioux, however, including a rising Lakhota headman named Sitting Bull, objected not only to the amendment but to the treaty in its entirety.

It was not long before the stipulations of the treaty were broken. The Sioux never ceased bullying the three tribes at every opportunity. When war broke out between the Lakhotas and the United States following the Grattan Massacre in 1854, the Arikara chiefs "rejoiced when they heard that their Great Father had sent soldiers in the country to chastise those who had violated their treaty stipulations, and protect those who have and are disposed to observe them."[90]

Cut off from annuities and trade goods while the war was in progress, the Sihasapa and Hunkpapa Lakhotas demanded trade from the Arikaras. They warned the Arikaras that "should they be refused powder and balls, and such articles as they desired, they would enter the houses and take what they wanted." These bands also told Arikara chief White Shield "that when they left here, that they intended killing every white man they met in the prairie."[91]

The war between the United States and the Sioux ended after the Battle of Blue Water (1855), so the three tribes once again faced the Sioux alone. Arikara relations with the government became increasingly strained. Apart from the government's failure to provide adequate protection against the Sioux, inadequate annuities and corrupt Indian agents were also sources of frustration. To make matters worse, another smallpox infection plagued the Arikaras at Fort Clark in 1856. Though less virulent and deadly than the 1837 epidemic, it nevertheless caused heartbreak.[92]

Once again the Arikaras suspected that the whites had introduced the disease among them. In May 1857, an Arikara named The Man That Don't Run, also known as The Male Crow, killed a carpenter named Le Blond, an employee of Honore Picotte's trading outfit. Picotte claimed that one of Pierre Chouteau's men, named Francois de Taille or de Tallie, had encouraged the murder. A subsequent investigation by Agent Redfield revealed that De Taille had an Arikara wife with whom he had several children, two of whom had died of the smallpox. The Male Crow assured Redfield that De Taille was innocent and that he had acted on his own because he blamed whites for the disease. Apparently unable to arrest The Male Crow, Redfield did not pursue the case further.[93]

By June 1858, all-out warfare had resumed between the Sioux and the Arikaras. On June 14, Redfield reported, "Horses have been stolen on both sides and a Ree has just been killed here at the Fort [Pierre] while in the act of stealing the horses of the Sioux." Redfield feared the violence would spread. "The stipulations of the Laramie treaty are not being observed at all," he wrote. "Nearly all the nations and tribes being at war and depredating on each other and white people also."[94]

Numerically small and poor in powder and balls, the Arikaras were clearly at a disadvantage in this conflict. Arikara frustrations with the government's failure to protect them came to a head on June 19, 1858, when Redfield visited Fort Clark to deliver annuities. Painter Charles Wimar, who accompanied Redfield, wrote that the Arikaras were "very desperate." When their steamboat landed, it was quickly surrounded by people from the town; guards had to be placed to prevent the Arikaras from plundering the boat. When Wimar took a stroll through the town, he was surrounded by begging women. The Arikaras were angry at Redfield for failing to protect them against the Sioux. Some Arikaras called to get rid of the treaty. When Redfield stepped of the steamboat, he was met by a group of young warriors, one of whom discharged his gun between Redfield's feet. Redfield then moved his council with the chiefs to the steamboat. Chief White Shield led the Arikara delegation. He and the other chiefs refused the annuities. They demanded that the government do something about the Sioux. The meetings dragged on for five hours. At the end of the talks, the chiefs accepted the annuities but received little else.[95]

FINAL YEARS AT FORT CLARK AND REMOVAL TO FORT BERTHOLD

In 1859 White Shield was head chief of the Arikaras. Behind him was The One Who First Rushes on the Enemy. This was probably the legendary Son of Star, whose name is sometimes given as Rushing Bear. Other chiefs included The Brother, Yellow Wolf, Chief Bear, He Who Strikes the Foe between Two Fires, and He Who Strikes Many.[96]

The chiefs faced a hard decision. Following the decimation of the buffalo population, the overstocking of eastern markets, and the financial crisis of 1857, the AFC began to phase out Fort Clark. The fort was abandoned later that year and burned down by the Sioux.[97]

The closing of Fort Clark left the Arikaras without access to necessary trade goods. Without adequate supplies of powder and balls, they were defenseless against Sioux raiders. In the winter of 1860–61, the Yanktons ran off almost two hundred Arikara horses in a single raid. With the situation becoming desperate, White Shield and the chiefs contemplated moving their people to Fort Berthold.[98]

Four Bears, Bear's Nose, and Lean Wolf of the Hidatsas and Long Mandan and Little Walker of the Mandans approved of the Arikara plan to move to Fort Berthold.[99] But before preparations for the move were finalized, a large Sioux war party attacked in August 1861. Although the Arikaras killed thirty Sioux in the affair, several Arikaras were killed also. After the harvest was brought in, the Arikaras abandoned Fort Clark. During the winter of 1861–62 they lived in two separate winter camps. One of the camps, Heart Village, was built on an island in the river.[100]

In the spring of 1862, the Arikaras moved north. They started constructing two towns on the west bank of the Missouri River opposite Like-A-Fishhook. The Mandans and Hidatsas invited the Arikaras to move their towns to the east bank of the Missouri River and closer to Like-A-Fishhook so they could combine their forces. The Arikara chiefs rejected the invitation. They argued that their ancestors had always lived on the west side of the river and stated that they had "put their medicines in the ground at that place."[101]

One of the new towns was named Star Village after Chief Star. White Shield and Tall Bull also resided there. Yellow Wolf and Eagle-on-Hill were the first and second chiefs of the smaller sister village. Star Village was surrounded by a defensive ditch between twelve and fifteen inches deep. Dirt from the ditch was piled up outside to form a breastwork. At the center of the town was the medicine lodge, in front of which was Grandfather Rock. The lodges of the leading families of the town were located around the medicine lodge and the plaza. Like-A-Fishhook was so close that messages could be shouted across to it. The name of the second village was not recorded.[102]

In a final effort to persuade the Arikaras to join them at Like-A-Fishhook, the Mandans and Hidatsas sent a delegate named Wooden Bowl to the Arikaras. Wooden Bowl carried a pipe. Star and the other chiefs politely refused. Wooden Bowl, angered by the Arikara refusal, raised the pipe and said, "My medicine is the bear who lives above. These people have refused to take the pipe so I ask you, my god, to send them across in four days."[103]

Wooden Bowl's prayer was answered a few days later when, in August 1862, the Sioux attacked Star Village after a trade dispute. The fight began at the trader's lodge. Dissatisfied with the price paid for their blankets, a few Sioux visitors killed the post trader. Because the trader had been married to an Arikara woman, the Arikaras at once attacked the Sioux in retaliation. But they possessed few guns, and sixteen Arikaras were killed. In 1912 Strikes Two, Running Wolf, and Red Star remembered the attack. Red Star's mother and five-year-old sister had been killed. Although Wooden Bowl had called on the sacred powers to punish the Arikaras, the Mandans and Hidatsas crossed the river to aid the Arikaras. Together the tribes drove off the Sioux. The next day the Arikaras abandoned their towns and joined the Mandans and Hidatsas on the other side of the river.[104]

When Blackfeet agent Henry W. Reed met the Arikaras later that year, he found them greatly demoralized as a result of Sioux harassment. "All of the above Indians are looking, as their only hope, to this government for help," Reed wrote. "If we aid them soon, they live; if not, they die."[105]

With the Sioux now openly hostile to the United States, Agent Samuel N. Latta called upon the US Army for protection. A rumor said that Bear's Rib, a friendly Hunkpapa chief, had been murdered for being too accommodating to the whites. Though the rumor turned out to be false, Captain John Pattee of Company A, Fourteenth Iowa Infantry, the commanding officer at Fort Randall, responded by asking his superiors to send troops to the Heart River region to offer assistance to the three tribes. It appears that troops were indeed sent, but they were too far removed from the tribes to be of real help. The following year Latta begged for additional troops. When Latta arrived to deliver annuities on July 4, 1863, he announced that troops were on their way. "They were greatly rejoiced at the near approach of troops," Latta reported, "as they were shut off from the Buffalo and the rest of mankind and in a starving condition." Once again, however, the military support was insufficient or only temporary, for the next year Jesuit missionary Pierre-Jean DeSmet wrote, "It will be necessary, and the Indians desire it greatly, to establish a military post near their town or Fort Berthold as this would give them protection against the numerous marauding bands of Sioux who are constantly lurking around them and from whom they have suffered greatly for these several years past."[106]

Unfortunately, despite many promises, it would take until 1864 until their pleas were finally heard.

8 MILITARY ALLIANCE WITH THE UNITED STATES, 1864–1881

> My boys, I have a letter from a white man asking for some of you boys to serve as scouts.
>
> —CHIEF RUSHING BEAR, ALSO KNOWN AS SON OF STAR, 1876

> We hardly knew what a good night's rest was then. We used to have to be out scouting night and day.
>
> —RED STAR, ARIKARA SCOUT

In 1903 Arikara tribal chief Sitting Bear told how the Sioux once tried to destroy his town. The Sioux even brought in allies to overwhelm and annihilate the people. The Arikaras were spared destruction through the intervention of a man who owned a sacred robe decorated with images of the sun, moon, and stars. The man wrapped himself in the robe, took a gourd rattle, and climbed on top of his lodge. When the enemy attacked, he shook his robe. Each time he shook the robe, enemy warriors fell from their horses, bleeding from their lungs and heads. This frightened the attackers and they ran off. The Arikaras gave chase and killed many. That night there were great celebrations and the people danced with scalps taken from the enemy. Years later, after the intertribal wars had ceased, some Sioux visitors told Sitting Bear that "at that time many tribes had got together to annihilate the Arikara."[1]

Warfare had been part of the Arikara experience ever since Neešaanu created it to keep the world's population in check. Mother Corn had sacrificed herself on the field of battle, to be born again as a cornstalk. The Arikaras carried on the military tradition. They staunchly resisted enemy nations. In the nineteenth century, however, Sioux pressure brought them to the brink of annihilation. Since the early 1800s certain Sioux bands had waged genocidal warfare against the Pawnees, and as Sitting Bear indicates, they made at least one attempt to exterminate the Arikaras as well.[2]

Sioux pressure prompted the Arikaras into a military alliance with the Mandans and Hidatsas, but by the mid-1860s Arikara leaders White Shield and Rushing Bear also recognized the value of a military alliance with the United States. By allowing Arikara men to serve as scouts for the US Army in the 1860s and 1870s, they pursued a strategy that would take war away from their towns and into Sioux territory. Through this military alliance, for the first time in decades the Arikaras placed the Sioux on the defensive and so staved off the prospect of annihilation.

Arikara men welcomed the opportunity to serve as scouts, earn war honors, and avenge past injuries. Between 1865 and 1881, they served honorably in several military campaigns, including the Yellowstone expeditions of 1872 and 1873, the Black Hills expedition of 1874, and the ill-fated Little Bighorn campaign of 1876. Although several scouts lost their lives while fighting in army blue, their sacrifice kept the people at home safe. The strategy pursued by White Shield and Rushing Bear paid off.

THE ARIKARAS IN 1864

In 1864 White Shield was the head chief of the Arikaras. Rushing Bear, a renowned warrior, emerged as second chief. He was the son of Chief Star and for this reason was often called Son of Star. Both men were capable leaders, keeping their people together despite formidable challenges, such as poverty and warfare with the Sioux. White Shield and Rushing Bear also negotiated with government agents, of whom many turned out to be unreliable and outright corrupt.

When agent Mahlon Wilkinson visited the three tribes in June 1864, White Shield and Rushing Bear complained that they needed guns to defend themselves against the Sioux so they could go hunt buffalo. Even after successful harvests, their supplies often ran out at the end of winter. Shortages led to nutritional deficiency diseases and even starvation. The Arikaras, Mandans, and Hidatsas now depended on government annuities for goods they formerly obtained by hunting and trading, but the fifteen-year term of government annuities would expire in 1866. White Shield, therefore, was anxious to negotiate a new treaty to provide for his people. He told Wilkinson that the Arikaras were willing to sell some of their land in return for annuities.

On July 2, 1864, White Shield dictated a letter to President Abraham Lincoln in which he reminded the president that the government had promised, but failed, to protect them. "Has our Great Father forgotten his children?" White Shield asked. The Sioux had driven the Arikaras from their country, and they had been forced to seek shelter with the Mandans and Hidatsas. "We want to live in our country," he said. But if that was not possible, he would accept compensation for it. This compensation ranged from "guns to hunt with" to "a school for our children."

White Shield had another reason to write this letter. In 1862 war had erupted between the United States and the Santee Sioux in Minnesota. The next year the conflict spilled onto the plains, drawing the western Sioux into the fight. The Sioux now changed course and tried to pressure the Arikaras to join them against the United States. Hunkpapa chief Sitting Bull, especially, was in favor of recruiting the Arikaras. Though undoubtedly some Arikaras urged White Shield to accept Sitting Bull's offer, he rejected it. In his letter to Lincoln, he reaffirmed the Arikaras' commitment to peace and friendship with the United States. "We like to see our white brothers come among us very much," he said. "We hear bad talk [from the Sioux], but have no ears." He added, "When we hear good talk we have ears."[3]

When the Arikaras, Mandans, and Hidatsas refused to join the war against the United States, the Sioux turned against them in anger. In 1863, determined to destroy the three tribes, about seven hundred Sioux warriors attacked Like-A-Fishhook. Carrying only bows and arrows, the defenders sent their women and children to nearby Fort Berthold for protection while they waited in the town to ambush the Sioux. Afraid to enter the town, the Sioux built a fire to smoke out the defenders, who were forced to withdraw to the fort as well. When the attackers turned against the fort, one of its defenders, Pierre Garreau, overheard a Sioux who planned to set fire to the fort. Garreau shot the man, and Man Chief of the Arikaras gave the coup de grâce. They hung the corpse from a rope in clear sight as a deterrent for his comrades. When the wind turned, the smoke of the fires finally drove the Sioux away.[4]

Refusing to give in to Sioux intimidation, White Shield was now eager to hear "good talk" from Washington. But the government remained silent. White Shield's message was lost in the Office of Indian Affairs. The military alliance desired by White Shield would not be forged by Washington officials but by US Army officers in the field.

BLOODY KNIFE AND ARIKARA MILITARY SERVICE, 1865–1871

The military alliance between the Arikaras and the United States was more the result of expediency than policy. In late August 1864, around the time White Shield dictated his letter for President Lincoln to Agent Mahlon Wilkinson, General Alfred Sully stopped by Fort Berthold on his way back from a military campaign against the Sioux, which had culminated in the Battle of Killdeer Mountain on July 28.[5]

White Shield, Son of Star, and the chiefs of the Mandans and Hidatsas welcomed Sully to Like-A-Fishhook. They told Sully of their problems with the Sioux and of their many requests for protection. Sully ordered Captain A. B. Moreland's Company G, Sixth Iowa Cavalry, to garrison Fort Berthold. Moreland's task was not only to protect the three tribes but also to keep communication on the Missouri River open. A few days later Sully continued his march and Moreland's company moved into the old fort.[6]

The troops did not stay long. When Sully returned to Fort Berthold for a new expedition against the Sioux a year later, he again found the three tribes in poor condition. Over the previous year alone they had lost four hundred horses to Sioux raids. "I urge upon the government to do something to better their condition," Sully wrote to Washington. Though the men of the three tribes were brave enough to fight, Sully wrote, they were outnumbered by the Sioux, and as a result their numbers were "fast decreasing." Sully emphasized their civilized habits as tillers of the soil and praised the industrious character of both men and women. The chiefs also expressed a desire for teachers to instruct the children to read, write, and converse in English. Once again, Sully left behind a company to protect the tribes and to prevent possible illegal trading with the Sioux as well. Then he took an unprecedented step: "I have also organized about 40 [Native American] soldiers to whom I have issued arms, and I would recommend that a cheap uniform be issued to these soldiers," he wrote. "I do not think on some accounts it is a good plan to give them United States uniforms. There should be some distinction."[7]

While at Fort Berthold, Sully learned that the Sioux planned an attack against Fort Rice. The sudden appearance of his troops, however, caused the Sioux to call off the attack. Determined to chase the hostiles, Sully enlisted the assistance of an accomplished Arikara soldier named Bloody Knife to act as a guide.[8]

Bloody Knife was the child of an Arikara mother and a Hunkpapa father. Born around 1840, he spent his childhood living among his father's people. Other children often ridiculed him because of his mixed heritage. According to legend, one of his greatest tormentors was a boy later known as Gall. When Bloody Knife's parents separated in 1856, his mother took him back to Fort Clark. Life there was difficult as a result of frequent Sioux attacks. Despite being part Hunkpapa, Bloody Knife was not safe during such attacks. One day, while traveling to his father's camp, he was ambushed by Gall and his friends, stripped of his clothes, savagely beaten with coup sticks, and told never to return. In the fall of 1862, a Sioux war party killed two of Bloody Knife's brothers in an ambush. Not surprisingly, Bloody Knife was eager to join Sully's command.[9]

Bloody Knife delivers a dispatch to an American officer. Apart from the name glyph, Bloody Knife is also recognizable by the chevrons on his uniform. Arikara scouts treasured military insignia such as chevrons, epaulets, and sabers in the same way they valued coup marks. National Anthropological Archives, Smithsonian Institution, MS 154064A #08510521.

Because of his bravery and his familiarity with the Sioux, Bloody Knife was a useful guide for Sully's expedition. They followed the Sioux trail across the Badlands and the Little Missouri River to Beaver Creek and from there to the Powder River. Unable to cross the river, Sully had to abandon the chase. But he was thoroughly impressed with Bloody Knife's skills as a scout and commended him in his report. At the conclusion of the expedition, Sully returned to Fort Rice and Bloody Knife returned to Fort Berthold.[10]

Bloody Knife continued to assist the soldiers. In November 1865, he guided troops from Fort Berthold to Gall's camp. When Gall resisted arrest, the soldiers stabbed him with their bayonets in the body and neck. Seeing that Gall was still breathing, Bloody Knife stepped forward to finish the job with his gun. He was about to deliver the fatal shot when an officer kicked his gun aside, causing the charge to miss. To Bloody Knife's dismay, the officer then ordered his men to leave Gall's body where it lay. Gall eventually recovered from his wounds and, according to legend, later avenged himself against Bloody Knife in the Battle of the Little Bighorn.[11]

Although Bloody Knife had shown that the Arikaras could make valuable contributions to the army, prejudiced and ethnocentric military officials at Fort Rice and Fort Berthold hesitated to enlist them as scouts. Instead, the army tried to keep the nomadic tribes under control by building a series of forts at strategic points, such as roads and rivers. Among these forts were Fort Berthold (1864–1867), Fort Rice (1864–1878), Fort Stevenson (1867–1883), Fort Buford (1866–1895), and Fort Abraham Lincoln (1872–1891). These posts formed a tremendous nuisance for the Sioux by disrupting hunting grounds and attracting settlers, who used up valuable resources. While Oglala chief Red Cloud targeted forts and roads along the Bozeman Trail, Hunkpapa chief Sitting Bull attacked the forts on the upper Missouri. Sitting Bull's warriors surprised small army units detailed to collect hay, water, and wood, or that carried mail. In December 1866, Captain W. J. Rankin of Fort Buford reported that the Hunkpapa, Sihasapa, Sans-Arcs, Minneconjou, and Two Kettle Lakhota had vowed to "wipe out all the forts on the river after cleaning me out." As a result of frequent attacks, soldiers were often virtually prisoners in their own forts.[12]

Periodically, the army staged expeditions against the resisting tribes, but these rarely met with success. The frontier army was too small, too dispersed, unfamiliar with the terrain and the enemy, untrained in Native American warfare, relatively immobile compared to the nomadic Indians, and unable to live off the land. It was not an effective Indian-fighting force. Despite these problems, relatively few officers were willing to use Indian scouts. Racial prejudice, the language barrier, questions about the loyalty of the scouts, and the idea that their use diminished the army's prestige prevented many commanders from enlisting Indians.[13]

Not until 1867 did the Arikaras enter the picture again as possible military allies. In February of that year, Colonel J. V. D. Reese at Fort Rice suggested using friendly Indians as guides, messengers, and sources of information, "if not a few warriors," in campaigns against the hostiles.[14] But it was Colonel Philippe Régis de Trobriand, commander of the Thirty-First Infantry at Fort Stevenson, who systematically enlisted Arikaras for military service. De Trobriand was new to Indian warfare, but he was willing to experiment. Upon his arrival at Fort Stevenson he found the troops quite helpless against the Sioux. The infantry, De Trobriand concluded, was useless against mounted warriors. Furthermore, many of the new soldiers were so "frightened by ridiculous reports and absurd commentaries on the Indians... that they think more of avoiding them than of fighting them."

When De Trobriand visited Like-A-Fishhook in September 1867, he was impressed with the martial skills of the Arikaras. The Arikara tribe, he wrote later, was the strongest of the three tribes as well as "the most enterprising and the most warlike." De Trobriand was also impressed with Chief White Shield. The two men, both accomplished warriors, quickly became friends.[15]

In 1868 White Shield allowed fourteen warriors to enlist as scouts. After a health inspection by the post physician, De Trobriand enlisted ten of them. To the warriors' surprise, he selected young men over more experienced older men. Each enlisted man received discarded army clothing: underclothes, a flannel shirt, shoes, trousers, a jacket, and a blue overcoat. The scouts also insisted on a cavalry hat with black feathers and the cavalry emblem. The scouts caused some embarrassment among the officers' wives at the post when they changed into their new outfits in the middle of the parade ground. Apart from a uniform, each scout also received cartridge belts and bags for extra shells, as well as long breech-loading rifles, which were later exchanged for shorter carbines. In addition, they received tin plates, cups, kettles, and camp stoves. Bull Head was made sergeant and received the honor of wearing three stripes on his sleeves.[16]

Over the years, 150 Arikara men served as scouts. A few Mandans and Hidatsas also joined. Each scout had his own reasons for enlisting. First and foremost was a desire for revenge. Almost all enlistees had lost friends and relatives in fights with the Sioux. Red Star, who enlisted in 1876, had lost his mother and five-year-old sister during a Sioux raid in 1862. Bloody Knife had lost two brothers that same year. An Arikara named Soldier had been severely wounded in a battle with the Sioux in 1854. Most other scouts shared similar stories. Another reason for joining the army was the opportunity to leave the confines of Like-A-Fishhook and seek adventure. Peer pressure prompted Red Bear to sign up after Chief Rushing Bear expressed his surprise that he had not yet enlisted. "I hadn't thought of going," Red Bear said later, but Rushing Bear's words "touched my pride." Monetary rewards enticed Soldier, whose heart jumped with joy at the sight of green paper bills in his hands. The army also fed and housed the men and their families. Scout rations consisted of "square thick crackers [hardtack], salt, fresh bread, flour, bacon, sugar, plug tobacco, tea, beans, peas, hominy, and square, solid strips of beans and [cabbage] leaves (succotash), and occasionally fresh beef." Such rations were particularly welcome at the end of winter, when food supplies in town were running low. The most important reason to join the army, however, was the opportunity to defend their people against the Sioux. The army furnished them with the horses and weapons with which they could engage their enemies on more equal terms.[17]

Although military service drained Like-A-Fishhook of defenders, White Shield and Rushing Bear encouraged men to join. They reasoned that by taking the war to the enemy, the warriors gave people greater security at home. Furthermore, their alliance with the army gave them greater leverage in future negotiations with the government. Just as important, perhaps, was the fact that the army treated the Arikaras as men and not children, as agents of the Indian Office were prone to do.

Scout service also allowed men to earn war honors. At festive occasions, scouts proudly painted coup marks on their bodies and used paint to emphasize where they had been wounded in battle. Several scouts recorded their deeds of bravery in ledger book drawings. Scout service became an avenue for young men to climb the social ladder and to earn the respect of not only their people but the sacred powers as well.[18]

During their service, Arikara scouts guided troops through unfamiliar terrain in search of hostile Indian camps, carried dispatches between commands, escorted hay and water details, protected railroad survey crews, policed Indian reservations, and caught and returned army deserters. During military expeditions they protected the flanks of the column, hunted meat to feed hungry troops, and spearheaded attacks against enemy villages.

Recognizing the threat posed by the Arikara scouts, the Sioux tried to persuade the Arikaras to abandon the troops. In the spring of 1868, for example, the Minneconjous offered the three tribes horses if they agreed to join the Sioux against the army. De Trobriand may also have enlisted Arikara scouts to prevent a Sioux–Arikara alliance. When the Arikaras rejected the proposal, Sioux war parties deliberately targeted the scouts in their attacks. They sought to intimidate them and discourage others from joining the army.[19]

The scouts saw action almost right away. On May 17, 1868, a scout unit returning from a reconnaissance mission ran into a Sioux war party. Although outnumbered, the scouts charged the Sioux. During the fight, Sergeant Bull Head was thrown to the ground when his horse was shot out from under him. While he lay unconscious, Hunkpapa chief Sitting Bull rode up to him. Surprisingly, Sitting Bull did not kill Bull Head. According to Soldier, who witnessed the fight, Sitting Bull spared him because they both belonged to the New Dog Society. It is more likely that Sitting Bull, ever the statesman, had not given up of forming an alliance with the Arikaras. The fact that Sitting Bull had an Arikara stepmother may have also played a role in his decision to spare Bull Head.[20]

De Trobriand was pleased with the performance of his scouts, who in June 1868 prevented a Sioux war party from stealing horses at the fort. A month later they repulsed another Sioux war party that tried to run off some cattle. According to the army report, the scouts gave them "a good chase" and no animals were lost. De Trobriand wrote that the "Rees conducted themselves well."[21]

After 1868, Arikara scouts served at Fort Stevenson, Fort Buford, Fort Rice, and, later, Fort Abraham Lincoln. The scouts lived in separate quarters with their families. While the men were out on scout duty, their wives took care of the household. They cooked, cleaned, dressed skins, made moccasins for their husbands, mended their clothes, and looked after gardens near the river. Sometimes they also worked as laundresses at the fort. To earn extra income they sold corn, vegetables, and fish to the soldiers.[22]

THE YELLOWSTONE EXPEDITION OF 1872

In 1872 Arikara scouts accompanied General David S. Stanley's expedition to protect surveyors of the Northern Pacific Railroad (NPRR), scheduled to pass north of the Great Sioux Reservation. Lakhota leaders such as Sitting Bull objected to the railroad. They considered these lands, where buffalo still roamed in large numbers, essential for their survival. Construction of a railroad through this territory would inevitably lead to war.[23]

Although he was aware of Sitting Bull's opposition, commanding general William T. Sherman supported railroad construction for strategic reasons. Railroads allowed troops to move faster over long distances (allowing a reduction in military forts), made it cheaper to supply posts that remained, and encouraged white settlement that would destroy buffalo herds upon which the nomadic tribes depended. Sherman considered the railroads "the solution of our 'Indian affairs.'"[24]

When NPRR surveyors prepared to explore the territory between the Missouri and Yellowstone Rivers in 1872, Sherman ordered Stanley to escort them. Stanley gathered a force of about 580 officers and infantrymen, some artillery, and 120 wagons to carry supplies. He requested but did not receive any cavalry troops. He did, however, receive the assistance of thirteen Arikara scouts, including Bloody Knife, and a handful of Santee scouts. On July 26, 1872, the command left Fort Rice.[25]

On several occasions, Lakhota war parties under Sitting Bull and Gall skirmished with Stanley's command. On August 18, Gall's warriors attacked surveyor H. C. Davis. They were repulsed. Three days later, the Lakhotas launched an unsuccessful attack against the scouts. On October 2, the Lakhotas killed Lieutenant Eben Crosby of the Seventeenth Infantry. Two days later the Lakhotas attacked Stanley's camp and killed Stanley's Black servant Stephen Harris and mortally wounded Lieutenant

Lewis D. Adair. The foot soldiers were unable to pursue the attackers. On October 15 the troops returned to Forts McKeen and Rice after a march of six hundred miles.[26]

While Stanley's expedition was in the field, Lakhota war parties attacked Fort McKeen. They specifically targeted the Arikara scouts. Five scouts were killed. Te ta way rish ("Amongst" or "Ree Standing among the Hidatsa") was ambushed while scouting twelve miles from the fort on August 8. Shiis-u-two ("Spotted Eagle") was killed about twenty miles from the fort on August 26. On October 2, a Sioux war party surprised a small detachment of scouts near the fort. Coon-agh-wah ("Red Bear") and Ka naytan ("Crow Tail") were killed in the fight. Another scout, Paint, escaped to alarm the others. Among them was Red Bear's son Nee-noch-na-shaun-na ("Boy Chief"). Boy Chief rushed out to avenge his father and to prevent the Lakhotas from mutilating his corpse. He was killed close to his father's body. Strikes Two and others were just about to enlist when they learned about the deaths of their comrades. They were shown the place where their comrades had been killed. Strikes Two later recalled that the men had been killed close together. Their blood had dried and cracked in the sun. Though the attacks by the Lakhotas did not deter Strikes Two and other Arikaras from enlisting, the soldiers were thoroughly frightened. "These military fellows at this post are the worst frightened men on the Indian subject that I have ever seen," wrote a railroad surveyor.[27]

Stanley's expedition had not achieved its objective. The survey was only partially completed due to harassment by Sitting Bull's men. Stanley asked the division commander, General Philip S. Sheridan, to furnish him with cavalry troops for the next expedition to keep the Lakhotas at a safe distance.

ON THE YELLOWSTONE EXPEDITION OF 1873 WITH STANLEY AND CUSTER

In response to Stanley's request, Sheridan ordered Lieutenant Colonel George Armstrong Custer and the Seventh Cavalry to the upper Missouri. In 1873 Custer and the Seventh Cavalry arrived at Fort Lincoln. With his fringed buckskin outfit, red leather–topped boots, wide-rimmed soft hat, and long blond hair that reached to his shoulders, Custer made a great impression on Bloody Knife and the other scouts at the fort. William Jackson, a mixed-blood Blackfeet scout, recalled Bloody Knife saying "That long, yellow-haired one, he is a real chief; of all white chiefs, the greatest chief!" From that day on, the Arikaras called him Uxčes ("Long Hair").[28]

Over subsequent years, Custer and the scouts became close friends. The scouts admired Custer for his bravery and appreciated his efforts to help their people.

Bloody Knife, in particular, became a close personal friend. Although Custer shared many of the racist sentiments prevalent among white Americans at the time, he nevertheless respected the Arikaras. He often attended ceremonies of his scouts. "Custer had a heart like an Indian," said Red Star years later. "If we ever left out one thing in our ceremonies he always suggested it to us."[29]

Although George Custer is one of the most controversial characters in American military history, to the Arikaras he was a hero. Despite his charisma and bravery, he had certain flaws as a strategist and tactician. He believed that the real difficulty with Indians was finding them, not fighting them; that Indians would always avoid fixed battles; that the only way to engage them was in a surprise attack; and that when surprised, Indians always preferred to escape, even when they had superior numbers. Thus Custer relied heavily on Indian scouts to locate Indian villages. To surprise the enemy, he would risk being cut off from support lines. Furthermore, if necessary, he was willing to attack without adequate intelligence on the size or position of the opposing force. Although his tactics contradicted time-tested military principles, after his victory at the 1868 Washita Battle, Custer did not believe his plans were flawed.[30]

Twenty-seven Arikara scouts accompanied the 1873 Yellowstone Expedition, under Stanley's command. The expedition included no less than twenty infantry companies, the entire Seventh Cavalry, 353 railroad engineers, nine scientists, 275 wagons, 2,321 mules and horses, and seven hundred head of cattle to feed the men during the first few weeks. Fort Berthold trader Frederick F. Gerard acted as interpreter for the scouts.[31]

Three days before the expedition set out, a Lakhota war party attacked a group of railroad engineers on their way from Fort Lincoln to Fort Rice. Responding to the sound of battle, the Arikara scouts rode out to support the engineers. They killed eight Lakhota warriors and returned to Fort Lincoln with the bodies of two of them. Arikara women hacked the bodies to pieces and celebrated the scalp dance that night.[32]

On June 20, the expedition left Fort Rice. Heat, rain, and mosquitoes tormented the men on the first days on the trail. Nearly a month later, on July 15, they arrived at the Yellowstone River. Here Stanley ordered the construction of a stockade, where supplies were to be stored.

On August 4, while scouting ahead of the column, Bloody Knife discovered Sitting Bull's trail. He reported to Custer that they were within twenty-five miles of a large Lakhota village. That afternoon a few Lakhotas attempted to steal horses. The scouts, together with some soldiers, went in pursuit. Fearing an ambush, they stopped. Immediately, three hundred mounted Hunkpapa warriors attacked and a heavy fight ensued. Bloody Knife killed one of the assailants with a single shot from long distance. Custer estimated later that the scouts and the troops had killed about forty Lakhotas, which was undoubtedly an exaggeration. On their part, the Lakhotas had killed Private John Ball, army veterinarian Dr. John Honsinger, and regimental sutler Augustus Baliran. To Bloody Knife's dismay, Custer did not order the army to cross the river to pursue the enemy because many of his men could not swim. Bloody Knife scoffed that the soldiers could at least hang on to their horses' tails and be towed across. The scouts even made a few bull boats to ferry the men across the river, but by the time the boats were done, night had fallen and it was too late to continue.[33]

At 4:00 A.M. on August 11, the Lakhotas attacked Custer's camp. The Arikara scouts prevented the Lakhotas from crossing the river. During a lull in the fight, the Lakhotas and the scouts exchanged profanities and insults. Custer's troops were in danger but were saved by Stanley, who upon hearing the sound of battle pushed the infantry ahead. A few salvos from Stanley's artillery dispersed the Sioux and effectively ended the battle. Although there was never an official count of casualties, Custer again estimated that forty Lakhotas had been killed. The troops lost one soldier killed and several wounded. In his report, Custer commended the scouts for their "prompt and valuable information regarding the enemy's movements."[34]

Little of interest occurred on the remainder of the campaign. In September 1873, the scouts safely guided the troops back to Fort Lincoln.[35] The Yellowstone Expedition of 1873 was hailed as a success, in no small part due to the Arikara scouts. Stanley was very pleased with the performance of the Arikaras especially Bloody Knife, who received a bonus of $60 from the NPRR for his excellent services on the expedition.[36]

THE BLACK HILLS EXPEDITION OF 1874

By 1873 the NPRR had advanced as far as present-day Bismarck. Construction ended abruptly when an economic recession struck that year. To fund expensive projects like transcontinental railroads, some US congressmen called for opening up the Black Hills to gold prospectors. With gold, the government could issue new money to jump-start the economy. Since 1868, however, the Black Hills were officially part of the Great Sioux Reservation. Nevertheless, Philip Sheridan ordered Custer and the Seventh Cavalry to explore the Black Hills. Sheridan stated that the official purpose of the expedition was to locate a suitable site for a military post to control the Sioux. The presence of geologists and two "practical miners" nevertheless suggested that gold prospecting was another purpose as well. Once again, the Arikara scouts would render valuable assistance during the expedition.[37]

In 1874 Custer assembled his expedition at Fort Lincoln. The military escort consisted of all ten companies of the Seventh Cavalry, two infantry companies, three Gatling guns, one three-inch cannon, 110 supply wagons, a number of scientists, several journalists, a number of white scouts, and a group of Dakhota scouts, mostly inexperienced boys from the Santee Sioux Indian School. Custer also took the regimental brass band along, undoubtedly as a signal to the Lakhotas that they had come in peace. Finally, forty-one Arikara scouts joined the expedition. Bloody Knife was particularly eager to go because a few days before the scheduled departure, his child had been murdered in a Sioux ambush. Young Hawk later explained the purpose of the expedition. "We were told that this expedition was for the purpose of locating gold," he recalled. "We saw men in the party who were surveyors with instruments and they used them on the hills and streams." Later, while the expedition was under way, Custer put a yellow nugget in Young Hawk's hands and told the scouts to look for more of these.[38]

Apart from scouting the country and searching for hostile Indians, the scouts carried letters between the command and Fort Lincoln. Bloody Knife selected only the bravest and most experienced men to perform this important task. Only the names of a few of these couriers were recorded: Skunk's Head, Bull Neck, Lover, Horn in Front, Red Stone (possibly a Santee scout), and two scouts named Left Hand. Couriers received the best of revolvers and carbines, and plenty of ammunition and rations for their journey.[39]

The 1874 expedition was rather uneventful compared to previous expeditions. Not until July 17 came the first sign that the Lakhotas were near. Smoke signals could be seen at regular intervals. Custer believed that "the signals may be intended to let the [Lakhota] village know where we are, so that they may keep out of our way." Many of the scouts, however, believed that the Lakhotas were preparing for battle.[40]

On July 26 the scouts discovered a small Oglala camp of five tipis led by One Stab (or The Man Who Stabs). The scouts wanted to attack, but Custer restrained them and invited One Stab to his camp instead. One Stab and three other Lakhotas arrived that evening. When two of the Lakhota delegates got up and left the talks, Custer ordered the scouts to follow them. Soon a scuffle broke out between the Lakhotas and the scouts. The scouts seized One Stab, who confessed that he had come to distract the soldiers while his people prepared to get away.[41]

Despite Bloody Knife's pleas, Custer would not allow his scouts to scalp One Stab. According to Lieutenant James Calhoun, Bloody Knife demanded a scalp to avenge the death of his child. Other scouts were also outraged at Custer's refusal. According to one report, Bear's Ears resigned in disgust and Mad Bull harangued Long Hair publicly.[42]

On August 2, the expedition discovered gold. Arikara oral tradition credits Red Angry Bear with the find. Red Angry Bear reportedly decorated his saddle and gear with gold dust. Custer asked him to show the spring where he had found the gold and promised the scouts a share of the money. He then sent a courier back to Fort Lincoln to announce the discovery.[43] Some present-day Arikaras believe that the gold the scouts found is still in a safe in Washington, DC, and that it belongs to the tribe.

On August 16, War Eagle, one of the scouts, spotted four Indians. Although they were ordered not to harm the strangers, the scouts prepared for battle. "Their orders had been to talk with and not to fight them," wrote newspaper correspondent William E. Curtis, "but they couldn't help putting on their war paint, and they approach all strangers as they approach a foe."[44] The scouts quickly intercepted the four Indians, who turned out to be Cheyennes. The Cheyennes informed the scouts that six Lakhota villages were encamped on the east side of the Little Missouri River, waiting to attack Custer's command on its return march. The scouts reported their findings to Custer. Over the next days, the Lakhotas set fire to the plains to deprive the cavalry of forage for their horses, but they did not attack. The remainder of the return march was uneventful.[45]

On August 30, the expedition arrived at Fort Lincoln.[46] The scouts had conducted themselves well during the expedition. They had shown tremendous courage by moving into the heart of enemy territory. Professor Aris B. Donaldson, a scientist with the expedition, praised their work. "As scouts, they are invaluable," Donaldson wrote. "Where they scour the country, no ambush could be successfully laid. . . . White men could hardly equal them in the capacity of scouts." Custer was also pleased with their performance, particularly with Bloody Knife. He ordered the quartermaster to pay Bloody Knife a generous bonus for his "invaluable assistance."[47]

Custer deemed the Black Hills Expedition a great success. The country had been explored in detail, so new and more accurate maps could be made. In addition, gold had been found. But the expedition had serious consequences. The Lakhotas were outraged at what they saw as a violation of their treaty rights. Soon after news of the discovery of gold was printed in newspapers around the country, miners swarmed the Black Hills. Their camps sprang up all over the area. A confrontation between the United States and the Sioux seemed inevitable.[48]

THE GREAT SIOUX WAR OF 1876

Unable or unwilling to dislodge miners from the Black Hills, the government tried to purchase the territory from the Lakhotas. When the Lakhotas refused to sell, President Ulysses S. Grant ordered them back to their reservation by January 31, 1876. Any Indians found outside the reservation after that date would be considered hostile. Runners were sent out to the various Sioux and Cheyenne camps to notify them of the ultimatum. Meanwhile, the army prepared for war. As expected, Sitting Bull, Crazy Horse, and other resisting leaders defied Grant's order. They were joined by the Cheyennes under Dull Knife and Little Wolf. The Sioux War of 1876 was about to begin.[49]

According to Arikara oral tradition, when Chief Rushing Bear traveled to Washington in 1874, Grant personally asked him to furnish the army with scouts should war erupt. Grant promised that the scouts would be rewarded for their work. Those who received injuries would be paid for their wounds. Those who lost horses would be compensated also. Rushing Bear shook the president's hand and spoke: "Yes, I have boys [warriors], they will take part in the expedition."[50]

Two years later, in 1876, Son of Star received a letter from George Custer requesting more scouts. Rushing Bear told his warriors, "My boys, I have had a letter from a white man asking for some of you boys to serve as scouts." Most were eager to enlist. Others were already serving at various posts. Young Hawk needed some prodding by his father. Red Bear joined after being asked by Son of Star to do so. The recruits were first sent to regimental doctor James M. DeWolf for a physical examination. Then they were sent to Captain Thomas W. Custer's office, where they "touched the pen" and were sworn in. They received guns, clothing, and two gray blankets apiece.[51]

The campaign was again coordinated by Philip Sheridan. In Sheridan's plan, three army columns would descend on the Sioux and Cheyennes from different directions. General George Crook was to lead a column north from Fort Fetterman. Colonel John Gibbon's "Montana column" would march east from Fort Ellis. General Alfred H. Terry, finally, would march west from Fort Lincoln with the "Dakota column." Terry and Gibbon were to combine their forces on the Yellowstone River.[52]

Thirty-eight Arikara scouts served in the Little Bighorn campaign, part of Terry's Dakota column. Bloody Knife received an appointment as a civilian scout at $50 a month. The remaining scouts, under the command of Lieutenant Charles Varnum, whom the scouts nicknamed Peaked Face, received regular army pay. The scouts also had nicknames for other white officers: Terry was One Star or Man Wearing

Black Buffalo *(left)* and Long Knife *(right)*, Arikara scouts. Cavalry sabers had fallen into disuse during the Indian Wars, but the Arikaras still treasured them as emblems of military service. Scouts were usually given discarded uniforms. The coat worn by Long Knife may have previously been assigned to members of military marching bands. State Historical Society of North Dakota, A1197–00001

the Bear Robe. Tom Custer was Wounded Face, and Gibbon was called Chief with a Red Nose, or Red Face. Because Varnum did not speak Arikara, trader Frederick Gerard acted as interpreter.[53]

Terry gathered troops and supplies at Fort Lincoln. Apart from the Arikara scouts, the expedition consisted of the entire Seventh Cavalry, two companies of the Seventeenth Infantry, one company of the Sixth Infantry, and a battery of Gatling guns. Four Sioux scouts also joined the command. Custer was not yet present. He had been called back to Washington for publicly criticizing the Grant administration. At Terry's request, however, Custer was allowed to join his regiment at the last minute.[54]

A few days before the march, the scouts visited Long Hair. Custer gave Bloody Knife a black handkerchief and a peace medal. He appointed Bobtailed Bull with the rank of sergeant and made Soldier corporal of the scouts. He also told the scouts that this would be his last campaign. He needed one more victory, he said, to become president of the United States. He promised to make Bloody Knife a chief and promised the scouts that their families would have plenty to eat for all time to come.[55]

Historians dispute the claim, made by Red Star in 1912, that Custer desired the US presidency. They argue that the Arikaras must have either misunderstood Custer or misremembered what he had said to them almost forty years earlier. But one should not be too quick to dismiss the claim. In preliterate societies, the spoken word is extremely important. The Arikaras took great pains to remember information accurately. It is possible that Red Star's words were mistranslated in 1912. The Arikara word for "president" (*atipAt*) is very similar to that for "father" or "grandfather." At the same time, Orin G. Libby and the Arikara translators who conducted the interviews in 1912 undoubtedly checked for the correct translation. Historian Robert Utley suspected that Custer aimed for a general's star instead. Still, the original idea of the presidency is not far-fetched. After all, that same year, Custer's fellow Democrat Samuel Tilden nearly won the presidency. In subsequent years, numerous other Civil War generals ran for the presidency as well. A quick look at Custer's credentials make a successful run for the presidency look even more credible. He was a West Point graduate (admittedly last in his class), a general in the Civil War, a hero of Gettysburg, a brave cavalryman (the most "romantic" of all army branches), a victor at the Washita Battle, a published author, and a successful self-promoter who went after Sitting Bull and Crazy Horse with great determination. If he had defeated the Sioux and the Cheyennes that day at the Little Bighorn, it might have indeed launched his political career.

On May 17, Terry's column departed from Fort Lincoln. As always, the scouts led the way. They were organized in three platoons. Soldier and Crooked Horn led members of the New Dog Society. Young Hawk and Bobtailed Bull led men of the Grass Dance Society. Strikes the Lodge and Bull Stands in the Water led the Daroch'-pa Society. They sang war songs as they paraded past people who had come out to watch them. "As we passed the quarters of the scouts," observed mixed-blood scout William Jackson, "their women, crying, sang a sad song of farewell, a song that chilled us." Behind the scouts, the troops marched to tunes of the regimental band.[56]

During the march, the scouts scoured the land in front and to the sides of the column. They took turns guarding the camp at night. They usually camped near Custer's headquarters. Some of the scouts earned extra income by hunting for the soldiers.[57]

Scouting was hard work. "We hardly knew what a good night's rest was then," said Red Star later. "We used to have to be out scouting night and day." Despite the hardships, the scouts did their work conscientiously.[58]

Four Arikara scouts—Forked Horn, Young Hawk, One Feather, and William Baker (a mixed-blood Arikara scout)—accompanied Major Marcus A. Reno on a scout of the Powder River on June 10. On June 16, the scouts discovered the remains of a large camp consisting of four hundred tipi rings. They later found the remains of a large sun dance camp. They followed the trail, which led west and then south toward the little Bighorn River, before turning back to the Yellowstone River. When Reno returned on June 19, he reported that the Lakhotas were probably gathering in a large camp at the Little Bighorn River.

Two days later, on June 21, John Gibbon's Montana column joined Terry's troops on the Yellowstone River. Terry, Gibbon, and Custer met later that day to discuss a new plan based on information provided by Reno and the scouts. Terry agreed to send Custer in pursuit of the Lakhotas with the entire Seventh Cavalry, nearly two hundred pack mules, twenty-five Arikara scouts, and six Crow and several civilian scouts. Terry and Gibbon, meanwhile, would lead the infantry up the Yellowstone to the Little Bighorn River. Around noon the next day, Custer set out with his command. He was eager to discover the hostiles before Terry and Gibbon, or Crook coming up from below. Despite Bloody Knife's warnings that the hostile camp was too big for him to attack, Custer was confident he could whip the Lakhotas. Custer then issued orders to the scouts: when the battle started, he wanted them to capture the enemy horse herd.[59]

On June 24, Custer halted at the sun dance camp. The scouts believed the Lakhotas had been gathering spiritual power for the upcoming battle there. They also believed the Lakhotas were very confident. Custer ignored their reports. He did not know that exactly one week earlier, on June 17, Crook had been defeated by Crazy Horse's warriors on the Rosebud River. The Rosebud Battle had inspired the Lakhotas and Cheyennes.

Later that night, Crow scouts reported that the hostile camp was closer than expected. Custer sent Varnum and his scouts to a lookout place on a ridge, called the Crow's Nest. Forked (Crooked) Horn, Black Fox, Red Foolish Bear, Strikes the Lodge, Red Star, and Bull accompanied Varnum. Custer followed with the rest of his command.[60]

BATTLE OF THE LITTLE BIGHORN

At 3:50 A.M. on June 25, the scouts at the Crow's Nest discovered what later turned out to be the south end of the Lakhota–Cheyenne camp. Red Star, Crooked Horn, and Bull reported the discovery to Custer. Custer immediately broke camp and arrived at the Crow's Nest at 9:00 A.M. Although he was unable to discern the village, Bloody Knife reportedly assured him that there were enough Indians to keep them busy for two or three days. By this time it became clear that the troops had been discovered by some Cheyennes. Alarmed by this news, Custer decided to attack without delay. The scouts warned him that he was in for a big fight, but Custer was more concerned that the Indians would break up their camp and scatter as they had done in the past.

Stabbed, one of the Arikara scouts, prepared the younger and less experienced scouts for battle. He told the young men to keep their courage. "We have been told that there is a big Sioux camp ahead," he said. "We attack a buffalo bull and wound him, when he is this way we are afraid of him though he has no bullets to harm us with." Then he prayed to Neešaanu for power and protection, and rubbed paint on each of the young men.[61]

Around noon, the troops crossed the divide. Custer stopped briefly and divided his command into three battalions. He took five companies of the Seventh Cavalry to form the right wing. He placed Reno in charge of the Arikara scouts and three companies to form the center column. Then he ordered Captain Frederick W. Benteen and the remaining companies to the left. The pack train, protected by Company B, was to follow them twenty minutes later. Custer once again instructed the scouts to capture the enemies' horses.

While rushing toward the village, the scouts discovered a "Lone Tepee" standing on the Plains. Strikes Two counted coup on the tent with a whip. Young Hawk entered the lodge and found the body of a Sioux warrior who had died of wounds received in the battle with General Crook at the Rosebud River. Other scouts took food that had been left for the dead man before they continued the charge. As they rode toward the camp, some of scouts fell behind because their horses had become jaded after weeks of scouting. As a result, Soldier, Stabbed, Bull, White Eagle, Red Wolf, Strikes the Lodge, Charging Bull, and Pretty Face were unable to cross the river and partake in the upcoming battle.

At 3:05 P.M. the scouts crossed the river ahead of Reno's troops and fired the first shots of the battle. The Arikaras who made it into the village were Bloody Knife, Bobtailed Bull, Strikes Two, Young Hawk, Boy Chief, Little Sioux, One Feather, Red Foolish Bear, Goose, Little Brave, Red Bear, Red Star, and Forked Horn. In the valley they captured a number of horses and killed a number of Lakhotas. Strikes Two, Red Star, Boy Chief, Little Sioux, One Feather, Bull Stands in the Water, and Whole Buffalo drove the horses back. Others continued the fight, which grew increasingly intense. It became clear that the village, as the scouts had predicted, was much larger than Custer anticipated. More and more Lakhota warriors joined the fight and began to drive the troops back. Some scouts were caught in the crossfire. Bobtailed Bull, Black Fox, Little Brave, Red Bear, Young Hawk, Forked Horn, Red Foolish Bear, Goose, and Bloody Knife were in the thick of the fight.

Bloody Knife was the first scout to fall. A bullet crushed his skull. Blood and brain tissue splattered over Reno, who was standing next to him. Shaken by Bloody Knife's death, Reno lost his composure and hastily ordered his troops to retreat across the river, where they rushed to a small hill. In the chaos of the battle, the order did not reach the scouts. They saw the troops retreat and abandon the battlefield. They began to fall back under pressure from the Lakhotas. At the left end of the line, Bobtailed Bull was cut off from the rest. Despite attempts by Young Hawk and others to help him, he was killed. Red Bear spotted Bobtailed Bull's blood-covered horse, but when he grabbed its reins, it dragged him away. During the retreat, Little Brave was wounded and fell behind. He died also. Goose, despite a serious wound to his hand, and White Swan (a Crow scout) desperately held off the Sioux. Around 4:30 P.M., the fighting abated. Many Lakhotas left to join the warriors fighting Custer, who had launched his attack a few miles ahead. Taking advantage of the lull in the fighting, Goose and White Swan joined Reno on the hill.

Chaos reigned on "Reno Hill." When Benteen arrived there at 4:20 P.M., he found many wounded soldiers and a shell-shocked Reno unable to command. The Arikara scouts were in a state of confusion. They had just lost three of their best men and saw that the troops were in shock. Interpreter Frederick Gerard was missing. There was nobody to tell them what to do. Their commanding officer, Lieutenant Varnum, had in effect abandoned them. Sergeant Bobtailed Bull was dead. Uncertain what to do, the scouts fell back on Custer's earlier order. Under Stabbed's leadership, they retreated to join Terry and Gibbon at the base camp on the Powder River. Goose and some other scouts stayed to help the soldiers defend the hill.

Meanwhile, Custer and his command were fighting desperately at the other end of the battlefield. They were quickly surrounded on a small and indefensible hill. All of them died in the battle. Many were scalped and mutilated; their clothes and personal belongings were taken. After annihilating the troops at "Custer Hill," the Sioux and Cheyennes once again turned their attention to Reno's troops.

While Custer's troops were fighting for their lives on Custer Hill, the officers on Reno Hill could not agree on a course of action. Captain Thomas B. Weir took Company D in an attempt to reach Custer. Reno, Benteen, and the remaining Arikara scouts reluctantly followed him later. At a small hill ("Weir Point") all were forced back by Lakhota warriors returning from Custer Hill after annihilating Custer's troops. Reno and the troops returned to Reno Hill, where they dug in for the night. The men were exhausted and thirsty. Reno ordered some scouts to break through the enemy lines to alert General Terry, but they were forced back by the Lakhotas.

On the morning of June 26, the Lakhotas and Cheyennes attacked again. They were forced back but inflicted more casualties. A small group of soldiers, covered by sniper fire from the hill, reached the river to get water for the thirsty men on the hill. That afternoon the Lakhotas and Cheyennes disappeared. The scouts were the first to examine the battlefield. Forked Horn, Red Foolish Bear, Young Hawk, and others looked for Custer's body and found many dead horses and the mutilated corpses of soldiers. A soldier showed them a fresh scalp he had found in the village. The scouts believed it belonged to Bloody Knife. The next day, while searching for Bobtailed Bull's body, they discovered Bloody Knife's remains. He was nearly unrecognizable. Sioux women had pounded his head to a pulp with mauls.[62]

On June 27 Terry arrived. In a hurry to return the wounded to base camp for treatment, the troops were able to dig only shallow graves for the dead. Among the wounded was Goose. Red Foolish Bear made a travois for him because he could not ride a horse with his mangled hand. Young Hawk dressed Goose's wounds and transported him by travois to the steamboat *Far West*, which evacuated the wounded from the battlefield. When Goose did not receive medical attention, Horns in Front took him off the boat and dressed his infected hand.[63]

In the weeks and months following the Battle of the Little Bighorn, newspapers printed numerous theories explaining the disaster. Some accused irresponsible reservation agents for arming the hostiles. Others blamed Reno and Benteen for not having done enough to save Custer. Fingers were also pointed at Terry, Crook, and even the Arikara scouts.[64] Today, historians agree that Custer made some fatal errors of judgment by underestimating the size of the Indian forces, ignoring the warnings of his scouts, attacking without knowing the exact location of the enemy camp, and dividing his command, thus enabling the Lakhotas and Cheyennes to destroy him in detail.[65]

Though one of the most controversial figures in American history, to the Arikara scouts who served with him, Custer was a hero and a friend. They thought of him as a brave warrior who sympathized with the Arikara people and their struggle against the Sioux. The scouts faithfully followed him into battle despite their doubts about the wisdom of the attack. Viewed objectively, Custer acted rationally. He based his decisions on his previous experiences with Indian warfare. He paid a terrible price for his mistake. He died, like so many other brave men on both sides that day. Many years later, the surviving Arikara scouts honored him with a song: "Now I'm lonesome / I'm lonesome, I'm lonesome / Custer, he's the cause of my being lonely."

News of the battle reached the Arikaras at Like-A-Fishhook through scouts carrying mail. They learned more particulars from Goose, who was dropped off at

Fort Berthold later. When they learned that Bloody Knife, Bobtailed Bull, and Little Brave had been killed, the people mourned. Several weeks later a pinto horse strayed into the town. It had belonged to Little Brave. It was the horse on which he had charged the Sioux camp. It had made its way back over hundreds of miles without its rider. Eventually, the surviving veterans honored Little Brave in a song: "The pinto alone, he returned / The dancer, he didn't return / Bear's Trail,[66] he didn't return."

AFTER THE LITTLE BIGHORN

The Battle of the Little Bighorn shocked the Arikara scouts. They learned that the soldiers were not invincible. Indeed, many of the troops were badly demoralized. Still, although the scouts had also lost confidence in the army's leadership, they continued to serve loyally.

At the base camp on the Yellowstone River, General Terry and Colonel Gibbon awaited reinforcements for a follow-up campaign. The Seventh Cavalry received new recruits to replace those lost at the Little Bighorn. But many of these "Custer's Avengers" were inexperienced. Twelve infantry companies (of the Fifth and Twenty-Second Infantries) were added to the troops. When Terry's command set out in August 1876, his force consisted of more than seventeen hundred men, including seventy-five Arikara, Crow, and white scouts.[67]

On August 5, Terry's command left the base camp on the Yellowstone River. Terry planned to combine his forces with those of Crook on the Rosebud River. Each day the command marched at 5:00 A.M., with the scouts in advance.[68]

On August 10, the scouts discovered George Crook's command. Crook and Terry came up with a new plan. They sent the Fifth Infantry under Colonel Nelson A. Miles to the Yellowstone River to prevent Sitting Bull from escaping across the river. Meanwhile, Terry and Crook combined their forces to pursue Crazy Horse. From then on, the Arikara scouts spent most of their time carrying dispatches between Terry, Crook, Miles, and Fort Lincoln.[69]

Because Terry's inexperienced, demoralized, and exhausted troops slowed down his advance, Crook persuaded Terry to separate their commands again. Terry would pursue Sitting Bull while Crook continued his pursuit of Crazy Horse. Six Arikara scouts joined Crook. They were Soldier, Black Fox, Charging-up-the-Hill, Boy Chief, Young Hawk, and Running Wolf. Ca-roo, a Sioux scout, also accompanied them.[70]

Terry's campaign was a failure. On August 31, Sitting Bull crossed the Missouri River near Fort Berthold. Terry immediately sent Reno and some Arikara scouts in pursuit. By the time Reno and the scouts reached Fort Berthold, however, Sitting

Bull had already crossed the border into Canada. On September 3, Reno and the scouts returned from their mission and rejoined Terry's command. Two days later, having failed to capture Sitting Bull, Terry abandoned the campaign and sent the scouts back to Fort Lincoln.[71]

The scouts with General Crook, meanwhile, scoured the country in search of Crazy Horse. They were getting closer. On the night of September 3, while the scouts were sitting down for dinner, eight Lakhota warriors suddenly appeared in their camp. A fight ensued, but the Lakhotas escaped into the darkness. None of the scouts were wounded. Two days later, the scouts discovered a band of Lakhotas, consisting of ten warriors and twenty women and children, in the distance. They immediately started their horses in pursuit, chased the Lakhotas for five miles, and killed one of them.[72]

Crook was pleased with the service of the Arikara scouts, but he was fast running out of supplies. On September 6 he decided to follow a trail leading into the Black Hills. He sent the Arikara scouts back to Fort Lincoln with a letter to inform General Sheridan of his plan. This ended the involvement of the Arikara scouts in Crook's campaign. They played no part in the Battle of Slim Buttes on September 9, 1876, when Crook's troops surprised a small Lakhota camp near Slim Buttes, South Dakota. This small victory boosted soldiers' morale, but it would have been impossible without help from the Arikara scouts, who, according to Crook's aide-de-camp John Bourke, had "proved to be of great service while with our column." Undoubtedly, it was some consolation for the scouts that they were spared the subsequent "starvation march" with Crook's troops.[73]

The Arikara scouts were called into action one more time that year. In October 1876, they accompanied General Terry and the Seventh Cavalry from Fort Lincoln as part of General Sheridan's plan to dismount and disarm the Sioux at the Standing Rock Agency. The records do not list the names of the Arikara scouts who accompanied Terry, but the register of enlistments shows that some thirty-two scouts served at Fort Lincoln at this time. Undoubtedly, the Arikaras were anxious to avenge the deaths of their comrades at the Little Bighorn.[74]

The mission was conducted in great secrecy and was a great success. Terry's troops successfully surrounded the Sioux camps at Standing Rock. Then he sent in the Arikara scouts, who according to one witness lashed their ponies "into a mad run" and rode into the camps yelling with great delight "at the discomfiture of their hereditary foes." Although they did not get to take scalps in revenge, the scouts apparently "took delight in doing all the mischief possible." Instead of entering a tipi through the door, they would "slash an opening with their knives, and [they] did not hesitate to destroy all the property possible."[75]

An Arikara scout, most likely Red Bear, meeting Colonel William Babcock Hazen. Red Bear's arms are marked with coup strikes. His robe depicts that he suffered four bullet wounds and captured seven horses, as indicated by the quirts at the bottom of the robe. Hazen (1830–1887) served as commanding officer at Fort Buford at various times between 1872 and 1880. A bullet wound sustained in an encounter with Comanches in 1859 forced him to walk with a cane later in life. National Anthropological Archives, Smithsonian Institution, MS 154064B #08510605.

At the end of the surround, the scouts gathered up twenty-five hundred ponies and a large number of guns. The operation had taken the Standing Rock Sioux completely by surprise, but there were no casualties on either side.[76] Similar operations were staged elsewhere. Pawnee scouts under Major Frank North disarmed the Oglalas, led by Chiefs Red Cloud and Red Leaf, in northwestern Nebraska. By the end of October, the first part of Sheridan's plan had been executed successfully.

In the fall and winter of 1876–77, the army launched several successful attacks against the resisting Lakhotas and Cheyennes. Colonel Ranald S. Mackenzie defeated the Northern Cheyennes at the Red Fork of the Powder River on November 25. Colonel Nelson A. Miles engaged the Lakhotas at Cedar Creek (October 21), Ash Creek (December 18), and Wolf Mountain (January 8). The Arikara scouts were only indirectly involved in these battles, as mail carriers between the various posts from which some of the expeditions were launched. As a result of the army's pressures, most of the Lakhotas and Cheyennes surrendered at the various agencies in 1877. Little Wolf and Dull Knife of the Northern Cheyennes surrendered at Fort Robinson, Nebraska, in early 1877. Crazy Horse surrendered at Fort Robinson on May 6. Only Sitting Bull was still at large, living in exile in Canada with his followers.

Although the Sioux War had effectively come to an end in 1877, some Arikara scouts remained in service until 1882. Bear's Eye, Big John, Eagle Tail, Left Hand, Little Soldier, Only Brave, Vermillion, White Breasted Rat, Little Sioux, and Young War Eagle periodically served at the various forts in the area. They also patrolled the US–Canadian border to prevent Sitting Bull's followers from raiding in the United States. Mainly, however, they served as couriers between troops in the field and the military posts. Little Sioux, for example, earned $25 a month carrying mail for the army between 1878 and 1882.[77]

When Sitting Bull fled to Canada, the Canadian government allowed him to stay on the condition that he remained peaceful. But there was little to eat and life was hard for the exiles. Occasionally, Sitting Bull's warriors crossed the border to hunt buffalo or steal horses in the United States. More and more chiefs and headmen decided to surrender and return home. Spotted Eagle of the Sans Arcs band was the first. Gall surrendered with his followers in January 1881. Finally, on July 17, 1881, Sitting Bull surrendered with 187 followers at Fort Buford, Dakota Territory.

THE HARD ROAD TO PEACE

Arikara military service increased pressure on the Sioux, prompting various Sioux bands to negotiate with the Arikaras in the 1870s. The US Army often acted as a mediator in these peace talks. On July 11, 1870, for example, the three tribes concluded a peace with the Sissetons, a branch of the Santee Sioux who lived in the vicinity of Fort Totten. White Shield, Rushing Bear, and the chiefs of the Mandans and Hidatsas welcomed Sisseton chief Tepe Wasta and head soldier Ompe Okaga at Fort Berthold. After a brief council, both sides pledged to restrain their warriors from committing depredations and promised to pay compensations for theft, destruction of property, injury, and murder. If they were unable to provide adequate compensation, the chiefs agreed to surrender the offenders to US authorities to be tried and punished according to law.[78]

More significant were talks between the three tribes and Yanktonai chief Two Bears one week later at Fort Stevenson. A few chiefs of the Hunkpapas, Sans Arcs, and Blackfeet Sioux were also present. White Shield opened the talks with a strong condemnation of the Yanktonai chiefs, who often talked of peace but could not control their young men who violated agreements. He accused Two Bears of not being a real chief because his warriors would not listen to him.[79] Not believing that these Sioux were serious about peace, White Shield and the other chiefs nevertheless signed the treaty on July 17, 1870.[80]

White Shield's concerns came true a few weeks later when a Yanktonais faction attacked a group of Mandans. The chiefs complained that the government's attempt to "buy the good will of the Sioux" with presents was failing. White Shield advocated a more confrontational policy instead. The Great Father, he said, could put an end to Sioux hostility through swift and severe military action. Instead, the United States had tied the hands of the three tribes. "Before agents were sent to us we could hold our own against the Sioux," White Shield said, "but now when we listen to the whites we have to sit in our villages, listen to [Sioux] insults, and have our young men killed and our horses stolen, within sight of our lodges." He concluded that the Sioux "will never listen to the 'Great Father' until the soldiers stick their bayonets in their ears and make them."[81]

In 1874 a new attempt at peace was made with the Yanktonais at Fort Lincoln. This time the three tribes had the support of Lieutenant Colonel George A. Custer, who opened the talks. "What I desire you to understand," Custer told the Sioux delegates, "is that the Rees are not only warm and faithful friends to the whites, but that many of their chiefs and warriors as you may see here, have become soldiers of the 'Great Father,' and having done this, we look upon them not only as good friends but as brothers." He continued, "Whoever makes war upon the Rees will be considered making war upon the 'Great Father' and his children." Custer warned the Sioux that if they attacked the Arikara scouts, he would "follow them and kill them, even if their trail leads us to the doors of their agencies."[82] The following year, the talks were concluded with a new treaty signed at Fort Lincoln on May 29, 1875. This treaty proved more lasting than the previous agreement.[83]

By breaking the power of the Lakhotas, the war of 1876–77 was the most significant turning point in Arikara–Sioux relations. Although the specter of Sitting Bull across the Canadian border continued to concern the Fort Berthold tribes, relations between the Arikaras and the other Sioux bands normalized with surprising rapidity.[84] In fact, Sioux and Arikara delegations visited each other so frequently that Indian agent William Courtenay curtailed these visits in 1879. The Sioux and Arikaras grudgingly submitted to Courtenay's order.[85]

ARIKARA AMERICAN PATRIOTS

Sitting Bull's 1881 surrender at Fort Buford ended nearly two centuries of warfare between the Sioux and the Arikaras. Historians have often downplayed contributions made by the Arikara scouts in the Indian Wars of the northern plains. For these scouts, the alliance with the US Army was a matter of survival. Although the Battle of the Little Bighorn had ended in disaster, the scouts had enjoyed strategic success by taking the war away from their towns and into Sioux territory. By joining the army, the scouts had placed the Sioux on the defensive. Through the sacrifices of men like Bloody Knife, Little Brave, and Bobtailed Bull, their people were safer at home. Therefore, even after the Battle of the Little Bighorn, the scouts continued to serve faithfully with the army.

Scout service reinforced Arikara martial culture. Although the use of Native scouts was sometimes justified as a way to impart Euro-American discipline and "civilization" to Indians, the Arikaras did not see it in these terms. Instead they entered battle in Arikara fashion, albeit with arms provided by the Great Father.

Today the graves of the scouts are in a cemetery near White Shield, North Dakota. Each year on Veteran's Day, the Arikaras commemorate the sacrifices made by the scouts and other Arikaras who served in later wars. They remember the scouts as the first true Arikara-American patriots.

9 DEFENDING ARIKARA LAND AND CULTURE, 1864-1900

> The Indian must conform to "the white man's ways," peaceably if they will, forcibly if they must.... They can not escape it, and must either conform to it or be crushed by it.
>
> —THOMAS J. MORGAN, COMMISSIONER OF INDIAN AFFAIRS, OCTOBER 1, 1889.[1]

> They listen attentively and then immediately disobey.
>
> —DR. JOSIAH JANNEY BEST, AGENCY PHYSICIAN, 1889.[2]

In 1903, White Bear told the story of how he became a member of the powerful Arikara Bear Society. Among his prized possessions was a hide he had taken off a bear cub. His father, Strikes Enemy, had tanned and painted the hide for him. "I wore it in dances and kept it by my pillow in our lodge," White Bear said. Strikes Enemy had been proud when his son joined the Bear Society. "I was glad of this and encouraged the boy to remain in the lodge," Strikes Enemy said. But reservation life and government policies changed matters at Fort Berthold. Under pressure from white agents, White Bear's society became inactive. Strikes Enemy lamented the loss of culture. Pointing at his son, Strikes Enemy said, "He is a Bear by birth, but as we now have no more Bear dances, he does not show the ways of a bear." Around 1900, Strikes Enemy sold his son's bear hide to a white man. When White Bear returned home from a visit to the Sioux, he noticed the hide was missing. His parents told him they had sold it. "I was sorry," White Bear said, "but it was all right, for we do not have any more Bear dances."[3]

The account showed that life was changing on the Fort Berthold reservation. White Bear was one of many young people losing Arikara ways. The episode also shows a rift between the generations: White Bear's neglect of his responsibilities as a member of the Bear Society prompted his father to sell one of the symbols of his office. Other families told similar stories.

After the Sioux threat had been removed, the Arikaras confronted a danger of a different kind. In the 1870s and 1880s, the US government began to nibble away at both Arikara land and Arikara cultural practices. The government's assault on tribal land was accomplished through a series of agreements, most of which were simply imposed upon the Arikaras or made through extortion. Next was a policy designed to destroy Arikara ways and traditions in favor of Euro-American culture. Using new instruments such as schools, missions, and the Court of Indian Offenses, these "civilization policies" undermined traditional positions of chiefs, priests, and doctors and sought to abolish traditional Arikara marriage practices, social and ceremonial dances, and educational customs.

The Arikara response to these acculturation pressures was mixed. Some accepted change while others rejected it. Most simply sought the best of both worlds. Whatever the response of the Arikaras, government officials, teachers, missionaries, and other agents of change were never satisfied and impatiently called on the Arikaras to change faster.

"WE WANT A NEW TREATY WITH OUR GREAT FATHER": THE TREATY OF 1866

In the mid-1860s, as a result of Sioux pressure and diminishing resources, the Arikaras suffered from shortages of food, clothing, guns, and ammunition. White Shield's calls for help fell on deaf ears in the Indian Office. Although the commissioner of Indian affairs published White Shield's letter to President Lincoln of July 2, 1864, in his annual report to the secretary of the interior, the letter never received any serious consideration.[4]

Compounding the problems were corrupt Indian agents who defrauded the Arikaras of their annuity payments. When Chief White Shield accused Agent Mahlon Wilkinson of theft, Wilkinson responded by deposing White Shield as head chief in favor of Rushing Bear. Iron Bear, the head chief of the warriors, took over Rushing Bear's old position. In reality, however, Rushing Bear and the other Arikaras continued to defer to White Shield.[5] Because of their opposition to his administration, Wilkinson suggested to his superiors in Washington that the Arikaras be removed to join the Pawnees. His plea was unsuccessful.[6]

Pressure was building on the Arikaras from all sides. Congress planned to end annuity payments as agreed upon in the Fort Laramie Treaty of 1851. White Shield and the other chiefs requested a new agreement with the government to secure new annuities for their people.[7] Worse, that same year warfare with the Sioux resumed.[8]

White Shield's request came at an opportune time for the government. Anticipating increased travel across the northern plains to the Montana goldfields, the government wanted to obtain permission from the tribes to build a road across tribal land. In July 1866, a government delegation that included territorial governor Newton Edmunds and Major General Samuel R. Curtis arrived at Fort Berthold to discuss acquisition of land for the new road, supply stations, and a military fort and depot. White Shield, Rushing Bear, and the chiefs of the Mandans and Hidatsas welcomed them. On July 23, the parties met for the first time in the Arikara medicine lodge. White Shield, Rushing Bear, Iron Bear, and Yellow Knife were the principal speakers for the Arikaras.[9]

After the commissioners expressed their wishes, White Shield voiced his concern that the new road would disturb the buffalo herds. If the road was to be built, he said, his people should be compensated. He also pointed out that the term of annuity payments had been changed from fifty to ten and then fifteen years and that each year payments had gotten progressively smaller. Cheating traders stole annuities to sell them to tribes elsewhere.[10] Meanwhile, Canadian Indians were trespassing on Arikara territory to hunt buffalo, and the Sioux continued to wage war while the troops did little to stop them.[11] "We have always obeyed our Great Father and [have] been furnished with no arms, while our enemies [who] have continually done wrong, have plenty of ammunition," White Shield said. "Our enemies are strong in numbers and besides are well armed; all we want is guns and ammunition to take care of ourselves against our foes."[12]

Rushing Bear pointed out that the Great Father had told them not to make war against the Sioux, but the Sioux were never punished for depredations against the Arikaras. He demanded compensation for these losses: "They steal our horses and we do not pursue them because the Great Father does not want us to fight. Will you promise to bring back the ponies which they have stolen?" Like White Shield, he demanded more guns and ammunition for defense. He also wanted cattle to feed his people. "We all nearly starved last winter," he said. "That is the reason I want the cattle so I can eat them when the buffalo are scarce."[13]

Apart from guns, ammunition, and cattle, the chiefs wanted clothing for their people, a blacksmith to mend guns and fashion tools, educators so their children could read the treaties they had signed, and compensation for losses caused by steamboats and travelers. Iron Bear also insisted that the sale of liquor to young men by travelers should be forbidden. Foremost on their agenda, however, was protection against the Sioux.¹⁴

On the second day of the negotiations, a Sioux war party attacked Like-A-Fishhook just as the delegates sat down to resume talks. The council immediately adjourned and the chiefs prepared for battle. In the fight, the Arikara, Mandan, and Hidatsa warriors took five scalps and drove the Sioux away. The attack was a major embarrassment for the commissioners. They had been discouraging the tribes from making war on the Sioux but now learned that the Sioux were the main instigators and aggressors. "We approve your conduct [in chasing the attackers]," Governor Edmunds was forced to admit the next day. "You are right in defending your property, wives, and children." Nevertheless, Edmunds called upon the Arikaras to refrain from sending out revenge expeditions.¹⁵

On July 26, the commissioners announced that they wanted to purchase land for the road. The announcement surprised White Shield. "I did not expect that our Great Father would demand our lands but expected he would give us presents for our good behavior," he said. Nevertheless, he was willing to sell some land they had abandoned on the lower parts of the reservation, but he wanted fair compensation. The Mandan and Hidatsa chiefs, however, were not willing to sell at all.

By now the commissioners were becoming impatient. Annoyed with the position of the Mandan and Hidatsa chiefs, they increased the pressure. Curtis stated bluntly that if the tribes did not want to sell the lands, it did not matter, for the Great Father "goes with his roads where he pleases, whether the land belongs to the white man or the red man." Edmunds went a step further and threatened that if the chiefs did not sign the treaty, the government would not assist them against the Sioux: "We have made a treaty with the Sioux, binding them to be friends who make peace with us; and if you refuse to treat with us they will come and fight you." He added that the tribes would be at a disadvantage because "the Great Father having made a treaty with the Sioux he will send them goods, blankets, guns, powder and provisions, but having no treaty with you he can send you none of these things."¹⁶

Blackmailed by the commissioners, White Shield and Rushing Bear were forced to give up their resistance. On July 27, while the Mandans and Hidatsas still debated their response, the Arikara chiefs reluctantly signed the treaty.

Apart from the usual clauses concerning peace, trade, and the punishment for treaty violations, the treaty granted the United States "the right to lay out and construct roads, highways, and telegraphs" through Arikara country. In return, the government promised to pay the tribe $10,000 annually for twenty years. The money was to be spent at the president's discretion for the purchase of animal stock, agricultural implements, education, health care, and other programs. The head chief of the tribe would receive $200 annually, and each "soldier chief" would get $50. Several days later, the Mandans and Hidatsas also signed the treaty.[17]

For reasons not entirely clear, Congress never ratified the 1866 treaty. Historian Roy W. Meyer explained Congress's reluctance: the treaty "involved the cession of lands to which the Indians' claim had never been recognized." In any case, the government did pay the annuities over the following years. Although this may appear as government waste of taxpayers' money, the threat of withholding annuity payments provided the Indian Office with a convenient tool with which to control and manipulate the chiefs.[18]

ESTABLISHMENT OF THE FORT BERTHOLD RESERVATION

Although the Fort Laramie Treaty of 1851 had outlined the territorial claims of the three tribes, it had not established a formal reservation. As more and more white people passed through or settled in the area, the three tribes began to complain that these strangers stole their timber and chased game away. They desired a formal reservation for their exclusive use. In September 1869, the chiefs met with Captain S. A. Wainwright of the Twenty-Second Infantry Regiment to establish the boundaries of the reservation. After the approval of the new reservation boundaries by the secretary of the interior, President Ulysses S. Grant formally established the Fort Berthold Reservation by executive order on April 12, 1870.[19]

The Sioux did not recognize the new reservation boundaries and continued to hunt on land of the three tribes and to send war parties against the people at Fort Berthold. To protect the Arikaras, Agent Lyman B. Sperry suggested in 1873 moving the Arikaras to Indian Territory, where they could join their Pawnee cousins. In 1874, Chiefs Rushing Bear, Black Fox, and Bull Head traveled to Washington to discuss removal with President Grant. On their way to the capital they stopped in Indian Territory to talk with the Pawnee chiefs. After their visit, they informed Sperry that they did not want to move south; they said the climate was too warm for their people and that the journey would be too taxing for old people, infants, and the infirm. Undoubtedly, the tragic experience of the Pawnees, who had moved a year before, was a major factor in their decision. Above all, they were unwilling to depart from the Missouri River. There was a deep spiritual connection between the Arikaras, the river, and the surrounding land that agents simply did not understand.

Fort Berthold delegation to Washington, 1874. Sitting: Dancing Flag (Mandan), Rushing War Eagle (Mandan), Rushing Bear (Son of Star; Arikara), Bull Head (Arikara), and Black Fox (Arikara). Standing: Running Face (Mandan), Charles Packineau, unknown (sometimes listed as Peter Beauchamp Sr.), and Peter Beauchamp (Arikara interpreter). NARA RG106, 19–1307a.

Rushing Bear told Sperry that they preferred to remain on the Missouri River even if it meant they had to "work harder and have less."[20]

Rushing Bear defended his position to government officials in Washington. A few days later, the delegates returned home. They left Washington without any firm concessions for economic and military assistance, but removal to Indian Territory was off the table. Rushing Bear had achieved a diplomatic victory, although the government's decision may have been based on the fact that Arikara scouts were needed for the upcoming war against the Sioux.[21]

The Indian Appropriation Act of March 3, 1871, seriously weakened the position of the chiefs by abolishing the treaty-making system. In effect, Congress now reserved the right to make decisions affecting Indian peoples without consulting the chiefs first. Although the government continued to call on the chiefs to negotiate agreements, it technically no longer needed their approval.[22] In 1880 the government applied this principle to the Fort Berthold tribes. It stripped the Fort Berthold Reservation of a large part of its territory to make room for the Northern Pacific Railroad. In compensation the government added a smaller tract of land on the northeast side of the reservation. But this land was much less valuable than the land they lost in the involuntary cession. Despite their objections, the change went into effect through executive order, signed by President Rutherford B. Hayes on July 13, 1880.[23]

Because the tribes did not use the land they received in the exchange of 1880, Agent Abram J. Gifford urged them to sell this tract to the government. Strapped for financial help, the chiefs agreed and offered a large western section of the reservation in the sale as well. In December 1886, the tribes gave up nearly two-thirds of their 2.9 million–acre reservation in exchange for $80,000 annually for ten years in the form of supplies, schools, and other facilities. The agreement also contained provisions for allotment of the reservation. The surplus land that remained after allotment would remain in possession of the three tribes. Even though the agreement had the support of the three tribes, Congress did not ratify it until May 20, 1891, when President Benjamin Harrison formally signed it into law. In 1892 a small portion of land was added to the Fort Berthold Reservation to reattach agency buildings that had been accidentally included in the 1891 cession. However, that same year the government moved the agency buildings to a new site on the Missouri River named Elbowoods. The reservation had now basically reached its final boundaries.[24]

HOW THE RABBIT SAVED A WARRIOR

With Sitting Bull hiding in Canada, warfare with the Sioux had effectively ended by 1877. Nevertheless, North Dakota was still a dangerous place. The Turtle Mountain Chippewas briefly replaced the Sioux as a major nuisance. These Indians did not have a reservation yet and thus frequently border-hopped into Canada. On August 28, 1880, they attacked a local Indian named Walking Wolf who had been herding horses some sixty miles from the Indian agency of Fort Berthold. The three tribes responded by fielding an expedition of fifty men, who caught up with the Chippewas before they could sneak across the Canadian border. The two sides engaged in a pitched battle. Five Fort Berthold Indians were killed in the fight, and six more were wounded. Fort Berthold agent Jacob Kauffman, who reported the incident, was unable to determine the casualties among the Chippewas, but his Indians claimed to have driven them from the field.[25]

In 1903 Elk gave an account of these events. Several Arikaras were wounded in the fight with the horse thieves, he said. A bullet passed clear through the neck of one of the men. This man expected to die from loss of blood. As he lay dying, he saw a jackrabbit. It spoke to him: "You are not to die; you are to live." After the battle, the man was brought back to town and taken into the medicine lodge. Here a Rabbit Society medicine man attended him. Four days later the man was up and moving again. He became one of the leading doctors of the Rabbit Medicine Society and lived to old age. He died only a few years before Elk told his tale.[26]

Elk's account shows that Arikara beliefs in the traditional supernatural powers remained strong despite the presence of Christian missionaries, who first arrived among the three tribes in 1876. The story also shows how closely oral history accounts resemble oral traditions.

The murder of Walking Wolf by raiders coming from Canada and the subsequent Arikara attack against a Chippewa wagon train caused a brief but sharp diplomatic exchange between the US State Department and British authorities. But Arikara relations with the Turtle Mountain Chippewas improved after the latter received a reservation near the Canadian border in north-central North Dakota in 1882.

Two years after the fight with the Chippewas, the Arikaras nearly came to blows with a small band of Lakhotas. Both the Arikaras and the Lakhotas were out hunting about fifty miles east of Slim Buttes, South Dakota, when a Lakhota went missing. The Lakhotas accused the Arikaras of killing him. Both parties hastily prepared for battle. At the last minute, a Lakhota by the name of Running Antelope advanced toward the Arikaras holding a quill-ornamented peace pipe. The pipe was more sacred to Indians than a white flag of truce was to white soldiers. Running Antelope lit the pipe and raised it toward the north, east, south, and west, and then toward the earth and sky. As he advanced, he held the pipe's stem in the direction of the Arikaras, who had dismounted and held their muskets ready for battle. About this time, an Arikara whose name is unfortunately not recorded went through the same ceremony and advanced with his pipe to meet Running Antelope. The two men crossed the pipes, "scissor fashion." With peace now made, both sides discussed the matter and settled all difficulties.[27]

ADJUSTING TO LIFE AT FORT BERTHOLD INDIAN RESERVATION

In the spring of 1885, the Arikaras abandoned Like-A-Fishhook and built a new settlement several miles away. The reason for the move was that many of the lodges were too old and dilapidated to be repaired. Furthermore, the Sioux no longer threatened the people. Finally, the independent-minded Arikaras also wished to create some distance from their Mandan and Hidatsa neighbors. Agent Abram J. Gifford provided an extra incentive by giving horse teams and farming implements to those who left. The Mandans and Hidatsas soon followed the example of the Arikaras. After they left Like-a-Fishhook, Gifford ordered the destruction of their abandoned earth lodges.[28]

The Arikaras established several small settlements in the eastern district of the reservation. The main Arikara settlement was eventually called Armstrong, after Assistant Commissioner of Indian Affairs Frank C. Armstrong, under whose direction a school was built in 1894. The town was quite different in appearance from Like-A-Fishhook. Most people abandoned earth lodges and built log cabins instead. It was no longer necessary to build the houses close together or to surround them with a moat and palisade. Still, in 1888 the Arikaras completed the construction of a sacred lodge, showing that the old traditions were not forgotten despite the adoption of Euro-American housing styles. [29]

The strength of Native ideas was also exemplified by the Arikara adoption of the grass dance in the late 1870s. The origin of this warrior dance is obscure, but the Arikara version was heavily influenced by the Pawnees. Enemy Heart, an Arikara, was one of the principal instigators of the grass dance movement. He learned thirty-eight songs from a visiting Pawnee named Running Scout (also known as Pawnee Tom) and another set of songs from a Pawnee named Crazy Horse. Enemy Heart later sold the dance to the Crows and then to other tribes. While visiting the Pawnees in the early 1900s, another Arikara, Bear Goes Out (also called Ray Gough), learned the Pawnee origin myth of the dance. It told of a poor young man who was taken into an animal lodge, where the eagles and crows taught him the dance and songs of the society. The songs that formed the core of the grass dance are today called the Pawnee Songs, to distinguish them from a number of grass dance songs that were dreamed up by Red Star and Crow Ghost, both Arikaras, in the early 1900s.[30]

The grass dance had several distinct features. As part of the dance, the Pawnees served a kettle of dog meat and reenacted elements from battle. Four dancers wearing feather belts "scouted for" and "captured" the kettle. The leading scout counted coup on the dog's head. The dancers performed a similar act with a kettle of corn. The dance was supervised by several whip bearers, whose task was to prod tired dancers back into the circle. Among the Pawnees, whip bearers often carried swords that had been presented to Indians who had scouted for the army. Many of the old Arikara scouts also owned swords and treasured them as emblems of honor.[31] The Arikara grass dance underwent subsequent transformations. The baby grass dance (*haaNUtpiiraáu'*) was one of its incarnations. In the late 1800s, the Big Grass Society (HaanUtkúsu') became the dominant group in Arikara social and political life.[32] But Indian agents discouraged any expression of Native customs.

"THEY ARE ESSENTIALLY CONSERVATIVE, AND CLING TENACIOUSLY TO OLD CUSTOMS": THE GOVERNMENT'S "CIVILIZATION" PROGRAM

In the late 1880s, the government stepped up its efforts to eradicate Native American cultures. Its "civilization" policies were characterized by ethnocentrism, paternalism, and capitalism. Believing that acculturation was necessary for Indian people to survive, the Office of Indian Affairs adopted policies designed to eradicate Native forms of cultural and religious expression. "The Indian must conform to 'the white man's ways,' peaceably if they will, forcibly if they must" said Commissioner of Indian Affairs Thomas J. Morgan in 1889.[33]

Fort Berthold agents strongly supported the new policies. Agent William Courtenay believed that the tribes under his care had to change or perish, but he also recognized that the three tribes would not relinquish their traditional ways easily: "Indians are essentially conservative, and cling tenaciously to old customs and hate all changes," he wrote as early as 1879. Courtenay advocated policies designed to break up tribes by scattering the people onto allotments, abolishing Indian dances and ceremonies, and "compel[ling] them to labor or accept the alternative of starvation."[34]

How abolishing their dances and changing their religion would save the Arikaras from starvation, Courtenay and the other proponents of "civilization" never explained. But Indian agents did use the threat of starvation by withholding annuities to pressure Arikaras who rejected the civilization program.

To break Arikara resistance, the Indian Office sought to undermine the position of the chiefs. The position of head chief in Arikara society had been instituted by Neešaanu. The people looked to the chief for guidance, and his word carried the weight of law. Theoretically, he had dictatorial powers, but in reality he keenly kept the interests and desires of his people above his own. His was an important position. Through wisdom, strength, and diplomacy, he held the people together. The love the Arikara people felt for wise leaders like White Shield and Rushing Bear was genuine and heartfelt.[35]

Until 1871, agents tolerated chiefs because they could sign treaties and help enforce policies of the Indian Office. The Indian Appropriation Act abolished the treaty-making system and seriously weakened the position of chiefs. Although the government continued to call on chiefs to negotiate agreements, it technically no longer needed their approval.[36] Agents also undermined chiefs by distributing annuity goods directly to the people. Customarily this work had been the prerogative of the chiefs and confirmed their position as benefactors and providers for the tribe. Now the agent acted as provider and effectively as chief. In 1876 Agent Charles W. Darling reported that chiefs heavily criticized his policy of distributing annuities directly to the people. "It has done much to break up tribal relations," Darling wrote, "and there is a growing tendency on the part of the more intelligent to independence of thought and freedom from control of the chiefs."[37]

Apart from undermining the position of the chiefs, government agents also discouraged Indian dances. The Arikaras danced not only for their enjoyment but also as a form of religious expression. In the mid-1880s, the Office of Indian Affairs began to suppress Indian dances by withholding rations. Among the sacred dances that came under attack were those organized by the doctor, or medicine lodge, societies. Believing that these magical performances had a negative impact on the people at Fort Berthold, the agents banned them. By the time photographer Edward S. Curtis visited Fort Berthold in 1908, the Arikaras had not performed their magic at the medicine lodge ceremony for nearly two decades.[38]

Agents and missionaries targeted social dances as well. They objected to the grass dance because participants wore Indian dress, told war stories, and supposedly engaged in "promiscuous" activities. They also complained that dances resulted in the loss of productivity and kept the Arikaras from observing the sabbath.[39]

The Arikaras refused to give up social dances despite threats to withhold rations. Agency physician Josiah Best wrote in 1889 that it was "almost as easy to bridge the Atlantic Ocean as it is to get them to relinquish the heathenish custom." What particularly bothered agency officials was that Indians who had been educated at boarding schools often took the lead in organizing dances. Although they failed to abolish social dances altogether, government agents were able to limit their frequency.[40]

Agents also cracked down on Arikara marriage practices. They dismissed Arikara traditions of plural marriage as well as the relative ease with which couples separated.[41] In reality, most Arikara marriages consisted of loving couples who shared the burden of raising a family. Other stresses on family life, such as economic depression and long-term separation as a result of seasonal off-reservation work, must be taken into account in explaining the relatively high divorce rates.

To fight polygyny, agents enlisted the assistance of the Court of Indian Offenses. The measure seemed effective. In 1885 Agent Abram J. Gifford wrote that polygyny "is gradually disappearing as the result of our Indian court of offenses, and I am confident that in the course of a few years this practice will be entirely abolished, as this evil is confined almost entirely to those of somewhat advanced age, and who will soon pass out of existence."[42] Five years later, Agent John S. Murphy reported only four cases of polygyny on the entire reservation. But Murphy also noted, "Divorce has been of frequent occurrence, but I discourage such actions."[43] Four years later, Agent A. H. Clapp reported, "Plural wives are now unknown on the reservation [and] as a rule, the women are virtuous, and immorality, with its consequent train of diseases, is growing less each year."[44] Agents continued to discourage divorces and would threaten to withhold rations if a couple insisted on a divorce.

While agents prided themselves on having overturned the practice of polygyny, other factors, such as the disappearance of buffalo and the end of intertribal warfare, were more significant. Male mortality rates dropped, and disparities in wealth disappeared in the reservation economy of the late 1800s, so there was no longer a socioeconomic need for plural marriages.

The influence of government officials over family life also extended to Indian children. Missionaries and government agents gave Indian children Anglicized and Christian names. When Best was called to check on an Indian boy born on February 22, 1889, he named it George Washington. "I am going to name every one I can," Best wrote to his wife, "so that they won't give them Indian names." By bestowing English names on Indian children, agents symbolically changed the identity of individuals.[45]

Best and other agency doctors also set out to break the power of Arikara healers. They discredited Arikara tribal medical practices as unscientific and detrimental to health. Best believed that Arikara medicine men deceived their patients to improve their own status in the community. The "first blow made to the civilization of the Indian," Best argued, "must be at the 'medicine men.'"[46]

In reality, the state of white medicine was quite primitive at this time. Most white physicians were unfamiliar with germ theory and failed to recognize malnutrition as one of the leading causes of health problems on the reservation. Physicians often misdiagnosed their patients and blamed ailments on the Indians themselves rather than on external factors. To break the power of medicine men, agency physicians urged the construction of a hospital at Fort Berthold, which would not only allow them to provide better care for their patients but would also keep patients away from the influence of medicine men.[47]

Although agency physicians often claimed they had undermined the authority and power of native healers, the Arikaras continued to consult their own doctors. Even though, gradually, more and more patients called upon agency physicians for help, their belief in traditional medicine remained strong. The Arikaras did not regard white medicine as a replacement for but rather as a supplement to traditional Arikara medicine. As late as 1911, Arikara spokesman Red Bear stated before the Board of Indian Commissioners that the Arikaras continued to trust their own ways of healing. According to Red Bear, a former Arikara scout, Neešaanu had given the people medicines to cure themselves. "Our medicine has been proven in the generations gone," he said. "We used this medicine ... and it healed us, and that's why we try to keep this medicine, because we have proved it among ourselves." He added that "white men think there is something wrong with this medicine, but we know it is right."[48]

Despite the presence of white doctors, mortality rates among the three tribes remained high. In the winter of 1880–81, missionary Charles Hall reported that twenty-five or thirty Indians died from tuberculosis, "most of them children." Seven years later, he reported an epidemic of erysipelas and pneumonia that was fatal to a large number of Indians at Fort Berthold. The epidemic caused a panic among some. Several patients were abandoned by friends, who were afraid to attend them. At the end of the epidemic, more than forty people had died. The next year, 1889, measles broke out, "proving fatal in many cases." In most of these cases, agency doctors were unable to provide relief. Although they firmly believed in the superiority of white medicine, agency doctors were often powerless and unable to explain the causes of certain diseases. Consequently, Arikara belief in witchcraft remained strong.[49]

The Court of Indian Offenses at Fort Berthold assisted agents in combating Arikara dances, plural marriages, religious ceremonies, and Native medical practices. The court consisted of three Indian judges, one from each tribe. They were selected by the agent. The court not only tried and punished Indians who had violated "rules of morality" but also settled disputes between tribal members. The court met regularly, usually on ration days, when everybody traveled to the agency to pick up their supplies.[50]

The court was assisted by tribal policemen, who reported violations and arrested lawbreakers. The tribal police force at Fort Berthold consisted of a captain, a lieutenant or sergeant, and a number of privates. They were all selected from the three tribes and placed under the command of a white agency employee, who acted as chief of police. According to Agent Thomas Jones, the officers were all "influential men among their people, [who] do not shirk duty no matter how unpleasant."[51]

Overall, the police force and the Indian court worked to the satisfaction of the agents as well as the Indian people on the reservation. The police acted as guards and preserved order when annuity payments were issued. They returned truant

Young Snake and family, circa 1900–10. Young Snake here wears the uniform and sidearm of an Indian police officer. Police officers were charged with carrying out the policies of Indian agents but often served as mediators between the people and government officials. State Historical Society of North Dakota, A0150-00003-2.

children to schools, searched for lost property, and arrested horse and cattle thieves, whiskey sellers, and trespassers stealing timber. There were few troubles among the people. Public intoxication was virtually nonexistent. Agent Jacob Kauffman noted that there were few quarrels between the Indians under his care and that the Fort Berthold Indians compared favorably when judged against nearby white settlements of a similar size.[52] Because of the relative tranquility on the reservation, the agents eventually reduced the number of tribal policemen.

Although the tribal police force and the Indian court also investigated violations against "religious" and "moral" codes at Fort Berthold, their role there was much more ambiguous. After all, most officers of the court also attended religious ceremonies, consulted medicine men, and attended dances. In these cases, they were more lenient toward offenders, if they reported such cases at all.

"THE SACRED WHITE MAN HAS ONLY TO SPEAK THEIR NAMES ... AND THEY WILL DIE": CHRISTIAN MISSIONARIES AND THE ARIKARAS

Assisting the civilization program were missionaries. In May 1876, Congregational minister Charles Lemon Hall arrived at Fort Berthold. He had come to "save" the Indians and to show them the benefits of Anglo-American civilization. Like so many other devout Christians of his age, Hall believed that Indian religious practices were evil and had to be destroyed completely: "The new must take place of the old," he wrote in his diary. "There must be no compromise. It must be 'unconditional surrender,' if Christ's way is to remain pure."[53]

Although Rushing Bear and the other chiefs generously gave Hall land to build his mission, not all Indians were pleased with the missionary. Several Indians accused him of sending sickness and grasshoppers to the reservation.[54] When Hall built his house near the agency, a Hidatsa named Crow's Belly threatened to burn it down.

Hall began his work with energy and enthusiasm. With the help of two Arikara interpreters, Thick (also called Ernest Hopkins) and Bull Boy, Hall compiled an Arikara dictionary and translated Bible passages, the Ten Commandments, psalms, sermons, and hymns into Arikara.[55]

Many Arikaras objected to Hall's inflexible and uncompromising stance. Not merely content with spreading the Gospel but determined to change Native ways as well, Hall agitated against Indian dances, dress styles, marriage customs, medical practices, and even long hair on men. Many Arikaras objected to Hall's attempts to stop them from making sacrifices of calico, cloth, eagles, horses, and other objects to the supernatural powers. "I am trying to press home upon them the thought of the great sacrifice God made of his Son, making all other sacrifices useless and wrong," Hall wrote.[56]

Some Indians accused Hall of witchcraft. When White Bird, a student at Hall's mission school, fell seriously ill in 1879, his father, Spotted Horn, accused Hall of bewitching his son. "The sacred white man has only to speak their names and desire it, and they will die," Spotted Horn said. When White Bird was near death, Spotted Horn threatened to take his "tomahawk to the school-house and cut open the heads of all who are there." White Bird recovered and calm was restored.[57] Still, accusations of witchcraft continued to follow Hall over the next years.

Likewise, Hall dismissed Arikara priests and doctors as "conjurers." When an Arikara holy man died in 1891, Hall rejoiced that his secrets had died with him and that his children would be raised as Christians.[58] When attending the funeral of

Arikara headman Sharp Horn in 1888, Hall was appalled to see Arikara women making blood sacrifices in mourning. "Do you wonder," Hall wrote, "in the sight and knowledge of such things constantly going on about us that we long to push our work and do more and more to bring salvation—a new way—to this darkened people."[59]

Because he would accept nothing less than "unconditional surrender," Hall in effect prevented many Arikaras from joining his church. For years attendance at his church remained low. Curious Indians occasionally attended services to learn more about the white man's religion. Over time, more Indians regularly attended church services, but they hesitated to become actual members. In 1897, after twenty years of hard work, Hall admitted that the number of people who came in "contact with God's thought" was distressingly small. Nevertheless, he believed that much progress had been made: "In Ree and Gros Ventres [Hidatsa] we have now much Bible truth printed and taught."[60]

Apart from leading church services, Hall's assistants ran a school. Chief White Shield suggested that they provide food to attract students.[61] Following White Shield's advice, Hall's wife began to cook meals every Friday for students who had attended class all week.[62] Classes taught at the school included reading and writing English, history, geography, grammar, music, drawing, and "industrial" subjects, such as farming for boys and domestic skills for girls.[63] Student ages ranged from six to sixteen years. The grades of advancement also varied from student to student. Advanced students were often called upon to help less advanced ones.[64] Until 1900, between thirty and thirty-six students attended the school each year.[65] Many of the school's most promising students went on to boarding schools for further education.

The Congregational mission also provided basic health care. Hall and his assistants visited the old, the sick, and the dying. If any was available, they brought medication and food. Most of the time, however, they had only prayers to offer. To combat diseases, women from the mission visited homes to instruct families in basic hygiene and sanitation. In the mid-1890s, these women formed an organization called the King's Daughters. The group held weekly prayer meetings and cleaned two houses a week. Stella Bear, an Arikara and secretary of the organization, described how the members washed clothes, cleaned homes, and cooked. After they finished this work, they had supper together, "and after supper we just had a little prayer meeting in the house which we had just cleaned."[66]

To reach out to women in the community, Hall's wife and the other women of the mission organized "sewing meetings." Arikara women showed a great interest in making dresses with collars, buttons, and buttonholes. Perhaps the gifts of small quantities of sugar, coffee, tea, and biscuits induced some women to attend.[67]

Hall also constructed a small hospital. "This bodily help is indispensible to our work of saving this people here," one of Hall's assistants wrote. "They can now come to us with confidence, and abandon their medicine men."[68]

After years of tireless work, Hall recorded some modest successes. Black Fox, who had accompanied Chief Son of Star to Washington in 1874, asked Hall to baptize his baby in 1878.[69] Like most Arikaras, Black Fox attended church but was reluctant to join as a full member. Another reluctant churchgoer was Strikes Enemy, who in the late 1880s allowed Hall to conduct sabbath services in his home in the Arikara settlement some five miles from the mission.[70]

Initially the gains were small. Not until the mid-1890s did the first Arikaras become full church members. Among these were John Little Eagle and his wife, Mary. Both had attended Hall's church. In 1893 Little Eagle fell seriously ill. When Hall visited him on his sickbed, Little Eagle told him that he believed in Jesus and that he would attend services again when he got better. Later that year, on November 22, 1893, Little Eagle and Mary were married in a Christian ceremony at the Congregational church. In 1896 Little Eagle and Mary were baptized in the church. Little Eagle died not long thereafter. During his final weeks, the couple stayed with a neighbor. According to Hall, Little Eagle was tempted by an old Arikara woman to "wear his old beads and other heathen adornments," but he refused and told Hall he was ready to die. "I have one heart," he told Hall the day before he died: "I trust only in Jesus. I have said this to you often." Hall buried him on a Sunday.[71]

Another convert was Bull in the Water, a former army scout. Around 1894 he began to attend Hall's church regularly and became a staunch defender of the missionaries. When critics threatened Hall, Bull in the Water spoke up, "saying that we did not used to stand by Hall, but now it was differently; Now [Hall] is like a tree rooted deep down here." In 1896 he went before the congregation and gave his testimony of faith, signifying his full membership in the church.[72]

Yet another convert was Rough Horn, one of the leading members of the Arikara medicine societies. In 1894 he was thrown from his horse onto the frozen ground and broke his leg and some ribs. Since he was already an old man (in his late fifties), all feared for his life. First doctors from various medicine societies treated him, but they were unsuccessful. When Hall visited him on his deathbed, Rough Horn reportedly told him, "If I get better, I am coming up to join the church and unite myself with God's people." Miraculously, Rough Horn recovered. Soon he was attending morning services again. Rough Horn and Good Goods were married in the Christian way by Hall, and on January 22, 1895, they were examined before the congregation and received into the church. Later Hall baptized Rough Horn's adopted daughter.[73]

Other Arikaras who joined the church were Lena Chase and Richard Fox, who was baptized on his deathbed.[74] Many converts were former students. "Nearly one half of our present membership have been pupils in our school here or elsewhere," wrote Hall in 1896. "Four from Hampton and Carlisle, eleven from Santee, and twenty-eight from the home school."[75] Among these members were John P. Young, George K. Bassett, Stella Bear, Henry Karunach, Ernest Hopkins, and Charles Hoffman. The last two became church leaders.

Ernest Hopkins (also called Little Elk) was one of the first Arikara students to enroll at Santee Normal Training School in Nebraska. Hopkins enjoyed school and encouraged other young Arikaras to attend as well, so they could "learn how to be good men."[76] But after returning from the boarding school, he no longer felt at home among his own people. "When I went [to] my home I couldn't hardly stay [at] their house, so I go back to Mr. Hall," he wrote. He found employment at the Fort Stevenson boarding school as a teacher and organist. He also led prayer services in Arikara because the students "can understand what I say to God." At home, Hopkins was ashamed of his parents' culture. At a Fourth of July celebration in Bismarck, he watched a parade of the old Arikara scouts dressed in their Native clothes. "The White folks dress up nicely, except [the] Indian," he wrote. "I was ashamed for them, but could not help it."[77]

Another of Hall's protégés was Charles Hoffman, who after his Scottish father abandoned the family, and after his mother's death, grew up in Strikes Enemy's family. Like Hopkins, Hoffman went to Santee Normal Training School in Nebraska, where he excelled. At Santee, he published a number of traditional Arikara stories. He spent his summers working in the eastern states. In 1890 he traveled to Chicago, where he was impressed by all the tall buildings and fast-moving elevators. "Chicago is a great noisy place, and I was afraid if I stayed too long I might get crazy," he wrote. In 1894, after graduation, he returned to Elbowoods, but he found few opportunities to earn a living.[78] In fact, he noticed many returning students struggling after graduation. "After loafing and hanging round the Agency, store, or various places, and finding nothing to do in order to get a living, he feels that his education is worthless," Charles wrote. A few fortunate ones found jobs with the agency. Others became farmers, but like farmers all across the United States, they struggled due to droughts, high interest rates, and low crop prices. "If the whites have failed to farm," Hoffman wrote, "how can we expect the Indian student to be successful in farming on these poor, dry lands.[79]

Despite their struggles, Arikaras like Hopkins and Hoffman were pioneers on the Fort Berthold Reservation. Both men became important and well-respected community leaders. Hopkins became a pastor in the Arikara Congregational Church at Armstrong, while Hoffman was appointed superintendent in charge of the three tribes in 1908.[80] By 1900, when a new church building opened in Armstrong, a small but devoted Arikara Congregational community had been established.

The other main denomination on the reservation was Catholicism.[81] French fur traders had first introduced Catholicism to the Arikaras. Two eighteenth-century Arikara Catholics were Pierre and Antoine Garreau, the adopted sons of fur trader Joseph Garreau. In 1840 the Arikaras welcomed famous Belgian-born missionary Pierre-Jean DeSmet. DeSmet and his fellow *nAhkAxiikatít* ("black robes") impressed the Arikaras, who credited him with bringing rain and raising sick people to health.[82] DeSmet was also on friendly terms with White Shield and Rushing Bear.

In November 1887, Sitting Owl, Good Bear, Old Dog, and Scattered Village asked Agent Abram Gifford to ask Bishop Martin Marty of the Dakota Catholic Mission to send a missionary among them. Marty assigned Father Francis M. Craft to the post in 1888. Craft was a flamboyant character. At age ten or eleven, he had fought in the Civil War and had been wounded at Gettysburg. In 1870–71 he served in the Franco-Prussian War in Europe and then joined the Cuban war for independence. In 1876 he joined the Jesuits but later switched to the Benedictine Order. Before coming to Fort Berthold, he had served as a missionary among the Kalispel Indians in the Pacific Northwest and among the Sioux at Rosebud and Standing Rock. He was an energetic man with a remarkable talent for angering his superiors, but he appealed to the Arikaras. He sometimes incorporated Indian religious practices, including sacrificing his own blood at ceremonies.[83] One of Hall's assistants complained that many Catholic rituals and ceremonies were "very attractive to the Indian mind."[84]

Sitting Bear, who had succeeded Rushing Bear as head Arikara chief, granted Craft a site near Elbowoods for construction of the Sacred Heart Mission. To assist him with his work, Craft established an order of Indian sisters, mostly from Sioux reservations in South Dakota, although some women from Fort Berthold may have served briefly as well. Because the mission was poor, the sisters begged the three tribes for food and fuel. Craft's temperament sometimes angered the people at Fort Berthold. Frank Wells, Sitting Bear's son, wrote to the bishop, requesting a new missionary. "We would like to have a priest like they have at Standing Rock," Wells wrote. "The Priest here do nothing, only gets mad, sometimes."[85]

Although Craft established a fairly successful health clinic, his mission soon became embroiled in scandal. Some accused the sisters of sexual liaisons with agency personnel. Fearing a scandal from which the Protestant churches might benefit, the Catholic hierarchy withdrew its support from Craft and the sisters. Around 1898 they abandoned the mission. After serving as medics in Cuba during the Spanish-American War (1898), most of the sisters returned to their reservations. Craft spent the remaining years of his life as a pastor in Pennsylvania.[86]

Craft's successor at the Sacred Heart Mission was Father Joseph B. Wilhelm. Although Wilhelm established a log cabin church at the Arikara community of Nishu, he was not a successful missionary because of an unhealthy appetite for liquor. In 1900, after only two years at Fort Berthold, he was replaced.[87] The Catholic mission at Fort Berthold had made a slow start. Not until after 1900 would it begin to flourish.

MANY FATHERS: ARIKARA RESISTANCE STRATEGIES

Despite pressures to abandon traditional ways, the Arikaras managed to protect parts of their culture they held most dear. One way they resisted was to exploit frictions between different white officials at Fort Berthold. Apart from the Indian agent, whites there included Hall, the Indian trader, and the US Army at Fort Stevenson. These groups were often at odds with each other. The agent, the trader, and the missionary especially pursued different (and often selfish) interests. By appealing variably to these powerful men, Rushing Bear and other leaders were able to keep them somewhat in check.

For example, in May 1875 White Shield and Rushing Bear traveled to Fort Stevenson with head soldiers Hard Striker and Bear's Teeth to lodge a formal complaint against Agent Charles W. Darling, who had defrauded the people out of their annuities. In a letter addressed to the president of the United States, they complained that the issued rations were too small and of inferior quality and that Darling had given cowhides to the trader, who had compensated the Indians with supply checks valued at $2. "We would much prefer that the hides should be given direct to us as in the absence of buffalo we need the skins very much for manufacturing boats and to use as moccasin soles," the chiefs said. In addition, instead of delivering beef cattle on foot, Darling had the cattle butchered before delivering it to the Indians, causing unnecessary waste of heads, horns, feet, and entrails. The Arikaras concluded their petition by calling for more traders to increase competition that would lower prices.[88]

The petition had only limited effect. The next year Darling was removed as Indian agent, but he was subsequently appointed trader for the agency. In his new role, he continued to defraud the Arikaras. Still, the petition showed that the Arikaras were able to mobilize other institutions to act on their behalf.[89]

Another example of this strategy involved a scandal that broke in 1879, when Hall accused acting Indian agent William Courtenay of abuse of power, mismanagement, corruption, and loose sexual behavior involving Indians and whites. At this time, Courtenay, a former agency farmer, clerk, and physician, hoped to be appointed as the regular agent for the three tribes. Hall objected to the appointment because Courtenay was not committed enough to the civilization project. Hall persuaded Rushing Bear to mark a letter in which he objected to Courtenay's appointment of E. S. Winston as trader at Fort Berthold. Hall told Rushing Bear that Winston was a heavy drinker and a cheat. Alarmed by this news, Rushing Bear dictated a letter in which he requested that "no one be appointed here who is from the army or under army influence, or who is a drinking man, or a dishonest man." Rushing Bear worried that Winston would steal from the Indians. "They [Winston and Courtenay] ought to be kept away," he wrote. "Please send us a good true man who will help us to become like white people."[90]

Although the letter bore Rushing Bear's mark, its tone was distinctly Hall's. Hall also implored recently arrived Indian agent Thomas P. Ellis to investigate supposed sexual indelicacies between one of Winston's employees and an Indian woman nicknamed Monkey. Poor Ellis had unknowingly stepped into a hornet's nest. While the scandal was rocking his agency, he suffered a paralytic stroke and had to step down in favor of clerk Courtenay. Courtenay at once ordered agency physician Dr. James L. Neave to investigate Hall's charges that Winston's men were suffering from venereal disease, but Neave found no such evidence.[91]

Courtenay in turn saw an opportunity to put Hall on the defensive when Rushing Bear told him that Arikara students at Hall's school were taught the Indian language instead of English. Courtenay set out to investigate the matter. After speaking to Hannah Briggs, the school's teacher, Courtenay was able to report to Commissioner Ezra Ayers Hayt that the charge was based on a misunderstanding: "Son of the Star [Rushing Bear] appears to have formed the impression on which he made his complaint from a few hymns [that] have been translated into Sioux, and divine service at the school having been conducted in this language some time ago."[92]

Still, a few days after her interview with Courtenay, Briggs resigned as schoolteacher. Courtenay now suggested appointing Neave's wife or the wife of the agency issue clerk, both of whom belonged to Courtenay's inner circle. In his letter to Hayt, Courtenay noted that Indian attendance at the school was poor because the Halls repeatedly used the Sioux language in their dealings with the Indians. "The use of the Dakota tongue by Mr. and Mrs. Hall in holding divine service with the Indians and using this language in all communications with them [creates] a prejudice in the minds of these Indians," Courtenay wrote. He added, "The Arickarees especially dislike the Sioux, and at once form a prejudice against any white man who uses the

Dakota tongue in communicating with them." Apparently, the Arikaras were also suspicious of Hall's attempt to acquire "the Arickaree language." Indeed, "Son-of-the-Star . . . and other influential and leading Indians complain that the 'Great Father' did not send Mr. Hall to learn Arickaree but to teach English." They feared that knowledge of their language would put Hall into a superior position among them. Also, they feared that if Hall acquired their language, the students would not feel compelled to learn English.[93]

Perhaps Rushing Bear's insistence that students receive English instruction seems supportive of the civilization program, but in fact he wished students to learn English to gain some protection against abusive whites. After all, as the above examples show, both Hall and Courtenay often twisted the chiefs' words to support their agendas.

The scandal festered for another year. It ruined Courtenay's attempt to gain appointment as Indian agent. Likewise, Hall suffered a major blow to his reputation after he called Rushing Bear, Crow's Breast, and Bad Gun—who had on one point sided against him—the "worst" characters on the reservation."[94]

On this occasion, the chiefs threw their support behind Courtenay. They signed a petition to the Indian Office on Courtenay's behalf. Among those who signed were Rushing Bear, Black Fox, Bull Head, and Forked Horn, as well as the headmen of the Hidatsas and Mandans. "We the undersigned chiefs and head men of the Fort Berthold Agency Indians, respectfully petition that Mr. Wm. Courtenay be appointed our agent," the letter said. "We have known him for a good many years [and] we know that he tells us the truth, and that he would not steal from us . . . we have full and entire confidence in him." Then they criticized the white "Medicine Man," Hall, for failing to teach the children English. "We want the Great Father to send him away; he does us no good; we do not like him and we do not want him." Although Courtenay drafted the letter, he reportedly read it to the Indians sentence by sentence to make sure that was what they desired to say. "They were *emphatic* in saying that the paper was *their own production* and they did not want it changed," Courtenay wrote. Arikara interpreters Pierre Garreau and Peter Beauchamp also signed the statement. In a separate meeting with Indian Office inspector Robert Gardner, Rushing Bear reiterated his desire to have Courtenay assume control of the agency. "I do not speak for myself alone," he told Gardner, "but for all of my people, we all want him."[95]

Despite the chiefs' support for Courtenay, the Indian Office appointed a different agent: Jacob Kauffman. The episode shows that although the chiefs were able to voice their grievances and express their desires, their real power was limited. Still, they did not sit passively by as different "fathers" at the agency struggled with each other for power. When they wanted to complain about the agent, they appealed to the missionary. When they had grievances against the missionary, they would seek out the agent. Complaints against traders were directed to the agent or the missionary, depending on who also opposed the trader. Finally, they could appeal to the army for help.

Until they learned to speak, read, and write in English, the three tribes would be at the mercy of the agency. This fact explains why the chiefs were so anxious to have their children master the English language, for this would be the best way to communicate with the Great Father in Washington and to avoid manipulation by local white officials. Not surprisingly, the chiefs almost always preferred to speak directly to the Great Father in person. On many occasions they appealed for permission to travel to Washington to speak in person with the president, the secretary of the interior, or at least the commissioner of Indian affairs. Such requests rarely received approval.[96]

"THEY OFTEN CRY FOR THEIR HOMES AND WILD LIFE AFTER COMING TO US": ARIKARA STUDENTS AT SCHOOL, 1870–1900

The most important instruments to transform Arikaras and other Indians were schools. Education, white reformers believed, would not only turn Indian children into farmers (which the Arikaras already were) and skilled laborers but would also instill in them white cultural and religious values so they would become loyal and patriotic subjects.

Most Arikara elders and parents supported education. They recognized the need for their children to function in the white world and hoped the tribe would benefit from their training. But the school experiences of many young Arikaras were hard. At boarding schools especially, children entered into a strange and frightening world, one that was very different from the familiar and caring homes they had left behind. Although school experiences could be traumatic, many Arikara children returned from boarding schools with positive impressions. Thus the record of Indian schools is mixed. Still, separation from parents and the loss of culture and language should be weighed more heavily against the positive aspects of the schooling experience.

In 1870 Agent H. L Clifford opened the first government school at the Fort Berthold Agency. Despite offering students a meal once a day, Clifford failed to attract many students, except in winter months when tribal food supplies ran low.[97] During these early years, the school was not very successful. Teachers did not speak Indian languages and relied on interpreters, which made effective instruction difficult.

In 1880 Reverend Hall constructed a boarding school. Separation from their parents was especially hard for the youngest students. "They are happy little folks and often cry for their homes and wild life after coming to us," wrote Hall's wife, Emma Calhoun Hall, who taught at the school. The boys arrived in Native dress and long hair. "The braids are very dear to their parents," wrote Emma Hall. "The hair is cut as soon as they come to us and the mother or father, generally, wait to take the braids and old clothes and see the boys in their new ones."[98]

Numerous new schools followed in the 1890s. In 1891 the Catholic Sacred Heart Mission opened St. Edward's School. In 1894 the government established a school named after commissioner of Indian affairs Frank C. Armstrong. The school attracted mostly Arikara students and soon a new town, likewise named Armstrong, formed around the school. The town's name was changed eventually to Nishu ("Corn"). In subsequent years, the government built schools at Independence, Shell Creek, Red Butte, Beaver Creek, Santee, and Little Missouri. Of these schools, Beaver Creek served primarily Arikara children. As at Armstrong, towns soon grew around the schools. The government also built a boarding school at Elbowoods, which operated from 1894 to 1954.

Parents were often reluctant to see their beloved children go to boarding schools far away. "Their sacrifice," Hall wrote, "is truly great." The good-bye was often heartbreaking. When Stella Elizabeth Rogers (or Cedar Woman) desired to attend Hampton Institute in Virginia in 1898, her mother hesitated. "Every night after night I prayed to God to let my mother say yes," Rogers wrote later. After she expressed her determination, her mother allowed her to go. "She did not say anything for a while but her tears ran down [her] cheeks and then she said yes, you can go [as] we can not do anything to keep you back from going." On the day of her departure, Rogers described the scene as parents said good-bye to their children. "Oh how they did cry when we started," she wrote, "We felt so sorry for them."[99]

Many Arikara students attended Fort Stevenson Industrial Training School. The former military post had been transferred to the Indian Office in 1882. When it opened its doors for students a year later, many of the buildings were in poor condition. There was no sewer system, and garbage was dumped not far from school buildings. Contaminated drinking water caused sickness among students and employees.

The school hired several Indian graduates to teach the students. But relations between Indian employees and white school administrators were not good. Henry Karunach, an Arikara who taught shoemaking, resigned in the spring of 1888 after only one year. George Thomas, a Crow Indian graduate of Carlisle Indian School, also resigned in 1888. Superintendent George W. Scott charged teacher George

Bushotter, a Sioux Indian, with being a "troublemaker" who "is constantly talking his language to the pupils, and learning the Arickara language from them."[100]

If life at Fort Stevenson was difficult for Native teachers, it was even harder for the students. "I found out that their beds were not changed for some time and to my surprise not one sheet could be found on the beds but [they] slept between the folds of the blankets," reported school physician Dr. Carlos Montezuma, a Yavapai Indian, in 1889. "I discovered the bathroom was a filthy place with three wash tubs for 67 boys and when through [they] wiped on their dirty sheets." As a result of this unsanitary situation, many students suffered from skin infections such as eczema. Disgusted with the conditions at the school, Montezuma resigned from his post after only nine months.[101]

Because of the problems at Fort Stevenson, few parents would send their children to the school. To increase the number of students, Scott suggested in 1887 withholding rations from Indian families until the school was filled. When Agent Abram J. Gifford did not comply, Scott complained to the commissioner of Indian affairs, who ordered Gifford to fulfill Scott's request. The measure was effective. In 1888, sixty-two Arikara students attended Fort Stevenson.

Students were subjected to a rigid regime at Fort Stevenson. They received severe punishments, including physical punishment for violating school rules. Some instructors and administrators were outright cruel. Scott especially was known for his brutality. When an Arikara boy accidentally struck Scott on the foot with a manure fork, Scott knocked him down and beat him savagely.[102] In 1886 parents demanded Scott's removal "for treating their children ... in a manner unbecoming an Indian educator." Few students had fond memories of the boarding school. One former student compared the school to a prison reformatory and concentration camp. He was certain the fire that destroyed the main school building in 1894 had not been accidental.[103]

Arikara students at boarding schools elsewhere fared somewhat better. In 1878 six Arikara students entered Hampton Institute in Virginia. Although started as a school for Black freedmen during the reconstruction era, Hampton opened its doors to Indian students in 1878.[104] The six Arikara students were George Ahuka (White Wolf), Henry Karunach (Sioux Boy), Laughing Face, George Sharp Horn, and eight-year old Anna Dawson (Wild Rose) and her mother, Mary Dawson, who according to one report "would not let her little girl come without her." They were recruited by former army captain Richard Henry Pratt, who later founded Carlisle in Pennsylvania.[105]

The Arikara students had a difficult time adjusting to Hampton. Boys and girls not only stayed in different dormitories but were also kept in separate quarters from the Black students. They did not like the food served in the mess halls. The boys' clothes, especially the heavy shoes and stiff caps, were very uncomfortable. Girls received feathered hats, which they refused to wear because in Arikara culture, only men wore feathers. According to Booker T. Washington, the great African American educator who taught at Hampton in the late 1870s, the male Indian students dreaded having their hair cut off. "The things that they disliked most," Washington wrote in his autobiography, *Up from Slavery*, "were to have their long hair cut, to give up wearing their blankets, and to cease smoking." Washington also noted that Indian students responded better to "kind treatment" and that they deeply "resented ill-treatment."[106]

The rules at Hampton were strict. Male students were drilled like soldiers and required to do guard duty to make certain that no students left campus without permission. Student rooms were routinely inspected, and card playing, liquor, and tobacco were prohibited. Attendance was required at daily devotional services, sabbath school, and Sunday services. Every day students were marched off to their classrooms, where they received instruction in English, elementary arithmetic, geography, and vocal music. Boys also received training in farming and industrial trades such as carpentry, shoemaking, wheelwrighting, tinsmithing, tailoring, and mechanical engineering. Girls received instruction in domestic trades such as sewing, cooking, and cleaning. On Sundays, students received religious instruction. Saturday was their only day off.

Although many students suffered from homesickness, they were not allowed to go home in summer because school administrators feared this would endanger the civilization process. In summer girls continued to receive daily instruction in English and homemaking, while boys worked at the school farm. The school also sent individual students on summer internships in eastern cities, where they could gain practical experience.

One major concern was the health of the Indian students. Tuberculosis claimed several Arikara lives. Within a few weeks after his arrival at Hampton, George Sharp Horn fell ill with tuberculosis. He died on January 21, 1879, and was buried in the campus cemetery. Mary Dawson, who had joined the program to be with her daughter, Anna, also contracted the disease. She had to return to North Dakota, leaving her daughter behind. She would never see Anna again. On March 11, 1880, Mary died of tuberculosis, and perhaps a broken heart, at Fort Berthold.

Concerned with the well-being of their children, a delegation of chiefs from Fort Berthold visited the institute in 1880. Among them was Chief Rushing Bear, whose son George Ahuka was a student. Apparently the visit reassured the delegates somewhat.

Anna Dawson dressed as Minnehaha from Henry Wadsworth Longfellow's poem "The Song of Hiawatha," circa 1880. Dawson was one of the first students to attend Hampton Institute and was one of its earliest Native American graduates. She married Byron Wilde and returned to Fort Berthold, where she became a field matron and a highly respected community leader and tribal advocate. State Historical Society of North Dakota, 00088 0001 00019.

Rushing Bear was pleased to see the progress his son and the other children had made. He told them to work hard and learn how to read and write English. "I want them to learn every kind of work the white man does," Rushing Bear said. "They are very young and have a long time to live so I want them to learn to do everything."

Although many returned to Fort Berthold with high hopes for the future, quite a few Hampton graduates died not long after their return. George Ahuka and Laughing Face died within a few years after coming back from Hampton, possibly as a result of diseases contracted in Virginia. Henry Karunach used the money he made as a shoemaker at the Fort Stevenson school to go back to Hampton to continue his studies. He returned to Fort Berthold in 1884. Four years later, he too died. Because of these deaths, the Arikaras would not send children to Hampton for years.

Little Anna Dawson did not immediately return to Fort Berthold after her three years at Hampton. After the death of her mother, she became a ward of the school. In 1885 she became one of Hampton's first female Indian graduates. After graduation she stayed at the institute to teach before continuing her studies at the Boston YMCA Domestic Science School. In 1895 she returned to Fort Berthold to work as a field matron. She was instrumental in recruiting a new group of Arikara boys and girls to attend Hampton Institute.

The parents of these students were deeply worried about the safety of their children. Lottie Stiles's father did not want her to go. "He thinks if we come away from home we might die sooner," remembered Stiles, "but I asked my father, so he said that I should come and try to do my best up here." Despite the strict discipline maintained at the institute, many Arikaras enjoyed their stay. Peter Beauchamp enjoyed his agricultural and dairy classes very much. Stella Rogers fondly remembered her work as a maid and nanny in Rhode Island during her summer program. "I used to take care of the baby in the afternoon and I could go out in the evening," she wrote. "Oh I took care of the baby as I would my own brother and I like him so much."

The experiences of Arikara students at Pratt's Carlisle Indian School in Pennsylvania were similar to those of the Arikaras at Hampton. Pratt ran his school in quasi-military fashion. Male students received school uniforms and girls received Victorian-style dresses. The boys were organized in companies led by "officers" and marched to and from classes and to the large dining hall for meals. Discipline was strict. The school's court system tried and punished violations of school rules. Students received both academic and industrial instruction. But as at Hampton, quite a few Arikara boys and girls died of diseases during their stay.

Despite the hardships that Arikara students experienced at boarding schools such as Hampton, Carlisle, Santee, and Haskell, education did much to prepare a new generation of community leaders. Several white-educated students would rise to positions of importance after 1900. Among these were Charles Hoffman, Anna Dawson, Peter Beauchamp, and Albert Simpson. Although they had been trained to act and live like white people, many became staunch defenders of tribal elders and their ancient ways. Education, then, did not entirely obliterate the Arikaras' desire to preserve their traditional culture.[107]

REMEMBERING ORIGINS

By the late 1800s, Arikara culture was changing. First log cabins and then frame houses replaced earth lodges. Gardens were no longer the exclusive domain of women as more and more men took up farming. Families also began to raise stock. Men and women began to wear the clothes of the white people and attend churches devoted to Jesus. Children were no longer exclusively instructed in traditional ways but were sent to white-run schools, where they learned the English language and white society's ways.[108]

Although the pressure on Arikara society to change was great, the attempt by white reformers to destroy Arikara culture was only partially successful. A growing number of Arikaras adopted elements of Euro-American culture, but they nevertheless remained distinctly Arikara in outlook. Occasionally Arikara people donned themselves in the old style of Indian dress. When the agency doctor proved helpless to heal them, they consulted tribal doctors. Although some ceremonies disappeared as their keepers died out, others continued to be performed when agents, schoolmasters, and missionaries were not looking.[109]

Although the Arikaras were anxious to learn from the whites, they nevertheless rejected white criticisms of their tribal culture. "They listen attentively and then immediately disobey," agency physician Josiah Janney Best summed up in 1889.[110]

Despite outside pressures to transform, the main agents of change were the Arikaras themselves. They decided to send their children to white-run schools and churches and to dress in white clothing styles. Despite changes, however, they were always aware of their Arikara origins and identity.

10 CULTURAL REVIVAL, 1900-1934

> The old customs and beliefs have a much stronger hold on them than on the Dakotas. There are not less than six Indian dance halls among the 1200 Indians, and medicine men and women are still interfering with the work of the modern physician.[1]
>
> —WORD CARRIER

By 1900 many Americans believed that Native peoples like the Arikaras were doomed to vanish. Arikara population numbers had dwindled from an estimated eighty-eight hundred around 1700 to about twenty-two hundred in 1835 to less than one thousand by 1865. In 1904 the Arikara nation reached its nadir: the tribal census roll contained only 379 names.

As the older generations passed away, their knowledge of traditional ways disappeared with them. Arikara cultural survival looked bleak indeed. Still, the first three decades of the twentieth century witnessed a revival of Arikara culture and history. Assisted by historians, ethnologists, and artists, elders recorded and documented their stories, ceremonies, and history. Apart from reviving old ideas, these decades also witnessed the introduction of new ideas that strengthened Arikara identity.

HEALTH AND POPULATION GROWTH

Although Arikara population figures rebounded after 1904, growth was sluggish and often frustrated by occasional epidemics of influenza, measles, and whooping cough. By then, however, tuberculosis had become the biggest killer.

Agents decried the lack of medical care at Fort Berthold. "One of the crying needs of this reservation is a small hospital under the supervision of the agency physician assisted by a competent nurse," Superintendent Ernest W. Jermark wrote in 1917.

Too often, people traveled long distances only to find doctors having been called away to the other side of the reservation for a day or two. Without access to professional medical care, many people continued to rely on traditional Native doctors. For more than a decade, reservation officials repeated their pleas for a hospital.[2]

In the meantime, infectious diseases claimed lives. The 1919 Spanish flu pandemic "occasioned much suffering" and increased mortality. Jermark reported, "In many cases the physician was not given an opportunity to administer the proper treatment at the critical time." Still, Jermark put a positive spin on his report by claiming that there were fewer deaths at Fort Berthold than in other parts of the country.[3]

The year 1930 was also disastrous. Superintendent Ralph P. Stanion reported sixty-six births but also sixty-four deaths that year. No less than forty-two of those deaths were of children under three years of age. "This high death rate is attributed very largely to the severe epidemics of influenza and whooping cough," Stanion wrote, "which were followed in turn by measles ... as many children were left by such epidemics in an extremely debilitated condition." Based on the report's statistics, it appears that the diseases hit the Arikara community especially hard.[4]

The need for a hospital remained a priority for agency officials. Jermark's successor, Stephen Janus, wrote in 1926 that the construction of a hospital had been the subject of many letters. He recommended an appropriation of $35,000 for a twenty-bed hospital by 1928. Not until May 1930 did the hospital open. But difficult working conditions in the hospital and strenuous circumstances at Fort Berthold resulted in a high turnover in personnel, impairing the hospital's efficiency.[5]

The people of Fort Berthold only gradually gained trust in the hospital. In 1933 Superintendent H. D. McCullough reported that hospital visits were low. Out of sixty-nine births, only twenty-five were attended by a physician or nurse at the hospital. Either people felt more comfortable delivering at home in the presence of Native doctors and midwives or the distance to the hospital prevented many women from going there. By 1938, however, agency physician Fred Hamernik declared that more people relied on the hospital for treatment. Indeed, Hamernik proclaimed, population growth on the reservation was better than ever. He attributed this growth to the presence of the hospital.[6]

"WE WANT TO KEEP ALL OUR LAND FOR OUR CHILDREN": THE STRUGGLE TO RETAIN TRIBAL LAND

At the turn of the twentieth century, the leading Arikara chiefs included Sitting Bear, Strikes Enemy, Bear's Teeth, and Enemy Heart. They faced great challenges as

Table 4
Arikara Population Growth, 1920–1934

Year	Male	Female	Total	Hidatsa	Mandan	Total
1920	202	213	415	526	264	1,205
1921	202	216	418	521	263	1,202
1922	209	214	423	n.a.	n.a.	1,226
1923	204	222	426	547	273	1,246
1924	209	231	440	570	279	1,289
1925	213	230	443	584	283	1,310
1926	221	224	445	605	284	1,334
1927	225	226	451	605	296	1352
1928	233	219	452	621	300	1,373
1929	237	227	464	612	300	1,376
1930	239	226	465	650	300	1,415
1931	240	236	476	654	324	1,454
1932	252	262	514	648	337	1,499
1933	257	275	533	678	334	1,535
1934	279	278	557	n.a.	n.a.	1,569

Source: Frame 1172, Roll 46, Frames 0064, 0067, 0164, 0250–0251, 0329, 0419, 0442, 0576, 0630, 0692, 0754–0755, 0808, and 0911–0920, Roll 47, Microfilm 1011, RG75: Records of the Bureau of Indian Affairs, NARA.

their people entered the new century. Among these was the termination of annuity payments in 1901.

To secure financial support for the tribes, in 1901 Agent Thomas Richards suggested selling the northern part of the reservation. The Indian Office in Washington approved and sent James McLaughlin to Fort Berthold to negotiate the deal. Sitting Bear and the other chiefs knew McLaughlin personally from when he had served as the Sioux agent on the Standing Rock Reservation.[7]

In mid-June 1902, McLaughlin inspected the reservation and suggested that some 315,000 acres of unused land could be sold to the government. He believed that $1.25 per acre was a reasonable price for the land.[8]

On June 18, 1902, the chiefs gathered to meet McLaughlin in council. Sitting Bear, Strikes Enemy, Bear's Teeth, and Enemy Heart represented the Arikaras. Good Bear, Old Dog, and Enemy Dog represented the Hidatsas, and Spotted Weasel and Wounded Face spoke for the Mandans. McLaughlin told the chiefs that the government wished to buy the northern tracts of their reservation. "You have a much larger reservation than you need," he said. "You are using comparatively only a small portion of it, and deriving no benefit whatever from a considerable portion of it." With the money obtained from the sale, he said, they could buy farming implements, cattle, and other necessary articles. The rest of the money would be held in trust for future expenses and projects.[9]

The chiefs answered that evening. Sitting Bear spoke first. "Away back in the olden times we did not know how to make treaties with the Government," he said. "But now we begin to know the value of our land." He wanted to reserve the land for the young men and the children. They were learning how to raise stock and would need the land. "This is the way I think," he concluded, "and we don't want to sell any of our land at present."

Strikes Enemy and Bear's Teeth shared Sitting Bear's opinion. "Our land is small and I think we will need all of it," said Strikes Enemy. "These young men here have a good many cattle and our reservation is very small" added Bear's Teeth. "We need all the land we have, so we can become self-supporting."[10]

After Good Bear, Old Dog, and Spotted Weasel of the Mandans and Hidatsas responded in similar terms, the council adjourned. It was reopened two days later. Opening the meeting, McLaughlin told the chiefs that they had the right only to *occupy* the land and that the federal government *owned* the land. Now that Congress had determined to open up "surplus lands" to white settlement, it was better if the tribes agreed to a settlement or Congress would simply take what it wanted on its own terms. It was in the best interest of the tribes if the chiefs agreed to sell the land at a fair price while it was offered.

Faced with this ultimatum, the chiefs relented. A few days later, they agreed to sell the land, but for a price of $5 per acre. "We believe that we have a right to this land, but we have concluded to sell you part of it, the part that has been pointed out to you," Sitting Bear said. "We value this land and think it is worth what we ask for it; that is, $5 per acre."[11]

McLaughlin was authorized to offer only $1.25 per acre. Although the chiefs resisted for a long time, they eventually agreed to the price. Still, they won a significant concession: instead of 315,000 acres, the government agreed to buy "only" 208,000 acres.

On June 25, the twenty-sixth anniversary of the Custer battle, the chiefs and 179 eligible members of the tribe signed the agreement. Of the $260,000 they received for the land, some money would be used to erect a 110-mile wire fence around the reservation and to buy five thousand head of cattle, sixty spans of American mares, one hundred mowing machines, and one hundred one-horse hay rakes. Some $50,000 would be deposited in the US Treasury to be held in trust for the tribes for subsistence and clothing for the "old and the helpless." The remainder of the money would be paid out to all individual tribal members in three annual per capita installments. The agreement also included a provision for the further allotment of the reservation.[12] In December 1902, the agreement was submitted to Congress.

For reasons not entirely clear, the agreement was never ratified. Consequently, the reservation boundaries remained essentially intact. But pressures to sell tribal land kept up. In 1904 North Dakota senator Porter J. McCumber proposed, but failed to secure, a bill to withdraw land from the reservation to house some Turtle Mountain Chippewas.[13]

North Dakota businessmen also eyed reservation land and began to pressure the tribes to sell it. In 1909 they wrote Congressman Louis B. Hanna, urging the opening some four hundred thousand acres of reservation land. Hanna told the businessmen that it was advisable (but not strictly necessary) to get the consent of the three tribes. On June 1, 1909, these land boosters invited the three tribes to the town of Ryder for a council, "with the understanding that we would furnish a young beef a day with bacon, ham, flour, coffee, sugar, etc." After four days of negotiations, the businessmen reported that the three tribes were willing to part with some land.[14] Hanna immediately drafted a bill to open reservation land to white settlers by executive order.

The news of Hanna's bill angered some people on the reservation. Among them was Charles Hoffman, an Arikara and now superintendent of the agency. Hoffman appealed to Congressman Asle J. Gronna: "Are our Congressmen going to look upon these Indians as slaves, having no rights as to whether they are willing to dispose of any part of their lands or not?" The Bureau of Indian Affairs, charged with the protection of the interests of Indian people, sided with Hanna.[15]

On September 10, 1909, Hanna and Assistant Commissioner of Indian Affairs Frederick H. Abbott arrived at Fort Berthold for talks with the chiefs. After two days, the chiefs agreed to sell thirteen full and eight fractional townships north and east of the Missouri River to the government. Their exact reasons are not entirely clear. Perhaps they needed money for older people on the reservation or they wished improve houses and farms. After government surveyors appraised the land at market value, the money was credited to the tribes and placed in the US Treasury at a 3 percent interest rate. A portion of the proceeds would be used to establish new schools and other facilities. The ceded land would be opened up to settlers. Congress approved the bill on June 1, 1910.[16]

Several Arikaras protested the sale of tribal land. In 1911 Red Bear, Enemy Heart, and Alfred Young Hawk wrote the commissioner of Indian affairs. Now that all the surplus lands were gone, "they have got us now to our homes," they wrote. "The land has been taken away and we have only to defend our homes. The line has come close."[17]

Their protests fell on deaf ears in Washington. In June 1911, President William Howard Taft signed a proclamation opening 150,000 acres of the acquired lands to the public. Registration of interested buyers began on August 14 in Bismarck, Minot, Plaza, Garrison, and Ryder.[18] On the first day of registration, more than five thousand people filled out applications. Hotels in the registration towns were "crowded to capacity." Registration booths were placed on all principal streets and "good-natured crowds [filled] the streets from curb to curb." When the registration offices closed, on September 2, thousands had registered. The lottery by which lots were assigned took three days to complete.[19]

New towns sprang up around the reservation. Among them were Parshall, Van Hook, and Sanish. They became trading centers for Indians and allowed for increased contact between Indians and whites.[20]

Other lotteries followed. In 1915 the government offered seven hundred homesteads (110,000 acres) for sale. No less than 30,561 people registered for the lottery, which took place at the Minot Theater on November 8 of that year. On May 1, 1916, the lucky winners claimed their homesteads.[21]

The revenue from the sales was credited to the account of the three tribes in Washington. Tribal leaders wanted to distribute this money equally among the people, but the Bureau of Indian Affairs was reluctant. In 1916 a delegation from the three tribes traveled to the capital to discuss the matter with Indian affairs commissioner Cato Sells. They were informed that they had $776,360.51 in their account. Sells agreed to disburse part of these funds among tribal members. Between February and August 1917, the BIA distributed about $300,000. With the money, people paid off their debts, improved their farms, and bought new farming implements and animal stock.[22]

Meanwhile, the process of allotting land to Indian families and individuals continued. The first allotments had been issued in 1895. Subsequent allotments were made in 1910, 1912, 1915, 1923, and 1928. By 1928 a total of 599,700.4 acres had been allotted to tribal members.

Not all allotted land remained in Indian hands. Although the Allotment Act stipulated that allotted lands could not be sold for twenty-five years, to give Indians time to develop ranching or farming operations, the government soon loosened restrictions. For example, old people were allowed to sell their allotments to support themselves in the remaining years of their lives. Most of this land was sold to white settlers.²³

The story of territorial loss is a sad one. In 1851 the three tribes were assigned 12,618,301 acres. By 1870 the reservation had been reduced to 7,833,043 acres. A decade later only 1,193,788 acres remained. In 1886 tribal landholdings dipped under one million acres. By 1928 the tribes had 599,700 acres left, and by the time of President Franklin Roosevelt's Indian New Deal, which stopped the alienation of Indian lands, the three tribes occupied a reservation of only 536,190 acres, of which only the bottomlands along the Missouri River were of real economic value.

The allotment process and the alienation of tribal lands not only outraged Indians but also drew criticism from sympathetic whites. In his journal, Episcopalian missionary Aaron McGaffey Beede bitterly summed up the shameful way in which the Fort Berthold Indians had been treated. "[When] we are told in history that this and that was done with the free consent of the Indians one should remember that it was generally free consent under compulsion," Beede wrote. Though they were paid for the land, Beede noted, "They have it to their credit on paper and the income goes 'for their civilization,' as Washington terms that system which eats up tribal funds and payments etc. to give jobs to some 17,000 clerks in Washington, and some 8,000 men and women in the field and on the railways and automobiles. Hurrah for 'civilization'!"²⁴

"THE LIGHT OF THE WORLD IS JESUS": ARIKARAS AND MISSIONARIES, 1900–1934

After 1900 Arikaras increasingly attended Christian churches, which now included Episcopal congregations. Most converts were former students returning to Fort Berthold. This did not mean that traditional ways were abandoned. Older Arikaras continued to worship in the traditional ways while simultaneously attending Christian churches. Some Arikaras also switched easily from one church to the next or even attended meetings and services of all denominations.

The Catholic presence grew steadily after 1900. Under the guidance of Father Leon Favreau, the Arikaras built St. Andrew's Chapel at Nishu. Favreau also erected a statue of Christ on the cross near Elbowoods, prompting Porcupine, a resident of Fort Berthold, to exclaim, "Why didn't he come here? We would have fought for him and the whites would not have killed him!"²⁵ Favreau's successor, Father Paul Lotter, oversaw the construction of several churches and schools, including the belfry of St. Andrew's Church at Nishu, the Queen of Peace Church at Raub, a chapel at Shell Creek, St. Anthony's Church at Independence, and Lucky Mound Church. Also in 1910 the first Benedictine sisters arrived at Fort Berthold. The sisters worked primarily as instructors in the mission schools at Elbowoods, Lucky Mound, and elsewhere.[26]

Catholic priests relied greatly on the services of bilingual Arikaras to communicate with the people. William Deane served for many years as official interpreter. Poor roads and communications made travel difficult for the priests and sisters. As a result, many parishes saw a missionary only once or twice a month. For this reason, Fort Berthold Catholics staged the annual Catholic Indian Congress, which was hosted by a different tribe ever year. At these meetings, people attended Mass, listened to speeches, shared supper, and participated in various social activities, including songs, dances, and movie showings. The attendants camped out at the meeting grounds. In 1925 William Deane, Claire Everett, and Sam Newman organized the congress at Nishu. Chief Floyd Bear translated the various speeches into Arikara.

Problems of translation and distance also troubled the Congregational mission. When Charles Hall conducted his sermons, he was assisted by Hidatsa and Arikara interpreters on opposite ends of the chapel. Hymns were sung in both Arikara and Hidatsa.[27] To deal with expanding church membership, Hall appointed two Native assistants: Edward Goodbird for the Hidatsas and Ernest C. Hopkins for the Arikaras. "[Ernest] has had a good training in Bible studies and a good musical training which enables him to lead in the musical part of the worship, both vocal and instrumental," Hall wrote. "He sings hymns of his own translation, [and] is giving the gospel to his Ree people in their own tongue."[28]

Hopkins was the driving force behind expansion of Congregational worship among the Arikaras. After attending boarding school at Santee, he came home to spread the Gospel to his people. "We are told it is better to trust in God that we might see the light or the works what God had promised to do," he wrote later. With the help of fellow Arikaras, Hopkins raised money to erect a new chapel.[29]

By 1915 the Congregational church at Fort Berthold numbered more than one hundred families. That year, Hopkins was licensed to establish his own mission among the Arikara people. But he suffered what appeared to be a stroke and died on March 15, 1917.[30] Fellow Arikara Lawrence Howling Wolf took over the pastorate of the Congregational church at Armstrong. To prepare himself for this responsibility, he spent several months at Santee for further study.[31] As the congregation expanded, Thomas Enemy also became a preacher in the church.

Despite these successes, membership remained in flux. Arikaras frequently switched from one denomination to another. For example, when the Arikara

Congregationalists dedicated a new church building at Nishu in 1927, there were several singers in attendance who had left the church. One had joined the Episcopalians while two others had gone over to "Romanism" and a fourth had "slumped into paganism." They nevertheless joined the dedication of the church, singing "Wenihatauwi Jesus" ("The Light of the World Is Jesus").[32] Such religious flexibility was an interesting link to the past, when Arikara doctors could switch from one doctor society to another or hold memberships in multiple societies at the same time. Most Arikaras did not necessarily see a contradiction between joining different churches simultaneously. So when the Congregationalists held their annual meetings in the fall, members of other churches often attended.[33]

Around 1900 the Episcopalians established a mission at Fort Berthold.[34] The missionaries who brought this church, Thomas P. Ashley and William White Eagle, were Sioux men from the Standing Rock Reservation. They successfully converted Yellow Bear, an Arikara leader who previously had "vehemently opposed all aspects of white civilization, and especially Christianity." After conversion he changed his name to Paul Yellow Bear, after Saint Paul, the patron saint of the new mission. He soon became a leading figure in the Episcopal mission at Fort Berthold. Several other Arikaras also joined in mission work. While Paul Yellow Bear and Anna Dawson-Wilde worked primarily on the east bank of the Missouri River, Henry Red Dog assisted John S. Brown (a mixed-blood missionary from Standing Rock) on the western part of the reservation.

Unlike the Catholics and Congregationalists, the Episcopalians lacked outside financial support and grew more slowly as a result. The church also met a temporary setback when a nativist movement led by Winnie Enemy Heart weaned away many members. The financial problems of the church continued after the Great Crash of 1929 and the Great Depression, which forced the church's executive council to lower its budget for Indian missions by one-third. This hampered all efforts to carry on missionary work at the reservation.

CULTURAL PERSISTENCE AND REVIVAL

To the frustration of elder Arikaras, government agents continued to crack down on Arikara dances and ceremonies. Still, Arikaras found ways to circumvent restrictions. In February 1913, for example, they organized a dance in honor of George Washington's birthday.[35] On other occasions they staged dances illicitly. When the Beaver Society held its dance in 1905, Agent Amzi W. Thomas sent a police officer, Hunts Along, a Hidatsa, to break up the meeting. When Hunts Along appeared at the dance, he was attacked by the crowd. In self-defense, he shot a man and wounded another before he was overpowered, beaten down, and left for dead in the snow. The next morning Charles Hoffman found Hunts Along nearly dead but still breathing. Hunts Along survived. It later was revealed that Thomas had given conflicting orders, causing the confusion that led to the incident.[36]

In 1911 Charles Hoffman reported that Indian dances were "becoming a tamer affair each year." As agency superintendent, Hoffman had limited dances to four times a year. They had to close at "proper hours." Giveaways were restricted. Young people and returning students were not allowed to participate in dances; Hoffman hoped this would soon make dances "a thing of the past." In 1913 Hoffman's successor, Ernest W. Jermark, commented that dances were still popular among older Indians but that "younger people have adopted the white man's form of dancing." According to Jermark, most of the old dances were grass dances, and with the exception of giveaways, these were not "detrimental" because men and women danced separately. In 1918 Jermark cheerfully noted that interest in Indian dances was waning rapidly due to his policy of limiting the number of hours, which made it impractical for people who lived on distant allotments to attend. In addition, he said, younger Indians realized they could not leave livestock unattended for long periods of time.[37]

Jermark had declared victory too soon. In 1921 he complained that "more Indian dancing has been indulged in during the past year than is good for the Indian." Undoubtedly, some of these dances were held in honor of returning World War I veterans. Despite new policies to discourage dancing, Jermark wrote the next year that the Indians danced "to an extent which became harmful" to their best interests. He felt compelled to call a council with the chiefs to formulate new restrictions. Dances from then on required written permission from the superintendent and were limited to legal holidays. No giveaways were allowed, and big feasts were discontinued except under special permission. In addition, "No men under 21 or girls under 18 years of age [were] to be permitted to dance, or wear dance costumes at the dances." To stop "promiscuous running from one dance hall to another," dances were to be conducted in the evenings only and had to be stopped at 2:00 A.M., "and all Indians [had] to return home not later than the following morning."[38]

Though Jermark considered the dances "merely a form of amusement in which only the old Indians are allowed to participate," his successor, Stephen Janus, continued to enforce strict rules. In 1924 the tribal fair was discontinued because "it became merely a means of getting together and having dances, riding, roping, etc. causing the Indians to leave their homes at a time when it was necessary that they care for their crops and stock." In 1926 only two big celebrations were held: a fall fair and a July 4 feast that involved dances, rodeo, and concession stands. In 1929 Superintendent L. W. Page wrote, "The discontinuance of the Indian dance is merely a process of elimination, as the older Indians die there are fewer who participate in the Indian dances, and I believe it is a matter of but a comparatively short time when the old Indian dances will be a thing of the past." According to Page, young Indians were more attracted to modern dances, but in reality, the agency's own policies prohibited young people from participating in the dances.³⁹

The government's policies frustrated and puzzled the Arikaras, especially in light of the scandalous dances that white people enjoyed in their towns. In October 1915, "Captain" Alfred Burton Welch took Red Fish, a Lakhota, and Crow Ghost, an Arikara, to see a vaudeville show in Bismarck. The men were deeply troubled as they watched a dancing girl dressed in tights kick up her legs. The two men walked out of the theater before the performance ended. An affronted Red Fish expressed his disappointment. "The Agent forbids us to have our old religious dances and he breaks our hearts by not letting us [perform] our old religious songs," he said. "And the chief of the capital of North Dakota lets . . . girls sing nasty music and almost show the hole of motherhood before 500 men with their wives and children. I want you to write the President to come immediately and see with his own eyes what disgraceful things the white people have in Bismarck."⁴⁰

Government and missionary pressures on the Arikaras were so rigorous that they even prompted criticism from non-Indians. Ethnologist George A. Dorsey wrote the commissioner of Indian affairs that the Arikaras were treated shamefully. The Arikaras, Dorsey said, "have been made to think that they have absolutely no right on this earth to think about their own gods." As a result, they "have literally been compelled to hide away all their religious paraphernalia; and whatever of their rites or ceremonies they have held they have held with fear and trembling."⁴¹

Despite oppressive government policies, the Arikaras continued to express their independence in religious matters. In fact, new forms of religious expression, this time directed by the Arikaras themselves, swept across the reservation between 1900 and 1934.

Among these was the nativist movement led by eighteen-year-old Winnie Enemy Heart. She had graduated from a white mission school. Around 1906 she went out into the hills, where she stayed for several nights. There she had a vision of Jesus, who showed her a white lamb and a black dog. "I have power with both these," Jesus told her. The white lamb was the white man, and the black dog represented Indian people. But the whites had fooled the Indians and were seeking to destroy them. Jesus had returned to save the Indians. He told Enemy Heart the secret of salvation.

After descending from the hill, she began to preach among the Christian Indians, warning them that the white people were deceiving them. Jesus had told her that the white people had used him "bad" and killed him. She told the people that Jesus had shown her his body and it was half white and half dark. This meant that he was "just as much Indian as white man."

The white ways, Enemy Heart said, had corrupted and weakened the people. There were now fewer than four hundred Arikara people remaining, and the tribe was getting smaller each year. She called for a return to the old ways to restore the power and vitality of the tribe. She particularly criticized the missionaries who had invaded the community. "If whites want you to believe in their ways," Jesus had told her, "you say: 'No! White ways [are] good for white men, but Indian ways [are] good for Indians!'" Many people came to hear her message. She and her uncle convinced several Arikaras to leave the churches and renounce white forms of worship.

The recently established Episcopal mission lost many converts to Enemy Heart's movement. Among the Episcopalians, only Yellow Bear and Red Dog remained. When Enemy Heart reportedly threatened to kill Yellow Bear with lightning, he moved his family to the other side of the river. The Catholics apparently also lost some Arikara members to her movement, but Enemy Heart did not appeal to Christian Mandans and Hidatsas.[42]

In 1907 the *Word Carrier* reported that Congregationalist pastor Ernest Hopkins had his hands full, since the "old heathen craze has been making much headway on [the Arikara] part of the reserve." But the paper also reported that the "church has gained by the craze since it winnowed out the dross." One of the students "seduced" by Enemy Heart's teachings was Milo Gillette, a former Santee student. The *Word Carrier* reported, "We are sorry to report that Milo Gillette, a Santee boy, has been carried back to the old heathen ways by his environment and the prophesyings of a foolish girl who has had nightmares for a few months past."[43]

Revitalization movements, sparked by the poverty, population loss, and general demoralization on the reservation, were not uncommon among American Indian nations at this time. The best-known example is the ghost dance. Although heavily inspired by Christianity, these movements nevertheless emphasized distinctly Native forms of worship. Winnie Enemy Heart also argued that the Arikaras should return to their former ways. For reasons not entirely clear, the movement at Fort Berthold faded after a few years. Perhaps the agent was successful in suppressing it. In any event, Enemy Heart's followers began to drift back to the white man's churches.[44]

Other Arikaras called for protection of traditional ways. Despite advances made in Western medicine, many Arikaras continued Native healing practices. Among them was Red Bear, a former Arikara scout. In 1911 Red Bear told the Board of Indian Commissioners that the Arikaras continued to rely on their own ways of healing. The "Almighty," Red Bear said, "gave us medicine to cure us and heal up ourselves." The Arikaras were unwilling to part with these medicines, which had proven their value over the generations. "Doctors come to our reservation now, and are using white man's medicines and all that, and it is supposed that they want the Indian medicine cut off," Red Bear admonished. "But still these old people want to use their own medicine."[45]

As Red Bear indicated, Arikara faith in traditional medicines remained strong. The Reverend Aaron McGaffey Beede recorded in his diary that Mary Gates had given him $10 to send to Paul Yellow Bear, who treated her son Philip when he was ill. "Even the young Indians, most of them," Beede commented, "have more confidence in old Indian medicine than in any other."[46]

Arikara beliefs in witchcraft, ghosts, and other supernatural phenomena remained strong as well. Even Christianized Indians keenly felt the presence of traditional beliefs. On December 19, 1912, Mason W. Jones, an Arikara, fainted and apparently died. Jones, a Congregationalist, and had been suffering from tuberculosis. The previous summer he had started bleeding from his lungs. After he was laid out for dead but not yet placed in a coffin, he suddenly woke up. His first words were that he had been to the other world and seen people there. "I saw some in the other world who are [still] in this world," he said. "Some people who think they are in the other world are in this world. And some who think they are in this world are in the other world." He then called for two men, Sam Newman and Strieby Horn, who were only a few miles away. Fearful that Mason would identify them as the ones he had seen in the afterlife, the two men at first refused to go. Only reluctantly did they agree to visit Jones, who lay dying. Jones gave them the names of Black Hawk's wife and two other people. Not long after Jones died, the others he had named died as well.[47]

Belief in animal spirits also remained strong. One day Yellow Bear was digging with a crowbar made of a flattened and sharpened gun barrel. He thrust the bar into a layer of coal and a toad came out. It was bleeding from one of its feet where Yellow Bear had struck it. Yellow Bear felt so bad that he cried. After wiping the blood from the toad and speaking to the animal, he attached a fine elk's tooth, which he kept for good luck, to a string. He then tied the string to the toad's neck as an offering and placed the animal back in the coal bank. The next day, a young man appeared at Yellow Bear's house with the elk tooth and string. He had taken the string from the toad and had replaced it with three beads to pay for it. "You cheated the toad, and you have done wrong," Yellow Bear said. "You better go and give him back the same elk-tooth." The young man refused. The next day he broke his arm and leg when his horse stampeded and threw him to the ground.[48]

In the early 1900s, Red Star and Crow Ghost revived the Arikara grass dance. Red Star received a new set of songs in a vision while he was fasting on top of a hill. In his vision, the thunderbirds gave him power to call or divert the rain. Crow Ghost received his songs in a vision while fasting at a number of graves. According to one version of Crow Ghost's vision, a crow sat on his shoulder and taught him the songs by whispering them into his ear. Another version states that Crow Ghost visited a lodge inhabited by crow spirits, who taught him the songs and other secrets. Apart from the grass dance, Crow Ghost also tried to revive some of the older Arikara ceremonies. Today fifteen of Red Stars' songs and twenty-two of Crow Ghost's grass dance songs survive.[49] During the early decades of the twentieth century, the Big Grass Society (HanUtkusu') became the "dominant group in Arikara social and political life." In 1918 a number of younger Arikaras on the north side of the Missouri River built a dance hall at Nishu and formed the Dead Grass Society. This society was modeled after the Big Grass Society and eventually replaced it altogether. The Dead Grass Society continued until World War II.[50]

The persistence of Indian dances and traditions at Fort Berthold frustrated missionaries and other agents of "civilization." "The old customs and beliefs have a much stronger hold on them than on the Dakotas," wrote a visitor in 1921. "There are not less than six Indian dance halls among the 1200 Indians, and medicine men and women are still interfering with the work of the modern physician."[51]

Ironically, whenever important foreign visitors arrived, the Arikaras were often asked to appear in Native dress and reenact traditional ways. Such an occasion took place in 1926, when Queen Marie, Princess Ileana, and Prince Nicholas of Romania visited Fort Berthold as part of a tour of the United States. British-born Marie had achieved fame during World War I, when she persuaded Romania to join the Allies against the Central Powers. When she arrived at Fort Berthold on November 1, she was welcomed by a large crowd of Indians. According to the *New York Times*, they included White Bear, Crow Ghost, Foolish Bear, Holy Horse, White Cow Walking, and Red Tomahawk. "At a little distance," the *Times* continued, "the young Indian girls were massed, and they sang a prayer for plenty and prosperity, the corn song of the Arikara tribe." Red Tomahawk presented Queen Marie with a war bonnet and gave her an Indian name.[52]

Arikara elders welcomed visitors such as Queen Marie as well as scholars of Indian culture because they provided an opportunity to perform old dances and ceremonies. They also welcomed the opportunity to record the old customs before they disappeared. The Indian Office, however, was suspicious of such reenactments and in most cases refused to give permission.[53]

Despite government suspicions, the Arikaras welcomed a string of scientists to Fort Berthold between 1900 and 1934. In 1903 Skiri Pawnee scholar James Rolfe Murie (1862–1921) arrived at Fort Berthold to record traditional Arikara stories for ethnologist George A. Dorsey. Murie was an old friend of George Ahuka, Henry Karunach, and Laughing Face from Hampton Institute in Virginia. Although stories were ordinarily told only during winter, many Arikara elders were willing to share stories with him. Among the storytellers were Yellow Bear, Two Hawks, Hand, Star, Bear's Tail, Four Horns, Hawk, Standing Bull, Snowbird, White Bear, Antelope, Strikes Enemy, Elk, White Owl, Many Fox, Little Crow, Yellow Bull, Joe Reed, Cut Arm, New Man, Young Hawk, Sitting Bear, and Enemy Heart. The stories were told in Arikara, translated by Murie into English, and edited and published by Dorsey in 1904. The publication remains, to this day, the most important collection of Arikara stories, both sacred and profane.[54]

In the summer of 1908, photographer Edward Sheriff Curtis (1868–1921) and a small crew of assistants arrived at Fort Berthold to photograph Arikara people and to record Arikara stories, ceremonies, and history. Curtis had obtained permission from the Indian Office to photograph the Arikara medicine lodge ceremony. At Fort Berthold, he met with the members of the various doctor societies, including Red Bear, Bear's Belly, Little Sioux, Crow Ghost, Red Star, Frank Heart (the last keeper of the buffalo bundle), and others. The Arikaras were excited to perform the ceremony that had been banned for so long. They also were glad to have a pictorial record of the ceremony. Curtis and his crew also described the Arikara sun dance, the Arikara genesis story, several folk tales, an Arikara vocabulary, and songs from various medicine societies. Curtis's account was published in 1909.[55]

Another scholar interested in Arikara history and culture was ethnobotanist Melvin Randolph Gilmore (1868–1940). Although much of his work dealt with Native uses of plants, Gilmore also recorded information on Arikara history and culture. Gilmore's work, both published and unpublished, is of great importance to the study of Arikara ethnography. Gilmore witnessed and described the adoption, or calumet, ceremony. With Gilmore's support the Arikaras were also allowed to perform the Mother Corn, sacred cedar tree, and medicine lodge ceremonies in 1922. An incident during this performance almost ended Gilmore's attempt to record these important ceremonies. Despite careful preparations by Four Rings, Pat Star, and several other priests and doctors, one of the participants made a small error during the Mother Corn ceremony. That night a terrible wind and hailstorm

Arikara Mother Corn ceremony. Members of a doctor society sing to Cedar Tree and Grandfather Rock, August 14, 1930. This was one of the last times the ceremony was performed. Although women could be doctors, their participation in the Mother Corn ceremony is largely undocumented. State Historical Society of North Dakota, 00200–5×7 0000000 00691.

swept across the campsite. Many tents were destroyed, and the roof of Gilmore's automobile was severely damaged. Many believed the sacred powers created the storm because of the error made during the ceremony.[56]

Despite this setback, Arikara elders were determined to record their ceremonies. "I found they wanted their old customs preserved," Gilmore told the *New York Times* later. In July 1924, Gilmore returned and recorded the medicine lodge ceremony and several other customs on film. The most sacred parts of the ceremonies were not filmed in order not to offend the sacred powers.[57] This time the ceremonies proceeded without incident. Many of the performers were elderly men who still adhered strongly to their Native beliefs, even though they were all affiliated with Christian churches on the reservation. Strieby Horn, for example, was a lay reader in the Episcopal congregation but also an expert on the sacred plants used in ceremonies.[58] In addition to the sage dance, the Mother Corn ceremony, and the medicine lodge ceremony, Gilmore also recorded an Arikara hand game and filmed the manufacture of moccasins. Today this film is a unique and priceless cultural object for the Arikara people.[59]

Apart from these attempts to document the old customs, new forms of Native religious expression also found their way to the Arikaras. Between 1912 and 1920, the peyote religion appeared at Fort Berthold. It is not clear exactly how and when the new religion arrived there. According to one report, it was introduced by an Arikara who had learned the custom from the Pawnees in Oklahoma. Another source states that it was introduced by Winnebago Indian evangelist Albert Hensley. In any event, the movement appears to have attracted only a few Arikaras at this time. Perhaps many were reluctant to join the religion because the use of peyote was under heavy fire from Indian agents and missionaries.

Critics claimed that peyote was addictive and that its rituals were a perversion of Christian sacraments. In reality, peyote was not addictive and the worshipers were devout Christians. They believed that peyote was a gift from God to help them lead good and healthy lives. The new religion embraced Christian concepts such as brotherly love, care of the family, self-reliance, and sobriety. Members gathered at the church, carried crosses and Native symbols (such as eagle feathers, eagle bone whistles, rattles, and sagebrush), prayed to Jesus, sang sacred songs accompanied by drums, read biblical passages, and consumed peyote buttons as a sacrament. Gatherings lasted all night and ended with a ceremonial meal at dawn. Church members believed that peyote had the power to cure certain diseases, especially alcoholism, and considered the consumption of peyote buttons a sacrament. The ceremony itself emphasized purification, rebirth, and unification with the sacred powers. It gave people the strength to face their problems with renewed vigor.[60]

The appearance of peyote alarmed Fort Berthold officials. In 1922 Superintendent Jermark reported the first instance of peyote use on the reservation, but he "was unable to catch any of the suspects in the act in order to verify the report." He was puzzled where the peyote came from and suspected it had been sent by mail. The next year Jermark reported that peyote use had increased during the previous year, but he assured his superiors that "those using it are of a type that are not of the highest mentality." Jermark's successor, Stephen Janus, stated in 1924 that peyote use continued to increase. He attributed the increase to Prohibition. "This drug is used mainly by the Indians from 35 to 60 years of age," Janus wrote. "The younger people do not seem to care to join in the festivities at which Peyote is used." Two years later, Janus's successor, Lewis W. Page, reported that peyote was used by no more than three people on the reservation and was not a serious problem there.[61]

Despite the religion's distinctly Christian and Native character, many Arikaras also viewed it with suspicion. When North Dakota prohibited the use of peyote in 1923, the ban was welcomed by Arikaras affiliated with established churches.

Among them was Sam Newman, who denounced the use of peyote in an article in the *McLean County Independent* in 1924. "It is a good thing that peyote is stopped for it was doing more harm than good," wrote Newman. Denouncing it as the "devil's root," he warned that peyote and Christianity were incompatible. Peyotists "tried to make others believe that peyote is a God and a religion, but if one wants to believe in mysterious things it must be Christ or peyote."[62]

Although the religion had failed to get a firm hold among the people of Fort Berthold, it did not die out. Two Arikaras, Thomas Goodall and Walter Plenty Chiefs, kept the religious objects belonging to the ceremony. The religion was revived in the 1950s.[63]

At this time, alcohol abuse was not a major problem on the reservation. In 1910 Superintendent Charles Hoffman reported, "These Indians are remarkably free from the crime of drunkenness, though they often visit rail towns to buy provisions, and also to haul freight, and yet they never cause any trouble." He reported only two cases of public intoxication over the previous year. Indeed, Hoffman continued, the Indians were hard workers. Two years later, in 1912, Hoffman reported that a student returning from a school in Nebraska, from which he had run away to marry a Winnebago girl, tried to introduce *tiswin* on the reservation. Tiswin was an alcoholic beverage brewed from corn.[64]

Alcohol use remained a minor problem until the 1930s, when the growth of white settlements next to the reservation increased supply. In 1933 Superintendent H. D. McCullough reported that twenty-four arrests were made for drunken and disorderly conduct. Because there were no towns on the reservation itself, McCullough reasoned that "most of the Indians who get drunk do so off the reservation." In 1934 Superintendent W. Beyer reported forty-two arrests. "The number of arrests during the past year has nearly doubled over those made in 1933, indicating that law and order is breaking down," Beyer wrote as he called for permission to hire more police officers. Beyer blamed the increase on the proliferation of small towns next to the reservation, where the tribal police force had no jurisdiction. In 1935 sixty-four cases were brought before a judge. Although a few of these were cases of illicit cohabitation, most involved drunkenness. In 1936 the number of arrests rose to 137. Because of the increased workload for judges and police officers, Beyer suggested salary increases. He also recommended the construction of a new, safer, and larger jail that could also handle female prisoners. The following year, the number of arrests dropped to ninety-seven, but the continued presence of saloons and liquor stores in adjacent towns frustrated government officials.[65]

"THESE INDIANS HAVE SERVED THE GOVERNMENT LONG AND WELL": ARIKARA MILITARY SERVICE, 1903-1919

Warfare had always been an important part of male Arikara identity. After the Indian Wars, however, there were few opportunities for Arikara men to follow in the footsteps of their illustrious scout ancestors. Still, quite a few Arikaras enlisted in the US military between 1903 and 1920. One of these, Eli Perkins, saw action in the Philippines, while several others served in World War I. This military service led to a revival of certain war-related traditions.

At the turn of the twentieth century, the old Arikara scouts entered old age. Many suffered from poverty caused in part by injuries sustained during their military service. In March 1891, Agent Jonathan S. Murphy wrote the secretary of the interior, requesting that pensions be issued to the old scouts. "These Indians," Murphy wrote, "have served the Government long and well and ought, I think, be rewarded for their services well rendered."

Many scouts, Murphy explained, were suffering from "ailments originating in the course of their service." They had been wounded in battles with the Sioux while scouting for the army. Bull Neck, for example, had his "feet burned . . . his arm and legs cut, his head pounded to a jelly and his scalp partly taken." Murphy described him as a "physical wreck [who] richly deserves all that the Government can give him during the few remaining years of his life." The widows and children of deceased scouts often lived in destitution and were in dire need of support. In his letter, Murphy included a list and a description of sixty scouts, together with their discharge papers. He requested that the discharge papers be returned, as their owners "regard them as something to be treasured." Nothing came of the request.[66]

In 1910 a delegation consisting of Enemy Heart, Red Bear, and Alfred (Bear) Young Hawk, traveled to Washington to lobby on behalf of the scouts. Their cause was picked up by Louis Benjamin Hanna, a Fargo-based lawyer and congressman from North Dakota. On July 19, 1911, Hanna introduced a bill in the House of Representatives calling for pensions for Indian veterans who had served as scouts for the US Army in the Indian Wars. Hanna also submitted the scouts' discharge papers. Again, nothing came of the request. To make matters worse, it appears that the discharge papers were lost as they were shuffled from one office to the next.[67]

Meanwhile, the old scouts wished to have the story of their military service recorded, possibly to strengthen their pension cases. They granted interviews to several historians, including Walter Mason Camp (1867-1925), who visited with the

Custer scouts on several occasions between 1909 and 1913. However, Camp died before he could publish his findings.[68]

The scouts also granted an interview with Orin Grant Libby, secretary of the State Historical Society of North Dakota. Libby was interested in the Arikara side of the story of the Little Bighorn. In August 1912, Libby met with Sitting Bear, Soldier, Young Hawk, Red Bear, Boy Chief, Red Star, Strikes Two, Running Wolf, Little Sioux, Goes Ahead (a Crow scout), and former interpreter Frederick F. Gerard. For four days the veterans talked about their experiences. According to Libby, the scouts were "very scrupulous to confine themselves to just that portion of the common experience to which they were eye witnesses." Publication of the interviews was delayed until 1920, when they appeared under the title *The Arikara Narrative of the Campaign against the Hostile Dakotas, June 1876*. The book instantly became an important source on the battle at the Little Bighorn. It shed new light on the battle and revealed that Custer had presidential aspirations, which might have prompted him to ignore his instructions and rush to engage the Sioux and Cheyennes without adequate support. The interviews also showed that the Arikaras had fought bravely both during the initial attack and in the defense of Reno Hill.[69]

Around 1912 the surviving scouts organized the United States Volunteer Indian Scouts, or Old Scouts Society. Its membership was open to any Arikara who had served in the US armed forces. The society organized dances and feasts in honor of Arikara veterans. It also continued to appeal to the government for pensions for the old scouts and their families. Society members composed several songs in honor of their comrades who had died at the Little Bighorn. The association took care of the cemetery where the deceased scouts were buried and on Memorial Day held celebrations honoring the brave men who had fought in war.

The story of the scouts' struggle for pensions is rather painful. Both Custer and President Grant had promised to look after the scouts after their service. But bureaucratic hurdles and complications due to loss of the discharge papers caused long delays. Most scouts died before their claims were awarded. Only a handful of scouts successfully secured pensions. One of them was Goose, who had been shot in the hand at the Little Bighorn. Goose was proud of his service. "I never turned back from anything I was sent to do," he once told a white visitor.[70] For most other scouts, however, securing pensions was a long and frustrating process. Not untypical was the experience of Red Star, who, after a process that took two decades, was awarded a pension on July 24, 1939. But he had passed away less than two months before. Following his death, his wife, Daisy D. Red Star, received a widow's pension.[71]

CULTURAL REVIVAL 245

Studio portrait of Eli Perkins (also known as Bear Robe), US Army veteran of the Philippine occupation, circa 1920. In the early 1950s, Perkins protested construction of the Garrison Dam. He reminded the government that he had fought for the country and demanded that his voice be heard. His demand fell on deaf ears. State Historical Society of North Dakota, A3205–00001 (where he is listed as Clarence Perkins).

Despite the poor treatment of Arikara veterans by the federal government, young Arikara men continued to serve in the US military. Eli Perkins, son of former Arikara scout Four Rings, was the first Arikara to enlist as a regular soldier in the US Army. After graduating from Carlisle Indian School in 1903, Perkins joined the Eighth Cavalry. He was stationed at Jefferson Barracks for the first two years of his service. In 1905 his regiment was ordered to the Philippines to police the island of Luzon against bandits and Filipino freedom fighters.[72]

Although President Theodore Roosevelt had declared the Philippine-American War over in 1902, Filipino freedom fighters reorganized themselves into guerrilla commands. They hid in towns and jungles, supported by local populations, and occasionally struck at American bases and patrols. According to regimental history records, Perkins's regiment arrived at Manila on March 27, 1905. Perkins was stationed at nearby Fort McKinley, where he spent most of his twenty-five-month service in the Philippines.[73]

Apart from patrolling the countryside and protecting supply and communication lines, Perkins and the other men in his company built public works, such as roads and bridges. Life in the Philippines was hard. The climate was hot and humid, especially during monsoon season. The islands were covered with jungles, mountains, and mosquito-infested swamps and rice paddies. Thick brush, bamboo, razor-sharp grasses, rain, mud, rivers, and creeks hampered patrols. The local population was often hostile toward Americans. Apart from smugglers, bandits, and guerrilla fighters, the greatest threat came from diseases, especially malaria and dengue fever. It appears that Perkins's company largely escaped these infections.[74]

Perkins continued in the service for several more years, reenlisting in 1907. He was stationed in various places, including Fort D. A. Russell, Wyoming, and Fort Apache, Arizona. At the end of his second enlistment, in December 1910, he returned home to Fort Berthold. His company commander remarked on his discharge papers that Perkins had distinguished himself as a sharpshooter and that his service had been "honest and faithful." Like many of the old scouts, he was unsuccessful in securing a pension. Worse, perhaps, was the fact that people at Fort Berthold did not all believe his stories of service in the Philippines. For years, he served as a lay reader at the Episcopal church. He died on July 31, 1949, and was buried at the Episcopal cemetery in Nishu. Not until many years after his death did someone discover that he had indeed served honorably in the US armed forces abroad.[75]

When the United States entered World War I in 1917, the Arikaras, like many other Indian tribes, enthusiastically supported the war effort. Nine Arikaras served in World War I. They were Charles and Ernest Fox, Joe Young Hawk, Thomas Rogers, Daniel and Harvey Hopkins, Philip Star, William Deane Jr., and Robert Winans. Meanwhile, the three tribes purchased $79,000 in Liberty Bonds and donated $4,503.76 to the Red Cross.[76]

The enthusiastic support from the Fort Berthold tribes took Superintendent Jermark by surprise. "It is amazing to see how interested many of the older Indians have become," he wrote in 1918, "and how eager they are for an explanation of where the different armies are located which is explained to them by diagrams, the different kinds of arms used, different modes of defense, as the trenches, wire entanglements, etc., all of which is in such great contrast to the kinds of warfare known to them in the early days." Jermark remarked, "There are no more loyal people," and they "have certainly taken the war to heart and made every effort to do their part." Indeed, "in each instance the quota [for Liberty Bonds] was over-subscribed by adults and minors," and "many of the boys have been drafted but a great percent did not wait for the draft but volunteered, many of whom were not of draft age."[77]

Arikara men enlisted for a variety of reasons: patriotism, a desire for adventure, to escape the confines of the reservation and see the world, and to follow in the footsteps of their ancestors and gain war honors. Despite attempts to create all-Indian regiments, the Arikara soldiers were integrated into white units because the Bureau of Indian Affairs reasoned that this would speed up their assimilation into white society.[78]

Undoubtedly, the Arikara soldiers sometimes encountered racial prejudice. Many officers held stereotypical ideas and believed that Indians possessed superior instincts, physical qualities, and fighting skills that supposedly enabled them to spot, sense, and sneak up on the enemy without being detected. Some officers even believed that Indians were equipped with "night vision." Misled by such stereotypes, officers often assigned the most dangerous tasks to the Indian soldiers in their command, and such misconceptions contributed to the disproportionately high casualty rates of Indian soldiers in the war.[79] One historian estimated that at least "5 percent of all Indian servicemen died in action, compared to 1 percent for the American Expeditionary Force as a whole."[80]

One of the first Arikara soldiers to enlist was Charles Fox, who served in the 128th Infantry Regiment, Thirty-Second Division. This division, nicknamed the Red Arrow Division, saw heavy fighting in France. It first saw action in July and August 1918 at Soissons, where it earned the admiration of the French, who nicknamed the division Les Terribles. When not fighting, the men in the division spent their time training replacement troops in gas defense drills, target practice, and small unit attacks. During the Meuse-Argonne offensive in the fall of 1918, Fox's division served near Verdun. Despite cold weather, heavy packs, enemy fire, and gas and flame attacks, the division slugged on against the German Kriemhilde defenses of the Hindenburg Line.[81]

On October 8, 1918, Fox was wounded by a bullet in the neck. He was evacuated to a French hospital behind the lines. He was in the hospital recovering from his wound when he learned that the Germans had called for a ceasefire. At 11:00 A.M. on November 11, 1918, the ceasefire went into effect. Fighting ended. The Meuse-Argonne offensive was the costliest yet for the Thirty-Second Division, which suffered 6,046 casualties, included 1,179 men killed, 1,006 severely wounded (including Fox), and 3,321 lightly wounded. Since the beginning of the war, forty-five men in Fox's company had been killed. Many more had been wounded. Fox spent five more months in the hospital before setting out for home on March 16, 1919. A few weeks later, in April, he arrived in the United States, where he was mustered out of service.[82]

Two Arikaras served on the front lines in France with the First Infantry Division. They were Thomas E. Rogers and Joe Young Hawk. Both men enlisted as volunteers in Bismarck on August 1, 1917, and were at first assigned to the Forty-First Infantry Division. After receiving their training in North Carolina, New York, and New Jersey, Rogers and Young Hawk left for France, where they were reassigned to the First Division.[83]

Once they arrived in the trenches on the front lines, they patrolled no man's land and sometimes took part in small-scale assaults against enemy trenches. These raids required skill and daring and were performed by specialized troops. Their purpose was to capture prisoners and to learn more about the enemy's defenses, but the raiders often suffered casualties. In April 1918 the First Division took part in an attack on the town of Cantigny. Before the attack, the Germans launched a terrible bombardment on American positions using mustard gas and fifteen thousand artillery shells. After nearly three and a half hours, the Eighteenth Infantry Regiment, to which both Rogers and Young Hawk belonged, had suffered 850 casualties. Among the wounded was Young Hawk, who had to be treated for gas poisoning.

On May 23, Young Hawk was again severely wounded. Although the circumstances are not entirely clear, it appears he was wounded during a raid on German lines. At one point, he found himself surrounded by five Germans. He was wounded and taken captive but somehow managed to turn the situation around. He reportedly killed several of his captors and marched the remaining Germans back to his line. There he received medical attention for leg wounds, and he was evacuated to a hospital behind the lines. In the absence of antibiotics, doctors could do little but clean the wounds and hope that no serious infection resulted. But it eventually became necessary to amputate the leg. Young Hawk remained in a French hospital for several months before he was returned to the United States.[84]

As a result of his injury, he was unable to join Rogers in the attack on Cantigny, which was scheduled to begin on May 28. In the days before the attack, Rogers worked for the Intelligence Section, crossing into no man's land to locate enemy machine gun positions and determine the enemy's strength. Whether he realized it or not, his role was similar to that of the Arikara scouts who had served with Custer. According to one of his officers, Rogers would crawl to the enemy lines alone to capture lone guards and take them back for questioning. If a man resisted, Rogers killed him and brought his coat back as evidence. "In 90 nights he did not fail once to bring back his man or a coat," the officer reported. "He brought in 33 of the latter."[85]

Rogers joined in the battles of Cantigny and Soissons. Although the First Division suffered many casualties in these battles, Rogers survived. By the time the First Division was relieved, it had suffered 7,318 casualties. Of these, 1,714 had been killed in battle.[86] After the Battle of Soissons, Rogers was promoted to sergeant and sent back to the United States to train new troops for trench warfare at Fort D. A. Russell. He was still training soldiers when the armistice went into effect on November 11, 1918.[87] He received an honorable discharge from the service on July 5, 1919. On his discharge papers, his regimental commander wrote, "Sergeant Thomas E. Rogers ... [h]as throughout his service with this regiment on the front given proof of the highest qualities of the soldier, notably during the attack on Cantigny, May 28th, 1918, and the battle south of Soissons, July 18th to July 22nd, on both of which occasions his service with the Intelligence Section of this regiment proved him to be a soldier of the highest type."[88]

Another Arikara recruit was Harvey Hopkins, who served in the 352nd Infantry Regiment, Eighty-Eighth Division. On August 30, 1918, his division arrived in France, where the men continued their training. In preparation for a major offensive, the division first went to a quiet sector on the front to acclimate to front-line conditions. Hopkins was still at this sector when news of the armistice reached him. While in France, he contracted the dreaded Spanish flu. Hopkins recovered but spent six weeks in a French hospital before he was able to rejoin his division.[89] He was among the American troops who crossed the Rhine into Germany following the armistice in November 1918. At the city of Koblenz, they occupied a bridgehead to control the Germans while the details of the peace treaty were worked out.[90]

Several other brave young Arikaras enlisted in the army but never made it to the front. Daniel Hopkins was assigned to a supply company of the Thirty-Third Infantry Regiment of the Second Division. Philip Star was assigned to the Forty-Third Infantry Regiment, Fifteenth Division, at Camp Logan, Texas. William C. Deane Jr., had just turned twenty-one when he enlisted and was also sent to Camp Logan, where he joined Star in the Forty-Third Infantry Regiment. Robert Winans and Ernest Fox were both assigned to the Eighty-Eighth Division. Most of these men learned of the armistice while they were still in training and never made it to France.[91]

All veterans, regardless of whether they made it overseas, received a hero's welcome home. In accordance with ancient Arikara tradition, some received new names. In recognition for his bravery during the war, the Arikaras honored Thomas Rogers with the name Charges Alone. When the Arikaras organized an American Legion post on the reservation, they named it after Joe Young Hawk. New songs

Distinguished World War I veteran Thomas Rogers, also known as Charges Alone, in dance regalia, 1923. After receiving US citizenship, the Arikaras enthusiastically embraced the "powwow revolution." In some categories, dancers competed with each other for prizes. State Historical Society of North Dakota, 00410–00025.

were composed in honor of those who had gone to serve. The war experience, then, allowed the Arikaras to revive some of their traditions.

The effects of his wounds continued to trouble Joe Young Hawk. On June 16, four years after being gassed and wounded in both legs, Young Hawk died. His death was announced in the *New York Times*. "Tribal services will be held when Younghawk is buried on Monday at the Fort Berthold Indian reservation," the announcement said.[92]

In recognition of Thomas Rogers's service, President Calvin Coolidge made him a letter carrier at Fort Berthold. Coolidge appointed him "without regard to the civil service rules" but solely on the basis of his record in the war. When French general Ferdinand Foch visited North Dakota while touring the United States, he picked Rogers out of a crowd of Indians and told the audience, "Tom Rogers was the bravest soldier in France."[93]

Other veterans became esteemed in the community. They had fought for democracy and self-determination for peoples around the world and would not let government agents keep them from exercising the freedom to maintain traditional ways. Harvey and Daniel Hopkins became founding members of the Nishu Singers, a traditional Arikara singing group. Daniel Hopkins eventually purchased from Ella P. Waters (Yellow Bird Woman) the right to conduct the ritual for the death feast and conducted it on several occasions before he passed away himself on November 26, 1982, at the age of eighty-two.[94] William Deane Jr. became a tribal subchief and served as treasurer in the tribal council. He was an active member of the American Legion post and presided over the organization for several terms. He also participated in Arikara tribal functions.[95]

CITIZENSHIP

The assertiveness of the veterans when it came to staging traditional Arikara ceremonies and practices received an additional boost when Congress transferred citizenship to Indian veterans of the war in 1919.

The movement to grant citizenship to all Native Americans in the United States dated to 1913. One of the driving forces behind the movement was Joseph K. Dixon, a self-declared "friend of the Indian." In 1913 Dixon visited Indian reservations around the country to conduct "flag raising ceremonies," where tribes displayed their patriotism and loyalty to the United States.[96] In September 1913, Dixon and his crew arrived at Fort Berthold, where they received a warm welcome from Chief Sitting Bear and the other chiefs and headmen. On September 27, the ceremony was held at

Elbowoods. Sitting Bear, Bear's Belly, and Strikes Two were the Arikaras invited to raise the flag together with a number of prominent Mandans and Hidatsas. During the ceremony, Dixon played a recorded message from President Woodrow Wilson on a phonograph.[97] With thumb prints, the chiefs signed a pledge of allegiance, stating, "Through our presence and the part we have taken in the inauguration of this memorial to our people, [we] renew our allegiance to the glorious flag of the United States and offer our hearts to our country's service.[98]

Despite Dixon's efforts, the issue of citizenship did not gain momentum until after World War I, when policymakers recognized the irony that Indian soldiers had fought to protect democracy around the world while not enjoying democratic rights at home. In 1919, while Harvey Hopkins and other Indian soldiers were still in Germany as part of the Allied occupation forces, Congress adopted the act that granted citizenship to Indian veterans of the war.

Universal American Indian citizenship was not adopted until five years later, when Congress passed the Snyder Act. This act declared all "non-citizen Indians born within the territorial limits of the United States . . . to be citizens of the United States."[99] Citizenship entitled the Arikaras "to all the rights, privileges, and immunities" of US citizens. This meant, among other things, that they had the right to vote, file lawsuits, and appear as witnesses in court. From then on, the rights of Indians, including freedom of religion, were protected under the Constitution and the Bill of Rights. Citizenship made it more difficult for the Indian Bureau to crack down on traditional Indian practices and ceremonies. Nevertheless, the Indian Bureau continued its policy of limiting Indian people in an attempt to "civilize" them.

Although citizenship protected the Arikara people in some ways, it also posed new problems. Not only were Arikara citizens now required to pay taxes, but the transition to citizenship, with all the bureaucratic red tape it entailed, was particularly difficult for elderly people. "It will be rather hard for some of the real old people, as they cannot read nor write and need an interpreter in their transactions," an unnamed Arikara wrote. He added, "Something should be done to take care of the old people and even younger ones."[100]

A NEW GENERATION

Fortunately for these elders, a new generation of tribal leaders, most of whom had been educated in white-run schools, worked tirelessly for the well-being and the rights of their people. Among these new Arikara leaders were Charles Hoffman, Peter H. Beauchamp, Albert H. Simpson, William Deane Jr., and Byron H. Wilde.

Hoffman was appointed superintendent at Fort Berthold in 1908. Although an advocate of assimilation (he opposed Indian dances, for example), he was also a defender of the rights and interests of the people of Fort Berthold. For example, he allowed Orin G. Libby to conduct interviews with the surviving Arikara scouts in 1912. In his four years as superintendent, Hoffman proved to be a highly capable agent.

In 1910 Deane, Wilde, and Beauchamp, together with young educated Mandans and Hidatsas, founded the Fort Berthold Business Council. The purpose of the council was to represent the views and opinions of people on the reservation to the Indian Office. Council members served one-year terms and each represented a specific community. Although the council had no real decision-making authority, it did advise Superintendent Hoffman. Furthermore, it provided its members with valuable experience and a greater voice in reservation affairs. On several occasions the council petitioned the federal government and sent delegations to Washington to discuss issues of importance.

In 1924, the council hired attorney Charles J. Kappler to pursue land claims of the three tribes. In 1930 Kappler and his associate Charles H. Merillat successfully sued the government on behalf of the tribes. The attorneys showed that the government had taken almost 11.5 million acres from the tribes without adequate compensation. In 1930 the US Court of Claims ruled in favor of the three tribes. A year later, on March 2, 1931, Congress authorized a payment of about $2.1 million to the tribes. Most of the money was distributed among the people in a series of per capita payments. Most used the money to build or repair houses and to buy farm machinery, livestock, and automobiles. The money also allowed the people at Fort Berthold to weather the worst years of the Great Depression.[101]

The Fort Berthold Business Council proved to be an important instrument for helping young men gain political and managerial experience. This training turned out to be particularly useful after 1936, when the tribes gained greater political control under the Indian Reorganization Act of 1934. Several council members, such as Peter Beauchamp and Albert Simpson, would later serve as tribal chairmen and tribal judges. Despite their white education and Christian faith, both these men were proud and strong advocates of the cultural and historical heritage of the Arikara people. Simpson, for example, served as an interpreter for Melvin Gilmore in the 1920s, and through his work with the old doctors of the tribe, he learned many old Arikara ceremonies and practices.[102]

Peter Hayward Beauchamp was a son of Arikara scout Peter Beauchamp and a grandson of Pierre Beauchamp. After graduating from Hampton, Beauchamp returned to Fort Berthold, where he assisted the chiefs as an interpreter. During his life he held various positions: road foreman, rancher, farmer, superintendent of the Arikara Congregational Sunday School at White Shield, and minister in the Congregational Church. In addition to being a founding member of the business council, he served several terms on the tribal council and was tribal chairman between 1942 and 1944. After World War II he served as a tribal judge. Although he was a devout Christian, he could talk for hours about Arikara history and ceremonial life. He strongly disagreed with white people who said that the old Arikaras were simply "superstitious." He explained to a white reporter, "[They] had ceremonies which were gone through with but all the time there was an undercurrent of worship and respect for the great unknown and for this reason it was easy for them to take up the teachings as told in the Bible." While a tribal judge, Beauchamp supported tribal police officers who wanted to go on vision quests in the hills surrounding the reservation. He was also highly critical of the US government, once saying that it treated former enemies such as Japan and Germany better than it treated Indian people.[103]

CHANGE AND CONTINUITY

As the examples of Albert Simpson and Peter Beauchamp show, the government's attempts to destroy Arikara culture were unsuccessful. True, many traditions and customs disappeared as the older generations of Arikaras passed away. High mortality rates perhaps did more to eradicate tribal traditions than any government policy except allotment. Although some young Arikaras showed little interest in preserving the old ways, others, despite being reared in an increasingly white-oriented world, tried hard to protect and preserve what they could.

Arikara elders understood how difficult it was for younger generations to maintain the old ways because first and foremost, they had to learn how to survive in the white world. Therefore the elders welcomed historians and ethnologists to record the old history and ways. These records stand today as important repositories of the ancient Arikara wisdom.

The Fort Berthold reservation was changing. Frame houses had replaced earth lodges. The first cars appeared on the reservation, making cultural exchange between Indians and whites easier. Taking advantage of available land, white people moved to Fort Berthold in growing numbers. At the same time, young Arikara people looked for experiences and opportunities outside the reservation. Some moved away to study, others went into business as cattlemen, while a third group traveled around the world as members of the US armed forces.

It was the Reverend Charles Hall who realized that ironically, the changes he had hoped to effect themselves caused trouble. The automobile, he lamented, not only brought in Christians more easily but brought in the devil as well. Missionaries had fought to discourage Indian dances, only to see them replaced by "immoral" Western dances and jazz music. Meanwhile, although the government had discouraged Indians from waging war against each other, it now increasingly called upon them to fight in America's foreign wars.[104]

The old and the new coexisted, as they always do. Dance halls played popular music one evening and traditional Arikara songs on another. Young men returning from military service appreciated the honors bestowed upon them by their own people as much as the commendations signed by their commanding officers. Parents gave their children English names when they registered them at the tribal office but often asked an elder to bestow an Arikara name on a little one as well. And during the long winter nights, people gathered around the furnace to exchange stories. Some of these were stories of the old days, when Neešaanu created the world, Mother Corn guided the Arikara people, and warriors went out on their adventures. Other stories were new and told of distant cities, faraway lands, strange peoples, and wonderful things. For such is the nature of history, in which old stories are retold and new ones constantly added.

11 THE SECOND FLOOD

BETRAYAL OF THE ARIKARA NATION, 1934–1953

> When the dam came, [all] was gone, you know. I mean the family units, the societies, everything was disrupted. Never, ever to happen again. Never to come back again.[1]
>
> —RUSSELL "BUDDY" MASON, 1998

The period between 1934 and 1965 witnessed repeated policy changes that affected the Arikara people and their Mandan and Hidatsa neighbors. The Indian Reorganization Act of 1934 held the promise of a better future by granting more self-government to the people, though it also carried the seeds of political factionalism that would manifest itself in later decades. The three tribes reciprocated eight years later by fully supporting the US war effort in World War II. Nearly two hundred Indians from Fort Berthold served in the armed forces, among them some sixty to seventy Arikaras. But the sacrifices of these men and women were dishonored by the federal government shortly after the war, when Congress adopted a plan to construct a massive dam that threatened to flood the most productive and beautiful portions of the reservation.

It seemed that what the federal government gave with one hand, it took away with the other. Arguably, the construction of the Garrison Dam was the most devastating policy ever devised by the federal government against the three tribes. The dam did more than flood the valley, dispersing people wide and far: it destroyed three ancient ways of life.

THE INDIAN REORGANIZATION ACT

In 1933 the Arikara people lived quietly on farms and homes along the Missouri River. Here they grew crops as their ancestors had done for centuries. Some families also raised cattle, while the elderly leased their land to white farmers and ranchers. Despite intermarriage, the Arikaras preserved what was left of their language and customs. They continued to gather for tribal ceremonies, funerals, and social events. The two leading Arikara settlements were Beaver Creek and Nishu (formerly Armstrong), although a number of Arikaras lived near the agency at Elbowoods.

Elbowoods was the largest town on the reservation. Apart from agency headquarters, there was a courthouse, sheriff's office, jail, and a hospital. Because it drew its population from all three tribes as well as white agency personnel, Elbowoods was more "cosmopolitan" than other settlements. A telegraph connected it to the off-reservation world.[2]

Although Fort Berthold fared quite well compared to many other Indian reservations around the country, it nevertheless faced a number of problems, including continued land loss due to allotment, droughts, joblessness, and health-related issues. Franklin Roosevelt's New Deal promised to solve several of these problems. Hundreds of young Indians found jobs constructing roads, schools, bridges, and other public infrastructure through the Indian Department of the Civilian Conservation Corps. The new policies, proclaimed by Bureau of Indian Affairs (BIA) commissioner John Collier, also protected Native manufacturers of arts and crafts by authenticating Native-made objects and creating more efficient marketing networks.[3]

The centerpiece of Collier's legislative efforts was the Indian Reorganization Act (IRA), or Wheeler-Howard Act. Adopted in 1934, the act was designed to revive tribal cultures by ending allotment and by extending "certain rights of home rule to Indians." In short, the act overturned the 1887 General Allotment Act and provided for the establishment of tribal governments. Each tribe had the right to accept or reject the act. BIA officials visited Fort Berthold to explain the various aspects of the act. Apart from self-government, the act promised an economic stimulus plan. When the proposal came up for a vote on November 17, 1934, more than 93 percent of eligible voters on the reservation went to the polls. The plan was approved by a vote of 477 to 139.[4]

After endorsing the Indian Reorganization Act, the leaders of the Mandan, Hidatsa, and Arikara people gathered to draw up a tribal constitution and bylaws. The constitutional committee was composed of the ten members of the old business council and five former chiefs, including Sitting Crow, Bears Arm, Foolish Woman, and Spotted Horn. Chief Running Wolf, now eighty-one years old, represented the Arikaras. The committee was a perfect mix of school-trained young men and experienced elders. To help draft the constitution, they received legal counsel from John H. Holst, a BIA representative who arrived at Fort Berthold on October 29, 1935. The next day the constitutional committee met Holst for the first time.[5]

For nearly two weeks the committee met daily at the agency building at Elbowoods. The members took their task very seriously. Despite freezing weather (Holst wrote that temperatures outside sometimes dropped to -65°F), the delegates braved the elements to attend meetings. Not all delegates trusted Holst. One Arikara leader demanded that a stenographer be present to report all that was said in the meetings. "For the past hundred years," he said, "government representatives have been coming to us with lies and flowery promises which they later deny."

The meetings proceeded slowly. Few of the old chiefs spoke English, so all that was said had to be translated into Arikara, Mandan, and Hidatsa. Sometimes the delegates met for fifteen hours a day. Eight days into the process, Holst wrote in exasperation, "No constitution of any kind anywhere has ever received more intense consideration." The tribes took their responsibilities very seriously. "The members of the committee of fifteen have examined every clause and every phrase and every word of every clause," wrote Holst. "They have sought exact interpretation of the meaning of every word in three Indian languages."[6]

There were tensions and frictions between committee members. "There is bitter rivalry among members of the committee," Holst noted in his diary, but he also noted "a complete absence of any appearance of antagonism among the members of the different tribes." Holst believed that the three tribes had "learned through long years of hardship to live together and to respect each other." Despite the tensions, progress was made. On the fifth day of the meetings, the delegates agreed on the official title of the tribal organization: the Three Affiliated Tribes of the Fort Berthold Reservation. The chiefs liked the word "affiliated" because it implied a sense of brotherhood among the different tribes. At the insistence of Running Wolf and the other chiefs, the constitution included a clause offering protection for Native ceremonies and traditions. After the session on November 8, a delegation headed by Running Wolf told Holst "that the older people of the reservation appreciated the efforts which had been made to protect them and their traditions."[7]

Finally, on the morning of Sunday, November 10, the committee unanimously approved the constitution. A small celebration followed. Everybody was pleased with the result. Now the committee members returned to their communities to persuade the people there to accept the constitution and its bylaws as well. Over the next weeks and months, people gathered to discuss the issue. On May 15, 1936, the tribal constitution was laid before the people for approval. Voter turnout was high. About 90 percent of all eligible voters showed up at the polls. After all ballots had been tallied, the people of Fort Berthold had voted in favor of the constitution by a margin of 336 to 220.[8]

In the constitution, the people of Fort Berthold outlined how they would govern themselves. The document provided for a tribal council, elected every two years, composed of delegates from the eight major communities at Fort Berthold. Only tribal members over the age of twenty-one could vote. Elections were to be held on the first Tuesday in September. Among other powers, the tribal council had the power to present and prosecute claims on behalf of the people, set up rules and regulations for law enforcement, and manage economic affairs. Any member of the tribe could subject a decision of the council to a referendum if he or she submitted a petition signed by 10 percent of the eligible voters on the reservation. To prevent further land loss Article 9, Section 2 of the constitution stated that no part of tribal land could be mortgaged, sold, or ceded. Privately owned land did not fall under this provision. Although the constitution provided the people of Fort Berthold with a new name—the Three Affiliated Tribes—most continued to identify themselves as either Arikara, Mandan, or Hidatsa.[9]

The bylaws regulated the duties of the tribal council, the tribal chair, and other tribal officials. Each member of the council had to swear an oath to "support and defend the Constitution of the United States and the Constitution and Bylaws of the Three Affiliated Tribes of the Fort Berthold Reservation, and [to] faithfully and impartially discharge the duties of councilman to the best of my ability." Like the constitution, the bylaws were approved by popular vote on May 15, 1936. Shortly thereafter, the people voted in their first tribal council election. Arthur Mandan became the first tribal chair, Ben Goodbird became vice chair, Peter Beauchamp was made secretary, and George W. Grinnell became treasurer.[10]

Over the following years, several Arikaras served on the tribal council and a few were elected to the office of tribal chair. Albert H. Simpson and Peter Beauchamp led the council during the troubled years of World War II. It must be pointed out that council service was not easy. Council members often faced criticism from members of the other tribes and frequently from people of their own nation as well. Still, considering what little experience these people had, they served admirably during these years.

ARIKARAS IN WORLD WAR II, 1941–1945

More Arikaras served in World War II than in any other war before or since. They served in the US Army, US Navy, and US Marine Corps. Several Arikara women joined the war effort in the Women's Army Corps (WAC). Some men and women left the reservation to work in war-related industries around the country. Those who remained at home worked hard on their fields and ranches to increase agricultural production.

On Sunday, December 7, 1941, the people of the Fort Berthold Reservation quietly went about their business. The reservation had been slowly recovering from the drought years of the mid-1930s. With government loans, the tribal council, under the chairmanship of Arikara Albert Simpson, had begun an ambitious agricultural recovery program. That Sunday, people attended church and spent a cold afternoon at their homes or visiting relatives and neighbors. Reports of Japan's attack against the US fleet at Pearl Harbor filtered back only gradually to Fort Berthold. There was no phone service on the reservation; news spread mainly by word of mouth. But soon everything moved quickly. On December 18, 1941, Mason Two Crow, a Hidatsa from Elbowoods, was the first member of the Three Affiliated Tribes to volunteer for service. Two days later, Archie Hopkins, an Arikara from Nishu, joined the army. Many others followed.[11]

About twenty-five thousand Indian men and women served in World War II. This was more than one-third of all able-bodied Native people between age eighteen and fifty. Unlike African Americans, they were integrated into white units. Those who did not or could not serve planted Victory Gardens, bought war bonds, and contributed in other ways. In 1944 Indian farmers and ranchers produced enough beef, pork, mutton, and poultry to supply 233,365 soldiers with rations for one year. By 1945 Indians had purchased more than $50 million in war bonds and stamps. By war's end, forty thousand Indian men and women had left their communities to work in war-related industries in cities around the nation. Native American women contributed greatly to the war effort. The *New York Times* estimated in 1943 that some twelve thousand Indian women worked in industry; a smaller number served as army nurses or as members of auxiliary forces. Native men fought in all theaters of the war and earned military honors, including two Congressional Medals of Honor, thirty-four Distinguished Flying Crosses, forty-seven Bronze Stars, fifty-one Silver Stars, and seventy-one Air Medals.[12]

Nearly two hundred Fort Berthold Indians served in the armed forces during the war. Among them were some sixty or seventy Arikaras, as well as many men and women of mixed Arikara–Mandan–Hidatsa heritage. Not all of them saw action, but Fort Berthold Indians took part in all theaters of the war: on the Atlantic Ocean, in North Africa and the Middle East, in Europe, in mainland Southeast Asia, and on numerous islands in the Pacific Ocean. Two Arikaras, Donald Hosie and Thomas White, made the ultimate sacrifice.

BETRAYAL OF THE ARIKARA NATION   261

Of nearly two hundred Fort Berthold Indians serving in World War II, between sixty and seventy were Arikara. They served in all branches of the military and in both theaters of the war. Several Arikara women enlisted and served in supportive roles. Two Arikaras, Donald Hosie and Thomas White, were killed in the European campaign. Here Private Guy Bateman, an Arikara from Elbowoods, is interviewed before deployment. NARA, RG336, H-25-L12642.

Donald "Three Bears" Hosie was born on October 24, 1924. His parents were George Hosie and Lottie Styles. When Donald was sixteen, his father died. On May 5, 1943, he enlisted at Fort Leavenworth, Kansas, and was assigned to the 101st Airborne Division. This division, nicknamed the Screaming Eagles, consisted of paratroopers, who jumped out of planes, and glidermen, who traveled to targets in gliders made of canvas strapped over flimsy metal frames. These troops were dropped deep behind enemy lines to seize and hold bridges and roads until they were relieved by the regular infantry. They were only lightly armed. Hosie was a paratrooper in Company A, 501st Regiment. Its nickname was Geronimo.[13]

Hosie's division joined Operation Overlord, the invasion of France on D-Day, June 6, 1944. Early that morning, his company was dropped deep behind enemy lines to secure exits from Utah Beach. But darkness and German air defenses scattered the paratroopers along a wide area. The 101st Airborne suffered heavy losses when some men landed in the swamps of the Douve River. These paratroopers drowned when their parachutes dragged them down into dark waters of the marshes. Hosie survived the jump. Scattered over a wide area, individual paratroopers joined one another and formed small bands, skirmishing with German troops dispatched to destroy them. Though small and disorganized, these units succeeded in capturing roads inland from Utah Beach. They kept the German forces busy, allowing ground troops to land relatively safely at Utah. Over the next few weeks, US troops strengthened the beachhead and moved west to capture the port city of Cherbourg. Hosie was wounded in one of these fights and sent to a field hospital, where he was treated for his injuries.[14]

By September 1944, Hosie had recovered sufficiently to join his division for Operation Market Garden, the largest and most famous airborne operation in history. The purpose of the operation was to capture a series of bridges in the Netherlands, which would allow Allied forces to bypass German defenses of the Siegfried Line. From there, an invasion into Germany's industrial heartland could be launched. If it was successful, the troops would be home by Christmas. On September 17, 1944, planes and gliders took off from airfields in England. After crossing the English Channel, they encountered German air defenses. Hosie's regiment was dropped near the town of Veghel in the Netherlands.

On September 23, 1944, Hosie's company took up a position along a ditch on the outskirts of the little town of Eerde, along a crucial sector of "Hell's Highway," as soldiers named the road that stretched from Belgium to Arnhem. The men had been marching for days and were too exhausted to dig in, so they slept in the ditch. That night, German paratroopers troops occupied a ridge of sand dunes across from Hosie's position. On September 24, a US patrol captured some Germans and learned that the paratroopers had occupied the dunes. This unit had also fought the Screaming Eagles in Normandy; the Americans were anxious to attack the paratroopers and clear the dunes. The fighting was fierce. Crossing the field to the dunes was very dangerous. Artillery support was largely ineffective because the sandy dunes absorbed the impact of the shells. Hosie's company led the charge, but many men were wounded or killed before they were able to cross the field. Perhaps Hosie too was fatally wounded in this charge, although it is also possible that he was wounded while trying to clear the ridge of German soldiers. He died that night in a small café that had been turned into a field hospital. He was one month shy of his twentieth birthday. His body was initially buried at Wolfswinkel, the Netherlands, before it was moved to the United States for reburial.[15]

News of Hosie's death reached Fort Berthold in October 1944. His mother, Lottie, was working in her field husking corn when she received the news. A memorial service was held at the Congregational church at Nishu on October 22. Some three hundred people attended the service, which was conducted by the Reverend Lawrence Howling Wolf and the Reverend Harold W. Case. Part of the service was conducted in the Arikara language. Peter Beauchamp delivered a message of courage. Although Hosie's body had not yet been returned, members of the Joseph Young Hawk American Legion Post led a procession from the church to the cemetery. There, American Legion members sang the "Battle Song." Walter Old Rock played taps. Several years after the war, Hosie's remains were finally returned to Nishu. Reburial services were held, with the Joseph Young Hawk American Legion Post in charge of the military rites. Hosie was laid to rest in the cemetery of the Congregational church at Elbowoods.[16]

Although Hosie's division had seized all its objectives, the entire operation proved to be one bridge too far. Despite great sacrifices, British and Polish paratroopers were unable to capture the last bridge at Arnhem. Consequently, the war was not over by Christmas but continued into 1945. Nevertheless, a large portion of the Netherlands had been liberated from the Nazis. Germany's defeat was by now merely a matter of time.

Another Arikara who made the ultimate sacrifice was Thomas "Yellow Hawk" White. He had been born in Nishu on March 21, 1912. His parents were Rhoda Edison and Thomas White Sr. White was married and raising a family when, on March 26, 1942, a few days after his thirtieth birthday, he enlisted at Fort Snelling, Minnesota.[17] He was eventually assigned to the 358th Infantry Regiment of the Ninetieth Infantry Division. In 1943 his division was shipped to Britain, where it prepared for Operation Overlord. On D-Day, the first units of the Ninetieth Division landed on Utah Beach. White's regiment landed two days later. The regiment saw heavy fighting when it tried to break through the German lines. The Germans were determined to drive the Allies back into the sea. The country behind the dunes of Normandy was covered with hedgerows, behind which the Germans took up defensive positions. White's division sustained heavy casualties as it conquered hedges one at a time. He received commendation for his actions in Normandy.

In July the Ninetieth Division broke through the German lines and rushed forward. City after city fell: St. Hilaire, Louvigne du Desert, Landivy, Mayenne, Le Mans. In each town the Americans received a hero's welcome. During the Battle of Falaise Gap in August 1944, White's division cut off elements of the German Seventh Army, which was subsequently destroyed. In four days, the Ninetieth captured thirteen thousand prisoners, wounded or killed eight thousand more men, and captured three hundred enemy tanks, 250 self-propelled guns, 164 artillery pieces, and 3,270 vehicles. White received another commendation for his participation in this campaign.[18]

In late August White's division was reassigned to General George S. Patton's army. Patton drove his men forward. In November, they cracked the German Maginot Line. During the fight, White's regiment captured Fort Koenigsmacher, one of the strongholds in the line. After crossing the Mozelle River into Germany, they ran into the Siegfried Line. On November 23, the 358th Regiment launched its attacks. Violent artillery barrages and fire from German pillboxes caused many casualties. The Americans captured two towns before the advance was blocked. Fighting was heavy. Among the casualties was White, who was killed on November 26. The next day, his regiment was ordered back. For his sacrifices in this campaign, White posthumously received another commendation.

His remains were later found and buried with military honors at the American War Cemetery in Luxemburg. After the war, General Patton was buried there also. Each year, the people of Luxemburg honor the men buried here in a solemn ceremony.

Several Arikara women also served in uniform. Margaret E. Starr, Elizabeth Felix, and Laura Bell Huber served in the WAC. Carolyn White Bear served with the navy in the Pacific. Female volunteers performed noncombat-related duties to free up men for combat. Most were employed as clerks, typists, stenographers, and switchboard operators. Others were trained as car mechanics, motor pool drivers, weather observers, cryptographers, radio operators, sheet metal workers, parachute riggers, control tower operators, electricians, lab technicians, and aerial photograph analysts. Women received pay and benefits, including pensions, overseas pay, life insurance, medical coverage, and death benefits, equal to those of men of the same rank.[19]

Margaret Starr (born January 2, 1921), daughter of Philip Starr and Katherine Hopkins, enlisted on May 11, 1944, in Minneapolis. All her brothers had enlisted before her, and she did not want to be left alone. She received her basic training at Fort Des Moines, Iowa, and from there was sent to Fort Childers, Texas, where she worked as a clerk and a nurse at the camp hospital. As a private she earned $21 per month. She was later promoted to private first class and earned $28 per month. Although she was twenty-three at the time of her enlistment, she received the nickname Star Baby because she looked so much younger than her age. The army used a photograph of her for promotional purposes. In her spare time, she loved to dance and go to the movies. She was coming back from a movie theater with some friends when she learned that the war had ended. She remembered that it was raining very hard and the streets were flooded. She saw an enlisted man up to his knees in water. His shirt was open and he was soaking wet and crying with joy. She later met an officer covered in mud, crying tears of happiness. The officer grabbed her and her friends and walked them back to the base in celebration. When they arrived, the officer was scolded because army rules prohibited officers from fraternizing with enlisted men and women. Starr served in the army for nineteen months. Her parents were extremely proud of her. The Arikara people composed a song in honor of her services during the war.[20]

While young men and women served in the military, the people at home did their best to support them. Apart from caring for the children, the sick, and the elderly, women also took on the burden of running family farms and ranching operations. They had to learn many things, such as handling and repairing farm machinery and equipment. Some learned to load .22-caliber guns to scare coyotes away from hen houses.[21] The Fort Berthold women also established organizations to assist families whose fathers, mothers, or children were in the service. Organizations on the reservation included the Second World War Mother's Federation of Elbowoods, General MacArthur's Service Club of Elbowoods, Nishu War Mothers of WWII, Gold Star Mothers, War Mothers and War Sisters, and the Enemy Women Society. They organized dances and celebrations honoring those who were sent off to war or came back on leave. The Nishu Morale Club was organized in 1943 by wives and sisters of servicemen. It sent letters and gift packages to tribal members stationed around the world. It also organized welcome home dances, pie sales, and celebrations to raise money for returning servicemen. The work of these organizations lifted the spirits of men in combat.[22]

In 1942 the Indian Office asked the people of Fort Berthold to increase agricultural production. Mother Corn must have smiled upon them, because in response the people cultivated the largest acreage of farmland in reservation history. They planted potatoes, corn, and beans in large quantities, as well as carrots, squash, peas, lettuce, beets, turnips, cucumbers, tomatoes, and rhubarb in smaller patches closer to home. People also gathered large amounts of wild berries. Anna Dawson-Wilde's family "put up 100 quarts of juneberries besides 90 quarts of plums and 100 jars of plum butter and jelly, 200 quarts of chokecherry jam and syrup, and 10 quarts of buffalo-berry jelly." Many of these homemade delicacies were sent overseas to men and women in uniform. Unfortunately, a sudden frost on June 22, 1942, damaged nearly 40 percent of the crop. Nevertheless, over the following years agricultural production increased dramatically.[23]

Even children contributed to the war effort. They spent long hours working in the fields or took care of younger siblings when their parents were absent. Each school had a garden, where children grew vegetables for their lunches. Some schools raised pigs and chickens. Students saved money to buy war stamps and collected paper, aluminum, scrap iron, and other materials needed for the war effort.[24]

These were difficult years on the reservation. Important materials, such as rubber, fuel, coffee, sugar, and leather, were rationed. During the particularly cold winter of 1942–43, the people of the Fort Berthold Reservation suffered tremendously from a lack of fuels to heat their homes. But worse than the cold and the lack of supplies were the reports of tribal members who had been wounded or killed in the war. Apart from Donald Hosie and Thomas White, four other Fort Berthold Indians died in the war. In November 1942, Lester Crows Heart, a Mandan, was killed in North Africa. In August 1943, Wilfred M. Stone was killed in Sicily. Clarence Spotted Wolf was killed in Luxemburg in December 1944. Francis Irwin, a Hidatsa and husband of Flora Wells, an Arikara, was killed on the Philippine island of Luzon on May 3, 1945.[25]

After Japan surrendered on August 14, 1945, the war finally ended. One by one men and women who had served returned home, where people gave them a hero's welcome. As in the old days, the people composed songs in honor of those who had served. Burton Bell conceived several songs honoring the different branches of the military in which Arikaras had served.

One of the most popular songs was the "Flag Song." Fort Berthold tribes still cannot agree on who composed it. The Hidatsas claim the song was composed by one of their people. The Arikaras maintain that the song was created by Nicholas Fox (later named Nicholas Night). Fox had enlisted in the army in January 1942. He was sent across the Atlantic and fought in North Africa and Europe. According to the "Flag Song" origin story, Fox was in a foxhole one night when a spirit came to him. The spirit taught him the words. After he came back to North Dakota, he told the words to Davis Painte, an esteemed singer. Painte put the words to music. According to the Arikaras, the Hidatsas later put Hidatsa words to the song and claimed it as their own.[26]

Flag Song

Ee nataraakani eheeu naawiinsaawi'uu	Our friends, the flag
Oeiinaseenu nuuwenaanuuhaku	Ours waving [flying] over there
Paat niineeninuhnaanawaana	The enemy, where it is waving over their land

World War II changed the lives of people at Fort Berthold in many ways. Those serving in the army or working in off-reservation industries gained experience in new trades. Change was greatest for those who served in uniform. Some returned from the war scarred, both physically and emotionally. Others returned with a heightened sense of pride and self-esteem. They would play important roles in the postwar development of the Fort Berthold Reservation.

WAR AT HOME: INDIAN POLICY SHIFTS

After World War II, Indian policy shifted again. Conservatives in Congress feared increased government spending and expanded government interference in public and economic life. After the war, they sought to roll back some of the reforms instituted by the Roosevelt administration. One target was Indian policy. The government, they argued, should stop "coddling" Indians and should once again push for American Indian assimilation into mainstream society. Maintaining separate tribal identities, they reasoned, was "un-American" and weakened the nation against America's communist enemies.

In 1946 Congress created the Indian Claims Commission as a first step toward ending the federal government's relationship with Indian tribes. Its purpose was to wipe the slate clean for past treaty violations by the government. Tribes had several years to file claims with the commission. They had to prove their aboriginal title to lands that had been taken from them. The commission would then review their claims and determine the amount each tribe was due for its losses. Some tribes, such as the Taos Pueblo and the Lakhotas of South Dakota, rejected financial settlements for sacred lands. The Indian Claims Commission closed its operations in 1978 after settling some 285 cases and paying out around $800 million in compensation.[27]

The Three Affiliated Tribes filed several claims with the Indian Claims Commission. They sought compensation for the land cessions of 1886 and 1910, for which they had received insufficient payments. They also filed claims for the disappearance of the buffalo from their lands and for the construction of government buildings with tribal funds. In May 1954, the tribes also filed claims for compensation for the illegal executive orders made by Presidents Grant and Harrison. The cases lingered in the US Court of Claims for many years. They would not be settled until the 1970s.[28]

After the war, many Indian people, both veterans and industrial workers, returned to their reservations only to find that job opportunities there were limited. But instead of stimulating industries and job programs on reservations, in 1948 the government offered financial assistance to Indian people willing to leave their communities. The relocation program helped Indian people leave their reservations for distant cities around the country. Although designed to end poverty among

Indian people, the policy was also a means to wear down tribalism and stimulate assimilation. Between 1948 and 1960, more than thirty-five thousand Indians moved to cities such as Denver, Minneapolis, Phoenix, Albuquerque, San Francisco, Dallas, Los Angeles, Oklahoma City, Tulsa, and Chicago. But despite assistance from relocation officers, adjustment to urban life often proved difficult. Approximately 30 percent of all relocated Indians returned to the reservation after a brief stay in the city. Far removed from family and friends, many people struggled with loneliness and alienation. They also encountered racial prejudice, misunderstanding, and discrimination. Unemployment caused some to slip into poverty. Seeking to rebuild their own social networks, Indian people began to form new communities in the inner cities. Some of these communities were poor, but they provided urban Indian people with a sense of identity and mutual support. By 1975 more Indians lived in urban areas than on reservations. Since the 1970s, urban Indians have made great progress. They have developed new ways of dealing with the demands and stresses of urban life through the creation of Indian centers and "survival schools." Many urban Indians have entered the middle class.[29]

A major policy shift in the early 1950s was the termination policy. Initiated by Senator Arthur V. Watkins of Utah and Representative E. Y. Berry of South Dakota, this policy was designed to end the government's trust relationship with tribes and to eventually dismantle the Bureau of Indian Affairs. Watkins and Berry had a powerful ally in Commissioner of Indian Affairs Dillon S. Myer. During World War II, Myer had headed the War Relocation Authority, which oversaw the imprisonment of more than one hundred thousand Japanese Americans. With Myer's support, Watkins and Berry compiled a list of Indian tribes that supposedly no longer required government support. Among them were the Three Affiliated Tribes. In 1953 Congress passed House Concurrent Resolution 108, which terminated the federal relationship with the Menominees of Wisconsin and the Klamaths of Oregon.

Between 1953 and 1962, Congress stripped sixty-one other tribes of federal services and protection. The consequences were devastating. Terminated tribes were required to pay taxes. Furthermore, they were now solely responsible for providing municipal, educational, health, and other services previously provided by the federal government. To meet expenses, tribes began to sell tribal land and other resources. When the money ran out, hospitals, schools, and tribal industrial projects closed down. Within a few years, several thriving communities spiraled into poverty. Individual tribal members were forced to appeal to government welfare programs. Hailed as a cost-saving measure, the termination policy ultimately ended up costing the government more in welfare payments. Meanwhile, Indian families suffered.[30]

Termination entered a new phase when Congress adopted Public Law 280 in 1953. This law transferred jurisdiction over tribal lands in California, Oregon, Nebraska, Minnesota, and Wisconsin from federal to state and local governments. It also authorized other states to take over legal jurisdiction on reservations without Indian consent, so states could now regulate Indian reservations. Initially, North Dakota was reluctant to extend its power over the tribes, but a 1958 state constitutional amendment permitted it to maintain law and order on Indian reservations. The tribes objected to state interference in reservation affairs. Relations between North Dakota and its Indian tribes quickly deteriorated.[31]

In 1955 the BIA scheduled the Three Affiliated Tribes for termination. To induce the tribes to accept termination, Watkins and the new commissioner of Indian affairs, Glenn Emmons, linked it to compensation payments for the loss of land and property incurred by construction of the Garrison Dam. The tribes, the BIA proposed, would receive their money only if they also accepted termination. BIA officials reasoned that any tribe capable of handling $12.5 million in compensation money was also capable of handling its own affairs without the supervision of the bureau. To protest the linkage between compensation payment and termination, a tribal delegation visited Washington in 1955. Among the delegates were tribal chairman Martin Cross, Sam Mathews, and Arikara representative William Deane. They had come for their compensation money, they said. It was needed to help the old people on the reservation. The bureau would not budge. Cross then appealed to North Dakota's congressional caucus and the National Congress of American Indians to put pressure on the BIA. This tactic was successful. The Three Affiliated Tribes were taken of the list of tribes scheduled for termination. This provided little comfort for the people of Fort Berthold. They already suffered from the terrible disaster that was the Garrison Dam project.[32]

THE STRUGGLE OVER THE GARRISON DAM

In 1943 the Missouri River rose beyond ordinary flood levels. Rising waters flooded cities including Omaha and Sioux City. Thousands of acres of farmland also flooded. Crops were destroyed and animal stock drowned. Human activities were partially responsible for the flood. Dikes and levees upstream had prevented natural runoff, causing the river to swell to spectacular levels downstream.[33]

For years Congress had considered "taming" the Missouri. The Army Corps of Engineers and the Bureau of Reclamation had come up with plans to control the river's water levels. The most ambitious of these plans was designed by Lewis

Pick of the Army Corps of Engineers. It included the construction of a series of dams and reservoirs. The largest of these dams was to be built west of the town of Garrison, North Dakota, just southeast of the Fort Berthold Reservation. If constructed, the lake that would be created by the dam would flood nearly one-third of the Fort Berthold Reservation. The towns of Elbowoods, Nishu, Beaver Creek, Red Butte, Charging Eagle, Lucky Mound, Independence, and Shell Creek would all be covered by the lake, as well as hundreds of homes and all the best farmland on the reservation. A competing plan, designed by engineer W. Glenn Sloan of the Bureau of Reclamation, was much less invasive and expensive, but it lacked political support. Eventually, Washington bureaucrats agreed on a compromise called the Pick-Sloan Plan. The compromise still included the Garrison Dam. On December 22, 1944, Congress adopted the Flood Control Act, authorizing construction of the Garrison Dam.[34]

As soon as rumors of the proposed dam reached Fort Berthold, the Three Affiliated Tribes voiced their objections. On November 15, 1943, the tribal council adopted a resolution protesting the plan, because the lake that would be created behind the dam would destroy the most valuable lands on the reservation, "causing untold material and economic damage to the Three Affiliated Tribes." Copies of the resolution were sent to Congress, the White House, and the commissioner of Indian affairs. The resolution was ignored in Washington. In another resolution, shortly after Congress authorized construction of the dam, the tribal council stated that the dam was a violation of the Fort Laramie Treaty of 1851. In a statement to Congress, the council said, "We have permanently located on these lands, and our forefathers also have lived on these grounds and it is the hopes and plans to have our children and their children to occupy this land continuously forever; and money or exchange for other land will not compensate us for the land, landmarks, and sentimental attachments."[35]

In October 1945, a tribal delegation traveled to Washington to protest the dam before the Senate Select Committee on Indian Affairs. Expenses for the trip were paid for by a collection held among the people of the reservation. The delegates included Martin Cross, Jefferson B. Smith, Martin Fox, and Earl Bateman. On October 9, they appeared before the committee. Cross read a statement in which the tribes claimed they had treaty rights that exempted them from eminent domain, which allows the government, under certain circumstances, to take private property for public use in return for compensation. When asked if they were willing to sell their land, Cross answered simply, "I am not here to sell the land. I am here to keep the land." Rejecting a proposal to move his people to another reservation, Cross pointed out the devastating consequences of the dam. "There is no possibility for us other than destructive," he said. "There are no benefits to be derived from this dam."[36]

The tribal delegation left Washington confident that the Garrison Dam project could still be stopped. But on December 28, 1945, Congress decided that "no money could be spent on the construction of Garrison Dam until the tribes had been given suitable and sufficient land in exchange for the land they would lose in the flood." This meant, in effect, that the project would continue. The Army Corps of Engineers began to work out the details of its designs, and preparations for construction began.[37]

To assist in their struggle against the dam, the council hired lawyer Ralph Hoyt Case to represent their suit before the government. Case quickly realized that the government would not stop the project, but he hoped that an alternative plan might spare the Fort Berthold Reservation. In 1946 Case hired Daniel C. Walser, an engineer, to study the government plans and to come up with a viable alternative to the Garrison Dam. After a quick survey, Walser issued a report recommending the construction of a dam near the town of Sanish, in the northwest corner of the reservation. Not only would this dam flood only a small fraction of the reservation, but it would also be cheaper to build. In May 1946, the Fort Berthold Tribal Council endorsed Walser's recommendations and even offered to surrender that part of the reservation that would be inundated by the dam to the government, free of charge.[38]

As with the previous protests, Congress, the Army Corps of Engineers, and the Bureau of Indian Affairs chose to ignore the Fort Berthold Indians.[39] Instead, the government suggested that the Three Affiliated Tribes surrender their reservation and move to another location. It gave the tribes until January 1, 1947, to accept a new reservation elsewhere. But the people rejected this proposal almost unanimously. "This land is our home," said James Driver of Shell Creek. "Our people are buried in the hills of our lands. We are opposed to leaving our homes." Most people agreed. A Nishu woman protested. "I object to leaving my land and home where my children have walked and played," she said. "Our cemeteries will be molested—here we have placed flowers on the graves of those who have gone on ahead of us."[40]

Secretary of the Interior J. A. Krug aborted the removal plans when white communities in the surrounding area feared they would have to vacate lands to make room for the tribes. Instead of offering substitute land, the government offered financial compensation. This too was rejected by the tribes. Unwilling to reconsider its plans and growing impatient with the tribes' resistance, Congress adopted Public Law 296 in July 1947, forcing the tribes to "accept the inevitable." The law appropriated $5,105,625 in compensation and authorized construction of the dam to begin in

Tribal chairman George Gillette weeping as Secretary of the Interior Julius A. Krug signs the order that would destroy homes, lands, and the economy of the Fort Berthold Indians. Gillette later said, "We, Indians, are not obstructionists, we welcomed the impounding of the Missouri River to provide irrigation and electric power. We did not wish to disturb the overall plan for the development of the Missouri River Basin, however, we were anxious to avoid our own destruction." NARA, Kansas City, 45641547, RG75-FB-599.

Alice Young Bear's house and shed on the road during relocation following construction of the Garrison Dam. Scenes such as this took place on many parts of the reservation. NARA, Kansas City, 285353.

October. The act basically crushed the resistance of the Fort Berthold tribes. They were forced to sign an agreement they loathed. While construction was in full swing, tribal chairman George Gillette reluctantly signed an agreement on May 20, 1948. As he signed his name, he spoke: "The truth is, as everyone knows, [that] our Treaty of Fort Laramie, made in 1851 and our tribal constitution are being torn into shreds by this contract." Indifferent to the sentiments of the Fort Berthold people, Congress quickly ratified the agreement. Perhaps to soothe its own conscience, Congress adopted Public Law 437, which appropriated an additional $7,500,000 to appease the tribes. It was not nearly enough to cover the loss of so much valuable land.[41]

Between 1952 and 1954, the people moved away from the valley. Some moved into newly constructed houses. Others had their homes moved to new locations. Others simply left the reservation altogether. Until the trucks arrived to move them, many people were in a state of denial. They could not believe their land would be sacrificed. Russell Mason, who watched the construction crews as a young boy, later recalled that "a lot of people didn't want to believe that it was really happening, that it would go away.... I didn't think that anyone would have the sense to destroy something that was so beautiful."[42]

Marie Wells, daughter of William and Leona Dean, remembered the trauma of removal and its effect on her parents:

> I just couldn't believe it. I didn't want to come home after that. My folks didn't have to move but they were lost. My they were lost-like. My father ranched down below . . . right along by the river, the Missouri River. We put up the hay down there. . . . [Our] home site was about, oh I'd say about twelve miles from the Breaks and it was on top. . . . So he couldn't bring his cattle up. He sold it and they were sick about it, you know. . . . Oh they were sad. Even visiting and stuff was out. Kinda didn't know where this one settled. They settled very far apart from each other.[43]

The dam not only destroyed homes and communities but also threatened sacred sites and objects. Virgil Chase remembered how his family came to save Grandfather Rock:

> We moved up when the water came. That was a terrible time. Everyone was leaving and crying. Some of the old people didn't want to go. And we got ready to go and mom said to stop at the Ceremonial Hall. She didn't want to forget the stone, the medicine stone. We stopped there to get it, and my brothers got off and started to try to pick it up. But they couldn't pick it up. It was pretty heavy to lift it, you know. So mom went back and she had a bad knee. She was on a cane. She was elderly. But then I noticed she talked to that stone in a different language, it was a clicking sound. I never did get it. It was a clicking sound. And she patted that rock around and lifted it up with one hand, like a feather, and put it in the back of the truck. And my brothers looked at each other. None of us said anything.[44]

Lake Sakakawea, created after the dam was finished in 1954, covered almost 217,000 acres of reservation land. Of the 643,368 acres of the original reservation, only 426,393 acres were left. The remaining land was of lesser quality than the land in the valley and was not well suited for farming. Families were forced to live on allotments scattered over the reservation. The lake sliced the reservation into five different segments. While the Hidatsas and Madans settled mainly on the western and southern segments, most Arikaras settled on the eastern segment.

Problems arose almost immediately. New roads had to be built, and tribal monuments and cemeteries, including the Old Scouts Cemetery, had to be relocated. These operations swallowed up much of the money appropriated by Congress. The tribes also disagreed on the best location for the new agency, tribal headquarters,

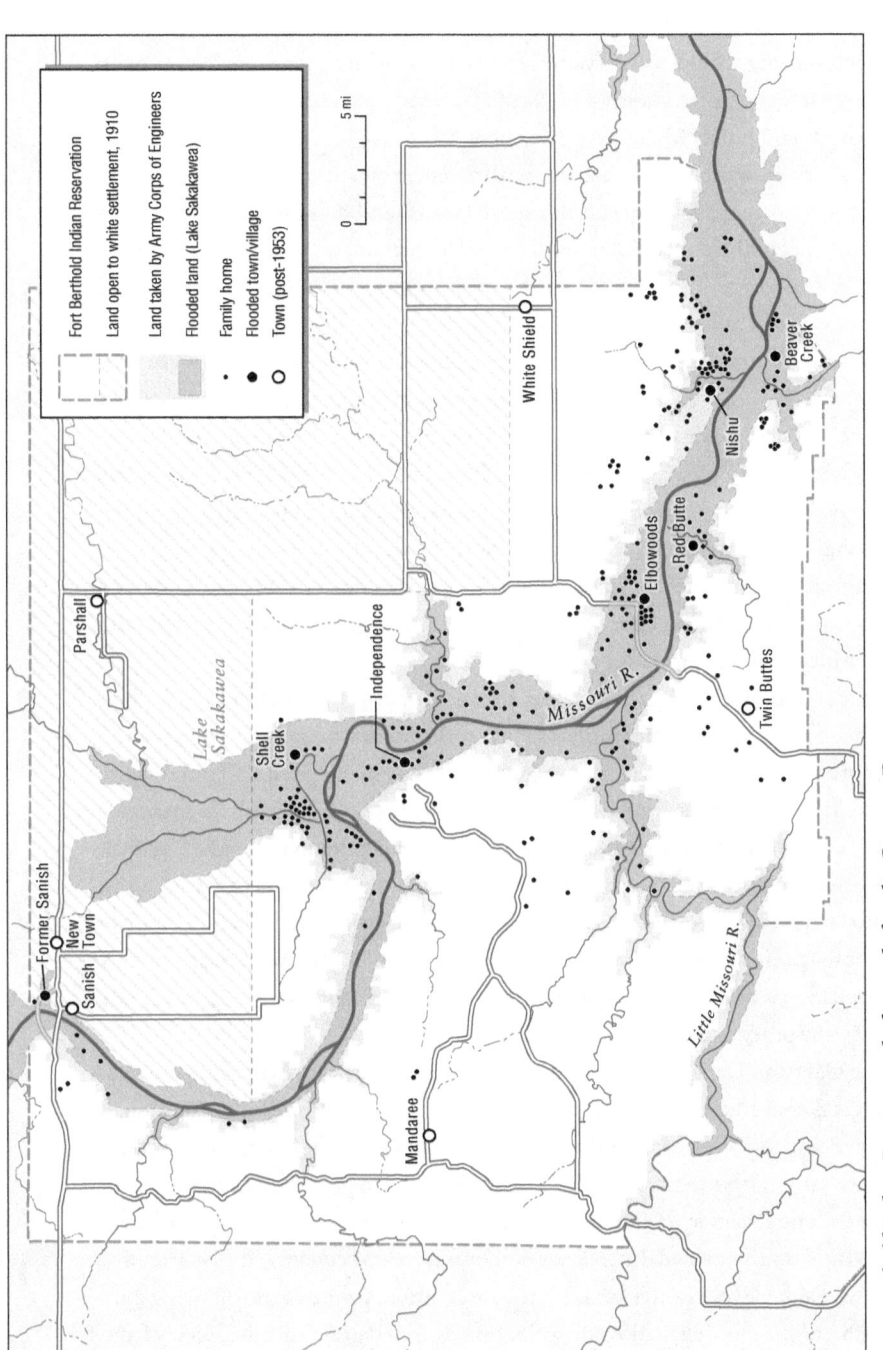

Fort Berthold Indian Reservation before and after the Garrison Dam

This map shows how Lake Sakakawea devastated the most fertile lands of the Three Affiliated Tribes and forced the dispersion of communities onto separate segments.

and other public buildings. Eventually it was decided to build the new agency on the northern edge of the reservation. The site soon received the name New Town. Although it was predominantly a Hidatsa settlement, some Arikara families from Elbowoods and Lucky Mound resettled here.[45]

New schools were constructed on the different segments of the reservation. As in the previous century, communities sprang up around these schools. In 1954 the BIA built a combined elementary and secondary school on the eastern segment, where the majority of the Arikaras lived. Three churches and a community hall soon followed. These buildings became the nucleus of the Arikara community on the eastern segment. It was named White Shield, after the old Arikara chief.[46]

Meanwhile, Arikaras living in the Beaver Creek area south of the river relocated to the southern segment of the reservation. Here the BIA built Twin Buttes Elementary School. Although quite a few Arikara families lived in this area, Twin Buttes was considered a Mandan community. Other Arikara families moved to the town of Parshall on the northeastern segment of the reservation. Parshall was a white community. Its residents were mostly of Scandinavian descent. Many of them did not approve of the sudden influx of Indian people among them. Racial tensions and discrimination were the result.[47]

Of all the problems the tribes faced, the issue of how to spend the $7.5 million was the most divisive. Some wanted to invest the money to develop industry and other programs. Others demanded that the money be distributed fairly among the people. They argued that families needed the extra money to deal with the problems caused by relocation. The issue kept the tribes in turmoil for many years. Finally it was decided to distribute the money among the people in per capita cash payments. The first payment of $200 was distributed in 1953. People used the money to improve their homes, buy ranch or farm implements, and pay off debts. Two more payments followed in 1955 and 1957. Then the money, like the land they had once owned, was gone. In the process, a way of life had changed forever.

The Garrison Dam relocations had tremendous political, economic, and psychological consequences for the people of Fort Berthold. Politically, the project poisoned relations between the Three Affiliated Tribes and the federal government. People were angry with the BIA, which was supposed to protect their interests but had abandoned them in their hour of need. They would never trust the government again. The dam also caused the collapse of the reservation economy. The lake flooded the most valuable and fertile lands on the reservation. In the years following construction of the dam, agricultural production declined dramatically. Money from leases (an important source of income for older people) declined as well. Many people were forced to look for jobs outside the reservation. Far more damaging were the psychological effects. The years following construction of the dam witnessed dramatic increases in alcohol and drug abuse, joblessness, domestic violence, child abuse, clinical depression, suicides, diseases, crime, and death. The economic crisis caused by construction of the dam further compounded these problems. More and more people became dependent on federal assistance.[48]

But there was another, almost invisible effect of the Garrison Dam. The dam not only deepened factional rivalries, but it also changed a way of life that had existed for centuries. People who had been part of tightly knit communities were now spread out over distant allotments in one of the five segments of the reservation. Roy W. Meyer, in his history of Fort Berthold and the Garrison Dam, wrote, "The sense of community that had existed in the old settlements was impossible to regain, for the new settlement pattern was more scattered, and the residents of a particular segment included several of the old communities." Instead of cooperation, people struggled to survive on individual allotments, without the help of friends, neighbors, and extended family. Some of the old societies disappeared because it was more difficult to get all the necessary bundles together. As the societies disappeared, so did many of the old songs. The disruption caused by the Garrison Dam weighed especially heavy on people born before the dam was built. The place they had grown up in was destroyed before their eyes. All they had left were memories of a world that had disappeared. Russell Mason said in 1998,

> I'm sixty-two years old, and life goes by so darn fast that I'll leave with those memories, and I can tell you where every place was at.... I can just imagine what my mother feels sometimes sitting on that deck, looking out there. You know, some of the older people, that's how they finish their life is talking about the way it was. Or sharing with you how it was with those stories. But that piece is gone. I mean, that's what's really, you know, that's what's really sad.[49]

12 AFTER THE FLOOD

> It will be the disturbance caused by the white man, and their conduct will be the basis of bringing about those difficulties you will not enjoy.
>
> —FRANK HEART, JULY 3, 1952[1]

When Frank Heart (1867–1964) was a little boy in the 1870s, he watched an old man named Hair Tufts on the Lip climb the roof of a lodge, from which he began to address the people. Everyone was quiet while the old man spoke. People restrained their dogs to prevent them from disturbing the speaker. Hair Tufts on the Lip reminded the people to put their faith in the sacred powers. He told women to work hard and men to be brave in war. He told the people to heed the ancient teachings and to worship in the traditional manner.

Little Frank watched Hair Tufts on the Lip through a crack in a wall of a lodge. He did not understand everything the old man said and decided to visit his grandmother who lived on the other side of town. He said, "I didn't know that that old man was watching my movements as I dashed across to my grandmother's. I heard loud talking from the old man saying 'Hey, you, with those horrible legs of yours, you probably will be the same person that will disregard and violate the teachings of my word. You will probably be the chief disturber of the rights as are taught you by these words.'"

Heart's grandmother admonished him for having interrupted the old man's speech. "My grandmother then told me that I had done wrong," Heart said. "[We] are not to do anything that would hinder or disrupt the recitation given by the old man and we were not to move about until the old man had ceased his speaking, then we were permitted to leave the lodges and go out and about our duties."[2]

In 1950 Heart, also known as Rising Eagle, was an old man himself. Now it was his turn to remind younger generations of the old teachings. But times had changed.

Would they listen to him? Would his words reach their hearts? Or would they go unnoticed? Undoubtedly, at some moments Heart felt like old Hair Tufts on the Lip, whom he had slighted many decades before.

In 1950 anthropologists from the University of Chicago arrived at Fort Berthold to do fieldwork while the Garrison Dam was under construction. For the next three years, they conducted interviews with Mandans, Hidatsas, and Arikaras. From their work emerges a picture of communities and cultures in crisis. The old ways were under pressure, and the Garrison Dam threatened to destroy rapidly what had been declining slowly.[3]

Among the men the anthropologists interviewed was Frank Heart, who seized the opportunity to express his concerns about the future of his people. That future, he said, was bleak. Instead of following tradition, the people were following the ways of the whites. Heart recalled Hair Tufts on the Lip's teachings about white people, which seemed prophetic in light of what was happening with the Garrison Dam project.

White people were coming, Hair Tufts on the Lip had prophesied. They would "overrule and destroy those things which belong to us." White people were reckless and greedy. "That which he will cast his eyes on, he will covet," Hair Tufts on the Lip warned. "It will be the disturbance caused by the white man, and their conduct will be the basis of bringing about those difficulties you will not enjoy."[4]

Now the people, Heart lamented, were losing their ways. They had abandoned old forms of worship. He saw a direct link between the passing of the old ways and the deteriorating health of the people. The creator had given medicines to the people on the condition that they would worship in the old manner, he said. If they did not observe the rituals, the people would be punished and die sooner. "People have been affected with unknown causes resulting in untimely death falling over in their trucks which is becoming quite common in our day," he said. Some of the poor health Heart attributed to changes in diet, such as canned food that sometimes sat on shelves for years, but in general he said it was the people's neglect of their sacred obligations that caused this misfortune:

> Now we have departed and violated the teachings so we have become weak and short-lived by reasons of non-observance [of] the teachings given by the old. It's becoming alarming. We hear from day to day reports of death among our people that that person has fallen off without warning and it's only the result of our non-heed what our old people preached. It's the result of our non-observance and disregard to revere the teachings of the old.[5]

Rather than seeing religious decline as a result of economic loss, social fragmentation, and demoralization following construction of the Garrison Dam, Heart attributed the decline in religious observance to lax attitudes among the people themselves. Young people were seduced by white ways. Heart especially mocked the latest trends among women, including hairstyles, cigarette smoking, and other behaviors they copied from white people.

Remembering the words of Hair Tufts on the Lip, Heart stated that the people would become disrespectful and troublesome: "They will make tumultuous disturbances, they will be aggressive and undertake and declare themselves worthy people when they are not." Heart did not mince words. "The old men of old proclaimed that we would have the habits of dogs. It will come to the point where incontinence will prevail; sexual ethics will become uncontrollable, that persons will indulge in sexual acts in daylight and places unashamed. Those practices will be committed between both sexes and of near kin."[6] Apart from sexual intemperance, Heart scorned laziness, immodesty, and alcohol abuse. He closed with the prediction that once he and his generation had passed away, all that remained of the teachings would pass with them. "When I pass on," Heart said, "you people as a tribe will no longer have the opportunity to learn what was preached by the old medicine men."[7]

Whether it was the passing of the last earth lodge generation that had known the old traditional ways before the white agents of civilization arrived, or the US government's disastrous engineering project to tame the Missouri River, Fort Berthold was at a crossroads in the early 1950s. Arikara history would forever be divided in two parts: before and after the flood.

"NOW WE ARE NOTHING!"

Frank Heart was not alone in blaming Arikara struggles on religious declension. Henry Snowbird, in 1952 one of the oldest and most respected tribal members, also scorned young people for failing to observe religious practices and social responsibilities, and for pursuing personal pleasures rather than work for the common good. Like Heart, Snowbird blamed the people's problems on their failure to worship properly. "We are living in the times of hardship, for the reason being that we have been negligent, undutiful for not perpetuating our rituals," Snowbird said. "Because of our failure the world and the earth is in bad ways, has become depraved." As a result, he said, "drought and other calamities have visited our earth."[8]

Snowbird's words seem surprising because he was also a committed member of the United Church of Christ. As strange as it might appear to readers today, to

Arikaras this duality was not at all contradictory. Both forms of religious expression shared an awe of the mysterious. To Arikaras like Snowbird, it was possible to worship in two (or even more) different churches and feel comfortable in all. Both ways came from the creator and thus had to be treated with respect. Both were worthy of preservation. Thus Snowbird could speak out in defense of the old ways while also being committed to the United Church of Christ.[9]

Female elders shared the concerns expressed by Heart and Snowbird. Elizabeth Gillette, also known as Chief Woman in the House, also lamented the passing of the old ways, especially where they pertained to women's work. Rather than admonishing people, however, Gillette chose to tell young women how things were done in the past.

When she was little, Gillette had been trained in gardening and domestic chores by her grandmothers, who prized industriousness above all other qualities in a woman. A woman not only had to work the field and maintain the lodge, but she also had to make certain that her male relatives looked clean and tidy. That included making bead- and quillwork for them and combing and braiding their hair. A good woman always worked. "I've now become an old woman," Gillette said, "and I've cultivated the habits of industry, and when I am about my home I long to do things about the place to keep it in tidiness and I feel sure that I have established myself in the habits of industry up to this time." Her grandmothers had warned her of the consequences of not living up to this ethic: "If on the other hand you are lazy and disregard the comforts of your husband, your husband will soon get tired of your lazy habits and will begin to despise you and will have no affection for you."[10]

Similar lamentations would be echoed by subsequent generations. More recently Fannie Whitman-Perkins (1914–2001) lamented the passing of the old ways. The Arikaras were once the greatest medicine people, she said, even greater than the Pawnees. Her grandparents were very strict. They taught respect. Back then, kids had to sit still during ceremonies. When people visited, children had to be quiet. People respected the medicines and ancient knowledge of the elders. "I had a strict grandmother," Whitman-Perkins said, "[but] she had a big heart." She and her grandmother used to tan hides together, and she made many moccasins when she was young. She also remembered dancing with garden hoes made of buffalo shoulder blades. She looked after grandfather White Face for many years. Her grandparents were mixed Ree and Gros Ventre, so she learned the languages of both. Back then, old people used to visit for days. She missed those days at Elbowoods, before the dam scattered eople. Back then the people were healthy too. "They had good teeth! Today we all have false teeth ... ghost teeth!" Whitman-Perkins chuckled.[11]

Now everything was different. "They were holy people back then," she said. "Now we are nothing! ... The Ree tribe is losing everything." New diseases, such as cancer, kidney stones, heart disease, and especially diabetes, were afflicting the people. "It's all because of the food we now eat." She used to teach at White Shield School but found the work challenging. The students did not want to listen. The old kinship ties were lost, together with the medicine ways and even the way to offer smoke to the sacred beings. The next generation did not care. They did not buy the old medicines. "Today," Whitman-Perkins said, "nobody respects the elders." Everyone is jealous of one another. Young people do not help anymore. They expect to be paid. "It's a wild life now," she said. Back in the old days, young men used to watch young women to see who worked hardest and was dressed well, indicating that they were good seamstresses. Then young men would tell their parents which woman they wanted to marry. Today, when intertribal couples have children, they only speak English and don't teach the tribal languages. Worse, people are even marrying their relatives. "We're coming to the end of the world, I think," Whitman-Perkins said.[12]

In her own way, she tried to preserve what she could. She was proud of an old gourd rattle she owned and took good care of it. She also owned two ancient ears of corn representing Mother Corn, the great Arikara prophetess. She taught her grandchildren old Arikara songs and derived great pleasure and pride from that. She passed away in 2001 at the age of eighty-seven.[13]

Elders such as Frank Heart, Henry Snowbird, Elizabeth Gillette, and later Fannie Whitman-Perkins blamed cultural declension—the failure to worship in traditional ways especially—for misfortunes such as the Garrison Dam. To them the Garrison Dam was not so much a cause but an effect of the people straying too far from tradition. In their minds, the flood was a case of history repeating itself.

FOLLOWING NATIONAL TRENDS

Arikara history after the Garrison Dam is a cycle of gains and setbacks. Although the elders blamed religious declension for the poor state of the people, the fact is that in almost every respect, Fort Berthold followed national trends for Native Americans in terms of health, economic problems, and cultural decline.

On a positive note, the Fort Berthold nations witnessed a remarkable population growth after World War II. Tribal enrollment rose from circa 1,200 in 1910 to 3,314 in 1958. By 1974 tribal enrollment had climbed to fifty-two hundred. Over subsequent decades it continued to climb steadily: to 8,750 by 1998 and to 12,204 in 2011. In February 2021, the Mandan, Hidatsa, and Arikara (MHA) Nation numbered 16,770 enrolled members. Of these, 5,395 were seventeen or younger, 9,808 were between the ages of eighteen and fifty-nine, and 1,567 were age sixty or older.[14]

These numbers mask a problem. Since the 1950s, most tribal members have lived away from the reservation. This complicates cultural preservation because the base for participation in cultural activities is smaller. Because of Lake Sakakawea, even those Arikaras remaining on the reservation often live too far away to regularly participate in forms of cultural expression. Only the annual Arikara powwow at White Shield attracts many off-reservation Arikaras.

The encouraging population growth numbers further obscure the fact that in matters of health and life expectancy, American Indians still lag far behind white Americans.[15] According to studies conducted by the Centers for Disease Control (CDC) American Indians "are more likely to have poorer health, unmet medical needs due to cost, diabetes, trouble hearing, activity limitations, and to have experienced feelings of psychological distress in the past 30 days" than any other ethnic group in the United States. A 2006 study showed an infant death rate that is 48.4 percent greater than the rate among whites. Native Americans also have "the highest rate of motor vehicle-related deaths, one of the highest rates of suicides, and the second highest death rate due to drugs (whether illicit, prescription, or over-the-counter) compared with other racial/ethnic populations."[16] In 2010 the ten leading causes of death among American Indians were heart disease, cancer, unintentional injuries, diabetes, chronic liver disease (cirrhosis), chronic lower respiratory diseases, stroke, suicide, influenza, pneumonia, and nephritis. The CDC linked these issues to poverty, high school dropout rates, and other socioeconomic factors.[17]

Many of these problems afflict the Fort Berthold nations as well. What is especially striking here is that diseases such as diabetes correlate with the decline of traditional forms of subsistence. As Fannie Whitman-Perkins and other elders pointed out, many Arikaras link the rise of diabetes to dietary changes due to European colonization. The ancient ways taught by Mother Corn—gardening especially—faded rapidly after construction of the Garrison Dam. But the path had been laid by US policies in the nineteenth and twentieth centuries that led to "food scarcity, unemployment, dependence on [low-quality] government rations, and later, commodity foods."[18]

A separate issue is mental health. Native American psychologists attribute certain modern-day problems such as depression, suicide, homicide, and substance abuse to past traumas. The creation of the Garrison Dam was one of these traumatic events. Even generations born after 1954 relive the pain sustained by parents and grandparents. The trauma sometimes manifests itself in self-destructive behavior, such as internalizing anger and other emotions, and "the resulting need for anesthetic self-intervention behaviors such as alcohol abuse, drug abuse, domestic violence, or suicide makes psychological sense." Whereas American Indian societies in the past had ways to deal with traumatic experiences, these old ways were systematically destroyed. Rites of passage designed to prepare young people to face the hardships of life were replaced by new and unhealthy forms of initiation that often involved alcohol use, sometimes with devastating consequences.[19] Western responses, such as the (sometimes involuntary) sterilization of American Indian women or the placement of Native children in non-Native foster homes, often made matters worse.[20]

Economic decline was a major contributing factor in cultural decline. Farming and ranching, once booming economic activities, declined drastically after construction of the Garrison Dam. The best farming lands and ranching pastures were lost. Rather than resuming agricultural activities on the rocky lands "up top," people searched for jobs in nearby towns. A drought in the 1950s exacerbated problems for those who persisted in farming. With these challenges, only capital-intensive operations could survive. By the late 1960s, farming and ranching had recovered somewhat, accounting for 40 percent of the total income on the reservation, but the sector was hit by new crises in the 1970s and 1980s, when global crop and beef prices dropped while domestic production costs increased. Despite government loan programs, farm debts increased, and in 1986 the tribes were in danger of losing nearly thirty-five thousand acres of reservation land. The tribal government responded with a program to buy up mortgaged lands to prevent them from falling into non-Indian hands. While well intended, the act caused new tensions within the tribes. Many indebted families felt that the tribes were more interested in saving tribal land than in helping struggling families, while nonagricultural tribal members were upset that tribal funds were used to help individual farmers rather than the tribe as a whole.[21]

The decline in agriculture is troubling considering the ancient connection of the Arikara people to Mother Corn and gardening. Corn was once the life source of the nation. As more and more people detached themselves from gardening to seek employment in other areas, fewer people recognized the association between corn and the vitality of Arikara culture. One could argue that modern-day religious declension, or secularization, owes some of its force to the detachment of people from their agricultural roots. Anxious to connect with any Native form of worship, some Arikaras started participating in foreign, mainly Lakhota, ceremonies.[22]

Over the decades since the Garrison Dam's completion, federal programs have tried to address unemployment and problems created by endemic poverty. These included programs that support arts and crafts, farming, clerical work, and carpentry. Construction projects to improve and build housing, schools, roads, health facilities, and community centers provided jobs from time to time. But such projects were only temporary. Once they were finished, many people again depended on government welfare.[23]

Compensation payments for past injustices brought some relief in 1970, 1974, 1975, and 1992, but they also caused divisions over how to spend the money. Most times, the people of Fort Berthold demanded per capita payments. Only small amounts went to fund tribal programs. Consequently, after bills had been paid and debts had been settled, most of the money was gone. The settlements made it appear that the tribes were doing well, but they did not offer structural solutions to the economic problems on the reservation.[24]

Presently, most jobs on the reservation are furnished by the Four Bears Casino and Lodge (built in 1993),[25] schools and other government-sponsored offices,[26] and the oil industry. Oil resources provide some revenue but also introduce new problems. The energy market is volatile, and fluctuating prices cause disruptive boom-and-bust cycles. Under pressure from the state and oil companies, the Three Affiliated Tribes reluctantly agreed to open the reservation to hydraulic fracturing (fracking), a process that causes pollution, earthquakes, and a range of other problems.[27]

None of the new industries truly connect the Arikaras to the way of life propagated by Mother Corn. To be sure, it may no longer be possible to have a feasible economy based on old models. Meanwhile, people have lost the spiritual connection with the land that existed with the ancient ways. Indeed, traditions gradually eroded as the reservation became impoverished.

"SOON IT WILL CEASE TO EXIST!"

After people were removed "on top" following completion of the Garrison Dam, old ceremonies and customs faded as elders who knew the old secrets passed away. Younger people were less interested in maintaining the cultural traditions of their ancestors. Popular music styles, such as rock and roll (and later hip-hop), proved more appealing than traditional music and dance. Many young people also left the reservation to go to school, seek work, or serve in the armed forces. The distance between the culture of the old generations and that of the new ones grew bigger with every mile and every day of separation. Still, the demoralizing effects of the Garrison Dam loomed largest. The dam sent the message to young people that they could not, both literally as well as figuratively, stem the tide.

Some people desperately tried to keep the memory of Arikara traditions and ceremonies alive. On July 22, 1952, for example, members of the Arikara Bear Society gathered at the home of Claire Everett near Nishu to initiate Wilbur Howard into the society. The ceremony was sponsored by Howard's grandparents Byron and Anna Wilde. Howard had been studying the Arikara bundle songs for ten years, and the ceremony would be the climax of many months of study and instruction. Albert H. Simpson, a graduate of three Indian boarding schools, led the ceremony. He was assisted by Burton Bell, Roy Gough, Snowbird, and an unidentified man who acted as fire keeper. Also in attendance were tribal head chief Robert Bear, Fred Fox, Claire Everett, Ralph Wells, Anna Wilde, and Arthur Mandan, as well as thirty or more spectators, mostly older people. The ceremony started around 11 A.M. First Simpson smoked and prayed. Then he placed incense on coals and purified Howard, a war bonnet and blanket Howard had brought as gifts, and finally the drum and rattles to be used in the ceremony. Songs were sung to honor all the sacred objects, followed by individual family songs. Many of the women in attendance wept when their family songs were sung and they thought of relatives who had died. Anna Wilde was overcome with emotion. An observer described the scene: "She went to the bearskins and knelt by them, weeping and stroking the bears' heads. Her grief was genuine, but the weeping seemed formalized. Mrs. Wilde then retired to the kitchen, but before leaving, waved her blue headkerchief over the heads of the bears, commonly an act of 'blessing.'"[28]

After several rounds of songs, food was brought in. It included boiled beef, beef soup, chicken, frybread, juneberry balls and sauce, pilot bread, soda crackers, pies, coffee, and cake. A small kettle of dog meat was also brought in and offered to the bearskins. Then the last round of songs started. Some of these referred to soldiers serving in Korea. The last songs referred to the old medicine lodge where the ceremony ordinarily would have taken place: "Now we are about to leave this earth lodge.... The ceremony is now over." Many of the men grunted like bears during these songs. After Howard gave the war bonnet and blanket to Simpson in payment for his initiation into the society, the feast began. One by one, everyone in attendance received a piece of the consecrated dog meat. Some rubbed the meat on their arms and chest to receive the maximum power from it. Then everyone ate. Some people got up and expressed their gratitude. Howard received a pipe that had been resting on the bearskin during the ceremony. It served as his badge of membership in the Bear Society.

At the end of the evening, Simpson asked two anthropologists who had attended the meeting if they had enjoyed the proceedings. They had. Simpson was pleased, but he also added with sorrow, "It is dying out.... Soon it will cease to exist."[29]

KEEPING TRADITIONS ALIVE

Still, in numerous small ways, people tried to keep traditions they had been taught by Mother Corn alive. Soldiers who returned from war received a hero's welcome. Following the Korean War, ceremonies for returning soldiers were organized by women's clubs. They ran "doin's" (events) to raise money for soldiers on furlough.[30] The clubs also provided food and drink at wakes and funerals for soldiers who had died in the war. On June 30, 1951, for example, they assisted in the traditional wake for Clyde Bearstail, who had fallen in the Korean War. A club called the War Sisters of Elbowoods prepared food for the ceremony. Bearstail's sister explained that the Arikaras "believe in spirits that stay around for four days. My mother wanted this to be done so we are having it. The men take some food and take it outside. Usually this is done at night. But he didn't die from any sickness, just from the war so it is being done in the day.[31]"

Since Korea, Arikara Indians served in every subsequent conflict, including those in Vietnam, Bosnia, Iraq, and Afghanistan. These soldiers were honored by the tribes in celebration. Many found their final resting place in the Old Scouts Cemetery, seven miles west of White Shield on land donated by Dan Howling Wolf. The cemetery had been moved there by the US Army Corps of Engineers in 1954. Unfortunately, the engineers placed the graves in the wrong direction. Instead of the heads pointing east, the graves were placed in a north–south direction, with the headstones facing south. Some people claimed that as a result, the spirits of the deceased scouts were restless.[32] The graves were not placed in the right direction until October 1995, after tribal council representative Austin Gillette called for a resolution of the issue at a public meeting.[33] The Joseph Young Hawk-Elmer Bear American Legion Post maintains the cemetery.[34]

Some individuals carried on the sacred traditions as best as possible. Among them was Joseph Reed (1931–1999), who was born near Nishu in the bottomlands now flooded by Lake Sakakawea. The mode of instruction in the old days was through stories that told young people what *not* to do. Until the mid-1940s, people addressed each other by their Indian rather than their English names. Reed's Indian name was Little Thunder. People in those days relied mostly on Indian doctors. "There were some powerful people in the old days," Reed said. "Back then you couldn't simply jump into a car to go to a clinic, so you went to an Indian doctor. They used to have apprentices, but when that stopped, a lot of it died. Nobody paid any attention anymore and it died out. People still have bundles, but they don't know what they're about. You have to be sure you want to learn about bundles."[35]

Reed learned some Arikara secrets and ceremonies through observation. When he was young, he was often invited by the different medicine societies to attend their ceremonies. Among those were the Buffalo, Bear, Deer, Owl, Mother Corn, and Duck Societies. Though he was grateful for this knowledge, it also required him to live a life of austerity, avoid bars, and abstain from certain indulgences. He regularly had dreams and visions that woke him up. He was often called to assist in funerals, for example to feed the spirits after four days. After each funeral, he had to cleanse himself with sweat baths to avoid becoming sick. He was also often called to name children. One time while he was bestowing names, a dead body was nearby. He feared the spirit would come and interfere, so he put tobacco down to keep the spirit away. A gopher appeared but was repelled by the tobacco. This showed that the medicine worked. People also asked him to interpret their dreams.[36]

Reed firmly believed in the sacred powers. One time doctors found spots on his liver and told him he would have to go to a sanatorium in Rapid City for treatment. Before leaving, he met a friend and they had a sweat together. During the sweat, an eagle came down. This happened a few days in a row. One day they found a little bird. On the fourth night, his friend said he was now cured. When the doctors X-rayed him in Rapid City, the spots on his liver had mysteriously disappeared.[37]

Reed went on several vision quests. The first time he went to sacrifice himself in a fast. He carried only a pipe. When he came back, the spirits told him what to do next, but he did not act upon it. He went a second time, and a cricket came and talked to him. It scorned him for not having done anything yet. Afterward, Reed never failed to do a ceremony when people asked him for one.[38]

He never had formal training in Arikara ceremonies. He just picked things up as he went along. Many times when he was asked to do a ceremony, he had no idea what to do until he got there. He did know that one could not do ceremonies when the ground was frozen, because then Mother Earth was asleep. "You can pray," he said, "but you can never take down the bundle until the grass is green." Once a group of people took down a bundle in March. "That was wrong!" Reed said. "Those people were older than me and should've known better."[39]

Though many people still possessed bundles, they did not know how to use them. They called on Reed for more information, but many refrained from learning more because of the responsibility that comes with this kind of knowledge.[40]

Thanks to efforts by Joe Reed and others, some traditional ways have survived. Indeed, many families and individuals preserve knowledge handed down orally by the older generation. But much of it is fragmented and scattered over different parts of the reservation. Still, efforts have been made to collect, gather, and preserve this knowledge in a more systematic manner.

The struggle to maintain traditional culture continued in the 1960s and 1970s. But few young people were interested in preserving the culture. "The young generation," said Arikara elder Thelma Hunter in 1973, "seem to refuse to learn their language and culture because of the white man taking hold and making them think more about white man's education and their ways." Such complaints were not uncommon, but Hunter also recognized the culpability of the older generations: "We as parents have not maybe taken too much effort to teach our children [because] we feel they have to learn the white man's way in order to be able to help themselves and be able to cope with the white people."[41]

Other elders also mourned the loss of cultural and historical knowledge. "Why [do] we have so much trouble today, the younger people do not have respect for anyone not even themselves," lamented George Gillette in 1973. "Why is there so many deaths among our people is because we have drifted away from our heavenly father. We need to go back to the old way of living."[42] Alfred Morsette agreed. "We have to teach the young people the old songs so that they will not forget," he said. "Now is the time to teach the people and [seek] the help of the recorders."[43]

Concerns about the loss of cultural patrimony caused the tribes to construct the Three Tribes Museum in 1962. The museum was erected with a generous financial contribution from Helen Gough, an Arikara elder who had earned a sizable fortune from oil leases. The museum was formally opened to the public on July 1, 1964. Apart from displaying priceless artifacts, it also informs visitors of the turbulent history of the three tribes.[44]

Many invaluable artifacts ended up in private collections and museums elsewhere in the country. The story of the Buffalo Society bundle is typical. In 1964 Frank Heart, the last keeper of the bundle, died at the age of ninety-seven. By the 1950s, the bundle's ceremony was no longer performed, and none of the younger Arikaras showed an interest in learning the bundle's secrets. Heart did not want the bundle to be passed on to an uninitiated Arikara because he feared that its powers might harm the Arikara people if it were handled improperly. He instructed his son Ben to either destroy the bundle or to sell it to the North Dakota State Historical Society in Bismarck, where it could not do any harm. After Frank's death, the bundle remained in Ben's house for a while. According to Ben, the two buffalo headdresses in the bundle would fight with each other by clicking their horns together and keeping the family awake at night. Ben asked Kenneth Leonard, a medical doctor from Garrison who shared an interest in Arikara culture, to buy the bundle and donate it to the historical society, which received it in August 1973.[45]

Today, only seven of twelve original bundles remain. A few of these bundles are still in the possession of Arikara people. Although they are no longer used in tribal ceremonies, they are still kept in places of honor on the west walls of private homes, where their keepers treat them with great reverence.[46] One such bundle is today in the care of Sidney Howard. It tells of the creation of the Arikara people and where they came from. Sidney's youngest sister Anita remembered seeing its contents when she was a child. Children were allowed to attend the opening of the bundle only if they could sit still. It was always kept in a special room, where children were not allowed to play. Anita never tried to get close because she knew the bundle was off-limits. The family still maintains the highest degree of respect toward this bundle.[47]

Apart from tribal bundles there are a number of privately owned personal bundles. One bundle owner is Yvonne Fox (White Buffalo Woman), who inherited a personal bundle from her grandmother Philamine Little Sioux-Felix. She was a kind-hearted woman who never talked bad about people and was generous to everyone. "She always gave visitors stuff to take home!" said Fox. Little Sioux-Felix used the bundle to treat people who were sick, because in those days "you couldn't jump in a car and run to the hospital or a clinic or anything." When Fox received the bundle she was given advice to honor it by living a good life. She devoted her life to teaching elementary school. She also served as treasurer of the Sahnish Cultural Society and was heavily involved in developing curriculum materials on Arikara history and culture for the White Shield School.[48]

Certain ceremonies, including naming and last supper rites, continued. Both ceremonies are of a sacramental nature because they deal with different stages in life, including the release of the spirit after death. Only people with a military record, veterans of good standing, chiefs, and medicine men and women (doctors) can give names.[49]

Although the Arikaras once had their own version of the sun dance, its secrets had been lost. In the 1990s, Arikara Glenn Perkins reintroduced the sun dance, although some of it was inspired by ceremonies from neighboring communities. The place of the dance was a patch of land donated by Austin Gillette for this purpose, about five miles southwest of the town of White Shield. One person instrumental in setting up the ceremony was Pearl Ross, who had attended Lakhota sun dances before. The sun dance was performed again in subsequent years but ended after Perkins's death in 2002.[50] Today many Arikaras participate in intertribal sun dances.

The Arikaras continued to express themselves creatively in other ways, including with pottery making, beading, quilting, painting, music, and other forms of expression. Perhaps the most accomplished Arikara painter was Miles S. Horn (1895–1977), who often depicted scenes from Arikara history and whose work was exhibited around the world. Unfortunately, most of his paintings ended up in one collection, which was later destroyed by fire.[51] Though a relatively modern craft form, quilting has taken on great meaning for Native Americans. They created a whole new type: star quilts. These quilts are not only functional items but are of great ceremonial value as well. They are given away at memorial feasts, naming ceremonies, and homecoming celebrations for veterans. They are displayed at family and community gatherings and draped over cars in parades. During funerals they are draped over caskets; sometimes the deceased is wrapped in a star quilt before being laid to rest. Star quilts replaced old painted buffalo robes as items that celebrate the lives of those who made or display them. The quilts are an excellent example of how old concepts and ideas live on through new technologies.[52]

Since the 1970s, tribal schools have been at the center of MHA cultural reawakening. For the Arikaras, the White Shield School was particularly important.[53] The school has invested heavily in language revitalization programs. In collaboration with Arikara elders and the school, linguist Douglas R. Parks developed lessons for Arikara students. As part of his work, Parks collected traditional stories and translated them into English. Among the speakers who contributed to Parks's study were Ella P. Waters, Lillian Brave, Mary Gillette, Eleanor Chase, Esther Perkins, Alfred Morsette Sr., William Deane Jr., Dan Howling Wolf, Dan Hopkins, Matthew White Bear, and Joseph Fox. Initially, some younger Arikaras objected to Parks's work, claiming that elders were giving away both the language and Arikara cultural secrets. The elders disputed that. Their intention was to preserve songs and stories for posterity and to allow Parks to develop language instructional materials.[54] With the language materials Parks developed, the White Shield School implemented an Arikara language program in 1975. That year, Delilah White-Yellow Bird came on board as the assistant language teacher at the school. Until her retirement in 2011, she taught hundreds of students the basics of the language. Arikara is required in kindergarten through sixth grade at White Shield School. Students are also required to take Arikara for at least one year in high school. But reviving a language when only a few (if any) active speakers are left is very difficult. In the absence of speakers at home, children are rarely encouraged to speak the language outside the classroom. Some people oppose teaching the language, partly because it drains resources from other important school subjects. The program has also been criticized by some who have unrealistic expectations about language acquisition, especially in regard to Arikara, which is an extremely difficult language to master. But there are also successes. Students become aware of the significance of the language and the culture that is taught to them. They recognize that the language and history of the tribe are important elements of their identity. Some actively use their acquired skills to compose songs and prayers. Such gains, however small they may seem, are nevertheless significant.[55]

On May 2, 1973, the Three Affiliated Tribes founded Fort Berthold Community College. In 1994 it was one of twenty-nine tribal colleges that received land grant institution status, enabling it to receive research grants from the US Department of Agriculture. Today, many of the teachers are Native Americans, who bring Native perspectives to the subjects they teach. In addition, the college offers courses in Native American art, ethnobotany, tribal government, hand games, singing, comparative spiritual beliefs, and several tribal languages, including Arikara.[56]

The most visible and popular form of cultural expression is the annual Arikara Powwow. After dispersal of the Arikara people following completion of the Garrison Dam, there was a growing need for a communal celebration that would bring the people together. Out of this need, the Arikara Powwow emerged. It allowed Arikara people from various segments of the reservation and even those who lived farther away to come together and renew family and tribal relationships.

The Arikara Powwow grew out of the grass dance. Although dances are at the center of the celebration, other events, such as giveaways, parades, rodeos, and pageants, often accompany the program. Over time a number of dance contests have been added to the program. Today's powwows usually feature contests in men and women's traditional dances, men's grass dances and fancy dances, women's jingle dress and shawl dances, and contests for dancers in different age categories. The increase in prize money has led to a growing professionalization among dancers and singers, some of whom travel the powwow circuit for much of the year. Dance outfits, especially those of the fancy dancers, have become not only increasingly elaborate and fantastic but also more expensive.[57]

Although dances can be staged at various times of the year, the Arikara Powwow traditionally takes place on the second weekend in July, at the height of the powwow season. It is held at an arena just outside the town of White Shield. It is an occasion for Arikara people who have moved off the reservation to return home and socialize with relatives, friends, and other tribal members, as well as guests from both Indian and white communities. It is a multiday event that includes various dance contests as well as activities such as horse races. Despite these attempts to maintain Arikara cultural identity, the era after the Garrison Dam was one of struggle and adjustment. The dam caused a wound that has never fully healed. Even the generations born after the second flood bear the scar inflicted by the US government's betrayal of the Mandan, Hidatsa, and Arikara nations.

AFTERWORD

LOOKING TOWARD THE FUTURE WITH ONE EYE TO THE PAST

> [Mother Corn] went down to the earth and she roamed over the land for many, many years, not knowing where to find the people.
>
> —HAND, "THE ORIGIN OF THE ARIKARA," 1903

When Arikara storytellers sat down with Pawnee ethnographer James Murie in 1903, they spoke with reverence about the great Arikara prophetess: Mother Corn. She had been sent by the Great Chief Above as his emissary. "You must go down to the earth and bring my people from the earth," he told her. Mother Corn descended from the heavens and wandered the world for many years. When she finally found the people, they were living underground. Through Neešaanu's power, Mother Corn moved underground. The people rejoiced when they saw her.[1]

Thus began the history of the Arikara people. With a dreadful flood, the Great Chief Above drowned the prideful giants who had mocked him. Then he sent lightning to place the people inside the earth in the form of seeds. Now it was Mother Corn's mission to lead the people from darkness to light, from poverty to civilization, from weakness to strength.

The old oral traditions have much to teach present-day generations. As bleak as the situation appeared in the decades after construction of the Garrison Dam, the people persevered. Mother Corn has not been forgotten. She is still present in the stories told by Arikara elders. The majority of these stories are still related orally, just as they were in the past, before white visitors such Dorsey, Curtis, Gilmore, Parks, and others recorded them. These stories continue to teach, entertain, warn, encourage, and inspire.

Considering the destructive power of US government policies and projects, changing economic tides, the pulls of modernity, the impact of globalization, and the distractions offered by new technologies, it is remarkable that so much of Arikara culture has survived. To be sure, it has not been easy. To the ancient stories of suffering and struggle, new stories of hardship are added daily. In that sense, rather than an end, the Garrison Dam was simply another chapter—though a dark one—in the often troubled history of the Arikara people. Yet, throughout the pain and suffering, the people carry on with optimism and determination.

They face many challenges. New engineering projects threaten the well-being of the Arikaras and their neighbors. Apart from the current fracking boom, construction of the Dakota Access Pipeline (DAPL) and Keystone XL Pipeline have caused great concern. Recalling the devastation caused by the Garrison Dam, numerous Arikaras, Mandans, and Hidatsas joined the 2016 Save the Water and No-DAPL protests on the nearby Standing Rock Reservation. Among the activists were representatives of all generations. It is especially heartening to see the commitment of young people in these protests. They will be the future leaders of the three nations.[2]

Presently, a new generation of Arikaras has been at work to rediscover and revitalize the Arikara language, customs, and ceremonies. Their efforts fall beyond the scope of this book. Still, Arikaras looking for answers for the future do not need to look far, because if they are willing to listen—though they may struggle to hear—Mother Corn still beckons.

She has not forgotten the people. Her voice can still be heard.

NOTES

PREFACE

1. Parks, *Myths and Traditions of the Arikara*, 80.
2. Hoffman, "Remarks on Indian Tribal Names," 294–296; Parks, "Arikara," 388–89.
3. Yellow Bird, "What We Want to Be Called," 1–21.

INTRODUCTION

1. Parks, *Myths and Traditions of the Arikara*, 85.
2. Dorsey, "An Arikara Story-Telling Contest," 240–43.
3. Aaron McGaffey Beede Papers, Journal 5, entry for February 26, 1915.
4. Aaron McGaffey Beede Papers, Journal 5, entry for March 29, 1915.
5. Aaron McGaffey Beede Papers, Journal 5, 1915 and entry for March 31, 1915. In his journals, Beede recorded several Arikara stories, including the story of the Standing Rock (Journal 8, entry for October 10, 1916).
6. Cooper, *Plato: Complete Works*, 551–52.
7. Liberty and Stands in Timber, *Cheyenne Memories*, 16.
8. Parks, *Myths and Traditions of the Arikara*, 28–29.
9. See Mason, *Inconstant Companions*.
10. Deloria Jr., *Spirit and Reason*, 344.
11. See Vansina, *Oral Tradition as History*; Nabokov, *A Forest of Time*; Echo-Hawk, "Ancient History in the New World," 267–90.
12. See Van de Logt, *Monsters of Contact*.
13. Echo-Hawk, *Enchanted Mirror*, 125.
14. Clements, *Native American Verbal Art*, 1.

CHAPTER 1

1. This reconstruction is based on Dorsey, *Traditions of the Arikara*, 11–37; Curtis, "The Arikara," 80–86; Gilmore, "The Arikara Book of Genesis," 95–120; Grinnell, *The Story of the Indian*, 186–94; Grinnell, "Pawnee Mythology," 113–30; Wilson, "The Arikara Cosmogony," Gilbert L. Wilson files.
2. These were likely the fossilized bones of dinosaurs or other extinct animal species. For a discussion of Native fossil folklore, see Mayor, *Fossil Legends of the First Americans*.
3. Grinnell, "Pawnee Mythology," 123.
4. Dorsey, *Traditions of the Arikara*, 11. The creation of land by a mosquito and ducks in the accounts by Two Crows and Yellow Bear symbolizes the marriage or sexual union between earth and sky, which is also typical of agricultural societies.

5. Dorsey, *Traditions of the Arikara*, 12.

6. The description of lightning also symbolizes sexual procreation: lightning crashes into wet earth, implanting people, in the form of seeds, into earth's womb.

7. Gopher, Skunk, Bear, and Fox are listed in other accounts. The emergence from the womb of the earth symbolizes birth. This metaphor is typical of societies relying on agriculture.

8. Star's version in Dorsey, *Traditions of the Arikara*, 18, implies the division between nomadic nations following the buffalo herds and the Arikaras, who relied on corn cultivation.

9. In Two Crow's account, the animal is a fish. In the account Bear's Tail gave to Dorsey, it was a gar-pike.

10. The Arikaras' long and troubled journey not only followed a historical path but also symbolized the development of the people from "primitive" to "civilized." Gilmore, "The Arikara Book of Genesis," 100, 110–18.

11. Linguist Douglas R. Parks stated that there is no translation for the term but suggests that it may be associated with the stem *huunawa* (to leave behind or abandon). Parks, *Traditional Narratives of the Arikara*, 3:3.

12. Dorsey, *Traditions of the Arikara*, 22.

13. Echo-Hawk, "Ancient History in the New World," 267–90, especially 277. See also Echo-Hawk, *Enchanted Mirror*, 21–22, 35.

14. Dorsey, *Traditions of the Arikara*, 33, 37.

15. Dorsey, 39–44.

16. Echo-Hawk, *Enchanted Mirror*, 39.

17. Echo-Hawk, 81–135.

18. Dorsey, *Traditions of the Arikara*, 14–15.

19. Dorsey, 16.

20. Grinnell, *Pawnee Hero Stories*, 224–25.

21. Grinnell, 225. Several versions of the Arikara creation account challenge the southern/southwestern hypothesis. Dorsey, *Traditions of the Arikara*, 33, 35.

22. Dorsey, *Traditions of the Arikara*, 14.

23. Mooney, *The Ghost-Dance Religion*, 1093–94; Dorsey, *Traditions of the Caddo*, 7–13.

24. Dorsey, *Traditions of the Skidi Pawnee*, 3.

25. Dorsey, *Traditions of the Skidi Pawnee*, 23–24; Echo-Hawk, *Enchanted Mirror*, 1–7.

26. Dorsey, 3–14.

27. According to Skiri Pawnee tradition, occasionally lightning carried the first humans to earth in a (uterus-shaped) "whirlwind sack." They were released from the sack by a wolf sent by Skiritióhuts, "Fool Coyote," a star who was jealous because the other stars had not consulted him. Dorsey, *Traditions of the Skidi Pawnee*, 14–20.

28. Dorsey, *Pawnee Mythology*, 38–41.

29. Guide Rock was once a much larger feature, but later settlers used much of the hill for construction materials and effectively destroyed it.

30. Dorsey, *Traditions of the Arikara*, 159.

31. Echo-Hawk, *Enchanted Mirror*, 72–80. According to Echo-Hawk, Closed Man's unification of the Skiris into a confederation occurred circa 1300.

32. Roaming Scout (Skiri), "Dispersion of the Gods and the First People," in Dorsey, *Traditions of the Skidi Pawnee*, 10. See also Hyde, *Pawnee Indians*, 52–54.

33. A few years after the great Pawnee prophet Closed Man died, his skull was taken from his grave and placed into the yellow calf bundle of his town. This bundle was henceforth also known as the skull bundle. Many years later, this skull was replaced with the skull of the second man. Roaming Scout (Skiri), "Dispersion of the Gods and the First People," in Dorsey, *Traditions of the Skidi Pawnee*, 13–14.

34. Dorsey, *Traditions of the Arikara*, 29.

35. Parks, "Caddoan Languages," 80–93; Parks, "Northern Caddoan Languages," 197–213.

36. Dorsey, *Traditions of the Arikara*, 114–15. For another Arikara version of their separation from the Pawnees, see Parks, *Traditional Narratives of the Arikara*, 3:363–65.

37. Gilmore, "Ethnobotany of the Omaha Indians," 330–31.

38. Ethnologist George Bird Grinnell pointed out that the Arikara version of this ceremony had replaced the sacrifice of humans with something else. Grinnell, *Story of the Indian*, 124. In his account, Hand states, "The Gods of the heavens are the four world quarters, for they are jealous. If you forget to give smoke to them they will get mad and send storms." Dorsey, *Traditions of the Arikara*, 17. This idea is similar to the four directions of the Olmecs and Aztecs, who were also jealous of one another's powers and every fifty-two years competed for primacy.

39. Parks, "Caddoan Languages," 80–93.

40. Kindscher et al., *Sahnish (Arikara) Ethnobotany*, 7.

41. Frison, "Hunting and Gathering Tradition," 131–45.

42. Johnson, "Plains Woodland Tradition," 159–72.

43. Wedel, "Plains Village Tradition," 173–85.

44. Wedel, "Plains Village Tradition," 185. See also Bob Bozell, "Pawnee Origins: Anthropology, History, and Oral Tradition," Nebraska State Historical Society, March 21. 2013, www.youtube.com/watch?v=-PJMFRm6-Uk. For an alternative history suggesting Cahokian ties between the Pawnees and Arikaras, see "Carlton Gover on Pawnee/Arikara History on the Plains," Pawnee Nation, October 28, 2019, www.youtube.com/watch?v=gAQJWjnbOGA. For the Oneota, see DeMallie, *Plains*, Part 1, 222–33.

45. DeMallie, *Plains*, Part 1, 186–95.

46. Krause, "Explication of Arikara Culture History," 308–35. See also Lehmer and Jones, *Arikara Archeology*; Krause, "Plains Village Tradition," 196–206.

47. Krause, "Plains Village Tradition," 206.

48. Lehmer, "Plains Village Tradition," 245–55.

CHAPTER 2

1. Grinnell, "Pawnee Mythology," 114.

2. Gilmore, "Arikara Book of Genesis," 104–9.

3. Dorsey, *Traditions of the Arikara*, 11.

4. Gilmore, "Arikara Ceremonies."
5. Gilmore, *Prairie Smoke*, 38–39. See also Dorsey, *Traditions of the Arikara*, 79–80.
6. Dorsey, *Traditions of the Arikara*, 72, 73–78.
7. Interview with Joseph Reed, Knife River Indian Villages National Historic Site, circa 1991.
8. Dorsey, *Traditions of the Arikara*, 156.
9. Dorsey, 114–15.
10. Parks, *Traditional Narratives of the Arikara Indians*, 3:287–89.
11. Interview with Joseph Reed, Knife River Indian Villages National Historic Site, circa 1991.
12. Aaron McGaffey Beede Papers, Journal 8, page 42.
13. Gilmore, "Arikara Book of Genesis," 99.
14. Gilmore, "Notes from Information on Ceremonies of Mother Corn."
15. Grinnell, "Pawnee Mythology," 114.
16. Gilmore, "Information on the Divine Gift of Corn."
17. Dorsey, *Traditions of the Arikara*, 15–16.
18. Dorsey, 22.
19. Clark, *Indian Sign Language*, 43.
20. See Will and Hyde, *Corn among the Indians*.
21. Will, "Notes on the Arikara Indians," 27–33; *Arikara Indians of North Dakota* (film); Gilmore, "Information on the Divine Gift of Corn." See also Bear's Tail's account in Dorsey, *Traditions of the Arikara*, 26–27.
22. Dorsey, *Traditions of the Arikara*, 110–18.
23. Dorsey, 110–18.
24. Gilmore, "Arikara Ceremonies."
25. Gilmore, "Arikara Ceremonies."
26. Gilmore, "Making Records of Ancient Rituals."
27. Curtis, "Arikara," 63–64.
28. Ubelaker and Willey, "Complexity in Arikara Mortuary Practice," 69–74.
29. Parks, *Traditional Narratives of the Arikara Indians*, vol. 4, 640–42.
30. Gilmore, "Arikara Consolation Ceremony," 256–74.
31. Dorsey, *Traditions of the Arikaras*, 152–53.
32. Curtis, "Arikara," 64–65.
33. Gilmore, "Arikara Ceremonies."
34. Holder, *Hoe and the Horse*, 50–52.
35. Holder, "Social Stratification among the Arikara," 210–18. See also Holder, *Hoe and the Horse*, 61.
36. Gilmore, "Making of a New Head Chief," 411–18.
37. Gilmore, "Information on the Divine Gift of Corn."
38. Aaron McGaffey Beede Papers, Journal 10, September 22, 1916, 94–95.
39. Rogers, *Objects of Change*, 57–58.
40. See Krause and Olson, *Prelude to Glory*, 106.
41. Van de Logt, "'Arikara *nituniisu*' Beliefs," 1–19.

42. Parks, "Historical Character Mythologized," 47–58.
43. Aaron McGaffey Beede Papers, Journal 4, February 6, 1915, 185–86.
44. Aaron McGaffey Beede Papers, Journal 4, February 6, 1915, 185–86.
45. For the role of women in Arikara society and beyond see Peters, *Women of the Earth Lodges*, especially 10, 34, 56–58, 63–64, and Albers and Medicine, *Hidden Half*, especially chapters 3–5. For a discussion of the role of women in contemporary Mandan, Hidatsa, and Arikara society, see Berman, *Circle of Goods*.
46. Gilmore, "Religious Teaching and Training."
47. Hyde, "Mystery of the Arikaras."
48. Parks, "Arikara," 376.
49. Gilmore, "Notes on Arikara Tribal Organization," 344–45.
50. Hyde, "Mystery of the Arikaras." For the debate over Pawnee-Arikara territorial locations, see *Nebraska History* 60, no. 2 (Summer 1979): 131–293.
51. Gilmore, "Indian Tribal Boundary Lines," 59–63.
52. Hyde, "Mystery of the Arikaras"; Deland, "Aborigines of South Dakota," 267–586.
53. Gilmore, "The Arikara Tribal Temple," 47–70.
54. Caldwell, "Fortified Villages in the Northern Plains," 1–7.
55. Parks, "Arikara." See also Hurt, "Seasonal Economic and Settlement Patterns," 32–37.
56. Holder, *Hoe and the Horse*, 61.
57. Gilmore, "Notes from Information on Ceremonies of Mother Corn."
58. Gilmore, "Old Arikara Method."
59. Gilmore, "Buffalo Skull from the Arikara," 75–79.
60. Gilmore, "Old Arikara Method"; Gilmore, "Arikara Order of Butchering a Buffalo," 21.
61. Gilmore, "Arikara Agriculture."
62. Gilmore, *Prairie Smoke*, 88–93, 104–10. See also Gilmore, "Account of the Piraskani Ceremony."
63. White Owl (Frank Heart) told Gilmore that the Arikaras were better than the Sioux at capturing eagles and that they traded eagle feathers to the Sioux for horses: "They could exchange one or two good horses with the Dakotas for one good eagle tail." Gilmore, "Arikara Commerce," 13–18. See also Gilmore, "Capturing Eaglets in the Aerie"; Gilmore, "Notes on Manufacturers and Intertribal Trade."
64. Gilmore, "Arikara Fish-Trap," 120–34; Denig, *Five Indian Tribes*, 50–51.
65. Wedel and Frison, "Environment and Subsistence," 44–60. See Gilmore, *Uses of Plants by the Indians*; Gilmore, "Wild Plants Used by the Arikara."
66. Curtis, "Arikara," 84.
67. Curtis, 84.
68. Dorsey, *Traditions of the Arikara*, 16.
69. The Arikara ceremony was very similar to the new fire ceremony of the Pawnees recorded by James Murie. Murie, *Ceremonies of the Pawnee*, 135–54.
70. Dorsey, *Traditions of the Arikara*, 166.
71. Lowie, "Societies of the Arikara," 646–78.
72. Willey, *Prehistoric Warfare*; Willey and Emerson, "Osteology and Archaeology," 227–69; Zimmerman and Bradley, "Crow Creek Massacre," 215–26.

CHAPTER 3

1. Dorsey, *Traditions of the Arikara*, 21.
2. Dorsey, 11.
3. Dorsey, 21.
4. Dorsey, 32.
5. Linea Sundstrom, *Storied Stone*, 3.
6. Hämäläinen, *Lakota America*, 168–69.
7. Though the hills were not an empty space, they functioned as a sort of neutral ground, where various groups could visit without fear of attack. After the mid-1700s, the Lakhotas took control of the hills and kept the Arikaras out. Archaeologists contend that it is unlikely that the Arikaras would have abandoned the Missouri River, though it is possible that small family groups scattered in search of safety. What complicates the search for traces of Arikara visits or occupation of the Black Hills is that archaeologists have no examples of Arikara rock art. Linea Sundstrom, personal communication, June 15, 2020.
8. Dorsey, *Traditions of the Arikara*, 26.
9. Owsley, "Demography of Prehistoric and Early Historic Northern Plains Populations," 75–86.
10. DeMallie, *Plains*, Part 1, 257.
11. According to Hyde, based on a publication by Clark Wissler, the "Iroquois came west and burnt a Skidi settlement, apparently in eastern Nebraska," in the late 1600s. Hyde, *Pawnee Indians*, 84.
12. Dorsey, *Traditions of the Arikara*, 22.
13. Thornton, *American Indian Holocaust*, especially chapters 3 and 4. Sharing a similar theme with the Whirlwind episode are Arikara accounts in which a murderous bear chases a girl and her brothers. In this case, the bear represented a disease (possibly rabies but more likely another, more easily transferrable infection) or an enemy tribe. Parks, *Traditional Narratives of the Arikara*, 3:179–85. For the versions by Ella P. Waters, Matthew White Bear, and Eleanor Chase, see Parks, *Traditional Narratives of the Arikara*, 4:591–95, 4:733–36, 4:775–76.
14. Dorsey, *Traditions of the Arikara*, 15.
15. See interview with Frank Heart, Action Anthropology Project.
16. See interview with Frank Heart.
17. Cox, ed., *Journeys of Rene Robert Cavelier*, 256–57. See also Hennepin, *Aenmerckelycke Historische Reys-Beschryvinge*, 38.
18. Lahontan, *New Voyages to North America*, 113–15.
19. Lahontan.
20. Lahontan; Thwaites, *Lahontan's New Voyages to North America*, 182.
21. Lahontan, *New Voyages to North America*, 115.
22. Sayre, *Les Sauvages Américains*, xiv–xvii, 123–29. See also Harvey, "The Noble Savage and the Savage Noble," 161–91.
23. Peter H. Wood, "Lahontan's Letter XVI: Frenchmen on the Missouri River in 1688," paper cited in Fenn, *Encounters at the Heart of the World*, 41–47.
24. Jantz and Owsley, "White Traders in the Upper Missouri," 189–201.

25. Willey, *Prehistoric Warfare on the Great Plains*; Willey and Emerson, "Osteology and Archaeology"; 227–69; Zimmerman and Bradley, "Crow Creek Massacre," 215–26.

26. See, for example, Brooks, *Captives and Cousins*.

27. Rushforth, *Bonds of Alliance*, 165–66.

28. For discussions on the changing identity of the Padoucas, see Grinnell, "Who Were the Padouca?" 647–70; Secoy, "The Identity of the 'Paduca,'" 525–42; DeMallie, *Plains*, Part 2, 926–40.

29. DeMallie, *Plains*, Part 2, 416.

30. DeMallie, Part 2, 400.

31. DeMallie, Part 2, 462.

32. Hämäläinen, *Comanche Empire*, 28, 174–75.

33. DeMallie, *Plains*, Part 2, 903.

34. Guillaume de L'Isle, "Carte de la Louisiane et du Course du Mississippi," Library of Congress, https://www.loc.gov/resource/g3701s.ct003028/. The Vermale map can be viewed at http://rla.unc.edu/Mapfiles/Marcel/Marcel%201893-25.jpg.

35. DeMallie, *Plains*, Part 2, 927–28.

36. Rushforth, *Bonds of Alliance*, 168. For samples of Panis entries at Michilimackinac, see "The Mackinac Register," Library of Congress, https://www.loc.gov/resource/lhbum .7689h_0025_0192.

37. Deliette, "Memoir of DeGannes (Deliette)," 302–95. The quote is on 386–88.

38. Dorsey, *Traditions of the Arikara*, 109–14.

39. Gilmore, *Prairie Smoke*, 166–72; Gilmore, "Study in the Ethnobotany of the Omaha," 330–31.

40. Gilmore, "Account of the Piraskani Ceremony."

41. DeMallie, *Plains*, Part 2, 907–25; Mooney, *Calendar History of the Kiowa*, 156, 158–61, 229, 251.

42. Grinnell, *Cheyenne Indians*, 1:6, 1:8–9, 1:37–38, 1:47, 1:240, 1:251–52, 1:302, 2:190, 2:205, 2:338; Moore et al., "Cheyenne," 863–85; Liberty and Stands In Timber, *Cheyenne Memories*, 16.

43. Howard, "Yanktonai Ethnohistory," 22–23.

CHAPTER 4

1. Parks, *Traditional Narratives of the Arikara*, 3:148–61.

2. Parks, 3:171–74. For discussions of cross stirrups and their uses, see Flint and Flint, *Latest Word from 1540*, 224, 226.

3. Rogers, *Objects of Change*, chapter 6.

4. Ubelaker and Bass, "Arikara Glassworking Techniques," 467–75. Gilmore, "Glass Bead Making by the Arikara," 20–21.

5. Garavaglia and Worman, *Firearms of the American West*, 343–60. See also Gluckman, *Identifying Old US Muskets*; Hamilton, *Indian Trade Guns*; Bohr, *Gifts from the Thunder Beings*, especially chapters 5–7.

6. Ewers, *Plains Indian History and Culture*, 48–50.

7. Douglas R. Parks, personal communication.

8. Ewers, *Plains Indian History and Culture*, 48–50.

9. See Secoy, *Changing Military Patterns*; Malone, *The Skulking Way of War*; Starkey, *European and Native American Warfare*.

10. Gilmore, "Arikara Code of Eagle Feather Honor Badges"; Gilmore, "Capturing Eaglets in the Aerie."

11. Interestingly, these positions do not correspond with the four sacred semi-cardinal directions, which may indicate that these horses became additional pillars in the Arikara system. Parks, *Traditional Narratives of the Arikara*, 3:101, 3:134–37.

12. Wilson, "Horse and the Dog in Hidatsa Culture," 125–311. See also Ewers, *Horse in Blackfeet Indian Culture*.

13. Levy, "Is This a System?" 985–91; Bridges, "Prehistoric Arthritis in the Americas," 76, 81–82; Hanson, "Adjustment and Adaptation," 93–107.

14. Ewers, *Horse in Blackfeet Indian Culture*, 279.

15. See Secoy, *Changing Military Patterns*.

16. Ewers, *Horse in Blackfeet Indian Culture*, chapter 10.

17. Wilson, "Horse and the Dog in Hidatsa Culture," 181.

18. Gilmore, "Arikara Code of Eagle Feather Honor Badges"; Gilmore, "Capturing Eaglets in the Aerie."

19. Lehmer, *Middle Missouri Archaeology*, 172.

20. Wescott and Cunningham, "Temporal Changes," 1022–36.

21. Posthumus, "Hereditary Enemies?" 361–82. For a recent history of the Lakhotas, see Hämäläinen, *Lakota America*.

22. Mallery, *Picture-Writing of the American Indians*, 297.

23. Howard, "Yanktonai Ethnohistory."

24. Greene and Thornton, *Year the Stars Fell*.

25. Greene and Thornton, 75–76.

26. Dorsey, *Traditions of the Arikara*, 170–71.

27. Greene and Thornton, *Year the Stars Fell*, 79; Curtis, *North American Indian*, 164.

28. Greene and Thornton, 73; Curtis, 161.

29. Greene and Thornton, 86; Curtis, 165.

30. Greene and Thornton, 79.

31. Warren W. Caldwell, "Fortified Villages in the Northern Plains," 1–7.

32. Greene and Thornton, *Year the Stars Fell*, 81, 91, 92.

33. Hämäläinen, *Lakota America*, 81.

34. See Secoy, *Changing Military Patterns*; Jablow, *Cheyenne in Plains Indian Trade Relations*.

35. Hämäläinen, *Lakota America*, 82.

36. Fenn, *Encounters at the Heart of the World*, 148–50. See also "The Narrative of Peter Pond" in Gates, *Five Fur Traders of the Northwest*, 11.

37. Guillaume Delisle, "Carte du Mexique"; Parks, "Bands and Villages of the Arikara and Pawnee," 215; Norall, *Bourgmont*, 110. Parks believes that both were Arikara and that the distinction merely reflects differences in dialect. Parks, "Bands and Villages of the Arikara," 217, 220, 228. Lehmer, *Middle Missouri Archaeology*, 168, 169–70.

38. Tucker, *Indian Villages of the Illinois Country*, 2:Plate XV. Lehmer, *Middle Missouri Archaeology*, 168, 169–70.
39. Margry, *Decouvertes et Etablissements*, 289–90, 293.
40. Margry, 395.
41. Margry, 455. See also Nasatir, *Before Lewis and Clark*, 25.
42. Burpee, *Journals and Letters of de la Vérendrye*, 335–37.
43. Burpee, 407–12.
44. Burpee, 18–23, 413. It is possible that the Beaux Hommes ("Beautiful Men"), Petits Renards ("Little Foxes"), Pioya, and Gens des Cheveaux ("Horse People") were Kiowa bands. However, this is only conjecture.
45. Burpee, 417–24.
46. Burpee, 424–26.
47. Burpee, 17, 427.
48. Burpee, 428–29.
49. Burpree, 429.
50. Nasatir, *Before Lewis and Clark*, 53.
51. Parks, "Arikara," 366.
52. Hyde argues that the Arikaras may have absorbed refugee groups (mostly Pawnees) trying to escape the Padoucas. Hyde, *Pawnee Indians*, 85.
53. Hämäläinen, *Lakota America*, 87–88.
54. Greene and Thornton, *Year the Stars Fell*, 89, 91; Curtis, "High Hawk's Winter Count," 166, 167.
55. Greene and Thornton, 96. In the description, the attackers are identified as Assiniboines, but the corn symbol makes it clear that the attackers were Arikaras. Curtis, "High Hawk's Winter Count," 167.
56. Greene and Thornton, *Year the Stars Fell*, 97.
57. Greene and Thornton, 97.
58. Greene and Thornton, 98. Other winter counts list this event in 1778–81.
59. Greene and Thornton, 81, 98.

CHAPTER 5

1. Greene and Thornton, *Year the Stars Fell*, 122–25.
2. Dorsey, *Traditions of the Arikara*, 36–37.
3. Thornton, *American Indian Holocaust*, chapters 2 and 3.
4. Mark Braun, School of Medicine, Indiana University, Bloomington, personal communication.
5. Trimble, "Infectious Disease and the Northern Plains Horticulturalists," 50.
6. Fenn, *Pox Americana*, 16–18.
7. Braun, personal communication.
8. Bradford, *Of Plymouth Plantation*, 302.
9. DeMallie et al., *Fur Trader*, 177.
10. See, for example, Dorsey, *Traditions of the Arikara*, 126–27.
11. Abel, *Tabeau's Narrative*, 124.

12. Lehmer, *Middle Missouri Archaeology*, 170.
13. Jablow, *Cheyenne in Plains Indian Trade Relations*, 65, 78–89.
14. Dorsey, *Traditions of the Arikara*, 125–26.
15. Lowie, "Societies of the Arikara Indians," 674–65.
16. Parks, *Traditional Narratives of the Arikara*, 3:209–12.
17. Owsley et al., "Demographic and Osteological Evidence for Warfare," 119–31.
18. Owsley et al., 119–31.
19. Greene and Thornton, *Year the Stars Fell*, 105; Fenn, *Encounters at the Heart of the World*, 166.
20. Greene and Thornton, 108.
21. Greene and Thornton, 111.
22. See, for example, Dorsey, *Traditions of the Arikara*, 120–22, 123–24, 148, 149–51, 151–52; Parks, *Traditional Narratives of the Arikara*, 3:334–57, 3:456–59, 4:614–19, 4:625–26, 4:684–88, 4:722–24.
23. Hämäläinen, *Lakota America*, 98–100.
24. Greene and Thornton, *Year the Stars Fell*, 115–16.
25. Greene and Thornton, 116, 117, 118. As is often the case with winter counts, different counts have small differences on chronology and content.
26. Nasatir, *Before Lewis and Clark*, 123, 126–27.
27. For information on Joseph Garreau, see census records for 1787 and 1797, "Census Collection, 1732–1980," Missouri Historical Society Archives; Nasatir, *Before Lewis and Clark*, 82, 95, 101n, 103, 105, 109, 233–35, 242, 248–50, 267, 274, 297–98, 334, 479, 503; Drumm, *Journal of a Fur-Trading Expedition*, 64, 68, 84, 90, 92, 93, 94, 97, 104, 107, 117, 158; Bonner, *Life and Adventures of James P. Beckwourth*, 378.
28. DeMallie et al., eds., *Fur Trader*, 163, 177.
29. DeMallie et al., 107.
30. DeMallie et al., 179.
31. Fenn, *Encounters at the Heart of the World*, 171–72.
32. For a biography of Truteau, see DeMallie, et al., eds., *Fur Trader*, 25–26, 27–28, 36–37.
33. DeMallie et al., 103, 109.
34. DeMallie et al., 163.
35. According to Waldo R. Wedel, the locations of the Arikara villages described by Truteau correspond with two archaeological sites (39ST50 and 39ST25) on Black Widow Ridge in present-day Stanley County, South Dakota. Both sites are now covered by the Oahe Reservoir. Wedel cited in DeMallie et al., *Fur Trader*, 117, 596, note 62.
36. DeMallie et al., 163–65.
37. DeMallie et al., 165.
38. DeMallie et al., 171.
39. DeMallie et al., 181–89.
40. DeMallie et al., 191–95.
41. DeMallie et al., 199. The Saone Sioux consisted of several bands, including the Sans Arcs and Hunkpapas.
42. DeMallie et al., 209.

43. DeMallie et al., 209–11. The two camps consisted of Suhtai and Ohmeseheso Cheyennes.

44. DeMallie et al., 211.

45. DeMallie et al., 213.

46. DeMallie et al., 219.

47. DeMallie et al., 221.

48. DeMallie et al., 223–25.

49. DeMallie et al., 225.

50. See Greene and Thornton, *Year the Stars Fell*, 120–21; Curtis, "High Hawk's Winter Count," 169; Howard, *British Museum Winter Count*, 17; Howard, "Yanktonai Ethnohistory," 41.

51. DeMallie et al., *Fur Trader*, 225.

52. DeMallie et al., 225–29.

53. DeMallie et al., 229–33, 239.

54. For discussions of the Mackay-Evans Expedition, see Wood, *Prologue to Lewis and Clark*; Nasatir, "John Evans," 219–39, 432–60, 585–608; Williams, "John Evans," 277–95, 508–29.

55. Collot, *A Journey in North America*, 271–301; locations and numerical overviews of nations given at 307–10.

56. Collot, 284–85.

57. Collot, 294.

58. Collot, 274, 283–84, and 309.

59. Dorsey, *Traditions of the Arikara*, 129–34.

60. Dorsey, *Traditions of the Arikara*, 84–88. "The Rabbit Boy," told by Elk, followed a similar theme; Dorsey, 109–14.

CHAPTER 6

1. Parks, *Traditional Narratives of the Arikara*, 3:376.

2. Yellow Bird, "Now I Will Speak," 79.

3. Moulton, *Journals of the Lewis and Clark Expedition*, 3:196–98. Fenn, *Encounters at the Heart of the World*, 195–96.

4. Greene and Thornton, *Year the Stars Fell*, 124–25.

5. Abel, *Tabeau's Narrative*, 52.

6. The small creek separating the two upper villages was called Kakawissassa Creek by William Clark in 1804. It was later called Cathead Creek. Moulton, *Journals of the Lewis and Clark Expedition*, 3:160, note 2.

7. For biographical information on Tabeau, see Abel, *Tabeau's Narrative*, 32–41.

8. Abel, 149–50.

9. Abel, 124.

10. Abel, 126.

11. Abel, 126.

12. Abel, 55–56, 130, 131, 136–37, 146.

13. Abel, 78, 151, 173, 174, 183.

14. Abel, 69, 91, 93–97, 149.
15. Abel, 87, 98, 137, 158, 162; Wood, *Prologue to Lewis and Clark*, 147.
16. Abel, *Tabeau's Narrative*, 104–5.
17. Abel, 130.
18. Abel, 127–28.
19. Abel, 130–33. See also Wood and Thiessen, *Early Fur Trade on the Northern Plains*, 165.
20. Abel, *Tabeau's Narrative*, 138–41.
21. Abel, 124, 141–42.
22. For an excellent discussion, see Ronda, *Lewis and Clark among the Indians*.
23. Ronda, chapter 2, "The Teton Confrontation."
24. The village was reportedly located on the upper end of the island. Moulton, *Journals of the Lewis and Clark Expedition*, 3:150–52, 11:97.
25. Moulton, 3:154–56.
26. Moulton 3:156–57. Also see Yellow Bird, "Now I Will Speak," 73–84.
27. Moulton, *Journals of the Lewis and Clark Expedition*, 3:157n, 3:183.
28. Ronda, *Lewis and Clark among the Indians*, 57.
29. Moulton, *Journals of the Lewis and Clark Expedition*, 9:79, 10:52–53, 10:54.
30. Moulton, 3:157, 9:84–85.
31. Moulton, 3:173–74.
32. Moulton, 3:159.
33. Moulton, 3:164–65.
34. Moulton, 3:165–66.
35. Moulton, 3:156, 3:160–64, 3:187, 3:208.
36. Moulton, 3:180, 3:173.
37. Moulton, 3:199–200.
38. Moulton, 3:208–12.
39. Moulton, 3:218–19, 3:224–25, 3:245.
40. Moulton, 3:225–26, 3:230–31.
41. Abel, *Tabeau's Narrative*, 127–28.
42. Abel, 129, 132–33; Moulton, *Journals of the Lewis and Clark Expedition*, 3:244–47, 3:251.
43. Abel, *Tabeau's Narrative*, 129–30; Moulton, *Journals of the Lewis and Clark Expedition*, 3:304–5, 3:308–9.
44. Abel, *Tabeau's Narrative*, 142–44.
45. Abel, 135.
46. Abel, 128, note 87; Moulton, *Journals of the Lewis and Clark Expedition*, 3:324.
47. Abel, *Tabeau's Narrative*, 128; Moulton, *Journals of the Lewis and Clark Expedition*, 3:332, 4:7, 4:10–11.
48. Jackson, *Letters of the Lewis and Clark Expedition*, 306, 559.
49. Moulton, *Journals of the Lewis and Clark Expedition*, 8:357.
50. James Wilkinson to President Thomas Jefferson, December 23, 1805, Jackson, *Letters of the Lewis and Clark Expedition*, 272–73.
51. Gilmore, *Prairie Smoke*, 38–39. See also Dorsey, *Traditions of the Arikara*, 79–80.

52. Dunlap, *Diary of William Dunlap*, 389–93.

53. Jackson, *Letters of the Lewis and Clark Expedition*, 305.

54. The location of Eagle Feather's grave is unknown. Historian Mark Chalkley writes that Eagle Feather was probably buried in Holmstead's Cemetery, near present-day Dupont Circle. In the mid-1800s the cemetery was removed. Chalkley, "Eagle Feather Goes to Washington," 6–10.

55. Henry Dearborn to James Wilkinson, April 9, 1806, Jackson, *Letters of the Lewis and Clark Expedition*, 303–5.

56. Steinke, "'Here Is My Country,'" 589–610; *We Proceeded On* 44, no. 2 (May 2018).

57. Parks, *Traditional Narratives of the Arikara Indians*, 3:287–89.

58. Steinke, "'Here Is My Country,'" 598–99.

59. Moulton, *Journals of the Lewis and Clark Expedition*, 8:311–17. For a biography of Sheheke (1766–1812), see Potter, *Sheheke*.

60. Moulton, *Journals of the Lewis and Clark Expedition*, 8:311–17.

61. Moulton, 8:315–16.

62. Moulton, 8:317.

63. Lewis and Clark met Gravelines on September 12, 1806. Moulton, 8:357–58.

64. Jefferson was not certain about Eagle Feather's proper name, further indication that he never met Eagle Feather in person. He first wrote Piaketo ("Eagle's Feather"), then Toone ("Whippoorwill"), and then Arketarnawhar ("Chief of the Town").

65. Jackson, *Letters of the Lewis and Clark Expedition*, 306.

66. Nichols, "The Arikara Indians and the Missouri River Trade," 81.

67. Dickson, "Hard on the Heels of Lewis and Clark," 23–24.

68. Jackson, *Letters of the Lewis and Clark Expedition*, 437n.

69. Oglesby, *Manuel Lisa*, 48–49.

70. Report from Nathaniel Pryor to William Clark, St. Louis, October 16, 1807. Jackson, *Letters of the Lewis and Clark Expedition*, 270, 432–37.

71. Kelly, *Lost Voices on the Missouri*, 67, 699.

72. Thomas Jefferson to Meriwether Lewis, Monticello, August 24, 1808. Jackson, *Letters of the Lewis and Clark Expedition*, 451–56.

73. Lewis's actions hint of corruption. See Wallace, *Jefferson and the Indians*, 266.

74. Lewis to Pierre Chouteau, St. Louis, June 8, 1809. Jackson, *Letters of the Lewis and Clark Expedition*, 451–56.

75. James, *Three Years among the Indians*, 173–74.

76. James, 173–74.

77. Report of Pierre Chouteau to William Eustis, St. Louis, December 14, 1809. Jackson, *Letters of the Lewis and Clark Expedition*, 451–56. Chouteau and Lisa left St. Louis with thirteen barges and 350 men. James, *Three Years among the Indians*, 2–9.

78. James, 174–75.

79. Potter, *Sheheke*, chapters 12 and 13.

80. Nichols, "Arikara Indians and the Missouri River Trade," 83.

81. Kelly, *Lost Voices on the Missouri*, 70, 90–91, 702.

82. Bradbury, *Travels in the Interior of America*, 163.

83. Oglesby, *Manuel Lisa*, 113; Rollins, *Discovery of the Oregon Trail*, 281–328; Irving, *Astoria*.

84. Brackenridge, *Views of Louisiana*, 238–40; Bradbury, *Travels in the Interior of America*, 90–96.

85. Brackenridge, 245–46.

86. Brackenridge, 245–46; Thwaites, *Early Western Travels*, 113; Bradbury, *Travels in the Interior of America*, 110–14, 116.

87. Brackenridge, 247–48; Thwaites, 114–15, 116; Bradbury, 114, 125, 165.

88. Brackenridge, 252–55.

89. Brackenridge, 250–51. Bradbury, 120, 121.

90. Brackenridge's journals disagree on the date of this event. For the exact date I have followed Bradbury. Brackenridge, *Views of Louisiana*, 261–62; Thwaites, *Early Western Travels*, 142–46; Bradbury, *Travels in the Interior of America*, 157–63. Jasper Young Bear clarified the meaning of the face paint. Interview with Jasper Young Bear, Bloomington, Indiana, January 30, 2007.

91. Bradbury, *Travels in the Interior of America*, 162–63.

92. Thwaites, *Early Western Travels*, 145.

93. Nichols, "The Arikara Indians and the Missouri River Trade," 77–93.

94. Nichols.

95. Drumm, *Journal of a Fur-Trading Expedition*, 64, 66–67.

96. Smith and Ludwickson, *Fort Manuel*.

97. Drumm, *Journal of a Fur-Trading Expedition*, 69, 73, 76.

98. Drumm, 87–89, 93.

99. Drumm, 80, 97, 104, 113, 115, 119–21.

100. Drumm, 124–26.

101. Drumm, 126.

102. Nichols, "Arikara Indians and the Missouri River Trade," 85.

103. Nichols, 79, 85–86.

104. Sunder, *Joshua Pilcher*, 38–39; Nichols, "Arikara Indians and the Missouri River Trade," 86.

105. Orser, "Understanding Arikara Trading Behavior," 101–7.

106. Nichols, "Arikara Indians and the Missouri River Trade," 86; Nichols, "Backdrop for Disaster," 93–113.

107. For an overview of the Arikara War (albeit flawed from the perspective of the Arikaras), see Nester, *Arikara War*. For original documentation, see Microfilm 567 and Roll 12, RG94: Records of the Adjutant General's Office, NARA. Roll 12 contains correspondence concerning the 1823 military campaign. See also US Senate, *Documents Accompanying the Message of the President of the United States to Both Houses*.

108. Robinson, "Official Correspondence of the Leavenworth Expedition," 181–234.

109. Robinson, 205.

110. Robinson, 206.

111. Robinson, 210, 213–14.
112. Robinson, 215.
113. Robinson, 216.
114. Robinson, 217; Strong, "Studying the Arikara and their Neighbors," 74.
115. Robinson, "Official Correspondence of the Leavenworth Expedition," 216–21.
116. Robinson, 222–23.
117. Robinson, 223–25.
118. Robinson, 225–26.
119. Robinson, 227–28.
120. Robinson, 228.
121. Robinson, 229.
122. Robinson, 229–30.
123. Robinson, 230–31.
124. Yellow Bird, "Now I Will Speak," 79.
125. Robinson, "Official Correspondence of the Leavenworth Expedition," 232.
126. Myers, *Saga of Hugh Glass*, 105.
127. Myers, 151–64.
128. Myers, 165, 167–68. Nichols, "Arikara Indians and the Missouri River Trade," 88.
129. Nichols, "Arikara Indians and the Missouri River Trade," 88–89; Myers, *Saga of Hugh Glass*, 180–83; Hall, *Letters From the West*, 302–4.
130. Colonel J. Snelling, April 11, 1824, Frame 0010–0012, Roll 883, Microfilm 234, RG 75: Records of the Bureau of Indian Affairs.
131. The Arikara War showed that there was considerable confusion between Indian agents and army officers about who had the ultimate authority in speaking for the government in discussions with Indians. Kelly, *Lost Voices on the Missouri*, 237.
132. For Pilcher's controversial status, see Kelly, *Lost Voices on the Missouri*, 251–55.

CHAPTER 7

1. The names of the chiefs appear on the peace treaty of 1825. See Kappler, *Indian Affairs*, 2:237–39. It is unlikely that Bloody Hands is identical with a legendary figure from Arikara oral tradition named Bloody Hands in Parks's collection or Burnt Hands (Stanapaat) in Dorsey's collection of Arikara stories. Dorsey, *Traditions of the Arikara*, 65–69, 69–70, 70; Parks, *Traditional Narratives of the Arikara Indians*, 4:485–514.
2. Jensen and Hutchins, eds., *Wheel Boats on the Missouri*, 1–2.
3. Kappler, *Indian Affairs*, 2:225–46.
4. Jensen and Hutchins, *Wheel Boats on the Missouri*, 128.
5. Jensen and Hutchins, 128–29.
6. Jensen and Hutchins, 130.
7. Jensen and Hutchins, 130–31. Kappler, *Indian Affairs*, 2:237–39.
8. Laidlaw to McKenzie, November 27, 1831, "Fort Tecumseh Letter Book, 1830–1832," 72–76, cited in Abel, *Chardon's Journal*, 311–12, note 439.
9. Chittenden, *American Fur Trade*, 1:313–45, 1:364–67.

10. Richard T. Holliday traded with the Arikaras in 1830 and 1831. In 1831 Honore Picotte, Pascal Cerre, and Dominique LaChapelle were also trading with the Arikaras on Apple Creek. Abel, *Chardon's Journal*, 205, note 30, 227–28, note 81.

11. Abel, *Chardon's Journal*, 205, note 30, 229–30, note 90; Barbour, *Fort Union*, 44.

12. Mitchell, "Extraordinary Indian Feats of Legerdemain," 657–58.

13. Letter by John F. A. Sanford, November 24, 1830, Frames 0288–0293, Roll 833, Microfilm 234, RG75: Records of the Bureau of Indian Affairs, NARA.

14. Donaldson, "The George Catlin Indian Gallery," 274, 470.

15. Donaldson, 78.

16. Wied-Neuwied, *Reise in Das Innere Nord-America*, 1:378–81.

17. It is possible that the LaChapelle Maximilian met was not David but Dominique LaChapelle. Abel, *Chardon's Journal*, 297, note 354; Goetzmann and Hunt, *Karl Bodmer's America*, 283.

18. For Maximilian's description of the Arikaras, see Wied-Neuwied, *Reise in Das Innere Nord-America*, 1:378–425.

19. Hyde, *Pawnee Indians*, 184.

20. The other man killed was Hugh Glass. Myers, *Saga of Hugh Glass*, 223–27; Bonner, *Life and Adventures of James P. Beckwourth*, 253–58. See also Wied-Neuwied, *Reise in Das Innere Nord-America*, 2:34–35, 336–39.

21. Hyde, *Pawnee Indians*, 184; Samuel Allis, "Forty Years among the Indians," 165. See Hulbert and Hulbert, *Marcus Whitman*, 94–95.

22. According to Hyde, only one group of Arikaras moved to the Skiris. Another group remained on the Platte River. Hyde, *Pawnee Indians*, 184.

23. Based on information furnished by the Sioux agent and former trader Joshua Pilcher, Allis reported that the Arikaras had murdered thirty-six white people since 1823. "I know of no other way to stop them than to kil [sic] them off," wrote Allis. Wedel, *Dunbar-Allis Letters*, 697, 701.

24. This information is based on Dodge, "Journal of the March," Dodge's journal and report of his 1835 expedition to the Rocky Mountains.

25. According to Dodge, hostilities between the Arikaras and the Cheyennes started after the Cheyennes had concluded an alliance with the Arapahos (around 1806). After the Arikaras stole Arapaho horses and killed a few traders who were doing business with the Arapahos, the Cheyennes determined to declare war against the Arikaras. Dodge, "Journal of the March," 30–31.

26. Van de Logt, *Monsters of Contact*, chapter 6.

27. Star was also known as Big Head. Perhaps this was the same person as Old (Man) Chief, one of the names Four Bears gave to Prince Maximilian in 1833.

28. Dodge, "Journal of the March," 2, 4–7, 8. For additional information on the expedition, see Pelzer, "Captain Ford's Journal," 550–79, and Perrine, "Hugh Evans' Journal," 192–214.

29. Dodge, "Journal of the March," 7–8, 12–14; Pelzer, "Captain Ford's Journal," 557–58; Perrine, "Hugh Evans' Journal," 200–201. John Dougherty, July 16, 1835, Frames 0736–0741, Roll 883, Microfilm 234, RG75: Records of the Bureau of Indian Affairs, NARA.

30. Dodge, "Journal of the March," 13–14; Pelzer, "Captain Ford's Journal," 558–59, 560; Perrine, "Hugh Evans' Journal," 202.

31. For a brief description of an Arikara sun dance, see Dorsey, *Traditions of the Arikara*, 164.
32. Dodge, "Journal of the March," 14–16.
33. Dodge, 16–17.
34. Dodge, 17.
35. Dodge, 17–18.
36. Dodge, 18.
37. Dodge, 30–31; Pelzer, "Captain Ford's Journal," 568–69.
38. Dodge, "Journal of the March," 30–31.
39. Dodge, 35; Hyde, *Pawnee Indians*, 193. Pelzer, "Captain Ford's Journal," 568–69.
40. Hyde, *Pawnee Indians*, 193–94.
41. Wedel, *Dunbar-Allis Letters*, 707.
42. Parks, *Traditional Narratives of the Arikara Indians*, 3:363–65.
43. Abel, *Chardon's Journal*, 80.
44. Abel, 100, 101, 105, 106, 109.
45. Abel, 109, 110, 111, 113.
46. William N. Fulkerson, September 30, 1837, Frames 0182–0194, Roll 884, Microfilm 234, RG75: Records of the Bureau of Indian Affairs, NARA.
47. Fulkerson.
48. Fenn, *Encounters at the Heart of the World*, 290–94. Arp Jr., "Rats at Fort Clark," 37–47. See also Hunt Jr., "Fort Clark Archeology Project, 2000–2001," 1–48.
49. Abel, *Chardon's Journal*, 118–19.
50. Trimble, "1837–1838 Smallpox Epidemic," 81–89.
51. William Fulkerson, September 20, 1837, and Joshua Pilcher, February 5, 1838, Frames 0273–0278 and 0287, Microfilm 234, RG75: Records of the Bureau of Indian Affairs, NARA.
52. Abel, *Chardon's Journal*, 126, 130, 131, 132, 133.
53. Abel, 123–24, 127, 130, 133, 136, 148, 149.
54. Abel, 124, 127, 132, 137, 138, 140.
55. Joshua Pilcher, February 27, 1838, Frames 0296–0297, Microfilm 234, RG75: Records of the Bureau of Indian Affairs, NARA.
56. Abel, *Chardon's Journal*, 123, 126, 128–29.
57. Abel, 126–27, 128.
58. Pearson, "Lewis Cass and the Politics of Disease," 9–35.
59. Aaron McGaffey Beede Papers, Journal 8, 1915 (mislabeled entry; the journal refers to events from 1916), entry for October 10, 1916.
60. Lowie, "Societies of the Arikara Indians," 662.
61. Abel, *Chardon's Journal*, 152, 153.
62. Abel, 165.
63. Abel, 160, 162–63, 164, 165, 166.
64. Abel, 167–68. Chittenden and Richardson, *Life, Letters and Travels of Father DeSmet*, 3:1135–39.
65. William Clark, February 21, 1838, and William N. Fulkerson, March 1, 1838, Frames 0289–0290 and 0307–0311, Roll 884, Microfilm 234, RG75: Records of the Bureau of Indian Affairs, NARA.

66. Joshua Pilcher, July 3, 1838, Frame 0323, Roll 884, Microfilm 234, RG75: Records of the Bureau of Indian Affairs, NARA.

67. Joshua Pilcher, September 15, 1838, Frames 0370–0372, Roll 884, Microfilm 234, RG75: Records of the Bureau of Indian Affairs, NARA.

68. McDermott, ed., *Up the Missouri with Audubon*, 91–92.

69. Morgan, "Stone and Bone Implements of the Arickarees," 131–34. Wood et al., *Fort Clark and Its Indian Neighbors*, chapter 4 and 5.

70. Lansing, "Plains Indian Women," 413–33.

71. Abel, *Chardon's Journal*, 144, 147, 148. Sunder, *Fur Trade*, 197.

72. Sunder, *Fur Trade*, 191.

73. Report of G. C. Matlock, Upper Missouri Agency, *Annual Report of the Commissioner of Indian Affairs* (hereafter *ARCIA*), 1847, 848; Report of G. C. Matlock, Upper Missouri Agency, *ARCIA*, 1848, 468; Report of William S. Hatton, Upper Missouri Agency, *ARCIA*, 1849, 1073.

74. Report of Alfred D. Vaughan, Upper Missouri Agency, *ARCIA*, 1853, 354. See also a letter by Agent Vaughan, April 1, 1854, Frames 0086–0087, Roll 885, Microfilm 234, RG75: Records of the Bureau of Indian Affairs, NARA.

75. Report of Alexander H. Redfield, *ARCIA*, 1858, 441–43.

76. Ray Mattison, *Henry A. Boller*, 99–102. See also "Journal of Dr. Elias J. Marsh," *Chicago Press and Tribune*, August 16, 1859, 117–18.

77. Report of Alfred D. Vaughan, Upper Missouri Agency, *ARCIA*, 1853, 355; Report of Alfred J. Vaughan, Upper Missouri Agency, *ARCIA*, 1855, 392–93; Report of Alfred J. Vaughan, Upper Missouri Agency, *ARCIA*, 1856, 630, 636.

78. Chittenden and Richardson, *Travels of Father DeSmet*, 3:857.

79. Barbour, *Fort Union*, 159–63.

80. Report of T. P. Moore, Upper Missouri Agency, *ARCIA*, 1846, 290.

81. Chittenden and Richardson, *Travels of Father DeSmet*, vol. 2, 650.

82. Sunder, *Fur Trade*, 178–79. Report of Alfred J. Vaughan, Upper Missouri Agency, *ARCIA*, 1856, 636, 637. Report of Alexander H. Redfield, *ARCIA*, 1857, 415.

83. Bowers, *Hidatsa Social and Ceremonial Organization*, 217.

84. Meyer, *Village Indians of the Upper Missouri*, 99–101.

85. In Alfred Morsette's account of the 1851 negotiations, the chief Arikara representatives were Son of Star and Carries Moccasins. He appears to be in error here. Parks, *Traditional Narratives of the Arikara Indians*, 3:377–82.

86. Report of David D. Mitchell, Superintendent of Indian Affairs, *ARCIA*, 1851, 322–26. Meyer, *Village Indians of the Upper Missouri*, 103. Prucha, *American Indian Treaties*, 216–17, 237–40, 440–42. The proceedings were published in several installments in the *Missouri Republican* in October and November 1851. A typed transcript of the newspaper articles was furnished by Raymond J. DeMallie, American Studies Research Institute, Indiana University, Bloomington.

87. Kappler, *Indian Affairs*, 2:594–96.

88. Meyer, *Village Indians of the Upper Missouri*, 103.

89. Report of Alfred D. Vaughan, Upper Missouri Agency, *ARCIA*, 1853, 358.

90. Report of Alfred J. Vaughan, Upper Missouri Agency, *ARCIA*, 1855, 392.

91. Alfred D. Vaughan, September 29, 1855, Frames 0237–0238, Roll 885, Microfilm 234, RG75: Records of the Bureau of Indian Affairs, NARA.

92. Alfred D. Vaughan, December 25, 1856, Frames 0294–0295, Roll 885, Microfilm 234, RG75: Records of the Bureau of Indian Affairs, NARA.

93. Alexander Redfield, February 6, 1858, and February 8, 1858, and Thomas Wright, July 15, 1857, Frames 0352–0353, 0354–0356, 0388–0389, 0391–0393, Roll 885, Microfilm 234, RG75: Records of the Bureau of Indian Affairs, NARA.

94. Alexander Redfield, June 14, 1858, Frames 0402–040, Roll 885, Microfilm 234, RG75: Records of the Bureau of Indian Affairs, NARA.

95. Report of Alexander H. Redfield, *ARCIA*, 1858, 438; Stewart, et al., *Carl Wimar*, 95–96; Rathbone, *Charles Wimar*, 21–22; Mattison, *Henry A. Boller*, 38–40. Alexander Redfield, June 21, 1858, Frames 0406–0408, Roll 885, Microfilm 234, RG75: Records of the Bureau of Indian Affairs, NARA.

96. Hayden, "Ari'karas," 351–62.

97. Sunder, *Fur Trade*, 208, 213–14.

98. Brown, "A Trip to the Northwest," 123–26.

99. Brown, 126.

100. Report of Indian agent Samuel N. Latta, *ARCIA*, 1862, 338.

101. Morgan, "Stone and Bone Implements of the Arickarees," 119; White, *Lewis Henry Morgan*, 164. Bowers, *Hidatsa Social and Ceremonial Organization*, 40–41; Samuel N. Latta, October 12, 1862, Frame 0840, Roll 885, Microfilm 234, RG75: Records of the Bureau of Indian Affairs, NARA.

102. Metcalf, "Star Village," 59–122; Report of Indian agent Samuel N. Latta, *ARCIA*, 1862, 338. Based on information provided by Bull Neck, O. G. Libby states that the second village was under the leadership of Wolf Chief and Yellow Knife, with Wolf Necklace as assistant. Bull Neck also gave a detailed list of families living in Star Village. See Libby, "Typical Villages," 506–8.

103. Bowers, *Hidatsa Social and Ceremonial Organization*, 40–41.

104. Libby, "Typical Villages," 506. According to Bull Neck, the battle took place in 1860, but this is obviously an error.

105. Report of Henry W. Reed, *ARCIA*, 1863, 283. See also Henry Reed, January 14, 1863, Frame 0869–0873, Roll 885, Microfilm 234, RG75: Records of the Bureau of Indian Affairs, NARA.

106. Captain John Pattee, July 21, 1862, Samuel Latta, March 7, 1863, and Pierre-Jean DeSmet, September 23, 1864, Frames 0841–0846, 0880–0884, 0891–0892, and 0917–0918, Roll 885, Microfilm 234, RG75: Records of the Bureau of Indian Affairs, NARA.

CHAPTER 8

1. Dorsey, *Traditions of the Arikara*, 159–61.

2. For genocidal warfare against the Pawnees, see van de Logt, *Monsters of Contact*, chapter 6.

3. Mahlon Wilkinson to Newton Edmunds, August 31, 1864, *ARCIA*, 1864, 407–8. In 1862 a Sioux faction also murdered Hunkpapa chief Bear's Rib for refusing to join the hostiles. Report

of Captain John Patter to Brigadier General Blunt, July 21, 1862, vol. 16, Fort Randall letters sent and received, RG393: Records of US Army Continental Commands 1817–47, NARA.

4. Kane, *Military Life in Dakota*, 90–93.

5. Utley, *Frontiersmen in Blue*, 261–80.

6. In 1866 Moreland's company was replaced with a company of "Galvanized Yankees" (former Confederate prisoners of war who had taken a loyalty oath to the Union) under Captain Benjamin Dimon. These troops chased away fifteen hundred Sioux warriors who said they had come to trade but who probably tried to intimidate the three tribes. Athearn, *Forts of the Upper Missouri*, 146–48, 171–72; Butts, *Galvanized Yankees*, 170.

7. Alfred Sully, August 15, 1865, Frames 0251–0255, Roll 886, Microfilm 234, RG75: Records of the Bureau of Indian Affairs, NARA.

8. Innis, *Bloody Knife*, 45.

9. Innis, 19–44.

10. Innis, 45.

11. Inniis, 46–47.

12. Captain W. J. Rankin, December 2, 1866, Fort Rice, letters sent and received, RG393: Records of US Army Continental Commands, 1817–47, NARA.

13. Dunlay, *Wolves for the Blue Soldiers*.

14. Colonel J. V. D. Reeve, February 24, 1867, Frames 0317–0320, Roll 887, Microfilm 234, RG75: Records of the Bureau of Indian Affairs, NARA.

15. Kane, *Military Life in Dakota*, 60, 95.

16. Kane, 276, 279. Libby, *Arikara Narrative*, 43–46. Peter Beauchamp interview, Action Anthropology Papers, Box 1, p. 016, AISRI, Indiana University, Bloomington.

17. Libby, *Arikara Narrative*, 46, 52, 186, 195, 200.

18. Greene, "Arikara Drawings," 74–85, 99. See also Greene, "Hazen Collection," 357–77. For information on Arikara marks of honor, see Hoffman, *Beginnings of Writing*, and Mallery, *Picture-Writing of the American Indians*.

19. Kane, *Military Life in Dakota*, 264; Utley, *Lance and the Shield*, 49.

20. Libby, *Arikara Narrative*, 46–48; Kane, *Military Life in Dakota*, 283–84.

21. Kane, *Military Life in Dakota*, 297, 326–27.

22. Custer, *"Boots and Saddles,"* 107–8, 195.

23. William Welch, February 3, 1872, Frames 0569–0574, Roll 886, Microfilm 234, RG75: Records of the Bureau of Indian Affairs, NARA; Utley, *Lance and the Shield*, chapters 8 and 9.

24. Athearn, *William Tecumseh Sherman*, 103.

25. Robertson, "'We Are Going to Have a Big Sioux War,'" 9–10.

26. Robertson, 10–14.

27. Strikes Two told Orin G. Libby in 1912 that five scouts were killed in the fight near Fort McKeen. According to Strikes Two, the other scouts were Spotted Eagle and Ree-Standing-Among-the-Hidatsas. The "Register of Enlistments," however, shows that these scouts had been killed earlier. Libby, *Arikara Narrative*, 189; "Register of Enlistments in the United States Army, 1798–1914," NARA; Robertson, "'We Are Going to Have a Big Sioux War,'" 14.

28. Schultz, *William Jackson*, 101.

29. Libby, *Arikara Narrative*, 77.
30. Arguably the best Custer biography is Utley, *Cavalier in Buckskin*.
31. Frost, *Custer's Seventh Cavalry*, chapter 2; Gray, "Bloody Knife," 93.
32. Frost, *Custer's Seventh Cavalry*, chapter 2, and 113.
33. Frost, chapter 5; Schultz, *William Jackson*, 117–20.
34. Frost, *Custer's Seventh Cavalry*, chapter 7.
35. Frost, 98–101.
36. Innis, *Bloody Knife*, 104.
37. Utley, *Frontier Regulars*, 244.
38. Utley, 243–44; Libby, *Arikara Narrative*, 48–50; Reiger, *Passing of the Great West*, 82, 85–86, 87. Carroll and Frost, *Private Theodore Ewert's Diary*, 126.
39. Custer, "Boots and Saddles," 150, 157–58. Merington, *Custer Story*, 274.
40. Reiger, *Passing of the Great West*, 103–5. Frost, *With Custer in '74*, 30, 35; Custer, "Boots and Saddles," 261.
41. Frost, *With Custer in '74*, 54–55, 64–66.
42. Frost, 55.
43. Libby, *Arikara Narrative*, 169–70. Parks, *Myths and Traditions of the Arikara*, 277–78.
44. Krause and Olson, eds., *Prelude to Glory*, 139–140.
45. Frost, *With Custer in '74*, 80.
46. Carroll and Frost, *Theodore Ewert's Diary*, 81.
47. Krause and Olson, *Prelude to Glory*, 72; Innis, *Bloody Knife*, 124–25.
48. Also in 1874 a number of Arikara scouts under the command of Major Marcus A. Reno accompanied the US Boundary Survey Commission, which surveyed the border between the United States and Canada. See Parsons, *West on the 49th Parallel*; Rees, *Arc of the Medicine Line*.
49. Utley, *Frontier Regulars*, 245–48.
50. Libby, *Arikara Narrative*, 38–40.
51. Libby, 50–53.
52. For two excellent works on the Great Sioux War of 1876–77, see Gray, *Centennial Campaign* and Gray, *Custer's Last Campaign*.
53. See Gray, "Arikara Scouts with Custer," 442–78.
54. Gray, *Centennial Campaign*, 69–71, 97–98.
55. Libby, *Arikara Narrative*, 58–59.
56. Libby, 59. Schultz, *William Jackson*, 124–25. Custer; "Boots and Saddles," 217.
57. Libby, *Arikara Narrative*, 61, 72.
58. Deposition by Red Star (Strikes Bear) in support of Red Bear's Disability Claim, August 23, 1911. Van de Logt, "'We Hardly Knew What a Good Night's Rest Was Then,'" 47.
59. Libby, *Arikara Narrative*, 74, 80–82, 145.
60. Libby, 78–80.
61. Libby, 84.
62. Libby, 105–13.
63. Libby, 113–15.

64. Lieutenant Varnum, who had been ineffective in leading the Arikara scouts, blamed them for abandoning the fight, prompting Reno to retreat. Carroll, *Custer's Chief of Scouts*, 65, 150.

65. Utley, *Cavalier in Buckskin*, 194–202.

66. The Arikaras also knew him as Bear's Trail.

67. Greene, *Yellowstone Command*, 39–40.

68. Koury, *Field Diary of General Alfred H. Terry*, 30–31.

69. Koury, 31–32.

70. Greene, *Slim Buttes, 1876*, 27–28, 31; Libby, *Arikara Narrative*, 146–47.

71. Greene, *Yellowstone Command*, 55–63.

72. Greene, *Slim Buttes*, 34–35; Libby, *Arikara Narrative*, 148.

73. Greene, *Slim Buttes*, 39, 59–96; Bourke, *On the Border with Crook*, 361.

74. The names listed include Barking Wolf, Bears Ears, Black Calf, Black Fox, Black Porcupine, Bull, Bull in the Water, Bush, Climbs the Bluff, Curley Head, Foolish Bear, Forked Horn, Good Elk, Good Face, Goose, Horn in Front, Howling Wolf, Left Hand, One Feather, One Horn, Owl, Rushing Bull, (Little) Sioux, Soldier, Strikes the Lodge, Strikes Two, Wagon, White Cloud (Sioux scout?), Running Wolf, Young Hawk, and Young War Eagle. Compiled from "Register of Enlistments in the United States Army, 1798–1914," NARA.

75. Cox, *Five Years in the United States Army*, 98 and 101.

76. Cox, 102.

77. "Register of Enlistments in the United States Army, 1798–1914," NARA.

78. Deloria and DeMallie, *Documents of American Indian Diplomacy*, 718–19.

79. Hurt and Lass, *Frontier Photographer*, 25.

80. Deloria and DeMallie, *Documents of American Indian Diplomacy*, 720–21.

81. Report of John A. Burbank, governor and ex officio superintendent Indian affairs to Commissioner E. J. Parker, *ARCIA*, 1870, 673–74.

82. Custer quoted in Frost, *Custer's Seventh Cavalry*, 128–29.

83. Deloria and DeMallie, *Documents of American Indian Diplomacy*, 723–24.

84. According to Agent E. H. Alden, Sitting Bull's presence a few days away on horseback retarded efforts to improve the economic conditions at Fort Berthold. Report of Agent E. H. Alden, August 23, *ARCIA*, 1877, 456.

85. Report of William Courtenay, August 19, *ARCIA*, 1879, 136.

CHAPTER 9

1. Prucha, *Documents of United States Indian Policy*, 177.

2. Brown Jr., "Letters from Dakota," 9.

3. Dorsey, *Traditions of the Arikara*, 174, 175–77.

4. Report of Mahlon Wilkinson, *ARCIA*, 1864, 408.

5. Kane, *Military Life in Dakota*, 155–57, 159–60; Dunn, "History of Old Fort Berthold," 60.

6. Mahlon Wilkinson to the commissioner of Indian Affairs, July 15, 1867, *ARCIA*, 1867, 237. The Arikaras frequently appealed to military commanders in their dealings with Wilkinson. See letters by Wilkinson, September 5, 1865, Frames 0060–0065 and

1139–1143, Roll 886, Microfilm 234, RG75: Records of the Bureau of Indian Affairs, NARA, and *ARCIA*, 1869, 754.

7. Governor Newton Edmunds to Acting Commissioner of Indian Affairs R. B. Van Valkenburgh, September 13, 1865, *ARCIA*, 1865.

8. General Samuel R. Curtis, May 30, 1866, Frames 0372–0375, Roll 886, Microfilm 234, RG75: Records of the Bureau of Indian Affairs, NARA.

9. See letters in Frames 0380–0381, 0657, 0665–0673, and 0781, Roll 886, Microfilm 234, RG75: Records of the Bureau of Indian Affairs, NARA.

10. Treaty commission report of August 25, *ARCIA*, 1866, 168–76.

11. For problems caused by trespassing Métis hunters, see the report of Agent John E. Tappan, *ARCIA*, 1871, 938. See also the letter by General Alfred Sully, September 14, 1866, Frames 0267–0269, Roll 886, Microfilm 234, RG75: Records of the Bureau of Indian Affairs, NARA.

12. Sahnish Culture Society, "Fort Laramie Treaty, 1866," treaty minutes, July 23–August 3, 1866, http://www.natureshift.org/Whawk/resource/treaty.html.

13. Sahnish Culture Society.

14. Sahnish Culture Society.

15. Sahnish Culture Society.

16. Sahnish Culture Society.

17. Kappler, *Indian Affairs*, 2:1052–56. See also treaty of July 27, 1866, with addenda, Frames 0909–0925, Roll 886, Microfilm 234, RG75: Records of the Bureau of Indian Affairs, NARA.

18. Meyer, *Village Indians of the Upper Missouri*, 111.

19. Kappler, *Indian Affairs*, 1:881–83.

20. Meyer, *Village Indians of the Upper Missouri*, 123–24.

21. *New York Times*, June 5, 1874.

22. Prucha, *Documents of United States Indian Policy*, 134–35, 136.

23. Kappler, *Indian Affairs*, 1:883; Meyer, *Village Indians of the Upper Missouri*, 112–13.

24. Kappler, *Indian Affairs*, 1:425–28, 883–84, 948–49; Meyer, *Village Indians of the Upper Missouri*, 134–37, 149.

25. Meyer, *Village Indians of the Upper Missouri*, 131–32. See also Kauffman to Trowbridge, January 8, 1881, "Papers Relating to the Foreign Relations of the United States, Transmitted to Congress, with the Annual Message of the President, December 5, 1881," US Department of State, https://history.state.gov/historicaldocuments/frus1881/d354.

26. Dorsey, *Traditions of the Arikara*, 154.

27. Aaron McGaffey Beede Papers, Journal 16, 1917–1919, 129–30.

28. *Word Carrier* (new series) 2, no. 4–5 (June–July 1885): 1; Meyer, *Village Indians of the Upper Missouri*, 135.

29. *Word Carrier* (old series), 17, no. 9 (September 1888), 29.

30. Murie, "Pawnee Indian Societies," 629; Parks, *Traditional Narratives of the Arikara Indians*, 3:323–24, 3:325–30.

31. Murie, "Pawnee Indian Societies," 629–30.

32. Parks, "Arikara," 386.

33. Prucha, *Documents of United States Indian Policy*, 177.

34. Agent William Courtenay, August 19, *ARCIA*, 1879, 136.

35. In 1875 Agent William Courtenay described White Shield as "straight-forward and truthful, and possesses a good deal of practical common sense." He described Son of Star as "commanding in presence" and as one who "speaks in a low, modulated, persuasive tone, and is cautious in expressing his opinions. He has great influence with his tribe, and is considerably over the average of Indians." William Courtenay, "Ft. Berthold, D. T., Indians," *Iapi Oaye* 4 (March 1875): 12.

36. Prucha, *Documents of United States Indian Policy*, 136.

37. Report of Agent C. W. Darling, September 8, *ARCIA*, 1876, 434.

38. Howard, "Arikara Buffalo Society Medicine Bundle," 257.

39. *Iapi Oaye* 7, no. 8 (August 1878): 32; *Iapi Oaye* 8, no. 10 (October 1879), 40.

40. Brown, "Letters from Dakota," 14.

41. Brown, 9.

42. Agent Abram J. Gifford, *ARCIA*, 1885, 257.

43. Agent John S. Murphy, *ARCIA*, 1890, 30–36.

44. Agent H. Clapp, *ARCIA*, 1894, 222.

45. Brown, "Letters from Dakota," 11.

46. Brown, 16–17.

47. Brown, 24.

48. Red Bear quoted in King, "Indian Service Physician on the Northern Plains," 33.

49. *Iapi Oaye* 10, no. 4 (April 1881): 31; *Word Carrier* (old series) 17, nos. 10–11 (October–November 1888): 34; *Word Carrier* 17, no. 12 (December 1888): 39; *Word Carrier* 18:4–5 (April–May 1889): 10.

50. Prucha, *Documents of United States Indian Policy*, 161–62, 186–89.

51. Agent Thomas H. B. Jones, *ARCIA*, 1889, 150; Agent William H. Clapp, *ARCIA*, 1894, 222.

52. Agent Jacob Kauffman, *ARCIA*, 1883, 91.

53. Meyer, "Fort Berthold and the Garrison Dam," 227. For a biography of Hall, see Case and Case, *One Hundred Years at Fort Berthold*.

54. *Word Carrier* 44, no. 4 (July–August 1915): 13.

55. *Iapi Oaye* 5, no. 8 (August 1876): 32; *Iapi Oaye* 7, no. 2 (February 1878): 8; *Iapi Oaye* 8, no. 2 (February 1879): 8; *Iapi Oaye* 8, no. 10 (October 1879): 40; Case and Case, *One Hundred Years at Fort Berthold*, 173–74.

56. *Iapi Oaye* 9, no. 3 (March 1880): 23.

57. *Iapi Oaye* 8, no. 10 (October 1879): 40.

58. *Word Carrier* (old series) 20, nos. 7–8 (July–August 1891): 27.

59. *Word Carrier* (old series) 17, nos. 10–11 (October–November 1888): 33.

60. *Word Carrier* (old series) 26, nos. 6–7 (June–July 1897): front page.

61. *Word Carrier* (old series) 45, no. 5 (September–October 1916): 19.

62. *Iapi Oaye* 7, no. 2 (February 1878): 8; *Iapi Oaye* 7, no. 4 (April 1878): 16; *Iapi Oaye* 8, no. 10 (October 1879): 40.

63. *Word Carrier* (old series) 19, no. 11 (November 1890): 31.

64. *Word Carrier* (old series) 17, no. 5 (May 1888): 20.

65. *Word Carrier* (old series) 23, nos. 7–8 (July–August 1894): 23.
66. *Word Carrier* (old series) 25, nos. 6–7 (June–July 1896): 23.
67. *Iapi Oaye* 8, no. 10 (October 1879): 40; *Word Carrier* (old series) 17, no. 5 (May 1888): 19; *Word Carrier* (old series) 25, no. 5 (May 1896): 18–19.
68. *Word Carrier* (old series) 23:7–8 (July–August 1894): 23.
69. *Iapi Oaye* 7, no. 4 (April 1878): 16.
70. *Word Carrier* (old series) 17, no. 9 (September 1888): 29.
71. *Word Carrier* (old series) 22, nos. 10–12 (October–December 1893): 23; *Word Carrier* 24, no. 10 (October 1895): 28; *Word Carrier* 25, nos. 8–9 (August–September 1896): 25.
72. *Word Carrier* (old series) 25, nos. 8–9 (August–September 1896): 28.
73. *Word Carrier* (old series) 24:3 (March 1895), 10–11.
74. *Word Carrier* (old series) 22:10–12 (October-December 1893), 23.
75. *Word Carrier* (old series) 25, no. 5 (May 1896): 18.
76. *Word Carrier* (new series) 1, no. 3 (April 15, 1884): 3.
77. *Word Carrier* (old series) 18, no. 8 (August 1889): 17.
78. *Word Carrier* (new series) 4, no. 1 (January 1887): 2–3; *Word Carrier* 4, no. 3 (March 1887): 2; *Word Carrier* 4, no. 7 (July 1887): 3–4; *Word Carrier* (old series) 19, nos. 7–8 (July–August 1890): 22; *Word Carrier* 21, no. 3 (March 1892): 7; 21:6–7 (June–July 1892): 20; *Word Carrier* 23, no. 7–8 (July–August 1894): 23; *Word Carrier* 24, no. 3 (March 1895): 12; *Word Carrier* 24, no. 8–9 (August–September 1895), 23.
79. *Word Carrier* (old series) 24, no. 3 (March 1895): 12.
80. Meyer, *Village Indians of the Upper Missouri*, 179.
81. See Kardong, *Catholic Life at Fort Berthold*; Foley, *Father Francis M. Craft*.
82. *Word Carrier* 44, no. 4 (July–August, 1915): 13.
83. Foley, *Father Francis M. Craft*, chapters 1–7.
84. *Word Carrier* (old series) 25, no. 5 (August–September 1897): 27.
85. Foley, *Father Francis M. Craft*, chapters 14–15. Frank Wells's quote is on page 109.
86. Foley, *Father Francis M. Craft*, chapters 16–20.
87. Kardong, *Catholic Life at Fort Berthold*, chapter 2.
88. Frames 0101–0103, Roll 295, Microfilm 234, RG75: Records of the Bureau of Indian Affairs, NARA.
89. For Agent Darling's fraudulent practices, see Frames 0093–0100, Roll 299, Microfilm 234, RG75: Records of the Bureau of Indian Affairs, NARA.
90. Frames 0348–0350, Roll 297, Microfilm 234, RG75: Records of the Bureau of Indian Affairs, NARA.
91. Frames 0834–0837 and 1025–1026, Roll 297, Microfilm 234, RG75: Records of the Bureau of Indian Affairs, NARA.
92. Frame 1078, Roll 297, Microfilm 234, RG75: Records of the Bureau of Indian Affairs, NARA.
93. Frames 1193–1197, Roll 297, Microfilm 234, RG75: Records of the Bureau of Indian Affairs, NARA.
94. Frames 0235–0248, Roll 298, Microfilm 234, RG75: Records of the Bureau of Indian Affairs, NARA.

95. Frames 0726–0728, Roll 297, Frames 0166–0168 and 0169–0170, Roll 298, Microfilm 234, RG75: Records of the Bureau of Indian Affairs, NARA. See also Frames 0545–0550.

96. See, for example, Frames 1063–1064, Roll 292, Frames 0152–0156, 0165, 0554–0556, and 0645–0648, Roll 293, Microfilm 234, RG75: Records of the Bureau of Indian Affairs, NARA.

97. Meyer, *Village Indians of the Upper Missouri*, 142–48, 180–82, 197–200.

98. *Word Carrier* (old series) 20, no. 4 (April 1891): 16.

99. Stella E. Rogers file, Hampton University Archives, Hampton, Virginia.

100. Willard, "Montezuma on the Missouri," 34–38.

101. Willard.

102. Meyer, *Village Indians of the Upper Missouri*, 144.

103. Bruner, "Mandan," 255.

104. Hultgren and Molin, "'Long Rides across the Plains," 10–36.

105. For quick access to information on Arikara students at Hampton Institute, visit http://carlisleindian.dickinson.edu/.

106. Washington, *Up from Slavery*, chapter 5.

107. The case of Anna Dawson is especially instructive. Dawson became a field matron at Fort Berthold, where she was charged with educating Native women with new standards of sanitation, cooking, and other domestic work. She was extremely important in helping people transition to new modes of living and was a tireless champion for her people, which was not always appreciated by government officials. See Frames 0835–0845 and 1050, Roll 46, and Frame 0429, Roll 47, Microfilm 1011, RG75: Records of the Bureau of Indian Affairs, NARA.

108. Matthews, *Ethnography and Philology of the Hidatsa*, 12, 31.

109. Walker, "Old Fort Berthold as I Knew It," 30.

110. Brown, "Letters from Dakota," 9.

CHAPTER 10

1. *Word Carrier* 50, no. 3 (May–June 1921): 10.

2. Frame 1049, Roll 46, Microfilm 1011, RG75: Records of the Bureau of Indian Affairs, NARA.

3. Frame 1118, Roll 46, Microfilm 1011, RG75: Records of the Bureau of Indian Affairs, NARA.

4. Frame 0617, Roll 47, Microfilm 1011, RG75: Records of the Bureau of Indian Affairs, NARA.

5. Frames 0402, 0616, and 1137, Roll 47, Microfilm 1011, RG75: Records of the Bureau of Indian Affairs, NARA.

6. Frames 0782, 1138, and 1155, Roll 47, Microfilm 1011, RG75: Records of the Bureau of Indian Affairs, NARA. As late as 1936, some officials complained that hospital visits were small because people continued to consult Native doctors.

7. "Agreement with Indians on the Fort Berthold Indian Reservation, etc.," H.R. Doc. No. 194-57, at 9–11 (1902).

8. "Agreement with Indians on the Fort Berthold Indian Reservation."

9. "Agreement with Indians on the Fort Berthold Indian Reservation," 13–15.

10. "Agreement with Indians on the Fort Berthold Indian Reservation" 15–16.

11. "Agreement with Indians on the Fort Berthold Indian Reservation," 21.

12. "Agreement with Indians on the Fort Berthold Indian Reservation," 23–30.
13. Meyer, *Village Indians of the Upper Missouri*, 162–63.
14. "Diary of E. E. Fredeen," transcripts in O. G. Libby Collection, SHSND.
15. Meyer, *Village Indians of the Upper Missouri*, 163.
16. Meyer, 163–64; Kappler, *Indian Affairs*, 3:462–66.
17. Red Bear and others quoted in Meyer, *Village Indians of the Upper Missouri*, 164.
18. *Washington Post*, June 30, 1911, 14.
19. *Chicago Daily Tribune*, August 14, 1911, 13; *Chicago Daily Tribune*, August 15, 1911, 12; *Chicago Daily Tribune*, August 16, 1911, 14.
20. Meyer, *Village Indians of the Upper Missouri*, 165.
21. *Washington Post*, November 9, 1915, 9.
22. Meyer, *Village Indians of the Upper Missouri*, 166.
23. Meyer, 168–69.
24. Aaron McGaffey Beede Papers, Ledger 1919, entry for September 29, 1919.
25. Kardong, *Catholic Life at Fort Berthold*, chapter 2, 36.
26. Kardon, chapter 3.
27. *Word Carrier* 32, no. 5 (September–October 1903): 17.
28. *Word Carrier* 33, no. 5 (September–October 1904): 19.
29. *Word Carrier* 34, no. 3 (May–June 1905): 10–11.
30. *Word Carrier* 44, no. 4 (July–August 1915): 13; *Word Carrier* 45, no. 5 (September–October 1916): 19; *Word Carrier* 46, no. 1 (January–February 1917): 3; *Word Carrier* 46, no. 3 (May–June 1917): 11.
31. *Word Carrier* 50, no. 2 (March–April 1921): 7.
32. *Word Carrier* 56, no. 6 (November–December 1927): 29.
33. *Word Carrier* 57, no. 5 (September–October 1928): 17.
34. Anderson, *400 Years*, 138–44.
35. Aaron McGaffey Beede Papers, Journal 1, 1912–1913, entry for February 21, 1913.
36. *Word Carrier* 35, no. 1 (January–February 1906): 3.
37. Frames 0816, 0870, and 1094, Roll 46, Microfilm 1011, RG75: Records of the Bureau of Indian Affairs, NARA.
38. Frames 0031, 0036, and 0127, Roll 47, Microfilm 1011, RG75: Records of the Bureau of Indian Affairs, NARA.
39. Frames 0304, 0318, 0411, and 0555. Roll 47, Microfilm 1011, RG75: Records of the Bureau of Indian Affairs, NARA.
40. Aaron McGaffey Beede Papers, Journal 6, entry for October 15, 1915. Like many other entries in Beede's journal, this one seems to be out of order.
41. George A. Dorsey to Commissioner of Indian Affairs William A. Jones, cited in Parks, *Traditional Narratives of the Arikara Indians*, 3:18.
42. Information furnished by Goodbird, Hidatsa, to Gilbert L. Wilson, 1909. Gilbert L. Wilson files, American Indian Studies Research Institute, Indiana University, Bloomington.
43. *Word Carrier* 36, no. 2 (March–April 1907): 7.
44. Parks, *Traditional Narratives of the Arikara Indians*, 3:18.
45. Red Bear quoted in King, "Indian Service Physician on the Northern Plains," 33.

46. Aaron McGaffey Beede Papers, Journal 6, 1916, entry for July 27, 1916.
47. Aaron McGaffey Beede Papers, Journal 2, entry for January 2 and 10, 1913.
48. Aaron McGaffey Beede Papers, Journal 4, 1914, entry for December 3, 1914.
49. Parks, *Traditional Narratives of the Arikara Indians*, 3:330–34. Interview with Jasper Young Bear, Bloomington, Indiana, January 30, 2007.
50. Parks, "Arikara," 386.
51. *Word Carrier* 50, no 3 (May–June 1921): 10.
52. *New York Times*, November 2, 1926.
53. Meyer, *Village Indians of the Upper Missouri*, 178.
54. Parks, "James R. Murie, Pawnee Ethnographer," 86–104. See Dorsey, *Traditions of the Arikara*.
55. Curtis, "Arikara," 59–100, 148–52, 155–77, 178–80.
56. See Gilmore, *Uses of Plants by the Indians*; *New York Times*, September 23, 1924; "Oldest Indians Alone Can Tell of Long Sacred Native Dances," *Fargo Forum*, December 9, 1922; Gilmore, "Account of the Piraskani Ceremony."
57. Will, "An Arikara Sacred Ceremony," 266–67; Alexander, "Lucky-in-the-House," 616–26.
58. Will, "Magical and Sleight of Hand Performances by the Arikara," 50–65; Will, "Arikara Ceremonials," 247–65; Will, "Notes on the Arikara Indians," 5–48; Will "An Arikara Sacred Ceremony," 265–68.
59. The film remained at the National Museum of the American Indian in New York until tribal member Loren Yellow Bird brought a copy back to Fort Berthold in 2005. Government officials were suspicious of traditional games and sometimes called them forms of gambling. See reports from superintendents in Frames 0817–0818 and 0873–0874, Roll 46, Microfilm 1011, RG75: Records of the Bureau of Indian Affairs, NARA.
60. Stewart, *Peyote Religion*, 256–57.
61. Frames 0128, 0216, 0306–0307, 0336, and 0400, Roll 47, Microfilm 1011, RG75: Records of the Bureau of Indian Affairs, NARA.
62. Newman "Peyote Fails," quoted in La Barre, *Peyote Cult*, 119. The article first appeared in the *McLean County Independent* (Garrison, ND), date unknown. It was later published in the *Indian Leader* (Haskell Institute, Kansas), 27, no. 26 (1924): 1.
63. Stewart, *Peyote Religion*, 256–57.
64. Frames 0796, 0799, and 0489, Roll 46, Microfilm 1011, RG75: Records of the Bureau of Indian Affairs, NARA.
65. Frames 0778, 0881, 0998, 1148, and 1166, Roll 47, Microfilm 1011, RG75.
66. Agent Jonathan S. Murphy to the secretary of the interior, March 1891, Box 516643, letters received November 4, 1890–April 14, 1891, RG75: Records of the Bureau of Indian Affairs, NARA.
67. Viola, *Little Bighorn Remembered*, 147.
68. See Hardorff, *Camp, Custer, and the Little Bighorn*, and Hammer, *Custer in '76*.
69. Libby, *Arikara Narrative*.
70. Aaron McGaffey Beede Papers, Journal 8, 1915 (mislabeled entry; the journal refers to events from 1916), entry for September 30, 1916.

71. Viola, *Little Bighorn Remembered*, 147–51. Van de Logt, "'We Hardly Knew What a Good Night's Rest Was Then."

72. Enlistment records, Department of Veterans Affairs, Fargo, August 7, 2007.

73. Enlistment records.

74. Enlistment records.

75. Enlistment records. Douglas R. Parks and Jacqueline Peterson, interview with Grace Simpson-Flute, White Shield, ND, July 9, 1998.

76. "List of Indians in the World War," Joseph K. Dixon Collection, Mathers Museum, Indiana University, Bloomington.

77. Frames 1109–1111, Roll 46, Microfilm 1011, RG75: Records of the Bureau of Indian Affairs, NARA.

78. Wise, *Red Man in the New World Drama*, 324. See also Tate, "From Scout to Doughboy," 417–37.

79. Britten, *American Indians in World War I*, 99–115.

80. Barsh, "American Indians in the Great War," 278.

81. Charles Fox file, "List of Indians in the World War," Joseph K. Dixon Collection, Mathers Museum, Indiana University, Bloomington; Joint War History Commissions, *The 32d Division in the World War*, chapters 3, 5, 6, 7, 8, and 9.

82. "List of Indians in the World War," Joseph K. Dixon Collection, Mathers Museum, Indiana University, Bloomington; Joint War History Commissions, *The 32d Division in the World War*, chapters 9 and 10.

83. "List of Indians in the World War," Joseph K. Dixon Collection, Mathers Museum, Indiana University, Bloomington; Densmore, "Songs of Indian Soldiers during the World War," 421.

84. Joseph Young Hawk file, "List of Indians in the World War," Joseph K. Dixon Collection, Mathers Museum, Indiana University, Bloomington; *Chicago Daily Tribune*, May 24, 1918, 4; Densmore, "Songs of Indian Soldiers during the World War," 420, 421.

85. Densmore, "Songs of Indian Soldiers during the World War," 420; *Washington Post*, April 11, 1927, 6.

86. Society of the First Division, *History of the First Division*, chapters 4 and 5; Millet, "Cantigny," 149–85.

87. Thomas Rogers file, "List of Indians in the World War," Joseph K. Dixon Collection, Mathers Museum, Indiana University, Bloomington.

88. Densmore, "Songs of Indian Soldiers during the World War," 420.

89. Harvey Hopkins file, "List of Indians in the World War," Joseph K. Dixon Collection, Mathers Museum, Indiana University, Bloomington.

90. *Word Carrier* 48, no. 4 (July–August 1919): 13.

91. Files for Daniel Hopkins, Philip Star, William Deane, and Robert Winans, "List of Indians in the World War," Joseph K. Dixon Collection, Mathers Museum, Indiana University, Bloomington.

92. *New York Times*, June 17, 1923, 17.

93. *Washington Post*, April 11, 1927, 6; *Los Angeles Times*, September 30, 1926; *New York Times*, November 28, 1926, RP12.

94. Parks, *Myths and Traditions of the Arikara*, 42–43.

95. Roll 136, Indian Census Rolls, Fort Berthold, 1936–39, National Archives; Parks, *Myths and Traditions of the Arikara*, 40.

96. Pfaller, "James McLaughlin," 4–11; Trachtenberg, *Shades of Hiawatha*, 211–77.

97. For an excerpt of Wilson's message, see "Wanamaker Party Now with Pueblos," *New York Times*, June 29, 1913.

98. Pfaller, "James McLaughlin," 6.

99. Prucha, *Documents of United States Indian Policy*, 218.

100. *Word Carrier* 54, no. 1 (January–February 1925), 1.

101. Meyer, *Village Indians of the Upper Missouri*, 187–90. Used to big cash payments, some people overspent and soon found themselves broke. Frame 1165, Roll 47, Microfilm 1011, RG 75: Records of the Bureau of Indian Affairs, NARA.

102. "Albert H. Simpson," Indian student files, Hampton University Archives, Hampton, Virginia; *Red Man* 3, no. 10 (June 1911): 468; *Red Man* 6, no. 6 (February 1914): 240; Hudson, "'A Harvest of Hope,'" 3, 8; Sanstead et. al., *History and Culture of the Mandan, Hidatsa, Sahnish (Arikara)*, 140; Parks, *Myths and Traditions of the Arikara*, 34–35.

103. Case and Case, *One Hundred Years at Fort Berthold*, 46–48; Hultgren and Molin, "'Long Rides across the Plains,'" 10–36; *Word Carrier* 39, no. 5 (September–October 1910): 18.

104. *Word Carrier* 47, no. 1 (January–February 1918): 2.

CHAPTER 11

1. Interview with Buddy Mason, White Shield, ND, July 10, 1998.

2. VanDevelder, *Coyote Warrior*, 13–15.

3. Meyer, *Village Indians of the Upper Missouri*, 191–92.

4. Meyer, 194–95. Frames 0999–1000 and 1132, Roll 47, Microfilm 1011, RG 75: Records of the Bureau of Indian Affairs, NARA.

5. Holst, "A Field Agent's Diary."

6. Holst, 9.

7. Holst, 8–9.

8. Holst, 10; Meyer, *Village Indians of the Upper Missouri*, 195–96.

9. Meyer, *Village Indians of the Upper Missouri*, 196. Office of Indian Affairs, *Constitution and Bylaws of the Three Affiliated Tribes of the Fort Berthold Reservation, North Dakota* (Washington, DC: Government Printing Office, 1936).

10. Office of Indian Affairs, *Constitution and Bylaws*, 196.

11. Hudson, "'A Harvest of Hope,'" 3–4.

12. Hale, "Uncle Sam's Warriors," 408–29; Bernstein, *American Indians in World War II*, 40, 42, 67–68.

13. *Mandan-Hidatsa-Arikara Times* 7, no. 35 (November 10, 1995), 2.

14. *Mandan-Hidatsa-Arikara Times* 7, no. 35 (November 10, 1995), 2.

15. Erwin Janssen, Eerde, Netherlands, personal communication, August 7, 2012.

16. *Mandan-Hidatsa-Arikara Times* 7, no. 35 (November 10, 1995), 2, 4.

17. *Mandan-Hidatsa-Arikara Times* 7, no. 35 (November 10, 1995), 2, 4.

18. See US Army, *A History of the 90th Division*.

19. Bellafaire, *Women's Army Corps*.
20. Interview with Margaret Starr, White Shield, ND, May 30, 2007.
21. Hudson, "'Harvest of Hope,'" 5.
22. *Mandan-Hidatsa-Arikara Times* 7, no. 35 (November 10, 1995): 3.
23. Hudson, "'Harvest of Hope,'" 5.
24. Hudson, 5–6.
25. Hudson, 6–7.
26. Interview with Myrtle Painte, White Shield, ND, February 27, 2003.
27. Interview with Myrtle Painte, 422–24.
28. Meyer, *Village Indians of the Upper Missouri*, 254–55.
29. See Fixico, *Urban Indian Experience*.
30. Fixico.
31. Davis, *Native America in the Twentieth Century*, 211; Meyer, *Village Indians of the Upper Missouri*, 239–40.
32. VanDevelder, *Coyote Warrior*, 165–69.
33. VanDevelder, 81–83.
34. VanDevelder, 87–88, 98–104; Meyer, "Fort Berthold and the Garrison Dam," 239–40.
35. Meyer, "Fort Berthold and the Garrison Dam," 243.
36. US Senate, Committee on Indian Affairs, *Protesting the Construction of Garrison Dam, North Dakota, by the Fort Berthold Indians* (Washington, DC: Government Printing Office, 1945), 6, 8.
37. VanDevelder, *Coyote Warrior*, 122.
38. Meyer, "Fort Berthold and the Garrison Dam," 245–46.
39. Some Indians believe the site suggested by the three tribes was rejected because it would have flooded the ranch of a North Dakota senator. Interview with Buddy Mason, White Shield, ND, July 10, 1998.
40. Meyer, "Fort Berthold and the Garrison Dam," 251.
41. Meyer, 251.
42. Interview with Buddy Mason, White Shield, North Dakota, July 10, 1998.
43. Marie Wells interviewed by Helen M. Steckler, New Town, ND, June 23, 1999.
44. Program 204, Wisdom of the Elders, http://wisdomoftheelders.org/2011/08/01/program-204-elder-wisdom/ accessed January 29, 2013.
45. Parks, "Arikara," 387.
46. Parks, "Arikara," 387.
47. Parks, "Arikara," 387.
48. VanDevelder, *Coyote Warrior*, 32–33.
49. Interview with Buddy Mason, White Shield, ND, July 10, 1998.

CHAPTER 12

1. Interview with Frank Heart, July 3, 1952, Action Anthropology Project.
2. Interview with Frank Heart, July 3, 1952, Action Anthropology Project.
3. Among the scholars visiting Fort Berthold were Sol Tax, who started the Action Anthropology Project at the University of Chicago; Robert Merrill; and Edward Bruner.

Most of their papers ended up at the University of Chicago. I used photocopies of selected reports and interviews kept at the American Indian Studies Research Institute, Indiana University.

4. Interview with Frank Heart, July 3, 1952, Action Anthropology Project.

5. Interview with Frank Heart, November 23, 1952, Action Anthropology Project.

6. Interview with Frank Heart, July 3, 1952, Action Anthropology Project.

7. Interview with Frank Heart, November 23, 1952, Action Anthropology Project.

8. Interview with Snowbird, June 27, 1952, Action Anthropology Project.

9. Interview with the Reverend George Gillette, April 26, 1973.

10. Interview with Elizabeth Gillette, July 3, 1952, Action Anthropology Project.

11. Interview Fannie Whitman-Perkins, n.d. Audio recording made available by Loren Yellow Bird.

12. Interview Fannie Whitman-Perkins.

13. Interview Fannie Whitman-Perkins.

14. See DeMallie, *Plains*, Part 2, 397. Data for 2000, 2010, and 2011 from "Statistics & Data," North Dakota Indian Affairs Commission, www.nd.gov/indianaffairs/, accessed January 21, 2013. Tribal enrollment figures for 2021 from "MHA Nation," Mandan, Hidatsa and Arikara Nation, www.mhanation.com, accessed February 17, 2021.

15. Sahota, "Critical Contexts for Biomedical Research," 12.

16. National Center for Health Statistics, "Health Characteristics of the American Indian or Alaska Native Adult Population: United States, 2004–2008," *National Health Statistics Reports* 20 (March 9, 2010): 1–20.

17. "Minority Health: American Indian & Alaska Native Populations," Centers for Disease Control and Prevention, http://www.cdc.gov/minorityhealth/populations/REMP/aian.html, accessed September 18, 2014. For specific numbers for Native Americans in North Dakota, see North Dakota Indian Affairs Commission, *Facts and Profiles*, 7, and North Dakota Legislative Council, "Minutes of the Tribal and State Relations Committee" (New Town, ND: North Dakota Legislative Council, 2006), 4.

18. Sahota, "Critical Contexts for Biomedical Research," 15.

19. Duran et al., "Native Americans and the Trauma of History," 63, 65, 67, 68.

20. Lawrence, "The Indian Health Service and the Sterilization of Native American Women," 400–19; Carpio, "The Lost Generation," 40–53; "Killing Our Future: Sterilization & Experiments," *Akwesasne Notes* 9, no. (1977); Torpy, "Native American Women and Coerced Sterilization," 1–22; Duran et al., "Native Americans and the Trauma of History," 69.

21. See works by Castle McLaughlin, including "The Politics of Agricultural Decline on the Fort Berthold Indian Reservation, North Dakota," *Culture and Agriculture* 44 (1992): 20–22; "Nation, Tribe, and Class: The Dynamics of Agrarian Transformation on the Fort Berthold Reservation," *American Indian Culture and Research Journal* 22, no. 3 (1998): 101–38; McLaughlin, "Ranching an Important Part," 17–19, 22–24.

22. "[Our] food sources were critical for our culture and survival," argued tribal chairman Tex G. Hall before the US Senate Committee on Indian Affairs in 2001. He called on Congress to provide funds for irrigation projects to compensate for the precious bottomlands lost

due to the Garrison Dam. *Hearing before the Committee on Indian Affairs on Federal Obligation to Equitable Compensation to the Fort Berthold and Standing Rock Reservations, New Town, ND, August 30, 2001*, 107th Cong. (2001), 13. For Arikaras adopting Lakhota religious concepts, see Irwin and Liebert, *Two Ravens*.

23. McLaughlin, "Ranching an Important Part," 9; Meyer, *Village Indians of the Upper Missouri*, 252.

24. Deloria and Wilkins, *Tribes, Treaties, and Constitutional Tribulations*, 134–35; DeMallie, *Plains*, Part 2, 398.

25. North Dakota Indian Affairs Commission, *Facts and Profiles*, 8.

26. Tiller, *Tiller's Guide to Indian Country*, 491–92.

27. North Dakota Legislative Council, "Minutes of the Tribal and State Relations Committee," 2. *Oversight Hearing before Senate Committee on Indian Affairs on Impacts of Environmental Changes on Treaty Rights, Traditional Lifestyles, and Tribal Homelands*, 112th Cong. (2012) (written testimony of Tex G. Hall, chairman of the Mandan, Hidatsa and Arikara Nation of the Fort Berthold Reservation).

28. Howard and Woolworth, "An Arikara Bear Society Initiation Ceremony," 176.

29. Howard and Woolworth, 179.

30. "Fort Berthold Field Notes," 1951, Action Anthropology Project; Reifel, "Relocation on the Fort Berthold Indian Reservation," 245.

31. "Fort Berthold Field Notes," 1951, Action Anthropology Project.

32. Viola, *Little Bighorn Remembered*, 140–41.

33. Stockdill, "All's Right with Scouts," *Bismarck Tribune*, September 17, 1995.

34. "Fort Berthold Indian Reservation Goals 2000: Tribal Curriculum Project," undated instruction sheet.

35. Interview with Joseph Reed.

36. Interview with Joseph Reed.

37. Interview with Joseph Reed.

38. Interview with Joseph Reed.

39. Interview with Joseph Reed.

40. Interview with Joseph Reed.

41. Statement by Thelma Hunter, unpublished typewritten manuscript, American Indian Curricula Development Program, New Town, ND.

42. George Gillette interviewed by August Little Soldier, August 13, 1973.

43. Alfred Morsette interviewed by August Little Soldier, August 14, 1973.

44. Meyer, *Village Indians of the Upper Missouri*, 246, 249.

45. Howard, "Arikara Buffalo Society Medicine Bundle," 242–43.

46. Reportedly, in the summer of 2006, four of the seven remaining bundles (there once were twelve) were brought together in the Ralph Wells Memorial Complex in White Shield. The people in attendance prayed over the bundles. Some refused to attend because of a false rumor that one of the bundles would be opened. The meeting reminded people of their collective identity as Arikaras. For privacy reasons, the name of the source of this information is not revealed here.

47. Interview with Sidney and Anita Howard, White Shield, June 6, 2007.

48. Yvonne Fox, Turtle Island Storytellers Network, www.turtleislandstorytellers.net/tis_north_dakota/transcript_y_fox.htm, accessed August 31, 2006; interview with Yvonne Fox and Gloria Yellowbird, White Shield, June 2, 2007.

49. Rodney Howling Wolf, personal communication, March 13, 2005.

50. Jasper Young Bear, personal communication, January 30, 2007.

51. Snodgrass, *American Indian Painters*, 52, 58, 80, 147, 158, 216; Miles S. Horn file, SHSND.

52. Personal communication, Delilah Yellow Bird, May 2007.

53. Meyer, *Village Indians of the Upper Missouri*, 236–37.

54. Parks, *Myths and Traditions of the Arikara*, 25–47.

55. Patrick Springer, "Voices from the Past: Departed Tribal Elders Still Talking Thanks to Computers," *Forum*, September 20, 2003.

56. DeMallie, *Plains*, Part 2, 397.

57. Parks, "Arikara," 386.

AFTERWORD

1. Dorsey, *Traditions of the Arikara*, 13.

2. See *NAhtAsuutaaka' (White Shield) News Journal* 3, no. 42 (September 2016).

BIBLIOGRAPHY

ARCHIVAL SOURCES
AMERICAN INDIAN STUDIES RESEARCH INSTITUTE, INDIANA UNIVERSITY, BLOOMINGTON

"Fort Berthold Field Notes," Action Anthropology Project
Aaron McGaffey Beede Papers
Melvin Randolph Gilmore Papers
Preston Holder Papers
Alexander Lesser Papers
Gilbert L. Wilson files
Typed transcript of the 1851 Fort Laramie Council proceedings from the *Missouri Republican*, October–November 1851

DEPARTMENT OF VETERANS AFFAIRS, MEDICAL AND REGIONAL OFFICE CENTER, FARGO

Eli Perkins military service record file

HAMPTON UNIVERSITY ARCHIVES, HAMPTON, VIRGINIA

Individual Indian student files

MATHERS MUSEUM, INDIANA UNIVERSITY, BLOOMINGTON

Joseph K. Dixon Collection

MISSOURI HISTORICAL SOCIETY ARCHIVES, ST. LOUIS, MISSOURI

"Census Collection, 1732–1980"

NATIONAL ARCHIVES AND RECORDS ADMINISTRATION (NARA), WASHINGTON, DC

RG75: Records of the Bureau of Indian Affairs
    Microfilm 234, "Letters Received by the Office of Indian Affairs, 1824–81"
        Rolls 55–61, "Central Superintendency, 1851–1880"
        Rolls 292–99, "Fort Berthold Agency, 1867–1880"
        Rolls 747–56, "St. Louis Superintendency, 1824–1851"
        Rolls 883–88, "Upper Missouri Agency, 1824–1874"

Microfilm 1011, "Superintendents' Annual Narrative and Statistical Reports" from Field Jurisdictions of the Bureau of Indian Affairs, 1907–1938"
    Roll 46, "Fort Belknap, 1932–1935" and "Fort Berthold, 1910–1920"
    Roll 47, "Fort Berthold, 1921–1938"
RG94: Records of the Adjutant General's Office, 1780s–1917
Microfilm 567, "Letters Received by the Office of the Adjutant General, 1822–1860"
    Roll 12, correspondence surrounding the 1823 Arikara War
RG393: Records of US Army Continental Commands, 1817–47
    Fort Randall, letters sent and received
    Fort Rice, letters sent and received
"Register of Enlistments in the United States Army, 1798–1914," vols. 150 and 151, 1866–77, Indian scouts, M233, Rolls 70–71
Indian Census Rolls, Fort Berthold, 1936–39, National Archives Microfilm Publication M595, Rolls 132–36
"US Military Fatal Casualties of the Korean War for Home-State-of-Record: North Dakota," http://www.archives.gov/research/military/korean-war/casualty-lists/nd-alpha.pdf

STATE HISTORICAL SOCIETY OF NORTH DAKOTA (SHSND), BISMARCK

Ben Reifel Papers
Charles Lemon Hall Papers
Frances Densmore Papers
Orin G. Libby Collection

GOVERNMENT DOCUMENTS

"Agreement with Indians on the Fort Berthold Indian Reservation, etc.," H.R. Doc. No. 194-57 (1902).
Annual Reports of the Commissioner of Indian Affairs (ARCIA), 1842–1905.
"Reports of Explorations and Surveys, to Ascertain the Most Practical and Economical Route for a Railroad from the Mississippi River to the Pacific Ocean," H.R. Doc. No. 91-33 (1855).
"Status of Certain Patents, etc., Fort Berthold Indian Reservation, N. Dak," S. Rep. 5318-59 (1907).
US Senate. *Documents Accompanying the Message of the President of the United States to Both Houses*. Washington, DC: Government Printing Office, 1825.
US Senate, Committee on Indian Affairs. *Protesting the Construction of Garrison Dam, North Dakota, by the Fort Berthold Indians*. Washington, DC: Government Printing Office, 1945.

INTERVIEWS

Action Anthropology Project, Fort Berthold Indian Reservation, 1952. Various interviewers; interpreted by Peter H. Beauchamp. Copies of transcribed interviews available at the American Indian Studies Research Institute, Indiana University, Bloomington.

Elizabeth Gillette, Elbowoods, ND, July 3, 1952
　　　Frank Heart, n.p., July 3, 1952, November 23, 1952
　　　Snowbird, Parshall, ND, June 27, 1952
Arikara Language Project interviews, by Douglas R. Parks and Jacqueline Peterson. Tapes and transcripts available at the American Indian Studies Research Institute, Indiana University, Bloomington.
　　　Florence Badger, White Shield, ND, July 9, 1998
　　　Grace Simpson Flute, White Shield, ND, July 9, 1998
　　　Buddy Mason, White Shield, ND, July 10, 1998
　　　Angela Plante, White Shield, ND, July 10, 1998
David Little Swallow interviews. Transcripts available at the American Indian Studies Research Institute, Indiana University, Bloomington.
　　　Eleanor Chase, August 20, 1973
　　　Mary Gillette, August 30, 1973
　　　Dan Hopkins, July 31, 1973
　　　Dan Howling Wolf, July 31, 1973
　　　Alfred Morsette, August 31, September 7, and September 14, 1973
　　　Matthew White Bear, July 8, 1973
August Little Soldier interviews. Transcripts available at the American Indian Studies Research Institute, Indiana University, Bloomington.
　　　Mrs. Ralph Baker, August 1, 1973
　　　Edwin Bensin, August 27, 1973
　　　William Deane, August 15 and August 21, 1973
　　　George Gillette, August 13 and August 31, 1973
　　　Alfred Morsette, August 14 and August 16, 1973
　　　Mrs. John Starr, August 1, 1973
　　　Ella Waters, August 6, 1973
　　　Alice and Matthew White Bear, August 22 and August 30, 1973
　　　Matthew White Bear, August 7, 1973
Mark van de Logt interviews.
　　　Yvonne Fox, Gloria Yellowbird, and Gail Valenzuela, White Shield, ND, June 2, 2007
　　　Anita Howard, White Shield, ND, June 6, 2007
　　　Pearl Myrtle Painte Howard, Martina Ross, and Gloria Yellow Bird, White Shield, ND, February 27, 2003
　　　Pearl Ross, New Town, ND, June 2007
　　　Margaret Starr, White Shield, ND, May 30, 2007
　　　Rhoda Star, White Shield, ND, June 1, 2007
　　　Gerald White, New Town, ND, May 31, 2007
　　　Wendell White, New Town, ND, March 17, 2007
　　　Jasper Young Bear, Bloomington, Indiana, January 30, 2007
Miscellaneous interviews. Transcripts available at the American Indian Studies Research Institute, Indiana University, Bloomington.

George Gillette, n.p., April 26, 1973
Ben Heart, n.p., n.d.
Bill Lockwood, Fort Berthold Indian Reservation, ND, April 3, 1973
Miscellaneous interviews conducted by Eric Holland, National Park Service ranger, Knife River Indian Villages National Historic Site, circa 1991
    Fannie Whitman
    Joseph Reed
On the Road with ND Studies, North Dakota State Historical Society. Helen M. Steckler, interviewer. Transcript available at North Dakota State Historical Society.
    Marie A. Wells, New Town, ND, June 23, 1999.
Wisdom of the Elders interviews. Audio versions and transcripts available at http://www.wisdomoftheelders.org/index.html.
    Yvonne Fox, n.p., n.d.
    Rodney Howling Wolf and Virgil Chase, n.p., n.d.
    Leo Lockwood, n.p., n.d.
    Dorreen Yellowbird, n.p., n.d.

FILM

Arikara Indians of North Dakota. New York: Heye Foundation, Museum of the American Indian, 1924.

NEWSPAPERS

American Missionary, 1878–1901
Chicago Press and Tribune/Daily Tribune
Iapi Oaye/Word Carrier, Dakota Territory/South Dakota, 1875–1930
Indian Craftsman/Red Man, Carlisle, Pennsylvania, 1909–1915
Los Angeles Times
Mandan-Hidatsa-Arikara Times, New Town, ND
New York Times
Washington Post

BOOKS, ARTICLES, AND DISSERTATIONS

Abel, Annie Heloise, ed. *Chardon's Journal at Fort Clark, 1834–1839.* Lincoln: University of Nebraska Press, 1997.

———, ed. *Tabeau's Narrative of Loisel's Expedition to the Upper Missouri.* Norman: University of Oklahoma Press, 1968.

Albers, Patricia, and Beatrice Medicine, eds. *The Hidden Half: Studies of Plains Indian Women.* Lanham, MD: University Press of America, 1983.

Alexander, Hartley B. "Lucky-in-the-House." *Theatre Arts Monthly* 17, no. 8 (August 1933): 616–26.

Allis, Samuel. "Forty Years among the Indians and on the Eastern Border of Nebraska." *Transactions and Reports of the Nebraska State Historical Society* 2 (Lincoln: State Journal Company, 1887), 133–66.

Anderson, Owanah. *400 Years: Anglican/Episcopal Mission among American Indians.* Cincinnati: Forward Movement Publications, 1997.
Arp, Don, Jr. "The Rats at Fort Clark." *Rocky Mountain Fur Trade Journal* 10 (2016): 37–47.
Athearn, Robert G. *Forts of the Upper Missouri.* Englewood Cliffs, NJ: Prentice-Hall, 1967.
Athearn, Robert G. *William Tecumseh Sherman and the Settlement of the West.* Norman: University of Oklahoma Press, 1995.
Barbour, Barton H. *Fort Union and the Upper Missouri Fur Trade.* Norman: University of Oklahoma Press, 2001.
Barsh, Russell Lawrence. "American Indian in the Great War." *Ethnohistory* 38, no. 3 (Summer 1991): 276–303.
Bellafaire, Judith A. *The Women's Army Corps: A Commemoration of World War II Service.* Washington, DC: US Army Center for Military History, 1993.
Berman, Tressa. *Circle of Goods: Women, Work, and Welfare in a Reservation Community.* Albany: State University of New York Press, 2003.
Bernstein, Alison R. *American Indians in World War II: Toward a New Era in Indian Affairs.* Norman: University of Oklahoma Press, 1991.
Bohr, Roland. *Gifts from the Thunder Beings: Indigenous Archery and European Firearms in the Northern Plains and the Central Subarctic, 1670–1870.* Lincoln: University of Nebraska Press, 2014.
Boller, Henry A. *Among the Indians: Four Years on the Upper Missouri, 1858–1862.* Lincoln: University of Nebraska Press, 1972.
Bonner, Thomas D. *The Life and Adventures of James P. Beckwourth.* Lincoln: University of Nebraska Press, 1972.
Bourke, John G. *On the Border with Crook.* Columbus, OH: College Book Company, 1950.
Bowers, Alfred W. *Hidatsa Social and Ceremonial Organization.* Lincoln: University of Nebraska Press, 1992.
Brackenridge, Henry Marie. *Views of Louisiana: Together with a Journal of a Voyage up the Missouri River in 1811.* Chicago: Quadrangle Books, 1962.
Brackenridge, Henry Marie. "Journal of a Voyage up the River Missouri: Performed in Eighteen Hundred and Eleven." In *Early Western Travels, 1748–1846,* vol. 6, edited by Reuben Gold Thwaites. Cleveland: Arthur H. Clark, 1904. Reprint, AMS Press, 1966.
Bradbury, John. *Travels in the Interior of America.* Ann Arbor: University Microfilms, 1966.
Bradford, William. *Of Plymouth Plantation, 1620–1647.* New York: Modern Library, 1981.
Bridges, Patricia S. "Prehistoric Arthritis in the Americas." *Annual Review of Anthropology* 21, no. 1 (1992): 67–91.
Britten, Thomas A. *American Indians in World War I: At War and at Home.* Albuquerque: University of New Mexico Press, 1997.
Brooks, James F. *Captives and Cousins: Slavery, Kinship, and Community in the Southwest Borderlands.* Chapel Hill: University of North Carolina Press, 2002.
Brown, John Mason. "A Trip to the Northwest in 1861." *Filson Club History Quarterly* 24, no. 2 (April 1950): 103–36, 246–75.
Brown, Stuart E., Jr., ed. "Letters from Dakota; or Life and Scenes among the Indians: Fort Berthold Agency, 1889–1890." *North Dakota History* 43, no. 1 (1976): 5–31.

Bruner, Edward M. "Mandan." In *Perspectives in American Indian Culture Change*, edited by Edward H. Spicer, pp. 187–277. Chicago: University of Chicago Press, 1961.

Burpee, Lawrence J., ed. *Journals and Letters of Pierre Gaultier de Varennes de la Verendrye and His Sons*. Toronto: Champlain Society, 1927.

Butts, Michelle Tucker. *Galvanized Yankees on the Upper Missouri: The Face of Loyalty*. Boulder: University Press of Colorado, 2003.

Caldwell, Warren W. "Fortified Villages in the Northern Plains." *Plains Anthropologist* 9, no. 23 (February 1964): 1–7.

Carpio, Myla Vicenti. "The Lost Generation: American Indian Women and Sterilization Abuse." *Social Justice* 31, no. 4 (2004): 40–53.

Carroll, John M., ed. *Custer's Chief of Scouts: The Reminiscences of Charles A. Varnum, Including His Testimony at the Reno Court of Inquiry*. Lincoln: University of Nebraska Press, 1987.

Carroll, John M., and Lawrence A. Frost, eds. *Private Theodore Ewert's Diary of the Black Hills Expedition of 1874*. Piscataway, NJ: CRI Books, 1976.

Case, Harold W., and Eva Case, comp. *One Hundred Years at Fort Berthold: The History of the Fort Berthold Indian Mission, 1876–1976*. Bismarck: H. W. Case, 1977.

Chalkley, Mark. "Eagle Feather Goes to Washington." *We Proceeded On* 29, no. 2 (May 2003): 6–10.

Chittenden, Hiram Martin. *The American Fur Trade of the Far West*. Lincoln: University of Nebraska Press, 1986.

Chittenden, Hiram Martin, and Alfred Talbot Richardson, eds. *Life, Letters and Travels of Father DeSmet*. 4 vols. New York: Arno Press, 1969.

Clark, William Philo. *The Indian Sign Language*. Lincoln: University of Nebraska Press, 1982.

Clements, William M. *Native American Verbal Art: Texts and Contexts*. Tucson: University of Arizona Press, 1996.

Collot, Victor. *A Journey in North America*. Paris: Arthus Bertrand, 1826.

Cooper, John M., ed. *Plato: Complete Works*. Indianapolis: Hackett Publishing, 1997.

Cox, Isaac Joslin, ed. *The Journeys of Rene Robert Cavelier, Sieur de La Salle*, vol. 1. New York: Allerton, 1922.

Cox, John E. *Five Years in the United States Army*. New York: Sol Lewis, 1973.

Curtis, Edward S. "The Arikara." In *The North American Indian*, vol. 5. New York: Johnson Reprint Corporation, 1970.

———. *The North American Indian*, vol. 3. New York: Johnson Reprint Company, 1970.

Custer, Elizabeth B. *"Boots and Saddles": or Life in Dakota with General Custer*. Norman: University of Oklahoma Press, 1961.

Davis, Mary B., ed. *Native America in the Twentieth Century: An Encyclopedia*. New York: Garland Publishing, 1996.

Deland, Charles E. "Aborigines of South Dakota" *South Dakota Historical Collections* 3 (1906–1908): 267–586.

Deliette, Pierre. "Memoir of DeGannes (Deliette) Concerning the Illinois Country." In *The French Foundations, 1680–1693*, edited by Theodore C. Pease and Raymond C. Werner, pp. 302–95. Collections of the Illinois State Historical Library 23 (Springfield: Illinois State Historical Library, 1934).

Delisle, Guillaume. "Carte du Mexique et de la Florida des Terres Angloises et des Isles Antilles du Cours et des Environs de la Riviere de Mississipi." Paris: Chez l'Auteur sur le Quai de l'Horloge, 1703.

Deloria, Vine, Jr. *Spirit and Reason: The Vine Deloria Jr. Reader*. Golden, CO: Fulcrum, 1999.

Deloria, Vine, Jr., and Raymond J. DeMallie, eds. *Documents of American Indian Diplomacy: Treaties, Agreements, and Conventions, 1775–1979*. Norman: University of Oklahoma Press, 1999.

Deloria, Vine, Jr., and David E. Wilkins. *Tribes, Treaties, and Constitutional Tribulations*. Austin: University of Texas Press, 2001.

DeMallie, Raymond J. *Plains*, Part 1. In *Handbook of North American Indians*, vol. 13, edited by William C. Sturtevant. Washington, DC: Smithsonian Institution, 2001.

———. *Plains*, Part 2. In *Handbook of North American Indians*, vol. 13, edited by William C. Sturtevant. Washington, DC: Smithsonian Institution, 2001.

DeMallie, Raymond J., Douglas R. Parks, and Robert Vézina, eds. *A Fur Trader on the Upper Missouri: The Journal and Description of Jean-Baptiste Truteau, 1794–1796*. Lincoln: University of Nebraska Press, 2017.

Denig, Edwin Thompson. *Five Indian Tribes of the Upper Missouri: Sioux, Arickaras, Assiniboines, Crees, Crows*. Norman: University of Oklahoma Press, 1973.

Densmore, Frances "The Songs of Indian Soldiers during the World War." *Musical Quarterly* 20, no. 4 (October 1934): 419–25.

Dickson, Frank H. "Hard on the Heels of Lewis and Clark." *Montana: The Magazine of Western History* 26, no. 1 (Winter 1976): 14–25.

Dodge, Henry. "Journal of the March of a Detachment of Dragoons, Under the Command of Col. Dodge, during the Summer of 1835." *American State Papers: Military Affairs 6* (Washington, DC: Government Printing Office, 1861), 130–46.

Donaldson, Thomas, comp., ed. "The George Catlin Indian Gallery in the U.S. National Museum (Smithsonian Institution) with Memoir and Statistics." *Annual Report of the Board of Regents of the Smithsonian Institution*, Part II (July 1885).

Dorsey, George A. "An Arikara Story-Telling Contest." *American Anthropologist* 6, no. 2 (April–June 1904): 240–43.

———. *The Mythology of the Wichita*. Norman: University of Oklahoma Press, 1995.

———. *The Pawnee Mythology*. Lincoln: University of Nebraska Press, 1997.

———. *Traditions of the Arikara*. Washington, DC: Carnegie Institution, 1904.

———. *Traditions of the Caddo*. Lincoln: University of Nebraska Press, 1997.

———. *Traditions of the Skidi Pawnee*. New York: Kraus Reprint, 1969.

Drumm, Stella M., ed. *Journal of a Fur-Trading Expedition on the Upper Missouri, 1812–1813, by John C. Luttig, Clerk of the Missouri Fur Company*. New York: Argosy-Antiquarian, 1964.

Dunlap, William. *Diary of William Dunlap (1766–1839): The Memoirs of a Dramatist, Theatrical Manager, Painter, Critic, Novelist, and Historian*. New York: Benjamin Blom, 1969.

Dunlay, Thomas W. *Wolves for the Blue Soldiers: Indian Scouts and Auxiliaries with the United States Army, 1860–90*. Lincoln: University of Nebraska Press, 1982.

Dunn, Adrian R. "A History of Old Fort Berthold." *North Dakota History* 30, no. 4 (October 1963): 156–240.

Duran, Bonnie, Eduardo Duran, and Maria Yellow Horse Brave Heart. "Native Americans and the Trauma of History." In *Studying Native America: Problems and Prospects*, edited by Russell Thornton, pp. 60–76 (Madison: University of Wisconsin Press, 1998).
Echo-Hawk, Roger. "Ancient History in the New World: Integrating Oral Traditions and the Archaeological Record in Deep Time." *American Antiquity* 65, no. 2 (April 2000): 267–90.
———. *The Enchanted Mirror: Ancient Pawneeland*. Self-published, 2018.
Ewers, John C. *The Horse in Blackfeet Indian Culture: With Comparative Material from Other Western Tribes*. Washington, DC: Smithsonian Institution Press, 1955.
———. *Plains Indian History and Culture: Essays on Continuity and Change*. Norman: University of Oklahoma Press, 1997.
Fenn, Elizabeth. *Encounters at the Heart of the World: A History of the Mandan People*. New York: Hill and Wang, 2014.
———. *Pox Americana: The Great Smallpox Epidemic of 1775–82*. New York: Hill and Wang, 2002.
Fixico, Donald L. *The Urban Indian Experience in America*. Albuquerque: University of New Mexico Press, 2000.
Flint, Shirley Cushing, and Richard Flint. *The Latest Word from 1540: People, Places, and Portrayals of the Coronado Expedition*. Albuquerque: University of New Mexico Press, 2011.
Foley, Thomas W. *Father Francis M. Craft: Missionary to the Sioux*. Lincoln: University of Nebraska Press, 2002.
Frison, George C. "Hunting and Gathering Tradition: Northwestern and Central Plains." In *Handbook of North American Indians*, edited by William C. Sturtevant. Vol. 13, *Plains*, Part 1, edited by Raymond J. DeMallie, pp. 131–45. Washington, DC: Smithsonian Institution, 2001.
Frost, Lawrence A. *Custer's Seventh Cavalry and the Campaign of 1873*. El Segundo, CA: Upton & Sons, 1986.
———, ed. *With Custer in '74: James Calhoun's Diary of the Black Hills Expedition*. Provo, UT: Brigham Young University Press, 1979.
Garavaglia, Louis A., and Charles G. Worman. *Firearms of the American West, 1803–1865*. Niwot: University Press of Colorado, 1998.
Gates, Charles M., ed. *Five Fur Traders of the Northwest*. St. Paul: Minnesota Historical Society, 1965.
Gibson, Arrell Morgan. *The American Indian: Prehistory to the Present*. Lexington, MA: DC Heath, 1980.
Gilmore, Melvin R. "Account of the Piraskani Ceremony of the Arikara at Armstrong, ND, September 1922." Unpublished manuscript, American Indian Studies Research Institute, Indiana University, Bloomington, n.d.
———. "Arikara Agriculture." Unpublished manuscript, American Indian Studies Research Institute, Indiana University, Bloomington, n.d.
———. "The Arikara Book of Genesis." *Papers of the Michigan Academy of Science, Arts, and Letters* 12 (1929): 95–120.
———. "An Arikara Bundle." *Indian Notes* 8 (Summer 1972): 93–98.

———. "Arikara Ceremonies: Observed on Fort Berthold Reservation, North Dakota, August, 1921." Unpublished manuscript, American Indian Studies Research Institute, Indiana University, Bloomington, n.d.

———. "The Arikara Code of Eagle Feather Honor Badges." Unpublished manuscript, American Indian Studies Research Institute, Indiana University, Bloomington, n.d.

———. "Arikara Commerce." *Indian Notes* 3 (January 1926): 13–18.

———. "Arikara Consolation Ceremony." *Indian Notes* 3 (October 1926): 256–74.

———. "Arikara Fish-Trap." *Indian Notes* 1 (1924): 120–34.

———. "Arikara Order of Butchering a Buffalo." *Indian Notes* 9 (Winter 1973): 21.

———. "Arikara Origin Myth: Told by Four-Rings, an Arikara Living at Armstrong, Fifteen Miles East of Fort Berthold, North Dakota, August 1924." Unpublished manuscript, American Indian Studies Research Institute, Indiana University, Bloomington, 1925.

———. "The Arikara Tribal Temple." *Papers of the Michigan Academy of Science, Arts, and Letters* 14 (1930): 47–70.

———. "Buffalo Skull from the Arikara." *Indian Notes* 3 (April 1926): 75–79.

———. "Capturing Eaglets in the Aerie." Unpublished notes and manuscripts, American Indian Studies Research Institute, Indiana University, Bloomington, n.d..

———. "Glass Bead Making by the Arikara." *Indian Notes* 1 (January 1924): 20–21.

———. "Indian Custom of 'Carrying the Pipe.'" *Indian Notes* 3 (April 1926): 89–95.

———. "Indian Tribal Boundary Lines and Monuments." *Indian Notes* 5 (1928): 59–63.

———. "Information on the Divine Gift of Corn to the Arikara, and of Ceremonies of Religious Worship when the Hakawirat Sacred Bundle Is Opened." Unpublished manuscript, American Indian Studies Research Institute, Indiana University, Bloomington, n.d.

———. "Interesting Arikara Story of the Origin of the Tobacco." *American Indian* 4 (February 1930): 14.

———. "The Making of a New Head Chief by the Arikara." *Indian Notes* 5 (October 1928): 411–18.

———. "Making Records of Ancient Rituals of the Arikara Tribe in North Dakota." Unpublished manuscript, American Indian Studies Research Institute, Indiana University, Bloomington, n.d.

———. "Months and Seasons of the Arikara Calendar." *Indian Notes* 6 (July 1929): 246–50.

———. "Notes from Information on Ceremonies of Mother Corn. Patrick Star, informant, Albert Simpson, interpreter, August 27, 1924." Unpublished manuscript, American Indian Studies Research Institute, Indiana University, Bloomington.

———. "Notes on Arikara Tribal Organization." *Indian Notes* 4 (October 1927): 332–50.

———. "Notes on Manufacturers and Intertribal Trade." Unpublished manuscript, American Indian Studies Research Institute, Indiana University, Bloomington, n.d.

———. "Old Arikara Method of Butchering a Buffalo." Unpublished manuscript, American Indian Studies Research Institute, Indiana University, Bloomington, n.d.

———. "The Plight of Living Scalped Indians." *Papers of the Michigan Academy of Science, Arts, and Letters* 19 (1933): 39–45.

———. *Prairie Smoke*. New York: AMS Press, 1966.

———. "Religious Teaching and Training of Arikara Children." Unpublished manuscript, American Indian Studies Research Institute, Indiana University, Bloomington, n.d.

———. "The Sacred Bundles of the Arikara." *Papers of the Michigan Academy of Science, Arts, and Letters* 16 (1931): 33–50.

———. "A Study in the Ethnobotany of the Omaha Indians." *Collections of the Nebraska State Historical Society* 17 (1913): 314–57.

———. *Uses of Plants by the Indians of the Missouri River Region*. Lincoln: University of Nebraska Press, 1991.

———. "Wild Plants Used by the Arikara People in the Old Days." Unpublished manuscript, American Indian Studies Research Institute, Indiana University, Bloomington, n.d.

Gluckman, Arcadi. *Identifying Old US Muskets, Rifles and Carbines*. Harrisburg, PA: Stackpole Books, 1965.

Goetzmann, William H., and David Hunt. *Karl Bodmer's America*. Lincoln: University of Nebraska Press, 1984.

Grafe, Ernest, and Paul Horsted. *Exploring with Custer: The 1874 Black Hills Expedition*. Custer, SD: Golden Valley Press, 2005.

Gray, John S. "Arikara Scouts with Custer." *North Dakota History* 35 (Spring 1968): 443–78.

———. "Bloody Knife, Ree Scout for Custer." *Chicago Westerners Brand Book* 17, no. 2 (February 1961): 89–96.

———. *Centennial Campaign: The Sioux War of 1876*. Fort Collins, CO: Old Army Press, 1976. Reprint, Norman: University of Oklahoma Press, 1988.

———. *Custer's Last Campaign: Mitch Boyer and the Little Bighorn Reconstructed*. Lincoln: University of Nebraska Press, 1991.

Greene, Candace S. "Arikara Drawings: New Sources of Visual History." *American Indian Art Magazine* 31, no. 2 (Spring 2006): 74–85, 99.

———. "The Hazen Collection: A New Source on Arikara Material Culture." *Plains Anthropologist* 65, no. 256 (2020): 357–77.

Greene, Candace S., and Russell Thornton, eds. *The Year the Stars Fell: Lakota Winter Counts at the Smithsonian* Lincoln: University of Nebraska Press, 2007.

Greene, Jerome A. *Slim Buttes, 1876: An Episode of the Great Sioux War*. Norman: University of Oklahoma Press, 1982.

———. *Yellowstone Command: Colonel Nelson A. Miles and the Great Sioux War, 1876–1877*. Lincoln: University of Nebraska Press, 1991.

Grinnell, George B. *The Cheyenne Indians*. Lincoln: University of Nebraska Press, 1972.

———. *Pawnee Hero Stories and Folk Tales*. Lincoln: University of Nebraska Press, 1990.

———. "Pawnee Mythology" *Journal of American Folklore* 6, no. 21 (April–June 1893): 113–30.

———. *The Story of the Indian*. New York: D. Appleton, 1908.

Grinnell, George Bird. "Who Were the Padouca?" *American Anthropologist* 39, no. 4 (1937): 647–70.

Hale, Duane K. "Uncle Sam's Warriors: American Indians in World War II." *Chronicles of Oklahoma* 69 (Winter 1991–92): 408–29.

Hall, Charles L. *Nikutati Isatau Natcitcitu (I Am the Bread of Life): Bible Translations and Hymns in the Ree Language*. Self-published.

Hall, James. *Letters From the West; Containing Sketches of Scenery, Manners, and Customs, and Anecdotes Connected with the First Settlements of the Western Sections of the United States.* London: H. Colburn, 1828.

Hämäläinen, Pekka. *Lakota America: A New History of Indigenous Power.* New Haven, CT: Yale University Press, 2019.

Hämäläinen, Pekka. *The Comanche Empire.* New Haven, CT: Yale University Press, 2008.

Hamilton, T. M., comp. *Indian Trade Guns: Missouri Archeologist* 22 (December 1960).

Hammer, Kenneth, ed. *Custer in '76: Walter Camp's Notes on the Custer Fight.* Provo, UT: Brigham Young University Press, 1976.

Hanson, Jeffrey R. "Adjustment and Adaptation on the Northern Plains: The Case of Equestrianism among the Hidatsa." *Plains Anthropologist* 31, no. 112 (May 1986): 93–107.

Hardorff, Richard G., comp., ed. *Camp, Custer, and the Little Bighorn: A Collection of Walter Mason Camp's Research Papers on General George A. Custer's Last Fight.* El Segundo, CA: Upton and Sons, 1997.

Harvey, David Allen. "The Noble Savage and the Savage Noble: Philosophy and Ethnography in the 'Voyages' of the Baron de Lahontan." *French Colonial History* 11 (2010): 161–91.

Hayden, Ferdinand V. "Ari'karas." *Transactions of the American Philosophical Society* 12, no. 2 (1862): 351–62.

Hennepin, Lodewyck. *Aenmerckelycke Historische Reys-Beschryvinge door Verscheyde Landen veel grooter als die van geheel Europa, onlanghs Ontdeckt.* Utrecht: Anthony Schouten, 1698.

Hewitt, J. N. B., ed. *Journal of Rudolph Friederich Kurz.* Lincoln: University of Nebraska Press, 1970.

Hoffman, Walter J. *The Beginnings of Writing.* New York: D. Appleton, 1895.

———. "Remarks on Indian Tribal Names." *Proceedings of the American Philosophical Society* 23, no. 122 (Philadelphia, 1886): 294–96.

Holder, Preston. "The Fur Trade as Seen from the Indian Point of View." In *The Frontier Re-examined*, edited by John Francis McDermott, pp. 129–39 (Urbana: University of Illinois Press, 1967).

———. *The Hoe and the Horse on the Plains: A Study of Cultural Development among North American Indians.* Lincoln: University of Nebraska Press, 1974.

———. "Social Stratification among the Arikara." *Ethnohistory* 5, no. 3 (Summer 1958): 210–18.

Holst, John H. "A Field Agent's Diary." *Indians at Work* (1936): 7–10.

Howard, James Henri. "The Arikara Buffalo Society Medicine Bundle." *Plains Anthropologist* 19, no. 66 (November 1974): 241–71.

———. *The British Museum Winter Count.* London: British Museum, 1979.

———. "Yanktonai Ethnohistory and the John K. Bear Winter Count." *Plains Anthropologist* 21, no. 73 (August 1976).

Howard, James Henri, and Alan Woolworth. "An Arikara Bear Society Initiation Ceremony." *North Dakota History* 21 (October 1954): 169–79.

Hudson, Marilyn. "'A Harvest of Hope': WWII Years at Fort Berthold." In *Produce for Victory: Posters on the American Home Front, 1941–45*. New Town, ND: Three Affiliated Tribes Museum, 2004.

Hulbert, Archer B., and Dorothy Printup Hulbert, eds., *Marcus Whitman, Crusader*. Colorado Springs: Steward Commission of Colorado College, 1936.

Hultgren, Mary Lou, and Paulette Fairbanks Molin. "'Long Rides across the Plains': Fort Berthold Students at Hampton Institute." *North Dakota History* 61, no. 2 (Spring 1994): 10–36.

Hunt, William J., Jr. "The Fort Clark Archaeology Project, 2000–2001 Historical Archeological Investigations." Paper presented at the Fifty-Ninth Annual Plains Anthropological Conference, Lincoln, November 1, 2001.

Hurt, Wesley R., and William E. Lass. *Frontier Photographer: Stanley J. Morrow's Dakota Years*. Vermillion: University of South Dakota Press, 1956.

Hurt, Wesley R. "Seasonal Economic and Settlement Patterns of the Arikara." *Plains Anthropologist* 14, no. 43 (1969): 32–37.

Hyde, George E. "The Mystery of the Arikaras." *North Dakota History* 18 (October 1951): 187–218.

———. "The Mystery of the Arikaras." *North Dakota History* 19 (January 1952): 25–38.

———. *The Pawnee Indians*. Norman: University of Oklahoma Press, 1988.

Innis, Ben. *Bloody Knife: Custer's Favorite Scout*, edited by Richard E. Collin. Bismarck: Smoky Water Press, 1994.

Irving, Washington. *Astoria or Anecdotes of an Enterprise beyond the Rocky Mountains*. Norman: University of Oklahoma Press, 1964.

Irwin, Louis and Robert Liebert, *Two Ravens: The Life and Teachings of a Spiritual Warrior*. Rochester, VT: Destiny Books, 1996.

Jablow, Joseph. *The Cheyenne in Plains Indian Trade Relations, 1795–1994*. Lincoln: University of Nebraska Press, 1994.

Jackson, Donald, ed. *Letters of the Lewis and Clark Expedition with Related Documents, 1783–1854*. Urbana: University of Illinois Press, 1962.

James, Thomas. *Three Years among the Indians and Mexicans*. New York: Garland, 1978.

Jantz, Richard L., and Douglas W. Owsley, "White Traders in the Upper Missouri: Evidence from the Swan Creek Site." In *Skeletal Biology in the Great Plains: Migration, Warfare, Health, and Subsistence*, edited by Douglas W. Owsley and Richard L. Jantz, pp. 189–201 (Washington, DC: Smithsonian Institution Press, 1994).

Jensen, Richard E., and James S. Hutchins, eds. *Wheel Boats on the Missouri: The Journals and Documents of the Atkinson-O'Fallon Expedition, 1824–26*. Lincoln and Helena: Nebraska State Historical Society and Montana Historical Society Press, 2001.

Johnson, Alfred E. "Plains Woodland Tradition." In *Handbook of North American Indians*, edited by William C. Sturtevant. Vol. 13, *Plains*, Part 1, edited by Raymond J. DeMallie, pp. 159–72. Washington, DC: Smithsonian Institution, 2001.

Joint War History Commissions of Michigan and Wisconsin. *The 32d Division in the World War, 1917–1919*. Madison: Wisconsin War History Commission, 1920.

Kane, Lucile M., trans., ed. *Military Life in Dakota: The Journal of Philippe Regis de Trobriand*. Lincoln: University of Nebraska Press, 1982.

Kappler, Charles J., comp., ed. *Indian Affairs: Laws and Treaties*, vols. 1–3. Washington, DC: Government Printing Office, 1902–13.

Kardong, Terrence. *Catholic Life at Fort Berthold, 1889–1989*. Richardton, ND: Assumption Abbey Press, 1989.

Kelly, Mark W. *Lost Voices on the Missouri: John Dougherty and the Indian Frontier*. Leavenworth, KS: Sam Clark, 2013.

"Killing Our Future: Sterilization and Experiments." *Akwesasne Notes* 9, no. 1 (1977): 4–6.

Kindscher, Kelly, Loren Yellow Bird, Michael Yellow Bird, and Logan Sutton. *Sahnish (Arikara) Ethnobotany*. Tacoma, WA: Society of Ethnobiology, 2020.

King, Charles R. "Indian Service Physician on the Northern Plains: Dr. James L. Neave at Fort Berthold, Dakota Territory, 1878–1885." *North Dakota History* 58, no. 4 (1991): 20–34.

Koury, Michael J. ed. *The Field Diary of General Alfred H. Terry: The Yellowstone Expedition, 1876*. Bellevue, NE: Old Army Press, 1970.

Krause, Herbert, and Gary D. Olson, eds. *Prelude to Glory: A Newspaper Accounting of Custer's 1874 Expedition to the Black Hills*. Sioux Falls, SD: Brevet Press, 1974.

Krause, Richard A. "An Explication of Arikara Culture History," *Plains Anthropologist* 61, no. 240 (2016): 308–35.

———. *The Leavenworth Site: Archaeology of an Historic Arikara Community*. Publications in Anthropology 3. Lawrence: University of Kansas, 1972.

———. "Plains Village Tradition: Coalescent." In *Handbook of North American Indians*, edited by William C. Sturtevant. Vol. 13, *Plains*, Part 1, edited by Raymond J. DeMallie, pp. 196–206. Washington, DC: Smithsonian Institution, 2001.

La Barre, Weston. *The Peyote Cult*. 5th ed. Norman: University of Oklahoma Press, 1989.

Lahontan, Baron de. *New Voyages to North America*. London, 1703.

Lansing, Michael. "Plains Indian Women and Interracial Marriage in the Upper Missouri Trade, 1804–1868." *Western Historical Quarterly* 31, no. 4 (Winter 2000): 413–33.

Lawrence, Jane. "The Indian Health Service and the Sterilization of Native American Women." *American Indian Quarterly* 24, no. 3 (Summer 2000): 400–19.

Lehmer, Donald J. *Introduction to Middle Missouri Archaeology*. Washington, DC: National Park Service, 1971.

———. "Plains Village Tradition: Postcontact." In *Handbook of North American Indians*, edited by William C. Sturtevant. Vol. 13, *Plains*, Part 1, edited by Raymond J. DeMallie, pp. 245–55. Washington, DC: Smithsonian Institution, 2001.

Lehmer, Donald J., and David T. Jones. *Arikara Archeology: The Bad River Phase*. Publications in Salvage Archeology 7. Lincoln, NE: Museum of Natural History, Smithsonian Institution, 1968.

Levy, Jerrold E. "Is This a System? Comment on Osborn's 'Ecological Aspects of Equestrian Adaptations in Aboriginal North America.'" *American Anthropologist*, 86, no. 4 (December 1984): 985–91.

Libby, Orin G., ed. *The Arikara Narrative of Custer's Campaign and the Battle of the Little Bighorn*. Norman: University of Oklahoma Press, 1998.

———. "Typical Villages of the Mandans, Arikara, and Hidatsa in the Missouri Valley, North Dakota." *Collections of the State Historical Society of North Dakota* 2 (Bismarck: Tribune, State Printers and Binders, 1908), 498–508.

Liberty, Margot, and John Stands in Timber. *Cheyenne Memories.* New Haven, CT: Yale University Press, 1967.
Lowie, Robert H. "Societies of the Arikara Indians." *Anthropological Papers of the American Museum of Natural History* 11, no. 8 (New York: American Museum of Natural History, 1915): 647–78.
Mallery, Garrick. *Picture-Writing of the American Indians.* Washington, DC: Smithsonian Institution, 1893.
Malone, Patrick M. *The Skulking Way of War: Technology and Tactics among the New England Indians.* Baltimore: Johns Hopkins University Press, 1993.
Margry, Pierre. *Decouvertes et Etablissements des Français Dans l'Ouest et Dans le Sud de l'Amerique Septentionale, 1614–1754, Mémoires et Documents Originaux,* Vol. 6, *Exploration des Affluents du Mississippi et Découverte des Montagnes Rocheuses, 1679–1754.* New York: AMS Press, 1974.
Marsh, Elias J. "Journal of Dr. Elias J. Marsh: Account of a Steamboat Trip on the Missouri River, May–August, 1859." *South Dakota Historical Review* 1 (January 1936): 79–127.
Mason, Ronald J. *Inconstant Companions: Archaeology and North American Indian Oral Traditions.* Tuscaloosa: University of Alabama Press, 2007.
Matthews, Washington. *Ethnography and Philology of the Hidatsa Indians.* Washington, DC: United States Department of the Interior, Geological and Geographical Survey, 1877.
Mattison, Ray H., ed. *Henry A. Boller: Missouri River Fur Trader.* Bismarck: State Historical Society of North Dakota, 1966.
Mayor, Adrienne. *Fossil Legends of the First Americans.* Princeton, NJ: Princeton University Press, 2005.
McDermott, John Francis, ed. *Up the Missouri with Audubon: Journal of Edward Harris.* Norman: University of Oklahoma Press, 1951.
McLaughlin, Castle. "Nation, Tribe, and Class: The Dynamics of Agrarian Transformation on the Fort Berthold Reservation." *American Indian Culture and Research Journal* 22, no. 3 (1998): 101–38.
———. "The Politics of Agricultural Decline on the Fort Berthold Indian Reservation, North Dakota." *Culture and Agriculture: Bulletin of the Anthropological Study Group on Agrarian Systems* 44 (1992): 20–22.
———. "Ranching an Important Part of Ft. Berthold History." *MHA Times,* August 10, 1991.
McLaughlin, James. *My Friend the Indian.* Boston: Houghton Mifflin Company, 1910.
Merington, Marguerite, ed. *The Custer Story: The Life and Intimate Letters of General Custer and His Wife Elizabeth.* New York: Devin-Adair, 1950.
———. "Star Village: A Fortified Historic Arikara Site in Mercer County, North Dakota." *River Basin Survey Papers, Smithsonian Institution, Bureau of American Ethnology Bulletin* 185 (Washington, DC: Government Printing Office, 1963): 57–122.
Meyer, Roy W. "Fort Berthold and the Garrison Dam." *North Dakota History* 35 (1968): 218–355.
———. *The Village Indians of the Upper Missouri: The Mandans, Hidatsas, and Arikaras.* Lincoln: University of Nebraska Press, 1977.

Millet, Allan R. "Cantigny, 28–31 May 1918." In *America's First Battles, 1776–1965*, edited by Charles E. Heller and William A. Stofft, pp. 149–85. Lawrence: University Press of Kansas, 1986.
Mitchell, David D. "Extraordinary Indian Feats of Legerdemain." *Southern Literary Messenger* 1, no. 12 (August 1835): 657–58.
Mooney, James. *Calendar History of the Kiowa Indians*. Washington, DC: Smithsonian Institution, 1979.
———. "The Ghost-Dance Religion and the Sioux Outbreak of 1890." In *Fourteenth Annual Report of the Bureau of Ethnology to the Secretary of the Smithsonian Institution, 1892–93*. Washington, DC: Government Printing Office, 1896.
Moore, John H., Margot P. Liberty, and A. Terry Strauss. "Cheyenne." In *Handbook of North American Indians*, edited by William C. Sturtevant. Vol. 13, *Plains*, Part 2, edited by Raymond J. DeMallie, pp. 863–85. Washington, DC: Smithsonian Institution, 2001.
Morgan, Dale L., ed. *The West of William H. Ashley*. Denver: Old West Publishing, 1964.
Morgan, Lewis Henry. "The Stone and Bone Implements of the Arickarees." *North Dakota History* 30, no. 2–3 (April–July 1963): 115–35.
Moulton, Gary E. *The Journals of the Lewis and Clark Expedition*, vols. 1–11. Lincoln: University of Nebraska Press, 1987–97.
Murie, James R. *Ceremonies of the Pawnee*. Part I, *The Skiri*. Washington, DC: Smithsonian Institution Press, 1981.
———. "Pawnee Indian Societies." *Anthropological Papers of the American Museum of Natural History* 11, no. 7 (New York: American Museum of Natural History): 546–644.
Myers, John M. *The Saga of Hugh Glass: Pirate, Pawnee, and Mountain Man*. Lincoln: University of Nebraska Press, 1976.
Nabokov, Peter. *A Forest of Time: American Indian Ways of History*. Cambridge: Cambridge University Press, 2002.
Nasatir, Abraham P. *Before Lewis and Clark: Documents Illustrating the History of the Missouri, 1785–1804*. Lincoln: University of Nebraska Press, 1990.
———. "John Evans: Explorer and Surveyor." *Missouri Historical Review* 25, nos. 2–4 (January–July 1931): 219–39, 432–60, 585–608.
Nester, William R. *The Arikara War: The First Plains Indian War, 1823*. Missoula: Mountain Press Publishing Company, 2001.
Nichols, Roger L. "Backdrop for Disaster: Causes of the Arikara War of 1823." *South Dakota History* 14 (Summer 1984): 93–113.
———. "The Arikara Indians and the Missouri River Trade: A Quest for Survival." *Great Plains Quarterly* (1982): 77–93.
Norall, Frank. *Bourgmont: Explorer of the Missouri, 1698–1725*. Lincoln: University of Nebraska Press, 1988.
North Dakota Indian Affairs Commission. *Facts and Profiles: Indians in North Dakota*. Bismarck: North Dakota Indian Affairs Commission, 1999.
Oglesby, Richard Edward. *Manuel Lisa and the Opening of the Missouri Fur Trade*. Norman: University of Oklahoma Press, 1984.

Orser, Charles. "Understanding Arikara Trading Behavior: A Cultural Case Study of the Ashley-Leavenworth Episode of 1823." In *Rendezvous: Selected Papers of the Fourth North American Fur Trade Conference, 1981*, edited by Thomas C. Buckley, pp. 101–7. St. Paul, MN: North American Fur Trade Conference, 1984.

Owsley, Douglas W. "Demography of Prehistoric and Early Historic Northern Plains Populations." In *Disease and Demography in the Americas*, edited by John W. Verano and Douglas H. Ubelaker, pp. 75–86 (Washington, DC: Smithsonian Institution Press, 1992).

Owsley, Douglas W., Hugh Berryman, and William M. Bass. "Demographic and Osteological Evidence for Warfare at the Larson Site, South Dakota." *Plains Anthropologist Memoir* 13 (1977): 119–31.

Parks, Douglas R. "Arikara." In *Handbook of North American Indians*, edited by William C. Sturtevant. Vol. 13, *Plains*, Part 1, edited by Raymond J. DeMallie, pp. 365–90. Washington, DC: Smithsonian Institution, 2001.

———. "Bands and Villages of the Arikara and Pawnee." *Nebraska History* 60, no. 2 (Summer 1979): 214–39.

———. "Caddoan Languages." In *Handbook of North American Indians*, edited by William C. Sturtevant. Vol. 13, *Plains*, Part 1, edited by Raymond J. DeMallie, pp. 80–93. Washington, DC: Smithsonian Institution, 2001.

———. "An Historical Character Mythologized: The Scalped Man in Arikara and Pawnee Folklore." In *Plains Indian Studies: A Collection of Essays in Honor of John C. Ewers and Waldo R. Wedel*, edited by Dougas H. Ubelaker and Herman J. Viola, pp. 47–58. Washington, DC: Smithsonian Institution Press, 1982.

———. "James R. Murie, Pawnee Ethnographer." In *American Indian Intellectuals of the Nineteenth and Early Twentieth Centuries*, edited by Margot Liberty, pp. 86–104. Norman: University of Oklahoma Press, 2002.

———. *Myths and Traditions of the Arikara Indians*. Lincoln: University of Nebraska Press, 1996.

———. "The Northern Caddoan Languages: Their Subgrouping and Time Depths." *Nebraska History* 60, no. 2 (Summer 1979): 197–213.

———. *Traditional Narratives of the Arikara Indians*. 4 vols. Lincoln: University of Nebraska Press, 1991.

Parks, Douglas R., Janet Beltran, and Ella P. Waters. *Sahnis Wakuunu': An Introduction to the Arikara Language*. Roseglen, ND: White Shield School District, 1998.

Parsons, John E. *West on the 49th Parallel: Red River to the Rockies, 1872–1876*. New York: William Morrow, 1963.

Pearson, J. Diane. "Lewis Cass and the Politics of Disease: The Indian Vaccination Act of 1832." *Wicazo Sa Review* 18, no. 2 (Fall 2003): 9–35.

Pelzer, Louis, ed. "Captain Ford's Journal of an Expedition to the Rocky Mountains." *Mississippi Valley Historical Review* 12 (March 1926): 550–79.

Perrine, Fred S., ed. "Hugh Evans' Journal of Colonel Henry Dodge's Expedition to the Rocky Mountains in 1835." *Mississippi Valley Historical Review* 14, no. 2 (September 1927): 192–214.

Peters, Virginia Bergman. *Women of the Earth Lodges: Tribal Life on the Plains*. North Haven, CT: Archon Books, 1995.

Pfaller, Louis L. "James McLaughlin and the Rodman Wanamaker Expedition of 1913." *North Dakota History* 44, no. 2 (Spring 1977): 4–11.

Posthumus, David C. "Hereditary Enemies? An Examination of Sioux–Arikara Relations Prior to 1830," *Plains Anthropologist* 61, no. 240 (2016): 361–82.

Potter, Tracy. *Sheheke, Mandan Indian Diplomat: The Story of White Coyote, Thomas Jefferson, and Lewis and Clark*. Helena, MT: Farcountry Press, 2003.

Prucha, Francis Paul. *American Indian Treaties: The History of a Political Anomaly*. Berkeley: University of California Press, 1994.

———. ed. *Documents of United States Indian Policy*. 2nd ed. Lincoln: University of Nebraska Press, 1996.

Rathbone, Perry T. *Charles Wimar, 1828–1862: Painter of the Indian Frontier*. St. Louis: City Art Museum of St. Louis, 1946.

Rees, Tony. *Arc of the Medicine Line: Mapping the World's Longest Undefended Border across the Western Plains*. Nebraska: Douglas & McIntyre, 2008.

Reifel, Ben. "Relocation on the Fort Berthold Indian Reservation: Problems and Programs." PhD dissertation, Harvard University, Cambridge, MA, 1952.

Reiger, John F., ed. *The Passing of the Great West: Selected Papers of George Bird Grinnell*. New York: Winchester Press, 1972.

Robertson, Francis B. "'We Are Going to Have a Big Sioux War': Colonel David S. Stanley's Yellowstone Expedition, 1872." *Montana: The Magazine of Western History* 34, no. 4 (Autumn 1984): 2–15.

Robinson, Doane, ed. "Official Correspondence of the Leavenworth Expedition into South Dakota in 1823." *South Dakota Historical Collection* 1 (August 1902): 181–234.

Rogers, John Daniel. *Objects of Change: The Archaeology and History of Arikara Contact with Europeans*. Washington, DC: Smithsonian Institution Press, 1990.

Rollins, Philip A., ed. *The Discovery of the Oregon Trail: Robert Stuart's Narratives of His Overland Trip Eastward from Astoria in 1812–13*. Lincoln: University of Nebraska Press, 1995.

Ronda, James P. *Lewis and Clark among the Indians*. Lincoln: University of Nebraska Press, 1984.

Rushforth, Brett. *Bonds of Alliance: Indigenous and Atlantic Slaveries in New France*. Chapel Hill: University of North Carolina Press, 2012.

Sahnish Culture Society. "Fort Laramie Treaty, 1866," treaty minutes, July 23–August 3, 1866, http://www.natureshift.org/Whawk/resource/treaty.html, accessed circa 2006; link corrupted.

Sahota, Puneet. "Critical Contexts for Biomedical Research in a Native American Community: Health Care, History, and Community Service. *American Indian Culture and Research Journal* 36, no. 3 (2022): 1–18.

Sanstead, Wayne G., ed. *The History and Culture of the Mandan, Hidatsa, Sahnish (Arikara)*. Bismarck: North Dakota Department of Public Instruction, 2002.

Sayre, Gordon M. *Les Sauvages Américains: Representations of Native Americans in French and English Colonial Literature*. Chapel Hill: University of North Carolina Press, 1997.

Schultz, James Willard. *William Jackson, Indian Scout*. Cambridge, MA: Riverside Press, 1926.

Secoy, Frank R. *Changing Military Patterns of the Great Plains Indians: 17th Century through Early 19th Century*. Lincoln: University of Nebraska Press, 1992.

———. "The Identity of the 'Paduca': An Ethnohistorical Analysis," *American Anthropologist* 53, no. 4 (1951): 525–42.

Smith, G. Hubert. *The Explorations of the La Verendryes in the Northern Plains, 1738–43*. Lincoln: University of Nebraska Press, 1980.

Smith, G. Hubert, and John Ludwickson. *Fort Manuel: The Archeology of an Upper Missouri Trading Post of 1812–1813*. Vermillion: University of South Dakota Archaeology Laboratory, 1982.

Snodgrass, Jeanne O., comp. *American Indian Painters: A Biographical Directory*. New York: Museum of the American Indian, 1968.

Society of the First Division. *History of the First Division during the World War, 1917–1919*. Philadelphia: John C. Winston Company, 1922.

Starkey, Armstrong. *European and Native American Warfare, 1675–1815*. Norman: University of Oklahoma Press, 1998.

Steinke, Christopher. "'Here Is My Country': Too Né's Map of Lewis and Clark in the Great Plains." *William and Mary Quarterly* 71, no. 4 (October 2014): 589–610.

Stewart, Omer C. *The Peyote Religion: A History*. Norman: University of Oklahoma Press, 1987.

Stewart, Rick, Joseph D. Ketner, and Angela L. Miller. *Carl Wimar: Chronicler of the Missouri River Frontier*. Fort Worth: Amon Carter Museum, 1991.

Strong, William D. "Studying the Arikara and Their Neighbors on the Upper Missouri." *Explorations and Field-Work of the Smithsonian Institution in 1932*, Publication 3213 (Washington, DC: Smithsonian Institution, 1933): 73–76.

Sunder, John E. *The Fur Trade on the Upper Missouri, 1840–1865*. Norman: University of Oklahoma Press, 1965.

———. *Joshua Pilcher: Fur Trader and Indian Agent*. Norman: University of Oklahoma Press, 1968.

Sundstrom, Linea. *Storied Stone: Indian Rock Art of the Black Hills Country*. Norman: University of Oklahoma Press, 2004.

Tate, Michael L. "From Scout to Doughboy: The National Debate over Integrating American Indians into the Military, 1891–1918." *Western Historical Quarterly* 17, no. 4 (October 1986): 417–37.

Thornton, Russell. *American Indian Holocaust and Survival: A Population History Since 1492*. Norman: University of Oklahoma Press, 1987.

Thwaites, Reuben Gold. *Early Western Travels, 1748–1846*, vol. 6. Cleveland: Arthur H. Clark, 1904. Reprint, AMS Press, 1966.

———. *Lahontan's New Voyages to North America*, vol. 1. Chicago: A. C. McClurg, 1905.

Tiller, Veronica E. Velarde, ed., comp. *Tiller's Guide to Indian Country: Economic Profiles of American Indian Reservations*. Albuquerque: BowArrow, 1996.

Torpy, Sally J. "Native American Women and Coerced Sterilization: On the Trail of Tears in the 1970s." *American Indian Culture and Research Journal* 24, no. 2 (2000): 1–22.

Trachtenberg, Alan. *Shades of Hiawatha: Staging Indians, Making Americans, 1880–1930*. New York: Hill and Wang, 2004.

Trimble, Michael K. "Infectious Disease and the Northern Plains Horticulturalists: A Human Behavior Model." *Plains Anthropologist* 34, no. 124 (1989): 41–59.

———. "The 1837–1838 Smallpox Epidemic on the Upper Missouri." In *Skeletal Biology in the Great Plains: Migration, Warfare, Health, and Subsistence*, edited by Douglas W. Owsley and Richard L. Jantz, pp. 81–89. Washington, DC: Smithsonian Institution Press, 1994.

Trobriand, Philippe Regis de. *Military Life in Dakota*. Lincoln: University of Nebraska Press, 1982.

Tucker, Sara Jones, comp. *Indian Villages of the Illinois Country*. Springfield: State of Illinois, 1942.

Ubelaker, Douglas H., and Patrick Willey. "Complexity in Arikara Mortuary Practice." *Plains Anthropologist* 23, no. 79 (1978): 69–74.

Ubelaker, Douglas H., and William M. Bass. "Arikara Glassworking Techniques at Leavenworth and Sully Sites." *American Antiquity* 35, no. 4 (October 1970): 467–75.

US Army. *A History of the 90th Division in World War II, 6 June 1944 to 9 May 1945*. Baton Rouge: Army & Navy Publishing, 1946.

Utley, Robert M. *Cavalier in Buckskin: George Armstrong Custer and the Western Military Frontier*. Norman: University of Oklahoma Press, 1998.

———. *Frontier Regulars: The United States Army and the Indian, 1866–1891*. Lincoln: University of Nebraska Press, 1984.

———. *Frontiersmen in Blue: The United States Army and the Indian, 1848–1865*. Lincoln: University of Nebraska Press, 1981.

———. *The Lance and the Shield: The Life and Times of Sitting Bull*. New York: Ballantine Books, 1993.

Van de Logt, Mark. *Monsters of Contact: Historical Trauma in Caddoan Oral Traditions*. Norman: University of Oklahoma Press, 2018.

———. "Arikara *nituniisu'* Beliefs and the Fur Trade." *Rocky Mountain Fur Trade Journal* 7 (2013): 1–19.

———. *War Party in Blue: Pawnee Indians in the United States Army*. Norman: University of Oklahoma Press, 2010.

———. "'We Hardly Knew What a Good Night's Rest Was Then': New Sources on Arikara Scout Service and the Battle of the Little Bighorn," Friends of the Little Bighorn, 2022, www.friendsofthelittlebighorn.com/markvandelogtarikarascouts0612.pdf.

———. "Whoever makes war upon the Rees will be considered making war upon the 'Great Father': Sahnish Military Service on the Northern Great Plains, 1865–1881." *Wicazo Sa Review* 32, no. 1 (2017): 9–28

VanDevelder, Paul. *Coyote Warrior: One Man, Three Tribes, and the Trial That Forged a Nation*. New York: Little, Brown, 2004.

Vansina, Jan. *Oral Tradition as History*. Madison: University of Wisconsin Press, 1985.

Viola, Herman J. *The Little Bighorn Remembered: The Untold Indian Story of Custer's Last Stand*. New York: Times Books, 1999.

Walker, James F. "Old Fort Berthold as I Knew It." *North Dakota History* 20, no. 1 (January 1953): 25–46.

Wallace, Anthony F. C. *Jefferson and the Indians: The Tragic Fate of the First Americans.* Cambridge, MA: Harvard University Press, 1999.
Washington, Booker T. *Up from Slavery.* New York: Oxford University Press, 2000.
Wedel, Waldo R., ed. *The Dunbar-Allis Letters on the Pawnee.* New York: Garland, 1985.
———. "Plains Village Tradition: Central." In *Handbook of North American Indians,* edited by William C. Sturtevant. Vol. 13, *Plains,* Part 1, edited by Raymond J. DeMallie, pp. 173–85. Washington, DC: Smithsonian Institution, 2001.
Wedel, Waldo R., and George C. Frison. "Environment and Subsistence." In *Handbook of North American Indians,* edited by William C. Sturtevant. Vol. 13, *Plains,* Part 1, edited by Raymond J. DeMallie, pp. 44–60. Washington, DC: Smithsonian Institution, 2001.
Wescott, Daniel J., and Deborah L. Cunningham. "Temporal Changes in Arikara Humeral and Femoral Cross-sectional Geometry Associated with Horticultural Intensification." *Journal of Archaeological Science* 33 (2005): 1022–36.
White, Leslie A., ed. *Lewis Henry Morgan: The Indian Journals, 1859–62.* Ann Arbor: University of Michigan Press, 1959.
Wied-Neuwied, Maximilian, Prinz von. *Reise in Das Innere Nord-America in den Jahren 1832 bis 1834.* 2 vols. Coblenz, Germany: J. Hoelscher, 1839, 1841.
Will, George F. "Arikara Ceremonials." *North Dakota Historical Quarterly* 4, no. 4 (July 1930): 247–65.
———. "An Arikara Sacred Ceremony." *North Dakota History* 16, no. 4 (October 1949): 265–68.
———. "Magical and Sleight of Hand Performances by the Arikara." *North Dakota Historical Quarterly* 3, no. 1 (October 1928), 50–65.
———. "Notes on the Arikara Indians and Their Ceremonies." *Old West Series* 3 (1934): 5–48.
Will, George F., and George E. Hyde. *Corn among the Indians of the Upper Missouri.* Lincoln: University of Nebraska Press, 1964.
Willard, William. "Montezuma on the Missouri: A Centennial of Sorts." *Wicazo Sa Review* 5, no. 2 (1989): 34–38.
Willey, Patrick S. *Prehistoric Warfare on the Great Plains: Skeletal Analysis of the Crow Creek Massacre Victims.* New York: Garland Publishing, 1990.
Willey, Patrick S., and Thomas E. Emerson. "The Osteology and Archaeology of the Crow Creek Massacre." *Plains Anthropologist* 38, no. 145 (1993): 227–69.
Williams, David. "John Evans' Strange Journey," Parts 1–2. *American Historical Review* 54, no. 2–3 (January–April 1949), 277–95, 508–29.
Wilson, Gilbert L. "The Horse and the Dog in Hidatsa Culture." *Anthropological Papers of the American Museum of Natural History* 15 (1924): 125–311.
Wise, Jennings C. *The Red Man in the New World Drama: A Politico-Legal Study with a Pageantry of American Indian History.* New York: MacMillan, 1971.
Wood, Raymond W. *Prologue to Lewis and Clark: The Mackay and Evans Expedition.* Norman: University of Oklahoma Press, 2003.
———. "Plains Village Tradition: Middle Missouri." In *Handbook of North American Indians,* edited by William C. Sturtevant. Vol. 13, *Plains,* Part 1, edited by Raymond J. DeMallie, pp. 186–95. Washington, DC: Smithsonian Institution, 2001.

Wood, W. Raymond, and Thomas D. Thiessen, eds. *Early Fur Trade on the Northern Plains: Canadian Traders among the Mandan and Hidatsa Indians, 1738–1818. The Narratives of John Macdonnell, Francois-Antoine Larocque, David Thompson, Charles McKenzie*. Norman: University of Oklahoma Press, 1985.

W. Raymond Wood, William J. Hunt, and Randy H. Williams. *Fort Clark and Its Indian Neighbors: A Trading Post on the Upper Missouri*. Norman: University of Oklahoma Press, 2011.

Yellow Bird, Loren. "Now I Will Speak (Nawah Ti Waako'): A Sahnish Perspective on What the Lewis and Clark Expedition and Others Missed." *Wicazo Sa Review* 19, no. 1 (Spring 2004): 73–84.

Yellow Bird, Michael. "What We Want to Be Called: Indigenous Peoples' Perspectives on Racial and Ethnic Identity Labels." *American Indian Quarterly* 23, no. 2 (Spring 1999): 1–21.

Zimmerman, Larry J., and Lawrence E. Bradley. "The Crow Creek Massacre: Initial Coalescent Warfare and Speculations about the Genesis of Extended Coalescent." *Plains Anthropologist* 38, no. 145 (1993): 215–26.

INDEX

References to illustrations appear in italic type.

adoption ceremony. *See* calumet ceremony
African Americans, 117, 160, 220–21, 260
agriculture, 76, 160, 260, 265, 278, 284. *See also* gardening; horticulture
Ahuka, George (aka White Wolf), 220, 221–22, 239
alcohol, 162, 242, 277, 280, 284
alliances, 77, 96, 115, 126, 153, 170–71; Hidatsas and, 130, 158; Mandans and, 94–95, 100–102, 105; Sioux and, 112, 119, 132, 176; US and, 195
allotments, 202, 205, 229, 230–31, 254, 274, 277
American Fur Company (AFC), 130, 145–46, 155, 162, 163, 166
Americans, 38, 160, 225, 283; Arikara conflicts with, 110–11, 141, 246; trade with, 112, 116–18, 127–35, 139–40, 143. *See also* fur trade; United States government
Ammon, 5
Amongst (aka Ree Standing among the Hidatsa), 178, 316n27
Anasazi, 14
animal lodges, 16, 204
animal powers. *See* terrestrial powers
annuities, 160, 162–67, 170, 209; and Indian agents, 146, 154, 215; termination of, 197–98, 227; withholding of, 200, 205–6
Antelope (person), 28, 239
anthropologists, 7, 78, 92, 279, 287. *See also* individual names
Apaches, 62–63. *See also* Padoucas

Arapahos, 103, 114, 148, 151, 163, 312n25
archaeology, 7, 15, 20–25, 55, 76, 302n7, 306n35; and evidence of massacres, 52, 61, 94
Archambeau, Louis, 133
Arikara Narrative of the Campaign against the Hostile Dakotas, June 1876, The (Libby), 244
Arikara Powwow, 283, 292–93
Arikaras: as confederation, 22, 25, 45, 47, 84, 108, 163; constitution of, 257–59, 273; and creation story, 9–16, 24, 27–28, 53–58, 93, 95; culture of, 70, 149–50, 215, 223–25, 233–40, 254–57, 281, 285–93; economy of, 48–50, 75–76, 276; identity of, 26, 32, 34–35, 67, 132, 224, 329n46; and land, 197–99, 227–31, 253; and marriage, 42–43, 85, 107, 206–7; and Missouri River, 142, 164, 200–201; society of, 37–46
Arikara War of 1823, 135–39, 143, 311n131
Armstrong (settlement), 204, 219, 257
Armstrong, Frank C., 204, 219
Army Corp of Engineers, 269–71, 287
Ashley, Thomas P., 233
Ashley, William, 134–35, 136, 138
Assiniboines (People of Cold Country, Pichia, Psi'a'), 11, 27, 57, 153, 158, 163
Astor, John Jacob, 130
Atkinson, Henry, 143–44
Awaáhu (Left Behind) band, 11, 19, 42, 45–46, 84, 114; sacred bundle of, 31, 35
Aztecs, 14, 299n38

353

Bad Bear, 142, 145
Bad Gun, 217
Bad River, 24, 46, 63, 91, 106, 107
Baker, William, 185
bands (tribal), 18, 19, 42, 45–47, 112–14
Bassett, George K., 213
Bateman, Guy, 261
Battle of Blue Water, 165
Battle of Killdeer Mountain, 171
Battle of Little Bighorn, 170, 174, 186–89, 195, 255
Battle of Slim Buttes, 191
Bear, Floyd, 232
Bear, Stella, 211, 213
Bear, The, 135
Bear Chief, 14, 163
Bear Goes Out (aka Ray Gough), 204
Bears Arm, 257
Bear's Belly, 239, 252
Bear's Eye, 193
Bear Society, 40, 196–97, 286–87
Bear's Tail, 13, 17, 19, 56, 239, 298n9
Bear's Teeth, 1, 3, 91, 92, 215, 226–28
Beauchamp, Peter, 217, 223, 252–54, 259, 263
Beaver Creek (settlement), 257, 270, 276
Beaver-Otter Society, 40
Beaver Society, 233
Beede, Aaron McGaffey, 3–4, 42, 44, 231, 237, 297n5
Benteen, Frederick W., 187, 188, 189
Bent's Fort, 151
Best, Josiah Janney, 206, 224
Beyer, W., 242
Big Axe, 148, 151
Big Black Meteoric Star, 55. *See also* Grandfather Rock
Big Grass Society, 204, 238
Big John, 193
Big Man, 130, 131, 133
Big Man Cheyenne, 119
bison (tanáha'), 39, 48–49, 50, 72. *See also* buffalo

Blackbird, 62
Black Buffalo, *184*
Blackfeet, 66, 123
Black Fox, 186–87, 190, 200, 212, 217
Black Hills (Waakatít), 90, 164, 302n7; as refuge, 53–56, 68, 85
Black Hills Expedition, 170, 180–82
Black Sun (Šakuúnukatít), 106–7
Black-Tailed Deer Society, 39
Bloody Hands (aka Little Hawk with the Bloody Hands, Stán-au-pat), 140, 142–54, 156, 158, 162, 311n1
Bloody Hands (oral tradition), 69–70, 311n1
Bloody Knife, 172–75, 177–84, 186–90, 195
Board of Indian Commissioners, 208, 237
Bobtailed Bull, 184, 185, 187–88, 189, 190, 195
Bourgmont, Etienne de Veniard, 80
Boy Chief (Nee-noch-na-chaun-na), 178, 187, 190, 244
Brackenridge, Henry Marie, 131, 132
Bradbury, John, 131, 132
Bright Star, 17
British, 65, 97, 100, 203
buffalo, 31–34, 55, 56, 63, 160–61, 166, 198; bundle, 239, 289–90; and storytelling, 1, 10, 13, 27, 30, 49, 73, 88, 123. *See also* bison; hunting
Buffalo Society, 39–40, 289–90
Bull (person), 186–87
Bull Boy, 210
Bull Head, 175, 176, 200, 217
Bull in the Water, 212
Bull Neck, 1, 3, 181, 243
Bull Stands in the Water, 185, 187
bundle lodges, 16
bundles, 19, 25, 28, 35–37, 286, 288, 329n46; Awaáhu, 31; buffalo, 239, 289–90; knot-in-the-tree, 13; medicine, 39; personal, 52, 290; sacred, 3–4, 11, 15, 24, 45, 47–48, 75, 108, 158; sacred arrow, 151; village (tribal), 21, 41, 42

Bureau of Indian Affairs (BIA), 229, 247, 252, 257; and termination, 268, 269. *See also* Indian Office; Office of Indian Affairs
Bushotter, George, 219–20

Caddos, 14–15, 19–20, 21–22, 24
California Trail, 163
calumet ceremony, 50, 66, 67, 97, 119, 121, 167, 239. *See also* pipe ceremony
Campbell, Collin, 137–38
Canada, 81–82, 84, 97; Sitting Bull in, 190–91, 193, 194, 202
Canyon de Chelly, 13–14
Canyon of the Ancients, 14
Carlisle Indian School, 220, 223
Ca-roo, 190
Catholicism, 214–15, 231–32, 236. *See also* religion
Catlin, George, *144, 146, 152, 161*
Cedar Fort, 135, 136
Cedar Tree (being), 53, 54–55
cedar tree (plant), 11, 28, 53, 54–55, 239
celestial powers, 31–33, 38. *See also* sacred powers; spiritual power
ceremonial lodge, 22, 40, *41*, 47, 53, 138
ceremonies, 19, 32–37, 47, 179, 209, 251–54, 257, 284–88; banning of, 205, 224, 233, 235; and bundles, 24, 51, 290; and Catholicism, 214; and Custer, 179; documenting of, 225, 238–40; Lakhota, 284; and priests, 41, 42, 48; protection of, 258; receiving of, 16; teaching of, 10, 17, 150, 295. *See also names of specific ceremonies*
Chardon, Francis A., 153, 154, 155–56, 158–59, 160
Charging Bull, 187
Charging-up-the-Hill, 190
Cheyenne River, 24, 81, 84, 96, 99–100, 101, 105
Cheyennes (Šaahé), 11, 27, 57, 67, 75, 79, 143, 148; and Arikara relations with, 66–67, 91–92, 103, 114–15, 143, 151, 163, 183, 312n25; and Battle of Little Bighorn, 186–89; and war with US, 192
Chief Horse, 46
chiefs (neešaanuu načitawi'U), 35, 38, 39, 48, 51; and Awaáhu band, 11, 19, 45–46; "civilization" policies and, 197, 205–6; competition among, 91, 108; disagreements among, 109, 112–14, 132–33, 135; subchiefs, 41–42; and treaties, 198–200, 201–2. *See also* priests (kuna'Uxwaarúxtii'u')
Chief Who Is Afraid, The, 142, 145
children, 28, 43, 52, 85, 94, 151, 266, 290; naming of, 207, 255, 288; and diseases, 62, 65, 208, 226. *See also* education
Chippewas, 202–3, 229
cholera, 55, 86, 89, 162
Chouteau, Pierre, 128–29, 165
Christianity, 32, 58, 210–13, 231–33, 241–242. *See also* Jesus Christ
citizenship, 251–52
Clark, William, 111, 112, 116–21, 126–27, 155, 159
Closed Man, 16–19, 22, 24–25, 56, 299n31, 299n33
Collot, Georges-Henri Victor, 105–7
Columbia Fur Company, 140
Comanches, 27, 63
Company of Explorers of the Upper Missouri, 100
Coolidge, Calvin, 251
corn (niishu), 14, 17, 70, 108, 284; growing of, 48, 49–50; and Mother Corn, 10, 26, 31–32, 169; trade of, 67, 72, 75–76, 78, 80
Coronado, Francisco de, 22
Corps of Discovery, 116, 128
Cottonwood Creek, 110, 142, 145, 147
Courtenay, William, 194, 205, 215–17, 320n35
Court of Indian Offenses, 197, 206, 208
Craft, Francis M., 214–15
Crane-Bald Eagle-Cormorant Society, 40
Crazy Bear (aka Foolish Bear, l'Ours Foux), 99–101, 102, 104–5, 112

Crazy Horse, 183, 185, 186, 190–91, 193
Crook, George, 183, 186, 189, 190–91
Crooked Horn (aka Forked Horn), 185–87, 189, 217
Crow Creek Massacre, 21, 52, 61
Crow Ghost, 204, 235, 238, 239
Crow Going Across (Kaakaawiisisa), 111–12, 116–19, 120, 126–27, 130
Crow Indians, 147, 163, 204
Crow's Belly, 210
Crow's Breast, 217
Crow Tail, 178
Curtis, Edward S., 36, 39, 53, 206, 239
Curtis, Samuel R., 198
Custer, George Armstrong (aka Long Hair, Uxčes), 178–89, 194, 244
Custer, Thomas W., 183
Cutis, William E., 182
Cut Nose, 13, 123

Dakhota Sioux. *See* Santees
Dakota Access Pipeline, 295
Darling, Charles W., 206, 215
Da-roch'-pa Society, 185
Dawson, Mary, 220, 221
Dawson-Wilde, Anna (aka Wild Rose), 220, 221–23, 233, 265, 322n107
Dead Grass Society, 238
Deane, William, Jr., 232, 246, 249, 251, 252–53, 291
Dearborn, Henry, 121–22
Deer-Elk Society, 40
d'Eglise, Jacques, 98, 101
De L'isle, Guillaume, 63, 80–81
Deloria, Vine, Jr., 6
de Neuville, Jean-Guillaume Hyde, 126
DeSmet, Pierre-Jean, 162, 168, 214
de Trobriand, Philippe Régis, 174
Dimon, Benjamin, 316n6
diseases, 7, 11, 42, 52, 114, 208; and Europeans, 57, 70, 283; and Whirlwind, 7, 11, 53. *See also names of specific diseases*

Dixon, Joseph K., 251–52
doctors (kunaananá, skunaananá), 31, 39–40, 44, 146, 197, 226, 288; and evil medicine (niitunísu'), 43. *See also* medicine men
doctor societies, 53, 206, 233
Dodge, Henry, 149, 150–51, 312n25
dogs, 11, 27, 49, 63, 74, 111
Dorsey, George A., 5, 64, 235, 239, 294
droughts, 21, 52, 55, 213, 280; 1700s, 85; 1800s, 147, 162; 1900s, 257, 260, 284
Duck Society, 40
Dull Knife, 183, 193
dysentery, 55, 86

Eagle Feather (father; aka Pi'a'hiitu', Too Né), 4–5, 29–30, 111–12, 116–19, 121–27, 128
Eagle Feather (son), 133, 142
eagles, 3, 50, 67, 77
Eagle Tail, 193
earth lodges, 21–23, 47, 48, 52, 60, 148; abandonment of, 204, 224, 254; and other tribes, 65, 67, 163
Echo-Hawk, Roger, 7, 12–13, 299n31
Edmunds, Newton, 198–99
education, 197, 206, 211, 213, 218; boarding schools, 219–23; learning English, 172, 216–18; traditional, 224, 287–88, 291–92
Elbowoods, 202, 214, 231, 257, 270; and Garrison Dam, 270, 276, 281; schools at 219, 232
Elk (person), 64–65, 77, 202–3, 239
Elkhorn River, 15–17, 19–20, 46
Elk's Tongue, 133, 139–40
Ellis, Thomas P., 216, 232
Enemy Dog, 227
Enemy Heart, 1, 204, 226–27, 230, 239, 243
Enemy Heart, Winnie, 233, 235–36
Eokoros, 59–60
epidemics, 54, 56–57, 225–26. *See also names of specific epidemic disease*

INDEX 357

Europeans, 38, 54, 61, 79, 89, 163; and first contact, 57, 58; and guns, 52, 62, 65, 70–71, 75–76
Evans, John, 105
Evening Star, 15, 17
Everette, Claire, 232, 286

Fish, Herbert C., 4
fishing, 39, 48, 50, 114
Flood Control Act (1944), 270
Fool Chief, 142, 145
Foolish Bear. *See* Crazy Bear
Foolish Woman, 257
Forked Horn. *See* Crooked Horn
Fort Abraham Lincoln, 174, 177–85, 190–91, 194
Fort Anthony, 140
Fort Assiniboine, 123
Fort Atkinson, 135, 143
Fort Berthold, 162, 163, 166, 168, 171–74
Fort Berthold Business Council, 253
Fort Berthold Community College, 292
Fort Berthold Reservation, 55, 200, 242, 254, 257; and Garrison Dam, 270–77; tribal council, 251, 259–60, 287; and World War I, 246–51; and World War II, 256, 259–67
Fort Buford, 174, 177, 193, 195
Fort Clark, 145, 153–60, 163, 165–66, 172
Fort Ellis, 183
Fort Fetterman, 183
Fort Henry, 135
Fort Laramie, 163
Fort Leavenworth, 155, 261
Fort Mandan, 120
Fort Manuel, 132–34
Fort McKeen, 178
Fort McKinley, 246
Fort Pierre, 145, 155, 165
Fort Randall, 167
Fort Rice, 172, 174, 177–78, 179
Fort Robinson, 193

Fort Snelling, 140, 263
Fort Stevenson, 174, 177, 193, 215; school at, 213, 219–20, 222
Fort Totten, 193
Fort Union, 145
four directional powers, 26, 30–31, 33–34, 35, 37. *See also* universe
Four Horns, 55, 239
Four Rings, 11–12, 15, 26, 32, 239, 245
Fox, Charles, 246, 247–48
Fox, Ernest, 246, 249
Fox, Yvonne (aka White Buffalo Woman), 5, 290
Fox Indians, 59
Fox Woman, 46
French, 58–65, 80–85, 97
French and Indian War, 85, 86, 97
Fulkerson William N., 153–54, 155, 159
fur trade, 80, 136, 159–62; Americans and, 110–11, 134, 139–40, 145–46. *See also* names of specific companies

Gall, 172, 173–74, 177, 193
Galvanized Yankees, 316n6
gardening, 28, 38, 80, 112, 121, 131, 266, 283; men and, 44, 50; women and, 32, 40, 48, 87, 177, 224. *See also* agriculture; horticulture
Garreau, Antoine, 144–45, 147, 154, 214
Garreau, Joseph, 98–99, 100–101, 115, 147, 214; as interpreter, 127, 131, 144–45
Garreau, Pierre, 144–45, 156, 171, 214, 217
Garrison Dam, 256, 269–77, 279–80, 282–86, 294–95
gathering, 21, 31, 48, 87
Gegare, Pennesha, 80, 83
General Allotment Act (1887), 230, 257
genetic testing, 20
Gerard, Frederick, 184, 188, 244
ghost dance, 236
Ghost Society, 39–40
Gibbon, John, 183–84, 186, 188, 190

Gifford, Abram J., 202, 203–4, 206, 214, 220
Gilmore, Melvin, 19, 44, 53, 239–40, 253; on bands (tribal), 40, 42, 46; on ceremonies, 35–36, 37
God Woman, 87, 109, 111
Gone with the Wind (Mitchell), 7
Good Bear, 214, 227–28
Goodbird, Ben, 259
Goodbird, Edward, 232
Goose (person), 187–89, 244
Gourd Rattle, The, 115, 119, 121
Grandfather Rock, 11, 53–55, 85, 167, 274
Grand River, 24, 47, 96, 111, 128, 130, 131
Grant, Ulysses S., 183, 200, 244, 267
grass dance, 204, 206, 234, 238, 292
Grass Dance Society, 185
Grattan Massacre, 164
Gravelines, Joseph, 116–18, 121, 122, 127
Great Chief Above. *See* Neešaanu
Great Depression, 233
Great Sioux Reservation, 177, 180, 183
Grey Eyes, 110–12, 116–17, 126–33, 135, 137, 138
Grey Prairie Eagle, 163–64
Grinnell, George Bird, 14, 149, 299n38
Grinnell, George W., 259
Guide Rock, 16, 298n29

Hair Tufts on the Lip, 278–80
Hall, Charles Lemon, 208, 210–12, 215–17, 232, 255
Hampton Institute, 219, 220–23
Hand (person), 13–14, 16, 32, 51, 57–58, 239
Hanna, Louis B., 229, 243
Hard Striker, 215
Harrison, Benjamin, 202, 267
Hawk (person), 11–13, 87–88, 239
Hay (aka PakUs, Straw), 112, 115, 116–18
Hayes, Rutherford B., 202
Heart, Frank (aka Rising Eagle), 58, 239, 278–80, 289–90
Heart Village, 166
Henry, Andrew, 134

Hidatsas, 21–24, 27, 79, 145, 157, 193, 232, 279; Arikara relations with, 96, 109, 111, 126–27, 132–34, 146, 161–67, 203–4; as scouts, 175; and smallpox, 156–58; and Three Affiliated Tribes, 258–60; and US government, 198–200. *See also* alliances
Hoffman, Charles, 213–14, 223, 229, 234, 242, 252–53
Holst, John H., 257–58
holy lodge, 26, 47, 87–88
Hopkins, Archie, 260
Hopkins, Daniel, 246, 249, 251, 291
Hopkins, Ernest (aka Little Elk, Thick), 210, 213–14, 232, 236
Hopkins, Harvey, 246, 249, 251, 252
Horn, Strieby, 237, 240
Horn in Front, 181, 189
horses (xaawaarúxti'), 66, 73–79; acquiring of, 62–63, 67; stealing of, 102–4, 131, 148, 165, 166, 172, 176, 179, 198
horticulture, 21, 42, 62, 90, 108, 158, 162; corn, 70, 75–76, 150, 154; harvesting, 49–50, 68, 170. *See also* agriculture; gardening
Hosie, Donald, 260–63
Howard, Anita, 5, 290
Howard, Pearl, 5
Howard, Wilbur, 286
Howling Wolf, Lawrence, 232, 263
Hudson's Bay Company, 79, 98
human sacrifice, 14, 19
Hunkpapas, 96, 143, 167, 180. *See also* Lakhotas
Hunt, Wilson P., 130–31
hunting, 21, 31, 39, 46, 48 52, 66; bison/buffalo, 50, 72–74, 92, 112, 132, 142, 150–53, 158
Hunts Along, 233–34

Iliad (Homer), 7
Indian agents, 146, 155, 189, 200, 204, 205–9; and corruption, 165, 197. *See also specific agents*

Indian Appropriation Act (1871), 201–2, 205
Indian Claims Commission, 267
Indian New Deal, 231, 257
Indian Office, 143, 159, 176, 197, 219, 239, 265; and chiefs, 200, 205–6, 217. *See also* Bureau of Indian Affairs; Office of Indian Affairs
Indian Reorganization Act (Wheeler-Howard Act, 1934), 253, 256, 257
Indian Territory (Oklahoma), 200, 201
Indian Vaccination Act (1832), 157
influenza, 89, 225, 226
Iowas, 21, 27, 65
Iron Bear, 197, 198
Iroquois (Wooden Faces), 11, 27, 56–57

Janus, Stephen, 226, 234, 241
Jefferson, Thomas, 5, 116, 121, 126, 127, 140
Jermark, Ernest W., 225–26, 234, 241, 246
Jesus Christ, 32, 57–58, 109, 235–36, 241. *See also* religion
Jones, Mason W., 237
Joseph Young Hawk-Elmer Bear American Legion Post, 263, 287

Kansas, 21, 27, 62–63
Karunach, Henry (aka Sioux Boy), 213, 219, 220, 222–23, 239
Kauffman, Jacob, 202, 209, 217
Kaws, 65, 121
Keystone XL Pipeline, 295
Kingsbury, Gaines P., 149, 150
Kiowa Apaches. *See* Padoucas
Kiowas, 27, 63, 67
Kitsais, 14, 20
Knife Chief, 143–44
Korean War, 286, 287

La Harpe, Jean-Baptiste Bénard, 63, 81, 84
Lahontan, Louis-Armand de Lom d'Arce, 59–61
Lake Sakakawea, 1, 274, 275, 283

Lakhotas (Tetons), 4, 27, 75, 106, 116, 143, 148; Arikara relations with, 76–77, 85–86, 203; and Battle of Little Bighorn, 186–89; in the Black Hills, 55–56, 90; and war with US, 177–82, 191–93. *See also* Sioux
language, 14, 20, 32, 34, 55; Arikara, 216–17, 257, 289, 291–92, 295; English, 218, 224, 282; Siouan, 63
Laocata band, 115, 119–20, 121
La Salle, Rene-Robert Cavalier, 58–59
Latta, Samuel N., 167–68
La Vérendrye, Francois, 58, 82–83, 84
La Vérendrye, Louis-Joseph, 58, 82–83, 84
Laughing Face, 220, 221, 239
Leavenworth, Henry, 110–11, 135–39, 141, 143
Left Hand, 181, 193
Left Handed (aka Le Gauche), 99, 130, 131, 133
Lewis, Meriwether, 111, 112, 116–20, 126–30, 141
Libby, Orin G., 4, 185, 244, 253, 316n27
Like-A-Fishhook, 163, 164, 166–67, 171, 175–76, 199, 203–4
Lincoln, Abraham, 170–71, 197
linguistics, 7, 19–20, 25, 45
Lisa, Manuel, 128–29, 131–34
Little Bear, 142, 145
Little Brave (aka Bear's Trail), 187–88, 190, 195
Little Cherry People, 82–83
Little Elk. *See* Hopkins, Ernest
Little Sioux, 187, 193, 239, 244
Little Soldier, 110, 135, 138–39, 193
Little Wolf, 183, 193
Long Knife, 184
Louisiana, 80, 97
Loup River, 17, 140, 144, 148
Lucky Man, 9, 27, 54

Man Crow (KaakaawiiA), 112, 114, 116, 120, 127, 130
Mandan, Arthur, 259, 286

Mandan, Hidatsa, and Arikara Nation (MHA), 282–83, 291
Mandans, 21–24, 27, 94–96, 98, 279; Arikara relations with, 84, 100–102, 109, 111–12, 118–21, 126–30, 139–40, 145–47, 161–67, 203–4; as scouts, 175; and smallpox, 156–58; and Three Affiliated Tribes, 258–60; and US government, 198, 199–200. *See also* alliances
Many Fox, 77, 239
maps, 60–61, 63, 80–81, 105; Eagle Feather's, 5, 30, 122–26
Mason, Russell, 273, 277
massacres, 52, 61, 94, 164
Mayas, 14
McCullough, H. D., 226, 242
McLaughlin, James, 227–28
measles, 55, 89, 162, 208, 225, 226
medicine lodge ceremony, 28, 40, 146, 206, 239–40
medicine lodges, 47, 93, 131–32, 167, 198, 286
medicine men, 207–8, 209, 238. *See also* doctors
medicine societies, 206, 288
men: first man, 10; gender roles of, 44, 50–51; and health, 74, 114
Mesa Verde, 14
Meso-America, 14, 19
Mexico, 19
migration, 13, 16, 28, 57, 65–66, 108
Miles, Nelson A., 190, 192
military societies (nanísu'), 43, 52
mining, 181–83
missionaries, 197, 210–12, 214–15, 232–33, 236. *See also* Christianity
Mississippi River, 14–15, 81
Missourias, 21, 27, 65
Missouri Fur Company, 110, 128–29, 130, 134–36, 141, 159
Missouri River (Tswaarúxti'), 30, 56, 58–59, 65, 172; in Arikara creation story, 9, 27–28, 33; as Arikara homeland, 10, 13, 15, 68, 79, 85, 112, 142, 148, 164, 166, 200–201; Big Bend of, 24, 46, 91; on Eagle Feather's map, 121–27; exploration of, 80–81, 97–101; flooding of, 114, 269
Mitchell, David D., 146, 163
Monroe, James, 143
Monsters of Contact (Van de Logt), 7
Moreland, A. B., 172
Morgan, Thomas J., 205
Morning Star, 15, 61, 69, 148
Morning Star ceremony, 19, 61, 148
Morsette, Alfred, Sr., 29, 69–70, 73, 91, 110, 289; and Douglas R. Parks, 6, 93–94, 291
Mother Corn, 10–12, 265, 285, 294–95; and Arikara culture, 30–32, 34–35, 37, 66, 84, 149–51, 287–88; and bundles, 19, 25; and gardening, 283–84; and Missouri River, 15–16, 142; sacrifice of, 26, 87–88, 109, 169; and Whirlwind, 53–55
Mother Corn ceremony, 22, 28, 32–33, 55, 85, 239–40
Mother Night Society, 40
Murie, James Rolfe, 5, 87, 239, 294
Murphy, John S., 207, 243
Mysterious River. *See* Missouri River

Nakotas, 76
National Library of France, 30, 126
Neešaanu (Chief), 9–10, 13, 27, 30–31, 34–35, 54, 70, 95; and chiefs, 41, 117, 205, 294–95; gifts from, 32, 48, 75; and medicine, 208; and Skiri Pawnees, 16; and warfare, 50–51, 169
Neešaanu NačitákUx (Great Chief Above). *See* Neešaanu
New Dog Society, 176, 185
Newman, Sam, 232, 237, 242
New Mexico, 84
New Town, 276
Nishu, 219, 270
Nishu Singers, 251
Northern Pacific Railroad (NPRR), 177, 180, 202

North Platte River, 147–48
Northwest Company, 79, 98, 123
Nuutawáčeš (serpent), 28, 122

O'Fallon, Benjamin, 135–36, 141, 143
Office of Indian Affairs, 171, 197. *See also* Bureau of Indian Affairs; Indian Office
Oglalas, 85; Arikara relations with, 94–95, 101, 103–4, 114, 119; war with US, 181, 192. *See also* Lakhotas
okipa ceremony, 67, 149
Old Dog, 214, 227
Old Scouts Society, 244
Olmecs, 14, 299n38
Omahas, 21, 27, 65, 84, 99, 157
One Feather, 185, 187
Oneotas, 21, 27
One Stab (aka The Man Who Stabs), 181–82
Only Brave, 193
oral history, 5, 8, 203
oral tradition, as history, 5–8. *See also* storytelling
Oregon Trail, 163
Osages, 27, 65
Otoes, 21, 27, 65, 157
Owl Society, 40

Padoucas (Apaches, Kiowa Apaches, Plains Apaches), 27, 62–63, 71, 82, 84, 93, 114
Pahukatawa (father), 148–49
Pahukatawa (son), 149
Pahur, 16
Paint, 178
Painte, Myrtle, 5
Painted Woods, 100
Palanis, 77–78, 85, 86
Pananas (Panaux), 81
Pananis, 81
Parks, Douglas R., 5, 6, 20, 93–94, 291, 294
Pawnees, 13, 24, 74, 169; and Arikara relations with, 19–22, 130, 140, 149–53; and grass dance, 204; and oral tradition, 14–15; as scouts, 192, 200, 204; and slaves, 57, 62–64. *See also* Skiri Pawnees, South Band Pawnees
Pawnee Songs, 204
peace ceremony (piireeškáni'). *See* calumet ceremony
Perkins, Eli, 243, 245–46
Perkins, Glenn, 290–91
peyote, 241–42
Phaedrus (Plato), 5
Pick, Lewis, 269–70
Pilcher, Joshua, 110, 134, 136–41, 155–57, 159
pipe ceremony, 103, 104, 131, 137. *See also* calumet ceremony
Place of Crying, The (Cha'kanǐ'nǎ), 15
Plains Apaches. *See* Padoucas
Plains Indians, 32, 55, 62, 64–65, 79, 163
Platte River, 16, 63, 150, 153
Poncas, 27, 65, 99, 143
Pontiac's War, 86
population, 54, 90, 130, 162, 225–27, 282–83
Pretty Face, 187
Pretty Voice, 107–8
priests (kuna'Uxwaarúxtii'u'), 3, 17, 45, 55, 108, 197; and Awaáhu band, 11, 19; and bundles, 13, 48; and calumet ceremony, 50, 66; and celestial powers, 31, 34; and separation of powers, 35, 41–42
Principal Medicine Society, 40
Pryor, Nathaniel, 128
Pueblo Indians, 14
puerperal fever, 86

Rabbit Boy, 64–65
Rabbit Medicine Society, 203
Rabbit-Sioux Society, 40
ranching, 230, 260, 265, 276, 284
Red Bear, 230, 239; as a scout, 175, 178, 183, 187–88, 243, 244; on traditional ways, 208, 237
Red Cloud, 174, 192
Red Dog, Henry, 233, 236

Redfield, Alexander, 161, 165
Red Foolish Bear, 186–87, 189
Red Leaf, 192
Red Star, 167, 204, 238, 239; as a scout, 175, 179, 185–87, 244
Red Wolf, 187
Reed, Joseph, 28–29, 30, 239
religion, 12, 26–27, 30–37, 52, 210–15, 231–33, 279–82, 284; and peyote, 241–42; rituals, 19, 28, 39, 42, 72, 251; sacrifices, 28, 38–39, 50, 51, 122; visions, 3, 17, 43, 58, 235–36, 238, 288
Reno, Marcus A., 185–86, 187–88, 190–91, 317n48
Republican River, 16, 148, 151
Rising Eagle. *See* Heart, Frank
Rocky Mountains, 13, 123, 147
Rogers, Thomas (aka Charges Alone), 246, 248–51
Roosevelt, Theodore, 245
Rose, Edward, 135, 139, 147
Rosebud Battle, 186
Ross, Martina, 5
Ross, Pearl, 5, 291
Running Antelope, 203
Running Wolf, 167, 190, 244, 257
Rushing Bear (aka The One Who First Rushes on the Enemy, Son of Star), 166, 170, 193, 197, 205, 214, 221–22; early life of, 47, 156, 160; and Indian agents, 214, 215–17, 320n35; and scouts, 175–76; in Washington, DC, 183, 200–201

sacred arrow ceremony, 67
Sacred Heart Mission, 214–15, 219
sacred powers, 30–31, 43, 70, 109, 240; and peyote, 241; and status, 37–39, 176; and storytelling, 4; and warfare, 51
Sacred River. *See* Missouri River
Sahnish, 45
Sanánat. *See* Sioux
Santa Fe, N.Mex., 62, 74, 79, 81, 122
Santa Fe Trail, 147

Santee Normal Training School, 213
Santees (Dakota Sioux), 27, 68, 76, 157, 177, 181. *See also* Sioux
Santee Sioux Indian School, 181
scalp dance, 64, 132, 179
scouts, 170, 172–93, 195, 201, 243–44, 317n48
Sharp Horn, George, 211, 220, 221
Sheridan, Philip S., 178, 180, 183, 191
Sherman, William T., 177
Shoshones, 127, 163
Simpson, Albert, 223, 252–53, 259, 260, 286–87
Sioux (Sanánat), 3, 44, 84–85, 107–8, 163–64, 183; Arikara relations with, 67–68, 76–79, 88–103, 109–12, 129–34, 145, 157–59, 161–62, 165–72, 175, 193–95, 198–200; and Arikara War of 1823, 136–37, 141; war with US, 171–74, 183–92. *See also* alliances
Sioux Boy. *See* Karunach, Henry
Sioux War of 1876, 183–92
Sitting Bear, 16, 46–47, 51, 169, 239, 244, 251–52; as chief, 214, 226–28
Sitting Bull, 164, 171, 176, 177; in Canada, 190–91, 193, 194, 202; and war with US, 174, 178, 179, 183, 185, 195
Sitting Crow, 257
Skiri Pawnees, 45, 61, 102, 151–52; Arikara relations with, 84, 104, 140, 142–44, 147–48; and Arikara tradition, 15–19, 24. *See also* Pawnees
Skunk (person), 142, 145
slaves, 54, 83–84, 108, 117; trade in, 57, 61–64, 68
smallpox, 23, 46–47, 56–57, 86, 88–91, 108–9, 162; at Fort Clark, 154–158, 165; in oral tradition, 93–95; and pictographs, 55
Snake Indians, 82, 84, 131
Snowbird, Henry, 13, 239, 280–81, 282
Snyder Act (1924), 252
Socrates, 5

Soldier, 175, 184, 185, 187, 190, 244
songs, 6, 32, 204, 235, 239, 244, 277, 286, 291; and bundles, 3, 17, 39; and grass dance, 238; and war, 132, 185, 244, 249, 266–67
Son of Star. *See* Rushing Bear
South Band Pawnees, 20, 22, 56, 59, 148. *See also* Pawnees
Spanish, 81–84, 97–98, 100; and horses, 62, 67, 71, 74, 79
Sperry, Lyman B., 200–201
Spiderman, 10
Spiderwoman, 10
spirits, 36–37, 43, 96, 102, 287
spiritual power, 37–38, 40–41, 43, 75, 118, 186
Spotted Eagle, 178, 193, 316n27
Spotted Horn, 210, 257
Spotted Weasel, 227–28
Squash Blossom, 69–70
Stabbed (person), 187–88
Standing Bull, 85, 239
Standing Rock, 4, 118, 123, 214
Standing Rock Agency, 191–92
Standing Rock Reservation, 4, 227, 233, 295
Stands All Night, 6, 67
Stanley, David S., 177–80
Star (chief), 149, 150–51, 154, 156, 160, 166–67
Star (storyteller), 13, 32, 47, 53, 54–55, 56–57, 239
Star, Patrick, 31, 239
Star, Philip, 246, 249
Star, Rhoda, 5
Star Boy, 69–70
Starr, Margaret, 5, 264–65
Star Village, 166–67
St. Edward's School, 219
Stephens, Aaron, 135
St. Louis, Mo., 98, 105, 121
storytelling, 1–8, 239, 294; snakes in, 28–29, 92–93; in winter, 50, 255
Strikes Enemy, 29, 196, 213, 226–28, 239

Strikes the Lodge, 185–87
Strikes Two, 46, 167, 178, 187, 244, 252, 316n27
Styles, Lottie, 223, 261, 263
Sully, Alfred, 171–73
sun dance, 149–50, 186, 239, 290–91
Swamp Bird Society, 39
Sweet-Scented Grass, 146, 152

Tabeau, Pierre Antoine, 91, 112–16, 119–20, 121
Taft, William Howard, 230
terrestrial (animal) powers, 29, 30–31, 37–39. *See also* sacred powers; spiritual power
Terry, Alfred H., 183–86, 188–91
They Who Went after Sinew (Niitaxkstaáwo), 27–28, 123
Thomas, Amzi W., 233–34
Thoth, 5–6
Three Affiliated Tribes, 258–59, 267, 285, 292; and Garrison Dam, 270–77; and termination, 268–69
Three Tribes Museum, 289
Tilton's Fort, 140
tipis, 29, 59, 63, 106, 158, 191; and traveling, 47, 148
tobacco, 19, 44, 65; as sacrifice, 28, 31, 50, 122
tools, 31, 198; bone, 49; metal, 71–72, 79, 108; stone, 55
Too Né. *See* Eagle Feather
trade, 75–81, 98–99, 108; with Americans, 112, 116–18, 127–35, 139–40, 143; with British, 100, 105; with Canadians, 101, 115, 132; with Europeans, 24, 48, 52, 70, 84; with French, 58, 120; with other tribes, 50, 67, 92, 102–3, 114–15; with Spanish, 67, 74, 83, 97, 100. *See also* fur trade; slaves: trade in
trading posts, 100, 123, 135, 160, 162
Traditions of the Arikara (Murie and Dorsey), 5

trapping, 98, 99, 130; beaver, 103, 133, 134; eagles, 50, 67, 77
treaties, 138, 144–45, 143, 194; Arikara negotiations of, 198–200, 201–2. *See also* Treaty of Fort Laramie
Treaty of Fort Laramie (1851), 163–64, 165, 197, 200, 270, 273
tribal government, 40–42, 45–46, 259–60; and police, 208–9, 242, 254
Truteau, Jean Baptiste, 90–91, 100–105
tuberculosis, 208, 221, 225, 237
Twin, The (Kah-béck-a), 146, 161
Two Bears, 193–94
Two Bulls, 149, 150–51, 154, 156, 158
Two Crow, Mason, 260
Two Crows, 9, 32, 58, 297n4, 298n9
Two Hawk, 29, 91, 92, 239
two-spirit person (kUxát), 44

United States Army, 143, 167, 171–74, 193, 243, 245. *See also* scouts
United States Boundary Survey Commission, 217n48
United States Congress, 143, 157, 164, 180, 197, 267; and Arikara land, 200, 201–2, 228–29, 253; and Garrison Dam, 256, 270–71, 273; and Indian citizenship, 251–52; and termination policy, 267–69
United States Court of Claims, 253, 267
United States government: alliance with Arikaras, 170, 195; and Arikara culture, 197, 205–8, 233–35, 254; and Arikara land, 197–99, 227–31, 253; Arikara relations with, 128–30, 140–41, 143–145, 157, 164; and Indian relocation, 267–68; war with Sioux, 171–74. *See also* Americans; scouts
United States Volunteer Indian Scouts (aka Old Scouts Society), 244
universe, 9, 27, 52; and bundles, 35; four corners of, 26, 33–34; and Lakhotas, 55. *See also* four directional powers

Universe and Everything Inside, The (Tiraáwaahat), 16
Up from Slavery (Washington), 221
Upper Missouri Agency, 141, 159

Valenzuela, Gail, 5
Varnum, Charles, 183–84, 186, 188
Vérendrye, Pierre Gaultier de Varennes, Sieur de la, 81–82
Vermillion (person), 193
veterans, 234, 243–45, 249; citizenship and, 251–52

Walking Wolf, 202–3
warfare, 24, 50–54, 60, 130–55, 157–59, 169–70, 242; and scalped ones, 37, 43, 96; and status, 39–41; 43; warriors and, 51, 71–75. *See also specific wars*
War of 1812, 134
warrior societies, 52, 131
Washington, Booker T., 221
Washington, DC, 126, 143, 151, 171–72, 182, 184, 230–31; Arikara visits to, 200, 243, 253, 269, 270–71; and Eagle Feather, 5, 111, 118, 121–22
Washington City. *See* Washington, DC
Washita Battle, 179, 185
water dogs, 29
Weir, Thomas B., 188
Wheeler-Howard Act (Indian Reorganization Act, 1934), 253, 256, 257
Whirlwind, 11, 27, 32, 53, 55, 57, 93; and Star Boy, 69–70
White, Gerald, 5
White, Thomas, 260, 263–64
White, Wendell, 5
White Bear, 50, 107–8, 196–97, 239
White Breasted Rat, 193
White Buffalo Woman. *See* Fox, Yvonne
White Coyote (aka Big White, Sheheke), 119, 126–27, 128–29
White Eagle, 187
White Eagle, William, 233

White Horse, 147, 156, 158
White Owl, 37, 239
white people (sahništaaká), 52, 70, 102, 141, 216, 279; Arikaras being like, 216, 223–24; and first contact, 57–58, 84; and religion, 32; and slave trade, 68
White River, 84, 106, 15
White Shield (chief), 162, 193–94, 205, 211, 214, 276, 320n35; and negotiating with US, 165–66, 170–72, 197–99, 215; and scouts, 175–76
White Shield (town), 276, 283, 293
White Shield School, 282, 290, 292
White Wolf. *See* Ahuka, George
Whitman-Perkins, Fannie, 281–82
Whole Buffalo, 187
whooping cough, 225, 226
Wichitas (Čirikuúnux, Witchcraft People), 11, 14–15, 19–20, 24, 27, 557, 148
Wilde, Anna, 3, 286–87
Wilde, Byron, 3, 252–53, 286–87
Wilkinson, James, 121, 122
Wilkinson, Mahlon, 170, 197
Wilson, Woodrow, 252
Winans, Robert, 246, 249
winter counts, 68, 77–78, 85–87, 88, 104
Wolf (being), 9–10, 27
Wolf Chief, 156, 158
women, 42–43, 71–72 74, 114, 280; first woman, 10; and gender roles, 44, 49, 76, 160, 281; as midwives, 39, 40, 226; as missionaries, 211, 214–15; during World War II, 259, 260, 264–65. *See also* gardening
Wooden Bowl, 167
World War I, 243, 246–51
World War II, 256, 259–66
Wounded Face, 228

Yanktonais, 68, 76, 99, 115, 143, 193–94. *See also* Sioux
Yanktons, 68, 76, 99, 143, 157, 163. *See also* Sioux
Yellow Bear, Paul, 233, 236, 237; and storytelling, 9, 28, 54, 239, 297n4
Yellow Bird, Michael, 20
Yellow Bull, 106, 239
Yellow Calf, 106–7
Yellow Knife, 198
Yellowstone expeditions, 170, 177–80
Yellowstone River, 164, 179, 186, 190
Young, John P., 213
Young Bear, Jasper, 5
Young Bird, Gloria, 5
Young Dog Society, 40, 131
Young Eagle (Neetahkaasiháni), 100, 106–7
Young Hawk, Alfred, 230, 239; as a scout, 181, 183, 185, 187–89, 190, 243–44
Young Hawk, Joe, 246, 248, 249, 251
Young Snake, 209
Young War Eagle, 193

www.ingramcontent.com/pod-product-compliance
Lightning Source LLC
Chambersburg PA
CBHW021334230426

43666CB00006B/287